Fields Watered with Blood

Fields

Edited by Maryemma Graham

The University of Georgia Press *Athens & London*

Watered
with Blood

Critical Essays on Margaret Walker

For permission to use copyrighted material, grateful
acknowledgment is made to the copyright holders listed
on pages xvi–xvii, which are considered an extension of
this copyright page

Designed by Walton Harris

Set in 10/13 Minion by G&S Typesetters

Printed and bound by Thomson-Shore, Inc.

The paper in this book meets the guidelines for
permanence and durability of the Committee on
Production Guidelines for Book Longevity of the
Council on Library Resources.

Printed in the United States of America

05   04   03   02   01   C   5   4   3   2   1

Library of Congress Cataloging-in-Publication Data

Fields watered with blood : critical essays on Margaret
Walker / edited by Maryemma Graham.

p.   cm.

Includes bibliographical references and index.

ISBN 0-8203-2254-7 (alk. paper)

1. Walker, Margaret, 1915– —Criticism and
interpretation.   2. Afro-American women in literature.
3. Afro-Americans in literature.   4. Women and
literature—United States—History—20th century.
I. Graham, Maryemma.

PS3545.A517 Z67 2001

818′.5209—dc21   00-032540

British Library Cataloging-in-Publication Data available

To the memory of

J. Saunders Redding

1903–1988

who challenged us all as teachers and critics

We with our blood have watered these fields and they belong to us.

—MARGARET WALKER, "Delta"

Contents

Preface *xi*

Acknowledgments *xv*

Chronology *xix*

Introduction: The Most Famous Person Nobody Knows *1*

PART 1 The Life and Political Times of Margaret Walker

"I Want to Write, I Want to Write the Songs of My People":
The Emergence of Margaret Walker *11*
  Maryemma Graham

Black Women Writers at Work:
An Interview with Margaret Walker *28*
  Claudia Tate

Margaret Walker: Black Woman Writer of the South *44*
  Joyce Pettis

Down from the Mountaintop *55*
  Melissa Walker

The "Intricate Design" of Margaret Walker's "Humanism":
Revolution, Vision, History *66*
  Minrose C. Gwin

PART 2 From *For My People* to *This Is My Century:*
The Poetry of Margaret Walker

The "Etched Flame" of Margaret Walker: Literary and Biblical
Re-Creation in Southern History *81*
  R. Baxter Miller

Fields Watered with Blood: Myth and Ritual in
the Poetry of Margaret Walker *98*
  Eugenia Collier

"Bolder Measures Crashing Through": Margaret Walker's
Poem of the Century *110*
  Eleanor Traylor

Folkloric Elements in Margaret Walker's Poetry *139*
  B. Dilla Buckner

Performing Community: Margaret Walker's Use
of Poetic "Folk Voice" *148*
  Tomeiko R. Ashford

The South in Margaret Walker's Poetry: Harbor and Sorrow Home *164*
  Ekaterini Georgoudaki

For My People: Notes on Visual Memory and Interpretation *179*
  Jerry W. Ward Jr.

Poet of History, Poet of Vision: A Review of *This Is My Century* *187*
  Florence Howe

PART 3 *Jubilee:* Folklore, History, and Vyry's Voice

Music as Theme: The Blues Mode in the Works
of Margaret Walker *195*
  Eleanor Traylor

"Oh Freedom": Women and History
in Margaret Walker's *Jubilee* *209*
  Phyllis R. Klotman

Black Folk Elements in Margaret Walker's *Jubilee* *225*
  James E. Spears

From *Uncle Tom's Cabin* to Vyry's Kitchen: The Black Female
Folk Tradition in Margaret Walker's *Jubilee* *231*
  Charlotte Goodman

"Rumblings" in Folk Traditions Served Southern Style *241*
  Jacqueline Miller Carmichael

The Use of Spaces in Margaret Walker's *Jubilee* *269*
  Hiroko Sato

The Violation of Voice: Revising the Slave Narrative *283*
  Amy Levin

Jubilee, or Setting the Record Straight *290*
  Esim Erdim

The Black Woman as Mulatto: A Personal Response
to the Character of Vyry *304*
  Michelle Cliff

Epilogue: "To Capture a Vision Fair": Margaret Walker and the
Predicament of the African American Woman Intellectual *315*
  Deborah Elizabeth Whaley

Selected Bibliography of Works by and about Margaret Walker *319*

Contributors *341*

Index *345*

Preface

Like many projects, this one began some years ago and moved with a rhythm all its own. The impetus had been given by Donald B. Gibson, whose *Modern Black Poets* (1973), a scholarly and interpretive guide to African American poets before the Black Arts Movement, excluded Margaret Walker.[1] Gibson acknowledged that Walker was "well-known," but found "simply little or no writing about [her]."[2] A little more than a decade later, Trudier Harris commented on the rather delayed critical reception to Walker's novel *Jubilee*, her earlier poetry, and her relationship to a new generation of writers: "She was looked upon as one whose achievements were in the past, someone who had earned respect but to whom no undue attention needed to be given. . . . Although her younger contemporaries might have been reluctant to praise [her], . . . [Walker] is a spiritual if not designated godmother to them."[3] In 1998, in an advertisement for the first film documentary on Walker, longtime friend Nikki Giovanni offered: "Margaret Walker . . . singlehandedly turned poetry upside down with her declaration of love and her challenge to the future of her people. . . . [She] is the most famous person nobody knows."

Although widely anthologized—over two hundred appearances to date—Walker is too often recognized among academic critics as the author of the extraordinary "For My People," while the novel *Jubilee* (1966) is far more widely read than it or its author is discussed. This "accident" of fate seems ironic for someone whose writing career spanned nearly seventy years. That career, however, was marked by periodic absences from the literary scene, corresponding with the moment when literary criticism was becoming a dominant force in the American academy. By the time Walker published a major work of fiction, it was twenty-four years after her first appearance as a poet, and the world had certainly changed. Not knowing where to place her critically literary scholars found it easier to leave her alone.

What fame Walker had managead to achieve had become notoriety by the late 1980s. She was still reeling from attacks by the established literary community, whose response to the appearance of *Richard Wright: Daemonic Genius* was unprecedented. This was the second time that negative public attention was directed toward her. The first occurred when she sued Alex Haley: she had found significant parallels between *Jubilee* and Haley's *Roots,* published a decade later, enough to lead her to believe that he had stolen her work. Most readers knew Margaret Walker as a poet and author of a widely read novel, but there is no denying that her reputation and credibility were badly damaged by these actions. She had written the book, many argued, as an embittered old has-been, forgotten by the literary establishment, her aborted relationship with Richard Wright still the source of unmitigated anger. Surrounded by such controversy, and continually denying that she was an "unrequited lover," Walker renewed her commitment to write to and for her people. Recovering from a minor stroke, she reentered public life in 1989 at age 74, with the zeal and passion of a woman many years younger. Giving sometimes as many as three readings a week, often in different cities to which she traveled by car—she flew only once in her life and vowed never to fly again—she soon found herself in the middle of new projects: her autobiography, a book about historically black colleges, and a sequel to *Jubilee*. Walker never openly admitted to disappointment, but "Fanfare, Coda, and Finale," the last of the new poems appearing in *This Is My Century*, rings a tellingly biographical note:

> Grant me one song to sing, America, out of my hurt and bruised
> dignity; let notes confused and bursting in my throat find
> melody. Reprieve the doom descending on my life. Remake
> the music stifling in my throat. Before my song is lost
> resound the tune and hear my voice.
> Out of my struggle I have sung my song; found hymn and flower
> in field and fort and dungeon cell. Yet now I have
> constriction in my heart where song is born. Such
> bitterness is eating at my vocal chords the bells within me,
> hushed, refuse to ring. Oh lift this weight of brick and stone
> against my neck, and let me sing.

As the dust of the Wright controversy settled, the need grew even more pressing to present critical opinions on Walker as a major twentieth-century author. The evidence of that had become increasingly clear in the last years of her life, when Walker was sought by interviewers and enjoyed the kind of public attention she had grown accustomed to receiving earlier. As perhaps the only African American woman writer who consistently privileges the black folk imagination as the source of creative expression, Walker challenges both new critical and conventional readings; at the same time she offers penetrating intellectual critiques. As a result Walker ruptures the critical categories such as "modernist," "feminist," or "nationalist" that we commonly engage. Those offering interpretations of Walker's work often find they have to modify if not "invent" a framework for discussion. As her two collections of essays indicate, Walker articulates a poetics of her own. *"How I Wrote Jubilee" and Other Essays on Life and Literature* and *On Being Female, Black, and Free* extended Walker's reputation as a world class intellectual and radical thinker who gave as much to her public as she demanded of them. In the end, she refused to allow her voice to be co-opted, whether the critics agreed with her or not.

Although I became the editor of the present volume, several scholars had been contacted, agreed to write original essays and committed to publishing a volume that would make its appearance on both sides of the Atlantic simultaneously. That effort, spearheaded by Myriam Díaz-Diocaretz in 1985, appealed to me because it gave Walker access to an international audience, one she clearly deserved. My role at that time was simple enough: to contribute an essay, outlining Walker's emergence as poet in the 1930s and '40s.

That book was not meant to be. But a book had to happen. I committed myself to documenting Walker's career and followed a scattered paper trail that led from the South to Chicago to Iowa and back South again. In time, the original group of essays expanded until Walker issued a proclamation one day. "When are you going to get that book done," she asked. "I want to know what are the critics saying about me. Or are they all waiting for me to die?" We both thought about Zora Neale Hurston and decided the book could wait no longer. In 1988, the project became a "Walker project," nurtured and supported by her, in much the same way that her writing had always been. Her tendency to hold things close to chest, to strive toward perfection, sometimes taking as many as thirty years to complete a single project, had begun to define this one as well. By the time Walker became critically ill in the summer of 1998, a decade had passed since we had first talked about this project. At that point, some fifty articles had been located, and a book manuscript culled from the best of these. From her bed, she fingered it admiringly, but did not read it. All things in time, we both thought.

I mention this rather personal story because it strikes a familiar chord for many of us doing foundational/archaeological work in African American literature. This volume comes later than it should have; its absence has handicapped our study of African American writing; and as the first of its kind, this single volume must bear the weight of several works still to come. Nevertheless, by focusing on the best essays appearing since the 1970s, those which offer extensive interpretations of Walker's poetry and fiction, we can place her within the context of both historical and contemporary critical discourse. There are no essays here on the Wright biography, although Walker's comments about it are included. It belongs to a genre, the study of which falls outside the goals of the present volume. Walker's essays, too, are not given focused attention as a whole here; however, they are consistently incorporated as evidence of her evolving aesthetic.

1. The Black Arts Movement refers to a literary movement of the 1960s and '70s that brought a number of identifiably "black" writers into prominence. See the *Oxford Companion to African American Literature* for a general discussion of the period and the poets involved. Although Walker published extensively during the Black Arts Movement, in 1973 she was still primarily identified with a school of writers who emerged during the 1930s and '40s.

2. Donald B. Gibson, ed., *Modern Black Poets: A Collection of Critical Essays* (Englewood Cliffs NJ: Prentice-Hall, 1973), 167.

3. Trudier Harris, "Black Writers in a Changed Landscape, Since 1950," in *The History of Southern Literature,* ed. Louis D. Rubin et al. (Baton Rouge: LSU Press, 1985), 367.

Acknowledgments

The work of this volume has involved a number of people over a number of years. I inherited a collection of essays from Myriam Díaz-Diocaretz of the University of Amsterdam, who initially proposed the volume. At the urging of several scholars as well as Walker herself, I picked up the volume again after an absence of several years and assumed full responsibility for seeing it through to publication. An enthusiastic thank you goes to Professor Diocaretz. Her spirit remains with this volume. Robert Anthony (Tony) Harris became the ideal graduate assistant/bibliographer, by tracking down and formatting citations in order to prepare the first comprehensive bibliography on Margaret Walker. Two people encouraged me in ways that I am still unable to describe: Alleane Curry, Walker's assistant for many years, and Bernice L. Bell, former librarian at Jackson State University and a bibliographic scholar in her own right. Because they both kept superb records and had flawless memories, I was able to fill in numerous gaps and identify additional primary works and uncollected criticism, which has made this a far better volume. This volume is in part possible, therefore, because I could locate work that others helped me to know existed. Deborah Elizabeth Whaley, a younger scholar, shared my vision of Walker's continued relevance for both our generations, working closely with the introduction. Because I believe, as Walker did, that mentoring our graduate students should not be exploitative, I have thanked her by including her epilogue.

During the twenty-year period between the earliest essay included here (1977) and the most recent one (1999), not only has the critical scholarship on Walker grown—primarily but not exclusively—outside of the South, but that scholarship has also become increasingly diverse, intergenerational, intercultural, and international. To give the reader some indication of the range of primary and secondary materials related to Walker, a bibliography is included, made possible by the combined efforts of our own intergenerational team, with Bernice Bell at one end, and Tony Harris at the other. Working with them allowed a process of cultural and intellectual transmission to emerge that has been lost to us in today's academy. For all of us this became, in Tony's words, "a labor of love." A host of colleagues and personal friends made the work of this volume more manageable with their attentive and intelligent editorial suggestions, nurturing, and general advice.

Were the collective history of the production for this volume to be told, the acknowledgments would be a chapter unto itself. Instead, I will thank all those, including students and staff from the University of Mississippi, Jackson State University, and Northeastern University, who gave various forms of assistance since the project began. I especially want to thank, at the University of Kansas, the office of the Chancellor, the Dean of the College of Liberal Arts and the Word Processing Center for facilitating the completion of this and other projects I brought with me when I joined the faculty. The English Department, then chaired by Richard Hardin, welcomed me warmly, refusing to allow me to feel like the newcomer that I was.

As always, my family, immediate and extended, encouraged and supported this project from its inception. I am humbled by the courage with which all of you—Ron, Malika, Robeson, Marona, and Rance—often gave up being first in order that "my writing projects" might get done. Finally, I thank Margaret Walker for forcing all of us to remember where we came from.

I wish to thank and publicly acknowledge the following publishers for granting permission to reprint the material that is contained in this volume:

From *Black Women Writers at Work.* Copyright 1983 by Claudia Tate. Reprinted by permission of the author.

"Margaret Walker: Black Woman Writer of the South," by Joyce Pettis. From *Southern Women Writers: The New Generation,* ed. Tonnette Bond Inge. Reprinted by permission of the University of Alabama Press, copyright 1990.

From *Down from the Mountaintop: Black Women's Novels in the Wake of the Civil Rights Movement, 1966–1989.* Copyright 1991 by Melissa Walker. Reprinted by permission of Yale University Press.

"The 'Etched Flame' of Margaret Walker: Literary and Biblical Re-Creation in Southern History," by R. Baxter Miller. *Tennessee Studies in Literature* 26 (1981). Reprinted by permission of the University of Tennessee Press.

"Music as Theme: The Blues Mode in the Works of Margaret Walker," by Eleanor Traylor; and "'Fields Watered with Blood': Myth and Ritual in the Poetry of Margaret Walker," by Eugenia Collier. From *Black Women Writers (1950–1980): A Critical Evaluation,* ed. Mari Evans. Copyright 1983 by Mari Evans. Used by permission of Doubleday, a division of Bantam Doubleday Dell Publishing Group, Inc.

"'Bolder Measures Crashing Through': Margaret Walker's Poem of the Century," by Eleanor Traylor. *Callaloo* 10.4 (fall 1987). Reprinted by permission.

"Folkloric Elements in Margaret Walker's Poetry," by B. Dilla Buckner. *CLA Journal* 33.4 (June 1990). Reprinted by permission of the College Language Association.

"The South in Margaret Walker's Poetry: 'Harbor and Sorrow Home,'" by Ekaterini Georgoudaki. *Cross Roads: A Journal of Southern Culture* 2.2 (summer 1994). Reprinted by permission of the author.

"Poet of History, Poet of Vision," by Florence Howe. *The Women's Review of Books* 7.10–11 (July 1990). Reprinted by permission of the author.

"'Oh Freedom'—Women and History in Margaret Walker's *Jubilee*," by Phyllis Klotman. *Black American Literature Forum* 11.4 (winter 1977). Copyright 1977 by Indiana State University. Reprinted by permission.

"Black Folk Elements in Margaret Walker's *Jubilee*," by James E. Spears. *Mississippi Folklore Register* 14.1 (spring 1980). Reprinted by permission of the author.

"From *Uncle Tom's Cabin* to Vyry's Kitchen: The Black Female Folk Tradition in Margaret Walker's *Jubilee*," by Charlotte Goodman. From *Tradition and the Talents of Women,* ed. Florence Howe. Copyright 1991 by the Board of Trustees of the University of Illinois. Used with the permission of the University of Illinois Press.

From *Trumpeting a Fiery Sound: History and Folklore in Margaret Walker's "Jubilee."* Copyright 1998 by Jacqueline Miller Carmichael. Used by permission of the University of Georgia Press.

Chronology

1915   Margaret Abigail Walker born 7 July in Birmingham, Alabama, the first of four children to Rev. Sigismund Constantine Walker, a Methodist minister originally from Jamaica, and Marion Dozier, a musician and teacher; grandmother Elvira Ware Dozier moves to Birmingham to live with family and care for her first grandchild.

1920   Parents go to teach at Haven Institute for Negroes in Meridian; Walker enters the first grade, after having learned to read at age four.

1925   Family moves to New Orleans; father gives her a daybook for tenth birthday; she begins writing poetry.

1926   Enters Gilbert Academy for high school.

1930   Graduates from Gilbert Academy at age fourteen; enters New Orleans University (now Dillard University) for college.

1931   Wins College Freshman writing prize.

1932   Publishes first essay, "What Is to Become of Us?" in *Our Youth*, a New Orleans magazine; meets James Weldon Johnson, Marian Anderson, and Langston Hughes; enrolls in Northwestern University as a junior.

1934   Returns for senior year at Northwestern; meets W. E. B. Du Bois and publishes first poem in *Crisis:* "Daydream" ("I Want to Write"); meets *Poetry* editor Harriet Monroe and vows to publish there.

1935   Drafts first three hundred pages of *Jubilee* for Creative Writing class; graduates from NU with B.A. in English in August at the age of twenty.

1936   Joins the Federal Writers Project in March as junior writer; meets George Dillon and Muriel Rukeyser through *Poetry;* meets Richard Wright and joins the South Side Writers group with Arna Bontemps, Frank Marshall Davis, Ted Ward, Russell Marshall, Marian Minus, Fern Gayden, St. Clair Drake.

1937 Publishes "For My People" in *Poetry* in October; Southside Writers group disbands.

1938 Publishes poems in *Opportunity, New Challenge,* and again in *Poetry.*

1939 Makes first trip to New York; breaks off friendship with Wright; leaves for graduate school at University of Iowa, with support from the National Youth Association and the Methodist church; publishes in *American Prefaces;* works closely with Paul Engel in poetry workshop; meets fellow student Elizabeth Catlett; edits and types dissertations for students to earn extra money.

1940 Graduates from Iowa with M.A., having completed the manuscript of *For My People;* publishes short stories in *Anvil* and *Creative Writing;* returns to New Orleans for eighteen months; suffers depression and burnout.

1941 "For My People" published in *Negro Caravan.*

1942 Joins faculty of Livingstone College in Salisbury, North Carolina, as English teacher for January semester; wins Yale Series of Younger Poets award; *For My People* published 20 October; goes to New York to promote book; listed on Honor Roll of Race Relations by New York Public Library; joins English Department at West Virginia State College in fall; inducted into Alpha Kappa Alpha Sorority; meets Firnist James Alexander on a train while returning from a reading.

1943 Marries "Alex" on 13 June in High Point (Guilford County), N.C.; sets up housekeeping in High Point; attends first black college professional conference (College Language Association); publishes "Growing Out of Shadow" in *Common Ground;* resigns from teaching job; writes poetry at Yaddo; signs contract with National Artists and Concert Corporation to lecture and read poetry.

1944 Gives birth to first child, Marion Elizabeth (19 July); receives Rosenwald Fellowship to continue *Jubilee* research; Elvira Ware Dozier (the basis for the character Vyry in *Jubilee*), Walker's grandmother, dies.

1945   Returns to Livingstone College for one year.

1946   Gives birth to second child, Firnist James Alexander Jr. (3 May); continues writing in journal and publishes less frequently.

1947   Suffers miscarriage.

1949   Gives birth to third child, Sigismund Constantine (26 July); joins English department at Jackson State College (now Jackson State University), Mississippi, in fall.

1951   Publishes "How I Told My Child About Race" in *Negro Digest.*

1953   Father, Rev. Sigismund Constantine Walker, dies in August; receives Ford Fellowship for *Jubilee;* spends one semester at Yale and conducts research in Georgia, Alabama, and at the University of North Carolina's Southern Historical Collection.

1954   Gives birth to fourth child, Margaret Elvira (17 June).

1955   Publishes in *Virginia Quarterly Review;* moves to new house on Guynes Street in Jackson; health begins to decline.

1960   Has surgery; experiences financial problems; returns to writing.

1961   Attends summer school in Iowa, taking two younger children; takes fiction workshop with Verlin Cassill; plans to use *Jubilee* for Ph.D. dissertation; begins revising chapters; returns to Jackson State in fall; organizes seventy-fifth anniversary celebration of JSU, reuniting Arna Bontemps, Melvin Tolson, Langston Hughes, Sterling Brown, Robert Hayden.

1962   Begins two-year leave from JSU in September; returns to Iowa for doctoral program; lives in the home of Alma Hovey, retired Iowa professor, and works as graduate teaching assistant in rhetoric program.

1963   While home in summer, neighbor and civil rights activist Medgar Wiley Evers is murdered in front yard of his Guynes Street house (12 June); writes elegy commemorating Evers.

1964   Completes Ph.D. comprehensive examinations; returns home to New Orleans and Jackson until December.

1965   Returns to Iowa in January; finishes *Jubilee* 9 April; receives Ph.D. in June; returns to JSU English department with book contract from Houghton Mifflin.

1966   *Jubilee* is published (25 September); wins Houghton Mifflin literary award, Mable Carney Student National Education Association plaque for scholar-teacher of the year, and Alpha Kappa Alpha Sorority Citation for Advancement of Knowledge; is honored at New York production of "A Hand is on the Gate"; meets Ruby Dee, Ossie Davis, Cicely Tyson, Moses Gunn, Roscoe Brown, James Earl Jones, and Gloria Foster (who performs Walker's poetry); attends party at home of Langston Hughes.

1967   Paperback rights to *Jubilee* sold to Bantam; accepts invitation to teach Creative Writing workshop in Craigville (Cape Cod); rejects movie offer for *Jubilee* after meeting the producers.

1968   Publishes "Religion, Poetry, History: Foundations for a New Educational System"; secures federal funding and establishes national Black Studies Program and the Institute for the Study of the History, Life, and Culture of Black People, one of the first Black Studies Programs (later the Margaret Walker Alexander National Research Center); prepares monograph, "Critical Approaches to the Study of African American Literature," planned as a book project on the history of black literature; hires full-time Institute secretary (Alleane Curry), who later becomes her personal assistant through retirement; receives key to city from Victor Schiro, New Orleans mayor; speaks at national NAACP convention; identifies with Black Aesthetic Movement that is sweeping the nation.

1969   Spends a semester as writer-in-residence at Northwestern.

1970   *Prophets for a New Day* published by Third World Press, marking a shift from mainstream publishers; publishes "The Humanistic Tradition of Afro-American Literature"; killing of James Earl Green and Philip Gibbs by highway patrolmen at Jackson State (May 14–15) inspires poem; serves as witness before President's Commission on Campus Unrest.

1971   Takes sabbatical for two years to work on book projects (1971–73); defers Fulbright Hayes Fellowship opportunity to teach at the University of Trondheim (Norway); conducts seminar, "A Brief Introduction to Southern Literature," at Mississippi Arts Festival; publishes "Richard Wright" essay.

1972   Receives National Endowment for the Humanities senior fel-
        lowship for independent study; conducts seminar at Atlanta's
        Institute of the Black World; *How I Wrote* Jubilee later pub-
        lished as monograph by Third World Press; speaks at centen-
        nial of Paul Laurence Dunbar in Dayton, Ohio, and conceives
        idea for festival of black women writers to honor Phillis
        Wheatley; delivers speech, "Agenda for Action: Black Arts and
        Letters," at Black Academy Conference to Assess the State of
        Black Arts and Letters in the United States, sponsored by John-
        son Publishing Company, Chicago; writes "Humanities with
        a Black Focus: A Black Paradigm"; delivers speech commemo-
        rating JSU massacre.

1973   *October Journey* published by Broadside Press; hosts Phillis
        Wheatley (bicentennial) Poetry Festival at JSU in October; gath-
        ering of black women in Jackson helps inaugurate the black
        women's literary renaissance; appears before Federal Commu-
        nications Commission regarding racial discrimination in the
        media; participates in Library of Congress conference on Teach-
        ing Creative Writing; presents "The Writer and Her Craft."

1974   *A Poetic Equation: Conversations Between Nikki Giovanni and
        Margaret Walker* published by Howard University Press; hos-
        pitalized for diabetes; outlines sequel to *Jubilee* in hospital; goes
        on speaking tour in Northeast; receives honorary degrees from
        Denison University, Northwestern University, and Rust College
        (Miss.).

1975   First granddaughter, Joy Dale Alexander, born 7 October; *Mar-
        garet Walker Reads Margaret Walker and Langston Hughes* and
        The Poetry of Margaret Walker Read by Margaret Walker re-
        corded by Folkways; appears as witness in Mississippi book
        censorship/adoption case; publishes "Chief Worshipers at All
        World Altars" in *Encore,* focusing on role of women in reli-
        gion; speaks on Richard Wright at University of Massachu-
        setts (Amherst); participates in Bicentennial Symposium on
        American Slavery with Carl Degler, James Blassingame, Benja-
        min Quarles; visits friend and sculptor Elizabeth Catlett (Mex-
        ico); publishes first major interview, with Charles Rowell *(Black
        World).*

1976   Publishes "Some Aspects of the Black Aesthetic" in *Freedom-ways;* premiere of Ulysses Kay's adaptation of *Jubilee* performed by OperaSouth; gives keynote speech, "Southern Black Culture," at Sojourner Truth Festival, Fort Worth, Tex.; commissioned to write essay, "Black Culture," for 1976 Bicentennial.

1977   Files suit against Alex Haley for plagiarism; judge rules in favor of Haley; Conference on Africa and African Affairs sponsored by the Black Studies Institute.

1978   JSU sponsors "Margaret Walker: A Woman for All Seasons" retirement tribute.

1979   Husband Alex is diagnosed with cancer; Walker retires from JSU; awarded Emerita status; receives President Jimmy Carter's "Potentially Unsung Heroes Award"; meets First Lady, Rosalyn Carter; begins work on Richard Wright book, under contract with Howard University Press.

1980   Publishes essay, "On Being Female, Black, and Free"; "Mississippi and the Nation," speech given at Governor William Winter's Inaugural Symposium; "Margaret Walker Alexander Day" proclaimed by Governor Winter (12 July); husband Alex dies in November; son Sigismund (Siggy) and his family move in with Walker; conducts lengthy interview with Claudia Tate for book *Black Women Writers.*

1981   Two grandsons born: Sigismund Walker Alexander II to Siggy and Norma Alexander and Jarrett Jamal Williams to Margaret and Vernon Williams; Guynes Street changed to Margaret Walker Alexander Drive; "A Bicentennial Pamphlet: Black Culture" monograph published; renegotiates contract with Howard University Press for publication of Richard Wright biography.

1982   Receives W. E. B. Du Bois award from Association of Social and Behavioral Scientists; delivers lecture, "Education and the Seminal Mind"; completes new book of poetry; reads excerpts to overflow crowd at Lincoln University (Pa.).

1983   Mother, Marion Dozier Walker, dies in April; "Moral Education: Who's Responsible?" delivered at Mississippi Committee for Humanities Conference, JSU.

1984   Serves as chairperson, Mississippi National Rainbow Coalition, supporting Jesse Jackson for President; elected delegate to Democratic National Convention in San Francisco; writes "Jesse Jackson: The Man and the Message"; featured in Smithsonian traveling exhibition, "Black Women Achievement Against the Odds."

1985   Keynotes at "Mississippi's Native Son: An International Symposium on Richard Wright" at University of Mississippi; fiftieth class reunion at Northwestern University; writer-in-residence at Randolph Macon Women's College (Lynchburg, Va.); honoree at Mary Church Terrell Literary Club Diamond Jubilee.

1986   Commissioned to write poems in honor of Jackson's historic black district, *For Farish Street;* gives reading at National Conference of Black Artists, Medgar Evers College, CCNY (N.Y.); honored at Langston Hughes Festival, City College of New York; meets James Baldwin and Toni Morrison; reads poetry at Library of Congress.

1988   *Richard Wright: Daemonic Genius* published after long battle with Wright's widow; celebration held at Old Capitol Museum, Jackson; serves as delegate from Fourth District to the National Democratic Convention in Atlanta; branch of Hinds County library named in her honor.

1989   *This Is My Century: New and Collected Poems* published; the Institute at Jackson State becomes the Margaret Walker Alexander National Research Center for the Study of the Twentieth-Century African American; receives three-year fellowship from Lyndhurst Foundation (1989–92); goes on East and West coast book promotion/lecture tour; attends Federal Writers Project reunion in Chicago; opening of "I Dream a World" exhibition (Brian Lanker), featuring Walker and other women, at Corcoran Gallery; appears on CBS's "Nightwatch" with Charlie Rose.

1990   Receives Living Legend Award for Literature from National Black Arts Festival, Atlanta; *"How I Wrote Jubilee" and Other Essays on Life and Literature* published by Feminist Press; U.S. Court of Appeals rules in favor of Walker's use of Wright's letters in the biography and against the Richard Wright estate; unveils historic marker at Richard Wright's home, site for the Natchez Literary Festival.

1991   Receives Senior Fellowship from the National Endowment for the Humanities for Lifetime Achievement and Contributions to American Literature; publishes essay "Natchez and Richard Wright" in *Southern Quarterly.*

1992   Celebrates seventy-fifth birthday in gala event at home; interviewed by Jack Switzer for national airing of "Open Air" (Mississippi Educational TV); fiftieth anniversary edition of *For My People* issued by Limited Editions and celebrated at Limited Editions Club, N.Y. (18 September); receives [Kirk Fordice's] Governor's Award for Excellence in the Arts, Lifetime Achievement Award from the College Language Association, and Golden Soror Award from AKA Sorority; receives, with Ralph Ellison, a tribute from the Modern Language Association; participates in five-day conference on "Black Women Writers and Magic Realism" sponsored by MWA National Research Center; Roland Freeman publishes *For My People: A Tribute,* a book of photographs in honor of Walker; is hospitalized for minor stroke.

1993   Receives American Book Award for Lifetime Achievement; accepts honorary degree from Spelman College (Atlanta); delivers keynote address, "Discovering our Connections: Race, Gender, and the Law," at Washington College of Law.

1994   Appears as witness in Ayers vs. Governor of Mississippi federal court case on segregation in Mississippi higher education.

1995   Margaret Walker Alexander National Research Center for the Study of Twentieth-Century African Americans hosts Margaret Walker Alexander Week (27 November–2 December); listed by *Ebony* magazine as one of "Fifty Most Important Women in the Past Fifty Years"; publishes "Whose 'Boy' Is This?" on Clarence Thomas, in *African American Women Speak Out;* completes first draft of autobiography.

1996   Honored at Cultural Olympiad, Agnes Scott College, and National Black Arts Festival, Atlanta; receives John Hurt Fisher Award from South Atlantic Association of Departments of English; donates private papers to MWA National Research Center; publishes "Setting the Record Straight."

1997   *On Being, Female, Black, and Free* published by University of Tennessee Press; reads poetry at Atlanta Arts Festival in July; Margaret Walker Alexander Research Center moves into remodeled Ayers Hall at JSU.

1998   Honored at Zora Neale Hurston International Festival, Eatonville, Fla., in January; reads poetry and is honored at George Moses Horton Society at UNC in April; diagnosed with cancer in June and undergoes radiation treatment, deciding against surgery; receives Major Arts Achievement award in Jackson in July; inducted into the African American Literary Hall of Fame at the Gwendolyn Brooks Writers' Conference in October; dies in Chicago at home of oldest daughter (30 November); funeral in Jackson on 4 December.

I wish to thank the Walker family for their help in preparing this chronology.

Fields Watered with Blood

Introduction: The Most Famous Person Nobody Knows

MARYEMMA GRAHAM AND DEBORAH WHALEY

Margaret Walker knew and understood the South intimately. It was a source of anger and righteous indignation; yet she thrived on its dual complexity: the natural beauty of its landscape in contrast to the unnatural horror of its racism. Growing up in the expanded Jim Crow era, she quickly captures for us the feeling of that experience: "I knew what it was to step off the sidewalk to let a white man pass before I was ten." She was known to credit much of her success to being born into a deeply religious family that fostered excellence and placed spiritual values and integrity above money.

Her birthplace was Birmingham, Alabama. On 7 July 1915, Margaret Abigail Walker was born and named in honor of her ancestors. She went to school in New Orleans but completed college at the Methodist-affiliated Northwestern University, where her father had gone before her. Although Walker had written and published before moving to Chicago, it was there that her talent matured. Writing as a college student, as a member of the wpa, and sharing intellectual, cultural and professional interests with many black and white artists who were gathered in Chicago, the most famous of whom undoubtedly was Richard Wright, Walker found her voice. Wright and Walker shared a close friendship until Wright left for New York in the late 1930s. Their friendship abruptly ended a year later. Walker herself left Chicago for graduate school at the University of Iowa in 1939, by which time she was well on her way to becoming a major American poet. In 1942, she completed the full manuscript of a volume she entitled *For My People,* the title poem for which had been written and published in *Poetry* in 1937. The volume served as her M.A. thesis in English from the University of Iowa; more importantly, its selection for the Yale Series of Younger Poets Award (1942) brought immediate recognition to her as the first African American woman, and the second African American after Richard Wright, to achieve national literary prominence. The volume along with its title poem quickly became an American classic.

Around the same time, Walker had begun work on a historical novel, based on her great-grandmother, Elvira Ware Dozier, a novel she would not finish until she returned to Iowa in the 1960s to complete her Ph.D. The book's long gestation period shaped much of Walker's life for thirty years. She returned to the South, began her teaching career at Livingstone College (Salisbury, N.C.), married, and had four children, all while doing intermittent research and writing on the novel. In 1949, after she settled her family in Jackson, Mississippi, so that she might join the faculty at Jackson State College, she slowly began to weave together the stories told to her by her grandmother. Unfortunately, Grandmother Dozier would not live to see the novel she had inspired; she died before *Jubilee*'s publication. The award-winning novel pushed Walker again to the forefront. *Jubilee* (1966) was enormously successful, appealing to a popular audience that her poetry could never reach. It has been translated into four languages and remains the first modern novel of slavery and the Reconstruction South, paving the way, as several critics point out, for Sherley Ann Williams's *Dessa Rose,* Ernest Gaines's *The Autobiography of Miss Jane Pittman,* J. California Cooper's *Family,* and Toni Morrison's *Beloved.* Other books followed soon thereafter: *Prophets for a New Day* (1970), *How I Wrote* Jubilee (1972), *October Journey* (1973), and *A Poetic Equation: Conversations Between Nikki Giovanni and Margaret Walker* (1974).

Throughout her literary career, Walker earned awards and honors for extraordinary achievement and for her lifetime contribution to American letters as a creative artist. "Her people" never failed to recognize her: eight honorary degrees, numerous certificates and citations, and in 1991 a Senior Fellowship from the National Endowment for the Arts. In 1992, Lifetime Achievement Awards came from both the historically black College Language Association and the Governor of Mississippi.

When Walker ended her teaching career in 1979, she quickly began another as one of the nation's most sought after black writers. After the controversial *Richard Wright: Daemonic Genius,* she turned her attention to poetry once again. The four volumes she had previously published and the new poems became *This Is My Century: New and Collected Poems.* A few years later, reflecting on the series of celebrations marking the fiftieth anniversary of *For My People* (1942–92), she explained:

> From my early adolescence, I've been dealing with the meaning of the turn of the century. I was born when it was barely fifteen years old. And now we have less than ten years left in this century. So, the body of my work springs from my interest in a historical point of view that is central to the development of black people as we approach the twenty-first century. That is my theme. And I have tried to express it, both in prose and poetry. I feel that if I've learned anything about this country and century—I've expressed it already in the books I've been writing and the few more I'd like to write. . . . Giving voice to all I have come to know and understand is still the most important thing for me as a writer—that has never changed for me, nor for the people I've known and worked with through all these years.

Recalling the past and present as symbols and myths drawn from a collective consciousness, giving it both secular and spiritual significance, was Walker's artistic mission. Although she turned to her imagination, her intellectual curiosity, and her training as a poet to realize that mission, she never failed to trust her emotions and the spirit that connected her to the folk.

Margaret Walker sought and acquired the necessary understanding to sustain a satisfying life early. She lived and grew old in a rather traditional way: with her children and her grandchildren, in her own home, not too far from where she was born, working hard and being severely underpaid, attending church and teaching a Bible class, enjoying the friends she had known most of her adult life. These were traditions that she revered, for they provided the balance between the intellectual and nonintellectual modes of being.

Whether it is the power of Walker's voice or the truth of her vision that invites the rich, lyrical and precise language of her poetry, fiction, or criticism, she reaffirms the values and the cultural distinctiveness of African American life through oratory as perhaps its central and most visible feature. Writers Sonia Sanchez, Toni Morrison, Alice Walker, Toni Cade Bambara, and Alex Haley seem to echo this sensibility in their own revisioning of the black historical experience. And Walker has an entire following of writers who have profited from her example, including Arthenia Bates Millican, Julia Fields, the late Raymond Andrews, the late Tom Dent, Robert Dean Pharr, Tina McElroy Ansa, and Pinkie Gordon Lane.

Given her self-prescribed role as a spiritual and intellectual leader—one her readers and reviewers gladly acknowledge—Walker's penetrating analyses and carefully constructed images of black life in America bespeak an uncompromising commitment to the integrity of an African American world view, one she considered essential for "saving" America from its own destruction. Perhaps no one has ever spoken as forcefully, as skillfully, or as truthfully as Walker about the range of complex problems we collectively face as Americans looking toward a common past, with full realization of the responsibility for preserving our common humanity. It is this simple truth pervading her work that has earned for her a permanent place in the cultural discourse of America.

Twenty-two essays here are all concerned to see Walker as a highly self-conscious artist, quintessentially female, black, and southern, who dared assume the burden of telling the "truth" of history. Intensely passionate and yet morally restrained, Walker was not content with a sentimental spiritualizing of nature, though admittedly her earliest poetry was modeled after the sentimental tradition. The heightened political awareness that she developed during the 1930s marked her for life and, together with her indigenous sensibilities, gave her a window to a world that her artistry constantly reinvented. The intergenerational, intercultural and international mix of scholars writing in this volume, representing the United States, the Caribbean, Japan, Greece and Turkey, all seem to be engaged in a critical intertextual exchange. Margaret Walker's texts are the focus, the elements and thematic concerns in them primary, with an eye toward the visionary possibilities they portend. Taken together, these essays attend to the multiplicity of ways that Walker's work has been interpreted by literary critics and scholars. The opening essay, "I Want to Write, I Want to Write the Songs of My People: The Emergence of Margaret Walker," explores various influences upon Walker's aesthetic vision, her initiation into the world of poetry, especially noting the subject position of Walker and her Harlem Renaissance legacy. Similarly, Jacqueline Carmichael's "'Rumblings' in Folk Traditions Served Southern Style" unearths the folk traditions and tropes of African American culture in *Jubilee,* which synchronizes African orality with material culture and cultural practices (e.g., Walker's use and description of quilts, architecture, candlemaking, and clothing). Dilla Buckner's "Folkloric Elements in Margaret Walker's Poetry" and James E. Spears's "Black Folk Elements in Margaret Walker's *Jubilee*" provide more detailed evidence of the text's vernacular traditions as "proof that she is a [fiction writer and] poet of the people, her people."

In "Music as Theme: The Blues Mode in the Works of Margaret Walker," Eleanor Traylor suggests that music is not simply a vernacular tradition that enriches the text of *Jubilee* but sees it, more importantly, as a didactic device. Traylor's text invites us to experience the music as she explores a dialectic that

Walker's prose creates between the characters and the reader. This "verbal music," then, is a dialogic idiom that encourages her poetry not only to be read and spoken but, as Tomeiko R. Ashford argues in "Performing Community: Margaret Walker's Use of Poetic 'Folk Voice,'" also to be heard. This polyrhythmic quality informs and invokes the oral and vernacular traditions so prevalent in African American expressive culture, indicative of the richness of Walker's poetry not only as spoken word but also as performance of African American culture through those words. In keeping with Walker's commitment to mine the depths of racial and gender memory, Phyllis Klotman's "'Oh Freedom': Women and History in Margaret Walker's *Jubilee*," Minrose Gwin's "The 'Intricate Design' of Margaret Walker's 'Humanism': Revolution, Vision, History," Claudia Tate's "Black Women Writers at Work," Michelle Cliff's "The Black Woman as Mulatto: A Personal Response to the Character of Vyry," Joyce Pettis's "Margaret Walker: Black Woman Writer of the South," Charlotte Goodman's "From *Uncle Tom's Cabin* to Vyry's Kitchen: The Black Female Folk Tradition in Margaret Walker's *Jubilee*," and Amy Levin's "The Violation of Voice: Revising the Slave Narrative" all focus on women as historical subjects.

Klotman writes that Walker's *Jubilee* is best understood as "historical fiction" and places it among those much-needed texts that record women's historical voices—the imaginative result of Walker's melange of African American historical processes and the part that women of African descent played in that process. Similarly, Minrose Gwin writes that *Jubilee* reflects the consciousness in Walker's civil rights poetry, arguing that both forms of work are "disruptive" and "creative," and "explore and explode patriarchal spaces of racism and oppression." Levin suggests that Walker's choices contribute to the dialogue on gender and African American cultural production by answering important questions about power, identity, family, and authenticity. While Klotman, Gwin, and Levin explore the sites of gender resistance (in *Jubilee* in particular) that shed light on the literary use of women's voices, Claudia Tate and Joyce Pettis provide nuanced and personal narratives of Walker's discussion of African American women's lives and histories. Tate, in "Black Women Writers at Work," uses a 1980 interview with Margaret Walker that enabled Walker to speak directly to gender concerns as presented in her written work, no doubt driven by Walker's own personal commitment to racial and gender uplift.[1]

Drawing from and responding to the struggle of self-representation for African American women in literature and culture, Michelle Cliff's "The Black Woman as Mulatto" concentrates on the stereotypes embedded in the American ideology of the "mulatto." Cliff compares works by Zora Neale Hurston, Nella Larsen, and James Fenimore Cooper to challenge the stereotype of the "tragic" mulatto in the white literary imagination by deconstructing the common narratives used to describe her. Cliff concentrates on the ways in which language, in this case a stereotype, renders the diverse realities of African American women's experiences invisible, but Joyce Pettis reads Walker's personal interests as political, a fact that her writing reflects. Pettis argues that the strength in Walker's work is not only in her allegiance to the ideologies of "race women" but also in her use of the South as a symbolic landscape and home for African Americans as a whole. It is precisely Walker's attention to the "everyday" aesthetics of African American women's experience that author Charlotte Goodman points to. Unlike the depictions of African American life in texts such as *Uncle Tom's Cabin,* Goodman cites Walker's *Jubilee* as an emergent text that reflects the subtle expressive forms and signifiers of African American antebellum culture and feminine subjectivity.

Margaret Walker's poetry involved the same literary innovation inasmuch as her poetry was committed to recasting cultural forms undergirded with cultural and "womanist" politics. The South represented a paradox: it was a place where African Americans would revivify culture and folkways, and yet it simultaneously signified marginality, invisibility, and race hatred. Ekaterini Georgoudaki's "The South in Margaret Walker's Poetry: Harbor and Sorrow Home" shows this well: Walker's poetry is celebration, ethnic revival, and mourning. Employing a deep structural analysis of poems such as "Jackson, Mississippi" and "Birmingham," Georgoudaki writes of the visual imagery merged with literary allegory that makes Walker's poetry prophetic. Esim Erdim shifts this focus on the structural aspects of Walker's work from the poetry to the novel. *Jubilee,* Erdim suggests, is a multivoiced text intended to reflect the paradoxical nature of southern life. Marginality, invisibility, and race hatred are indeed double-edged. The author wants us to hear Grimes's story, although he is the brutal overseer. Even though he is marginalized and deprivileged (in short, "white trash"), he invites a compassionate reading as much as the protagonist Vyry. Walker employs irony in the novel, one of several discursive strategies that complement the novel's central tensions. The authorial voice shifts in response to Vyry's vision of acceptance and understanding, and the novel alternates between a spiritual and a secular, a folk and a religious perspective, in order to achieve narrative closure.

The canon of Walker's work is a literary montage of Africa, America, and the South, Eleanor W. Traylor writes in "'Bolder Measures Crashing Through': Margaret Walker's Poem of the Century." A common thematic strand in Walker's work speaks of and to the historical complexities and transformations of twentieth-century America. As Florence Howe argues in "Poet of History, Poet of Vision: A Review of *This Is My Century,*" with prophetic and lyrical genius Walker emerges as the consciousness of a people, the poet of their history. It is indeed the attention to the expressiveness of African American culture and the quest to articulate a shared experience that makes Walker's poetry a mythical and material statement, as Eugenia Collier remarks in "Fields Watered with Blood: Myth and Ritual in the Poetry of Margaret Walker," on the use of diasporic traditions in American culture. The rituals and myths of a culture, Collier argues, are engulfed in racial memory; they form a comment on the future hopes and desires of African American men and women.

Margaret Walker's creation of literary and metaphoric spaces place her among those authors who make conscious connections to their art while aiming to visualize a sense of "place" in their work. Hiroko Sato's "The Use of Spaces in Margaret Walker's *Jubilee*," R. Baxter Miller's "The 'Etched Flame' of Margaret Walker: Literary and Biblical Re-Creation in Southern History," Jerry Ward's "*For My People:* Notes on Visual Memory and Interpretation," and Melissa Walker's "Down from the Mountaintop" examine Walker's use of cultural space. Sato writes that Walker "uses the concept of space in showing the reversal of power and the extent and limits of liberation," whereas R. Baxter Miller claims that the biblical references in Walker's work create a different type of space: a spiritual one. Miller writes that texts such as *For My People* and *Prophets for a New Day* are couched within a "historical sense of biblical implication," thus carving out a space for not only an emergent self but a spiritual one as well. Textual analyses of African conjure and aspects of Christianity lead Miller to conclude that the land and sense of space is analogous to Walker's overarching concern with the spiritual struggle of African Americans.

This very same textual framework is also examined in Melissa Walker's essay; she notes how *Jubilee* is representative of the historical moment in which it was created and embedded in later moments, such as 1960s cultural turmoil. Walker's novel is "not the story of a dead past but of the past as a precondition of the present," she writes. Thus civil rights metaphors of spiritual and material freedom such as the "mountaintop" become cultural tropes for a sense of political space, extending the notion of place to ideological spaces of contestation and cultural struggle—a common element in Margaret Walker's work. Foregrounding the inevitably cultural perspectives that readers bring to interpretation (our visual memories and subject positions), Jerry Ward argues that the intertextuality of Walker's poem "For My People" lends itself to multiple readings and meanings. For him, decoding and siting the visual space in Walker's literary work situates it as a dialogic text, leading the readers to negotiate their visual interpretations of Walker's poetry with their own material histories and sense of place.

This first full-length study of Margaret Walker's work appears at an important moment in the evolution of Walker criticism. For although Walker did not enjoy the mainstream critical success of Toni Morrison or Alice Walker, she has paralleled their successs outside the mainstream as a writer of unusual intellectual boldness and literary complexity, a genius with words. These essays open the door of interpretive inquiry by excavating from Walker's work the various elements of African American culture, threads of folk material, gender and race consciousness, prophetic poetry, prose, and place (the South), forming a cultural quilt. No matter which analytic lens one uses to view her work, Walker's reputation rests, we are reminded in Deborah's Whaley's timely epilogue, on the connection between her exemplary writing life and her social practice. The portrait revealed here is by no means a final one, but it is intended to uncover the shape of Walker's poetry and fiction and to trigger the quest to know more about an artist for whom the personal was always political. In her search to unite home and community with the world of poetry, literature, history, and theology, Margaret Walker became America's moral touchstone. That search was her obsession and her truth. Fortunately for us as readers and critics, Walker did not measure the worth of her life's work by institutional judgments. Being "the most famous person nobody knows" in the end may well have been her greatest strength.

NOTE

1. Walker began and served as the first director of the Institute for the Study of the History, Life, and Culture of Black People in 1968. In 1989, the Institute became the Margaret Walker Alexander National Research Center, with funding from the National Endowment for the Humanities and the State of Mississippi.

PART ONE

The Life and Political Times
of Margaret Walker

"I Want to Write, I Want to Write the Songs of My People"

The Emergence of Margaret Walker

MARYEMMA GRAHAM

Margaret Walker set out to be a writer at a most extraordinary time. Born in Birmingham in 1915 and growing up in New Orleans while the majority of America's black population were recovering from the ravages of slavery, Walker came of age as part of a unique generation. By the time she was ten, the Harlem Renaissance was in full swing in the urban centers of the North. In the South, those who chose not to migrate nevertheless felt the effects of this national cultural and social movement. At a time when old traditions were giving way to new ones, the Renaissance concerned itself with cultural achievement as well as political and social access. Its great success was that it produced writers and exemplars of black excellence on an unprecedented scale. Walker's life and conscious cultivation of a literary career followed on the heels of this Renaissance and took inspiration from it. In part, Walker's dual role as an artist and spokesperson for her people is the result of early exposure to the canonical figures of the era, including James Weldon Johnson, Marian Anderson, W. E. B. Du Bois, Roland Hayes, and Langston Hughes; listening to educated, deeply religious parents debate Booker T. Washington's and Du Bois's racial ideas; being nourished by the rituals of southern black culture; and her need for self-definition as a creative, intellectual, and psychological being, unhampered by proscriptions of race and gender. Aware though she was of the codes governing the moral and social behavior of middle-class women of her time, Walker refused to allow those codes to govern her personal advancement. In time she would see herself in the tradition of African American women who worked tirelessly to improve the conditions of people's lives. Her teachers were men, but her heroes were women like Phillis Wheatley, Frances Ellen Watkins Harper, Fannie Jackson Coppin, Nannie Burroughs, Angelina Weld Grimke, Georgia Douglas Johnson, Anne Spencer, Jessie Fauset, Nella Larsen, and Zora Neale Hurston. Walker grew up, in short, a "race woman," a New Negro, with a strong sense of her own power as an individual to impact the world at large. Some of this she inherited from her father, Sigismund Walker, a Jamaican who had immigrated to the United States to get a college education and an ordained minister in the Methodist Episcopal church, who taught philosophy and religion at New Orleans University (now Dillard) for most of his life. Some she got from her mother, Marion Dozier Walker, a wise woman of great musical talent, aggressive and controlling when it came to her children. Some of it was simply Margaret Walker herself, curious, intense, a lover of nature, a child whose passion for language was apparent to anyone around her. In any case, the context within which she grew to womanhood and initiated her career— before "For My People"—demonstrates intellectual borrowings and kinships that were invaluable to her literary apprenticeship.

As long as Walker could remember, she was "enthralled in . . . Grandmother's stories" and recalled her grandmother being chastised by her parents for telling "harrowing" tales of slavery rather than more acceptable bedtime stories. Elvira Ware Dozier, who would become the protagonist Vyry in *Jubilee*, with indignation rising in her voice, reportedly confessed to "telling the naked truth." The naked truth was available to Walker throughout her childhood because she was the first born and had the greatest access and exposure to her grandmother. The freedom of the narrative exchanges went uninterrupted for most of her early years. Learning from and listening to the stories from the oldest member of the household, a woman who had been born a slave, instilled in Walker the importance of history as told through stories.

It was her grandmother who gave Walker an early appreciation for the images and sounds of the black lived experience as they were recorded in a slave woman's memory. She was told repeatedly the story of her great-grandmother, Margaret Duggans Ware Brown, who had died one month before her birth. As was the custom, she was given the name Margaret, after her maternal great-grandmother and her father's mother, and Abigail after her maternal aunt. "As I grew older and realized the importance of the story my grandmother was telling, I prodded with more questions." This was the beginning of *Jubilee*, which took her thirty years to write. "While I was still hearing my grandmother tell old slavery-time stories and incidents from my mother's life, I promised my grandmother that when I grew up I would write her mother's story." [1]

Her early teachers in New Orleans had sung her praises. Until she left for Chicago to complete her final two years of college, Walker had lived in the South her entire life. Reading at three, writing her first poems at eight, graduating from high school at fourteen, publishing her first essay at sixteen, writing "For My People" at twenty-one, and winning the nation's top literary award at twenty-six, Walker was as extraordinary as the era in which she was born. A child prodigy, it seems apt to call her, Walker knew by the time she was five years old that she wanted to become a writer.[2] She entered school and made herself a vow. Everything she did would prepare her for a writing career. Walker recalled her early life being filled with opportunities to experience the joy of reading and trying to write, even though poetry eluded her at first:

> I was a small child only ten years of age. I must have already felt even earlier that although I loved books and especially poetry, there was something mysterious about the process and only the elite were elected to be poets. So my first composition at age ten was prose. I wrote a Thanksgiving piece for my seventh grade English class and I still remember how it began, "Picture to yourself a band of pilgrims." [3]

The four Walker children were taught the life of the mind. Sigismund, who distinguished himself as one of the best-trained ministers of his time, was keenly intellectual, bent on transmitting his affinity for books, ethics and philosophy, and his belief in the power of the rational to establish one's place in the world. Margaret, who looked like her mother, wanted most to be like her father. When it became clear to Marion, herself an accomplished musician, that of the two girls only Mercedes had the propensity for music, she was eager to cultivate her older daughter's literary abilities. Marion urged young Walker to write, circulated the resulting work to vanity presses, and actually paid for the first poems to appear in print.

To become a poet, a novelist, a scholar—as her parents intended and as she herself desired—meant rigorous and continuous training. Reading books from her father's library brought with it his bias: nineteenth- and twentieth-century British classics were more familiar to him than the fledgling American literature she would later come to love. As the oldest, she was also assigned the task of preparing outlines for her father's sermons, a habit that allowed her to become intimately familiar with the Bible and contemporary theological views. Years later, Walker remarked,

> When I went to school, I read history books that glorified the white race and described the Negro either as a clown and a fool or at best capable of very hard work in excessive heat. I discovered the background of chattel slavery behind this madness of race prejudice. Once we were slaves and now we are not, and the South remains angry. But when I went home to the good books and the wonderful music and the gentle, intelligent parents, I could see no reason for prejudice on the basis of a previous condition of servitude.[4]

The "gentle, intelligent" parents that Walker remembered held firmly to the traditional values in their religious and home life. They observed the strictest standards of social behavior, believing that high morals signified a good Christian and, in the case of their two daughters, defined a virtuous woman. They believed, too, as most high-achieving blacks did at the turn of the twentieth century, that racial uplift was directly tied to literacy and would result in social mobility and economic progress. The Walkers looked for and took advantage of the opportunity to advance themselves, and saw to it that their children did the same. Each move the family made, from Birmingham to Meridian to New Orleans, represented upward mobility. Sigismund went back to get his Master's in Theology from Northwestern, which earned him a permanent teaching position at New Orleans University. Marion returned to evening school and completed her college education so that she could teach music. The family set high expectations for their children: Margaret would be a writer; Mercedes would go to conservatory; Gwendolyn and Sigismund Jr. ("Brother," they called him) would follow the parents and become teachers.

If Sigismund Walker's high regard for the life of the mind and Marion Walker's passion for music and the arts supported a carefully constructed bourgeois environment for the family, it was Grandmother Dozier who brought a different sensibility to bear on the young writer. Grandmother Dozier was not only the immediate link to an African American slave past, but she personified traditions—both oral and aural—that Walker would learn to transform and call her own. To understand rationally the profound and subtle significance of racial memory—as represented by her grandmother—became the test of Walker's ability as a writer. It was therefore her grandmother's voice that she associated with her first acts of cultural recovery, her grandmother's memory that became a tool for regaining and reconstructing her own family history as a communal history of African Americans. As she grew older, she grew increasingly more conscious of developing her own voice, one that would both incorporate and transcend that of her grandmother. She viewed her ability to speak with her ability to exercise control over her environment. When she was puzzled about the contradictions she saw in the world around her, she could comfortably use her imagination to create the world another way. In time, Walker came to understand that her vocation was not just to be a writer but to permit her voice to be the instrument of reconciliation; she would become her people's memory.

That voice found its first major articulation in poetry, a choice that gave her control over an intimate and personal process and that challenged her ability to deconstruct and reconstruct a wide range of narratives, those she heard as well as those she lived. The lyric poems, sonnets, ballads, and narratives, just as the later novel, became a series of discursive affirmations of a humanistic vision. What she had learned by growing up in the South enlarged her frame of reference by anchoring the racial experience in a distinctly southern context. It fueled her imagination and fed her intellect, providing an opportunity to envision the world other than the way it was.

Although some of the earliest poems are lost, the first phase of Walker's professional poetry career dates back to her pre-Chicago experience. In 1932, in her last year at New Orleans University, she met Langston Hughes. On a tour of the South, Hughes read at her parents' college, under the sponsorship of the Lyceum program there. Walker's dream of becoming a writer took a giant leap forward when she met Hughes. Boldly she went up to him after his reading, pressed her poetry into his hands, and waited anxiously for his reply. Hughes was stunned; he knew the excited seventeen-year-old had talent and told her so. To Walker's parents, he made his now famous remark, "Get her out of the South." Two more years would pass before Walker would take a major first step in her publishing career. It happened in Chicago.

Walker went to Chicago to continue her education at Northwestern. Testing her wings in a northern white institution rather than the traditional black institution like Howard or Fisk affirmed the family's sense of their daughter's enormous potential . . . and their desire to push the racial barriers down a bit further. There were other reasons as well. Northwestern was a family tradition. Her father had done his graduate education there, as had her favorite teacher at Gilbert Academy. More importantly, Northwestern was affiliated with the Methodist Episcopal church (later the United Methodist Church), and it attracted Methodist families from throughout the country, offering special financial arrangements to those with needs. The Walkers knew families with whom their daughters could stay, since blacks were not allowed housing on Northwestern's campus.[5]

For two years Walker immersed herself in a highly competitive educational environment, ever aware that she was battling against a double sense of inferiority. Not only were African Americans generally thought to be intellectually inferior, but the southern system of education was also regarded as equally inferior. For Walker, nothing could be further from the truth. Her English professor there, E. B. Hungerford, must have been impressed by this tiny eighteen-year-old, more girl than woman, far more intelligent than her years. Walker was looking for a mentor, someone who could supervise the formal training she needed. Fully aware that a fairly solid middle-class background and superior early education had made her a thinking and highly motivated young woman, she was also steeped in the oral culture of the black South. She knew its folk-based rhythms and its ritualized behaviors. But Walker also knew that the voice of the South had to be the voice of change, of truthfulness, of strength and courage. It was in this voice that she would need to learn how to speak.

Under Hungerford, she learned all the forms of English poetry and the English metrical system; she learned how to do the scansion of a poem and memorized the versification patterns. She read the English poets, focusing on the Romantic writers, and developed a keen interest in Shakespearean sonnets, the odes of Shelley and Keats, and the long poems of Wordsworth, all important influences upon her future work. Hungerford had done something else for Walker, however, that she would never forget. He had managed to get her inducted into the Poetry Society of America.[6] During her senior year, she had taken a second course from him: creative writing. She was gaining increasing confidence in her ability to write both poetry and prose. Hungerford was more than encouraging, and she, in turn, wanted his approval. When she turned in her poems to him along with her first three hundred pages of *Jubilee,* she went to his office to find out her grade. Thinking that she had failed miserably, she asked what she would have to do to get an "A." Hungerford not only awarded her the highest grade in the course but provided her with a host of little magazines and poetry reviews, suggesting some places where she submit some of her work. One of the magazines was *Poetry;* its editor, Harriet Monroe, had been one of the speakers she heard at Northwestern. She secretly vowed that she would publish there.

In 1934, when Walker was eighteen, a junior at Northwestern, and looking for opportunities to publish, it was to an invitation by W. E. B. Du Bois that she first responded. He, too, had spoken at Northwestern. And when he suggested she send some of her poetry to him for *Crisis,* she leaped at the chance. Appropriately, Walker titled her first officially published poem "Daydream":

> I want to write.
> I want to write the songs of [my] people.
> I want to hear them singing melodies in the dark.
> I want to catch the last floating strains
> From their sob-stricken throats.
> I want to frame their dreams into words,
> Their souls into notes.
> I want to catch their sunshine laughter in a bowl;
> Fling dark hands to a darker sky
> And fill them full of stars,
> Then crush and mix such lights till they become
> A mirrored pool of brilliance in the dawn.
>
> *Crisis,* 1934[7]

Eleanor Traylor notes that this poem, Walker's "dawn song, . . . is a compelling . . . recitation, . . . a valediction at commencement, winning its audience through its elocution of the strategies of delight."[8] The psalmlike quality of the poem indeed offers it as a meditation, a dedication, a public acknowledgment of poetic commitment. It was the beginning of her soul journey.

In the poem, a spiral of moments from a recaptured past charged with symbolic significance inspire a creative vision. Although it is a "daydream," the poem emphasizes the movement from darkness ("melodies in the dark"; "darker sky"; "stars") to light. Art is viewed as that experience that changes things, and it is rooted in one's own culture. The poem offers a vision of possibility coupled with desire, symbolized by the repetition of "I want," as the poet establishes the essence of a poetic vocation. The poet must utilize all sense of feeling, thought, knowledge, and history, not only to interpret racial and cultural signs but also to change the course of history ("frame . . . dreams into words . . . souls into notes"). The lyrical phrases, rhythmic flow, and alliterative quality that we associate with the poems in *For My People* and *Prophets for a New Day* are prefigured in this apprentice piece, as Walker sets up the characteristic tension between consciousness and experience, between human will and historical circumstance. The underlying song motif signifies the process of transformation in which all art is engaged.

The poem is evocative as it explodes and explains the musical motif. From this ritual of music ("songs of my people"; "melodies in the dark"), the author discerns that a new kind of music can emerge from the "last floating strains /

From sob stricken throats." "Dark hands" create from the fragments of a dark past ("darker sky") that which becomes a "mirrored pool of brilliance in the dawn." The poet is indebted to the past for the "stars and sunshine laughter," which moves the poem deductively to a climax. The movement of discovery, from the general "I want to write" to the specific "I want to write the songs of my people," suggests that art must be purposeful and located within a definite cultural matrix. Further specificity is called for as Walker identifies a collage of metaphors, the raw materials that she wants "to catch . . . Then crush and mix." Invoking a routinely feminine activity as a site of artistic creation affirms the importance of the female writer. Walker, in this her first poem, has successfully inserted the female voice—her own voice—as she has synthesized various elements from the past to create a work of art.

Like Langston Hughes, whom she regarded as her mentor during their thirty-five-year friendship, Walker seemed to instinctively recognize the importance of drawing upon multiple traditions in her poetry. Hughes was innovative and experimental in his use of voice and imagery to construct poetic forms appropriate for and consistent with black historical reality. Walker invokes the dynamism of southern racial history by juxtaposing the pain and sadness emerging from historical memory with the joy and excitement of cultural recovery. The experience is neither transcended nor forgotten but is transformed into art. This revisioning of the dominant cultural narrative of black history is essentially a modernist project for Walker, whose Christian humanism could easily accommodate both American and African American poetic traditions. The philosophical bent of her father and her New England– trained high school instructors bequeathed to her the tradition of Emersonian transcendentalism and romantic individualism, stressing the continuity between the self and nature. Twentieth-century American poetry instruction in the first decades of the century also acknowledged the Whitmanesque tradition, which locates the sacred in ordinary human experience. Rigorous instruction in the classical forms of poetry, which Walker undertook at Northwestern, and the practice in the modernist forms she received in the Writers Program at Iowa gave her the sophistication and experience she needed to refine her voice. But Walker was ever comfortable with the Bible, where her instruction in literature had begun, and she found few places where the imagery and controlled cadences from the Bible could not be integrated. Into this mix must be added one other influential figure: Sterling Brown. Brown made it possible to comprehend black vernacular culture without tying it to the plantation dialect poetry of the past. Inspired by Hughes and Brown, therefore, Walker could easily expand upon received traditions and rename them at the same time.

By the time Walker graduated from college in 1935, just weeks after she turned twenty, she felt that her studies had served her well. What she took from her classes in poetry was an appreciation for the poet's ability to evoke human emotion within highly structured frameworks. When she looked to black poetry, she saw some similar structures, except that it honored a greater juxtaposition between written and oral expression and between the individual and the collective voice. Because she had grown up amid some of the most powerful expressions of human feeling imaginable, Walker had little difficulty recognizing the poetic sensibility inherent within black culture. With the South embedded in her memory, and the weight of her own personal and social history bearing down on her soul, Walker left Northwestern but remained in Chicago to honor her commitment to herself and her art.

Then began a period of Walker's life unlike any other. Suddenly the world looked very different from the one she had known at Northwestern. Even in that less-than-cordial environment, her education was being paid for, and she had her work and a professor who believed in her. Now on her own, she had to earn a living for herself. A career as a writer seemed to be dwarfed by the contemporary economic reality. Alone and unemployed, she began to comprehend the meaning of the Great Depression. An important poem, "People of Unrest and Hunger," evolved as a response to the perceived hopelessness of poverty. Like so many others in Chicago and throughout the country, she wanted to feel hope and sought to counter the intensity of a nation's hunger and loss. When placed within the context of Walker's complete canon, this poem appears atypical. Although the theme is reflected in the Walkeresque juxtapositions that became her trademark—the love for the natural landscape is contrasted with the social landscape with accompanying feelings of love and hate—the form is not:

> Stare from your pillow into the sun.
> See the disk of light in shadows.
> Through fingers of morning Day is growing tall.
> People of unrest and hunger
> Stare from your pillow into the sun.
> Cry with a loud voice after the sun.
> Take his yellow arms and wrap them 'round your life.
> Be glad to be washing in the sun.
> Be glad to see.

The poem shows the awkwardness of Walker's early experiments. Trying to reverse the pattern she tried in "Daydream," the poem charges ahead after the title is announced, speaking directly to the "people of unrest and hunger." Without setting the personal context, the poem emphasizes action as the poet assumes a certain authority over those to whom she speaks. The choice of the second person creates too much distance between the speaker and the reader, and while it is boldly affirmative, it becomes so through pronouncements. The logic of self-discovery apparent in "Daydream" or of cultural recovery as seen in "Southern Song" is lost. Instead, "People of Unrest and Hunger" shows a stiff lyricism, the statements undeveloped as the meaning is revealed. Each line is an independent thought, unconnected to the previous one, as we experience the metaphors ("disk of light"; "fingers of morning"; "yellow arms"). What Walker has attempted—to shift emphasis away from the material reality of poverty by offering compensation from nature—overstates the possibility of relief from human desperation through blind faith. The poet's effort to offer solace to the poor seems dismissive and insensitive at best, even though the poem ends by forecasting a better day ahead, "Be glad to see." On the other hand, if this piece is viewed as an apprentice work showing experimentation with voice, Walker must have realized its effect. She discontinued her use of the second person in her later work, preferring instead to find more effective ways to maintain the connection between herself as poet and the reader as other as well as between the spirit of the inner world and the reality of the outer world.

The Depression became a critical marker for Walker and a host of American and African American writers. While Franklin Delano Roosevelt and the U.S. Congress responded with a massive federal program intended to speed the recovery and restore hope to the nation, the popular response was more radical and explicit. Violent demonstrations in New York, Detroit, Los Angeles, the South, and Chicago contrasted with the decorum of the soup kitchens and relief lines. In Chicago, home to one of the largest urban populations and distinctively black and southern in character, the Depression fueled the activities of the Communist Party, which drew a host of writers into its orbit. An international Communist movement had brought attention to the condition of the poor and was organizing effectively among those "who had nothing to lose but their chains." The Great Depression permitted a convergence between those working toward reforming America's racial policies with those seeking a total restructuring of the American economic system. Believing that America was indeed on the verge of an economic collapse, which made the emergence of new leadership a necessary reality, blacks and radical activists found solidarity as they envisioned common solutions. The Communist Party especially targeted artists and writers, encouraging representation of the masses of people, whether black, ethnic, or poor. It was the writers who would impart their vision of a new America to the nation and the world.

Walker's search for employment took her to the Federal Writers' Project of the Works Progress Administration (WPA), where she eventually found a placement in 1936. The WPA not only meant getting paid for working with enough time left to write on her own, but it also meant meeting other writers, finding out about publishing outlets, and being exposed to new ideas. In addition to its radical contingent, Chicago had been the home of established writers who had helped to establish it as a major literary and industrial center outside of New York. A Chicago-identified literature, voiced by writers like Carl Sandburg, James T. Farrell, Theodore Dreiser, Hamlin Garland, Upton Sinclair, and Floyd Dell, had promoted naturalism in American writing. It was this naturalistic vision that had appealed to the newly arrived migrants to Chicago, those from the small towns of the Midwest and the prairie like Edgar Lee Masters, Margaret Anderson, and Vachel Lindsay, and those from the black South and Southwest like Richard Wright and Frank Marshall Davis. With the access and opportunity available to her on the WPA job, Walker soon made the acquaintance of radical white women poets like Leonie Adams, Elinor Wylie, Louise Bogan, and Muriel Rukeyser. After only a few months on the job, she was in a position to meet Geraldine Udell and George Dillon, the distinguished editor of *Poetry* magazine. Dillon advised her to read the French symbolists; armed with a substantial reading knowledge of French, symbolist poetry helped Walker advance her understanding of modernist literary forms.

Although Walker encountered other African American writers and artists at the WPA—notably Arna Bontemps, Ted Ward, William Attaway, and Richard Wright; Katherine Dunham, Frank Yerby, and Willard Motley—and attended frequent activities sponsored by the Communists, it was a more direct emotional and social connection that would prove to be her most personally rewarding experience during the three years she lived and worked in Chicago. Her chance meeting with Richard Wright in April 1936 resulted in an invitation to the organizing meeting of the South Side Writers' Group and the beginning of lifelong friendships, including a singular friendship with Wright that changed her life. The first meeting terrified her, but she quickly grew accustomed to its intense debates and exchange of ideas. She found herself among young black professionals whom she could regard as peers and who had similar expectations and varying degrees of commitment to Communist ideals.

Wright led the group and paid particular attention to the young woman who outstripped him in education and professional training, matched his intelligence and admired his political sophistication. Walker found his social theories strange but respected his criticism of her work, as he did hers. "Suspended in time somewhere between the Writers' Project and the South Side

Writers' Group, possibly in the parlor of the house where I lived, three forms of writing took place in our consciousness, conversation, and actions. We sat together and worked on the forms of my poetry, the free verse things, and came up with my long line or strophic form, punctuated by a short line."[9]

Only later would Margaret realize that the group she was part of formed a new kind of Renaissance among African American writers and artists, a Chicago Renaissance. These writers would shift allegiance away from the themes of Harlem, were decidedly more working class in background and consciousness, and believed that the problems of African Americans were primarily economic and not exclusively racial in nature. The Chicago Renaissance represented one of those rare moments when history and artistic greatness find a convergence. For African American writers living in Chicago during the 1930s and '40s, this Renaissance was a triumph of a new kind of consciousness rooted in a tradition of social protest. While this tradition was not new in and of itself, it was accompanied by the consolidation of a new literary leadership, one no longer based in the conventional African American middle class. The difference was in the way a new generation of writers, identifying with the experiences of southern blacks, expanded their sociological imagination and responded to the politics of Marxism. Arna Bontemps, Frank Marshall Davis, Ted Ward, William Attaway, and, especially, the sociologists St. Clair Drake and Horace Cayton along with Walker herself became a cohesive group challenging each other and articulating a vision of commitment and change. To them, the artist was not simply an exemplar of achievement and a sign of racial progress, she was also an agent of change. This sense of her own agency and an evolving political awareness matched her complex historical vision and her need to locate and restore a distinctive African American sensibility.

Encouraged by her positive experiences at the South Side Writers' Group and her developing relationships with other young writers in Chicago, Walker submitted the poems she had been working on to *New Challenge*, edited by Dorothy West, a transitional figure from the Harlem Renaissance who viewed the publication as an opportunity to introduce some newer voices. Four poems were published, two of which were to become part of Walker's collected works. "People of Unrest and Hunger" and "Southern Song" both had been shared and criticized at a meeting of the South Side Writers' Group. The other two poems, "Mess of Pottage" and "Hounds," never appeared again, no doubt because they showed some of the more glaring weaknesses of Walker's early work.

In "Southern Song," Walker returned to the first person, making herself a participant in the process of cultural recovery and this time allowing herself to be its site:

I want my body bathed again by southern suns; my soul
    reclaimed again from southern soil: I want to rest again in
    southern fields; in grass and hay and clover bloom; to lay
    my hand again upon the clay baked by a southern sun;
    to touch the rain-soaked earth and smell the smell of soil.
I want my rest unbroken in the fields of southern earth; freedom
    to watch the corn wave silver in the sun and mark the
    splashing of a brook—a pond with ducks and frogs;
    and count the clouds.
I want no mobs to wrench me from my southern rest; no forms
    to take me in the night and burn my shack and make for
    me a nightmare full of oil and flame.
I want my careless song to strike no minor key; no fiend to stand
    between my body's southern song—the fusion of the
    South, my body's [southern] song and me.

The New Challenge, 1937

In the poem, one in which the South is imaginatively reconstructed, Walker moves closer to the form that, in its full evolution, marked her signature: the long, incremental free-verse stanzas in which indented lines explore the meaning of the opening line for each stanza. Alliteration and repetition give the poem needed emphasis, and the catalog of images undercuts what at first appears to be a tranquil, pastoral scene. If "Daydream/I Want to Write" presented a record of Walker's awakening to the possibility of relationships among history, memory, art, and the artist, then "Southern Song" announced the writer's discovery of her own distinctive voice, one that can synthesize the natural and social worlds. The poem locates Walker's voice within a specific cultural matrix, while her vision is inclusive and holistic. "Southern Song" establishes a connection to that which is primal, as the mythic voice struggles to make experience intelligible and give order, meaning, and unity to the images, chaos, fragments, and phenomena from a dismembered culture. The memory of the South permits Walker to reenter history and make it sacred. For the creative artist, the poetic process remakes and transforms the old into the new.

"Southern Song" revoices the passionate outpouring of "Daydream," as individual memory is merged with cultural memory. Each stanza emphasizes the subjective aspect of desire: "I want my body bathed"; "I want my rest unbroken"; "I want no mobs"; "I want my careless song." The action of the poem centers around the author as agent as the South is reclaimed through a sensory experience, the sounds and smells of southern earth. But the pastoral imagery is juxtaposed with the South's other reality. The mood of desire soon becomes one of resistance. The contradiction is established linguistically; the object of desire expressed longingly in "I want my body," and "I want my rest" is replaced by a strident denunciation: "I want no mobs . . . no forms to take me in the night and burn my shack." The open embrace has now shifted to rejection and resistance in the third and fourth stanzas that complete the poem. "Nightmare full of oil and flame" suggests something unreal, that which exists in a semiconscious state. To evoke memory and imagination is also to risk the painful thought of violence and destruction: "mobs that wrench me from my southern rest . . . and make for me a nightmare full of oil and flame." The resistance expressed appears to be double-edged. While the nightmare of the past must not be repeated, we must also prevent the past from causing psychic divisions. The poem ends with reconciliation (the fusion of the South) and integration of the self, memory (my body's song), and history (my body's southern song). The threat of the violent past is evoked in a "careless song," but the resistant imagination asserts the humanistic self.

The contrasting images of the South—a place of beauty and ugliness, peacefulness and violence, suffering and joy, creativity and destruction—provide a constant source of tension in Walker's best poems. Taking this journey back in physical and spiritual time corresponds with the journey forward toward the integrated self on a personal and political level. "Southern Song" traces the formation of belief in the integrated self as the body becomes a site of creation and transformation.

The appearances in *Crisis* and *New Challenge* brought Walker much-needed recognition within the African American community, which would always be her most important social base. Because it was a time when a new vision was called for to meet the demands of a new era, these were stepping stones to the mainstream recognition that would be hers soon thereafter. The apprentice poems gave definition and meaning to her voice. Walker was indeed "growing out of shadow," the title she gave to her first autobiographical essay, which appeared shortly after *For My People* had won the Yale Series of Younger Poets Award. Walker was able to put into clearer focus the first steps in her literary journey:

When I went to school, I read the history books that glorify the white race and describe the Negro either as a clown and a fool or beast capable of very hard work in excessive heat. I discovered the background of chattel slavery behind this madness of race prejudice. Once we were slaves and now we are not, and the South remains angry. But when I went home to the good books and the wonderful music and the gentle, intelligent parents, I could see no reason for prejudice on the basis of a previous condition of servitude. . . . I went to church and I wondered why God let this thing continue. Why were there segregated churches and segregated hospitals and cemeteries and schools? Why must I ride behind a Jim Crow sign? Why did a full-grown colored man sit meekly behind a Jim Crow sign and do nothing about it? What could he do? Then I began to daydream: It will not always be this way. Someday, just as chattel slavery ended, this injustice will also end; this internal suffering will cease; this ache inside for understanding will exist no longer. Someday I said, when I am fully grown, I will understand and I will be able to do something about it. I will write books that will prove the history texts were distorted. I will write books about colored people who have colored faces, books that will not make me ashamed when I read them.[10]

Margaret Walker's emergence as a poet was as much about her own intellectual and artistic awakening and discovery as it was about molding and consequently affirming an identity for herself as a young black woman, whose individual will and creative spirit converged with the needs and expectations of her family, community, and her race. The first poems to appear in print represented the working out of her philosophical vision and her formal literary preferences, and her search for a place that would allow her to speak in her own voice. Walker often noted that she was not taught to think as a woman, because her parents had respected her intelligence and had imposed no limitations upon her abilities. She grew to womanhood understanding that the only things that would prevent her from achieving her goals were social prescriptions, which she could not control, and individual talent, which she could. The orientation that race was the major barrier to overcome in order to achieve success left little time to consider the implications of gender in this early stage of her life. When she expanded her political understanding to include the role of economics in shaping the reality of African American life, this only provided further affirmation that not only was change possible, it was also the responsibility of the artist to serve as an agent of change. The function of education was to cultivate the individual talent, and this dictated her educational and professional career goals: she left Chicago to pursue the M.A. at the University of Iowa, a place she returned to in 1961 to complete her Ph.D. Concurrently, she produced *For My People* and *Jubilee,* as indications that her intellectual potential was commensurate with her own vision of racial progress.

What mattered most for Walker was that she live up to her human potential. But it was a sense of her own human potential intimately connected to a communal racial destiny. Had not her sense of self been so completely bound to her sense of others, Walker would have made some very different personal choices as a woman and an artist. This is the humanistic appeal that pervades her work, one that is quintessentially feminine, as critics Minrose Gwin, Joyce Pettis, Charlotte Goodman, and others have pointed out. It is also that which marked her intellectual distance from Wright and other writers for whom Marxism had a strong appeal. When this personal vision combines with her philosophical understanding of African American culture, the result is a startling testament of faith. Nowhere is this clearer than in "The Humanistic Tradition of Afro-American Literature":

> No one questions the deep pathos of our sorrow songs sung in a minor key, the feeling-tone of our religious and gospel music, the melancholy note in our blues, or the rhythmic syncopation of our jazz; but what most white America still does not know is that our literature reveals how we have transmuted suffering into song and heartbreak into compassion. . . . Langston Hughes was the humanist par excellence—loving all mankind and celebrating life with a constant plea for social justice and a tender note of compassion for all the suffering poor. The black writer therefore has a heritage of fighting for freedom, for the liberation of mind and spirit from the hideous bondage of racism and all the shackles of fearful prejudice. We have a rich gift from America, but it is a spiritual gift. . . . It is a gift of wholeness from within, born out of our ancient heritage and from the unbroken tradition of humanistic values that did not spring from Renaissance Europe, but developed in Asia and Africa before the religious wars of the Middle Ages. This humanism includes a recognition that we are part of nature and the historical process, that we are implicit in the dynamic evolving of mankind to ever higher planes of being.

The "gift of wholeness from within" revealed itself in poetry and prose and was hers to share. As she uncovered more and more of the lived black experience, creating landscapes from myth and history that were both literal and symbolic, her work became synonymous with the transformative power of the poetic text. From the very beginning of her career to its abrupt ending when she died of cancer at eighty-three, Walker created by enacting meaning from memory and unifying the psychological and spiritual selves of history, in short, by becoming a living memory for her people. Humanism became her antidote for the fragmentation of history, revealing itself best as internal juxtaposition and controlled emotion, the essence of her form and style.

Her apprentice poems had served their function. The stage was set for "For My People," a poem that would know no comparison in terms of lyrical power, historical meaning, and the use of cultural memory. It, like Walker herself, was that passionately human response to the historical legacy of racism and the need for cultural reconciliation, demanding to be heard.

NOTES

1. "How I Wrote *Jubilee*," in *"How I Wrote Jubilee" and Other Essays on Life and Literature*, ed. Maryemma Graham (New York: Feminist Press, 1990), 51.

2. Mercedes, the second child born to the Walkers, was actually considered a musical prodigy, whose training the mother carefully supervised.

3. "My Creative Adventure," in *On Being Female, Black, and Free: Essays by Margaret Walker 1932–1992*, ed. Maryemma Graham (Knoxville: University of Tennessee Press, 1997), 12.

4. "How I Wrote *Jubilee*" 3.

5. Margaret and her younger sister Mercedes were sent to Northwestern together; Mercedes joined the freshman class.

6. Apparently Hungerford had broken a racial barrier by lobbying for Walker to be the first African American to be admitted in a college chapter.

7. "Daydream" appeared in Walker's subsequent volumes as "I Want to Write."

8. Eleanor Traylor, "'Bolder Measures Crashing Through': Margaret Walker's Poem of the Century," *Callaloo* 10.4 (fall 1987), 570–95.

9. Margaret Walker, "Richard Wright," *Richard Wright: Impressions and Perspectives*, ed. David Ray and Robert Farnsworth (Ann Arbor: University of Michigan Press, 1971), 51.

10. "How I Wrote *Jubilee*" 3–4.

Black Women Writers at Work

An Interview with Margaret Walker

CLAUDIA TATE

MARGARET WALKER: I would like to read this excerpt from my forthcoming autobiography from Howard University Press, which speaks for itself:

I graduated from Northwestern and [worked for] the WPA. After three years I went to graduate school in order to get a master's degree to enhance my teaching. Getting my master's in one school year nearly killed me. I was on NYA [National Youth Administration] and had so little money I ate lunch only once a week when a friend bought it. Like my college days at Northwestern, I went hungry unless friends fed me. When I went home in August, my father lifted me from the train. I was in a state of collapse. For eighteen months I was unable to work and could not find a job anyway. Meanwhile, one of my sisters graduated from music college and got a job teaching music at a small school in Mississippi. Her salary was forty dollars a month. Like my mother, she worked seven days a week, including playing for vespers and church on Sunday and practicing with the choir. She said the only time she had for herself was at night close to midnight until dawn. After teaching for two years in Mississippi, she went to Knoxville, Tennessee, for a larger salary; but she had the same back-breaking schedule.

As for myself, my teaching career has been fraught with conflict, insults, humiliations and disappointments. In every case when I have attempted to make a creative contribution and succeeded, I have been immediately replaced by a man. I began teaching in the early '40s at Livingstone College in Salisbury, North Carolina, for the handsome sum of $135 a month.

I was very happy to get it. I had a master's degree but no teaching experience. They would not have had a man for less than $150 to $200 a month. I arrived in Salisbury one cold February morning at two o'clock. Although I was expected, there was no one at the station to meet me. I finally found a taxi to take me to the campus, and I banged on the door of the girls' dormitory for a full half-hour before anyone opened the door. Less than three hours after I went to bed, the matron ordered me out for breakfast at six o'clock and told me I had an eight o'clock class. My life was arranged for me hour by hour and controlled by half a dozen people. I was resented in the town and by some faculty and staff people because I was replacing one of their favorites. And I didn't know this person from Adam's cat. I had absolutely no social life; I spent most of my afternoons and evenings in my room writing.

That summer I won the Yale award and began getting job offers from everywhere. I felt strong pressure to stay at Livingstone, but when I went home my mother had accepted a job for me at West Virginia State College. It paid the grand sum of $200 a month. My dear mother thought it her duty to grab it before somebody else did. While I was there I never had a stable living situation. The night I arrived I had no place to go. . . . Five places in one school year. I had had it. If I had been a man, no one would have dared to move me around like that.

But the real harrowing time of my life came at Jackson State College. In September 1949 when I began teaching in Jackson, Mississippi, I was married and was the mother of three children. My youngest was nine weeks old. For nine months everything went well, and they kept saying that they were honored to have me until I moved my family and furniture. When they saw my husband was sick and disabled from the war, that I had three children all under six years of age, that I was poor and had to work, then they put their foot on my neck. . . . If I had been single, I would have quit that day; but I had three children and a sick husband, and I had just moved. So I bowed my head and decided to stay on. Perhaps I should have taken another job. . . .

A year later I was ordered to produce a literary festival for the 75th anniversary of the college. I was told to write some occasional poetry and to write and produce a pageant for the occasion. I said, "If I succeed I must leave here, and if I fail I must leave here." I succeeded through much stress and strain and much public embarrassment. Then I secured a Ford Fellowship and left. I stayed away for fifteen months, and when I returned with a substantial raise, I also had another child.

While at Jackson State from 1954 until 1960, my salary remained well under $6,000. Meanwhile, I had devised a humanities program to suit the needs of black students in Mississippi, which not only raised the cultural level 75 percent but also provided credits on race in the modern world and on the great contributions of black people to the modern world. . . .

Then began the death struggle for me to return to graduate school. I contended that I was no longer content to be classified as the equivalent of a Ph.D. because I was a poet. My salary was not equivalent. I was determined to go back and get the degree that everybody worshipped. Then they would be forced to pay me more money. After all, my children were growing up and getting ready for college, and my husband was disabled. I absolutely needed the money. I was tired of living on borrowed money from one month to the next.

I borrowed $500 from the credit union, got another $300 from the college as salary, plus money from my husband and my mother. I took my two younger children, ages six and eleven, and went back to Iowa to summer school. There I inquired about my chances of returning for the Ph.D. degree and using my Civil War novel for my dissertation. I also inquired about financial assistance. In the fall I went back to Jackson State College for another hellish year, but in September 1962 I managed to get away.

I had two children with me who were in college during those three years. One graduated a week before I did. When I returned to Jackson with my degree, I asked not to be involved with the humanities; instead I tried to formulate a new freshman English program of writing themes from relevant reading. After a year, the college administration did not so much as give me the courtesy of saying they would not require my services in that capacity the next year; they simply replaced me with a man, and not a man with superior training, rank, or ability. I returned to an old interest in creative writing and taught courses in literary criticism, the Bible as literature, and Afro-American literature. After another so-so year, I devised the black studies program. Three years with that program have been the happiest of my teaching career at Jackson State College.

CLAUDIA TATE: What was it like to live with *Jubilee* for thirty years?

MW: You just become part of it, and it becomes part of you. Working, raising a family, all of that becomes part of it. Even though I was preoccupied with everyday things, I used to think about what I wanted to do with *Jubilee*. Part of the problem with the book was the terrible feeling that I wasn't going to be able to get it finished, since I was sick so much of the time. And even if I had the time to work at it, I wasn't sure I would be able to do it the way I wanted. Living with the book over a long period of time was agonizing. Despite all of that, *Jubilee* is the product of a mature person. When I started out with the book, I didn't know half of what I now know about life. That I learned during those thirty years. After all, I started writing *Jubilee* at nineteen, and I couldn't have dealt with, for instance, the childbirth problems. I couldn't have known about them then, not until I had become a mature woman who had her own problems. There's a difference between writing about something and living through it. I did both. I think I was meant to write *Jubilee*.

CT: *For My People* appeared in 1942, and [Gwendolyn] Brooks's *A Street in Bronzeville* in 1945. Was there any competition between these two works?

MW: I'll give you some historical background on the two pieces. I wrote the title poem of *For My People* in July of 1937, around my twenty-second birthday. It was published in *Poetry Magazine* in November of that year. I went out to Iowa in the fall of 1939 and got my master's degree in the summer of 1940 when I was twenty-five. I then went south to teach, though I actually didn't begin teaching until 1942. I met Gwendolyn Brooks in 1938, after I had written the title poem "For My People." Margaret Burroughs, a mutual friend, introduced us. I don't think Gwen had published in national magazines at that time. I'm two years older than Gwen.

For My People won the Yale award in the summer of '42. Yale had rejected it three times. Stephen Vincent Benét, the editor at that time, wanted to publish it the first time I sent it to him from the University of Iowa. Anyway, he kept it from February until July in '39, and he wrote to me telling me he thought the poems were as near perfect as I could make them. He asked me to resubmit them the following year, and I did. He said he'd keep them while he was trying to make up his mind. I didn't really know what was actually happening at Yale until I won. That year, 1942, was the last year Benét edited the Yale Younger Poet Series. I think he simply confronted his colleagues with the fact that if they wouldn't give the award to me, he wasn't going to name anybody else. In other words I think he was telling them he was through with them if they didn't give it to me. After all, he had repeatedly said the piece was as near perfect as I could make it. I think he felt they were refusing purely on the basis of race. I didn't know how much the issue had gone back and forth between them until I went up there. The woman with whom I'd corresponded said that they had "to come begging" because they had to ask for the manuscript. I hadn't submitted it that year because I got tired of sending it.

Three years after *For My People* was published, *A Street in Bronzeville* appeared in 1945. It was a very good book. I remember saying to Langston that the poetry was promising, technically and intellectually; the work had great potential. *Annie Allen* [1949] fulfilled that potential. I think *Annie Allen* is a superb book. Technically it is stunning. The subtleties come through it much better than they did in *A Street in Bronzeville*.

Getting back to your question . . . I never felt that I was in competition with Gwen. But I had this feeling; I may be very wrong, and I've been told I was wrong. I said in the book with Nikki [*A Poetic Equation: Conversations Between Nikki Giovanni and Margaret Walker*] that it was ironic that all the forces that had dealt negatively with my work dealt positively with Gwendolyn Brooks's work. I named them in that book. First, Gwen won a poetry prize at Northwestern. That never happened to me. Northwestern later gave me a lot of recognition. But when I was a student there, they didn't. Paul Engle was my teacher, and he was fighting mad with me for sending *For My People* to Yale. For years he was annoyed about it. I think he helped Gwen. Second, Richard Wright was a man whom I knew very well for three years. We were never intimate, but we were very dear and close friends. After we broke up and our friendship ended, he helped Gwen. I'm certain that Gwen got published at Harper because Wright was there. Nobody ever told me, but I think he interceded for her. Paul Engle, Northwestern, Richard Wright, and the Friends of Literature on the North Side, with whom my teachers at Northwestern were involved, all helped Gwen. Paul did do two things for me: he helped me to get a job and helped me find the ways and means to study at Iowa both times, in 1939 and in the sixties. But to answer your question—I never figured for one day I was in competition with Gwen.

I think *This Is My Century* is a good book. I haven't seen anything like it. The power is more sustaining than *For My People*. I've wanted to do it for a long, long time. It's been in me for half a lifetime. What I have here is a complete indictment of our present-day society, our whole world. What's wrong with it is money, honey, money. Inflation blues is what we got. What

I have tried to do in this piece is integrate what [Alex] Haley did to me to show that it's just part of the same corrupt scene.

CT: What's happening with the Wright biography? [1]

MW: I sometimes get very frightened because I know so much. I know I've been on the "black list" for a long time. Every time I pick up the Wright stuff, I get frightened. I realize that I'm dealing with very sensitive material. Sometimes I just turn away from it and wonder will I be signing my death warrant if I do what I know has to be done with that book. You see there are several very sensitive areas. One is communism itself, which concerned the great intellectual debate between black nationalism and the Communist Party: its dictates and policy on Negroes. If you tell the story the way it needs to be told, you're in trouble with both sides—the U.S. Government and the Communist Party. Neither one of them is a friend to black people. When Wright realized that, he got out of the Party.

Do I look like a crazy, foolish, superstitious woman to you? Well, I may be. I've fooled with astrology for forty years. When I first met Wright in 1936, *Horoscope Magazine* was published for the first time. I bought some of the first issues for a dime. I know how to set up charts. When Martin Luther King was killed in Memphis, I was in the Leamington Hotel in Minneapolis, Minnesota. I sat down and made his death chart. The chart shocked me. I didn't understand it at the time because what I saw all over King's chart was not so much death—I saw the gun, the government—as nothing but money—millions and millions of dollars. Money of all kinds, from all countries. Nothing but money.

Getting back to Wright . . . I remember the news flash on television about Wright's death. I was fixing breakfast. It upset me so that I sat down and began to tremble. Wright was just like somebody in my family. I had been that close to him. All that day I kept thinking about it, and I said to Eubanks, "They said he had a heart attack, but I believe it was tied up with his stomach." Because he had a delicate stomach. I know because I had cooked for him, and I knew he had to have simple foods. I didn't think about foul play. I didn't know his death had been kept out of the press for two days. No autopsy was ever performed. *Ebony* came out with an article, "The Mystery Around Richard Wright's Death." And John A. Williams's *The Man Who Cried I Am* suggested in a very symbolic fashion that Wright might have been murdered.

I felt Wright wanted me to write his biography because nobody is going to be more sympathetic and understanding than I. I was in love with him, and he knew it. He could not marry me. I was not what he could marry. That's the whole truth of that. You can't say he didn't love me; I knew he did.

People think that Wright helped me and my writing. But I was writing poetry as a child in New Orleans. I had published in *Crisis* even before I ever met Wright. He had a lot of influence on me, but it wasn't on my writing. It concerned social perspective—Marxism and the problems of black people in this country. I helped Wright. He couldn't spell straight; he couldn't write straight. I had just graduated from Northwestern with a major in English literature. Do you believe that I was just being introduced to literature by Wright?

Michel Fabre, Wright's biographer, recognized [that] Wright and I had a literary friendship. He wrote not too long ago on behalf of Yale, asking if I'd donate Wright's letters. Yale wants my letters. Harper & Row called and told me I had a debt to literary posterity. I said, "I'll pay the debt in the way I choose."

They know what I wrote to Wright, but they don't know what he wrote to me. Here's one of Wright's letters. You notice he lived in a different place with every letter: Gates Avenue, Carlton Avenue, Rutledge Place, 136th Street. . . . He lived at a dozen different addresses in three years' time.

You know, "Goose Island" was the story that Wright took from me for *Native Son.* I had written it for a project, and he read it. It was a slum story. The main character was a girl who went into prostitution. It was very much like Studs Lonigan stuff. I started writing that story in the writers' project, and I took three years. I was supposed to enter my story in the same contest Wright entered *Uncle Tom's Children.*

I remember Wright wrote me a Special Delivery letter, requesting that I send him all the newspaper clippings on Robert Nixon's trial. I sent him enough to cover a nine by twelve foot floor. Then he came to Chicago and asked me to help him for a day or so. We went to the library, and on my card I got that [Clarence] Darrow book, and I took him to the office of [Ulysses] Keys, who had been the lawyer on the case. I asked Keys for the brief. Those were integral parts of *Native Son.* I still didn't know what his story was about. When he did tell me, I said, "Oh, we're writing about the same thing, only your character is a man and mine is a woman." My character was a very talented girl, a musician who became a prostitute. That's what the environment did to her. Of course, I didn't have the violence and murder.

Wright returned to New York. From then on the relationship began to deteriorate. It still hadn't ended until the week he sent the manuscript to the publishers, and then he said that he didn't have any further need of me. He had used me to the fullest extent. He didn't intend to marry me, not ever. I'm glad of that because it wouldn't have worked.

Well, Wright's violence comes out of his anger. I gave a speech at Amherst in which I said the keys to Wright's fiction and personality were anger, ambivalence, and alienation. In the biography I start with him as a child and show how this anger builds up. If you knew him, you would not know how much of that anger is seething inside of him. He was always angry. I didn't understand it. He was like a demon possessed. One of my theses is that Wright was angry as a child. The Farnsworth piece [*Richard Wright: Impressions and Perspectives,* edited by David Ray and Robert Farnsworth] revealed how well I knew him and that I was the one to do the biography. It also revealed the literary content of our friendship. I didn't start out to do a definitive biography. What the editors discovered when I quoted from the letters was that I have a psychoanalytic treatment of Wright. Furthermore, I tied it in with the writing. I did what nobody could do. I dealt with Wright's formative environment: his family background with the broken home, the poverty, the racism, the hunger, and their effects. Horace Cayton was to write the biography. He collected interviews with people who knew Wright, and in '68 was on his way to Paris to complete the research. Vincent Harding suggested I should do the book, also Charles Rowell. I quit teaching with the full intention of writing full-time. I received a Ford grant in 1979 and completed the book in the fall of 1980, just two weeks before my husband died.

I organized it into five or six parts. In the introductory statement I state why I'm writing the book. I have a section on the psychic wound of racism the first nineteen years of his life. I took a quote from Wendell Berry, who said: "If the white man has inflicted the wound of racism on black men, the cost has been that he would receive the mirror image of that wound into himself. I want to know as fully and as exactly as I can what the wound is and how much I am suffering from it. And I want to be cured." I did the research. I talk about what's wrong with Constance Webb's book and Fabre's book. Fabre's book was written in the shadow of the widow. She determined what should go in that book. He was indebted to her. He wanted to please her. If he discovered something, he couldn't do anything with it. Then again, he never knew the man. He never saw him in his life. Constance Webb may have seen him, but that book is so disorganized. She talks about "Dear Richard," and anybody who knew Wright either called him Dick Wright or Wright. They didn't call him Richard. She's off-base. In '73 everybody felt that Fabre wrote the definitive biography. I beg to differ. A definitive biography should recreate the man for you so you see him and you know him. Neither one of those books did that. I knew the man, and neither book is Wright.

I went down to Natchez [Mississippi]. I made some contacts with his father's side of the family. That has never been treated. The Wrights still exist all over that area, in Mississippi, Louisiana, and in California. They are just as middle-class as the mother's side. As a matter of fact Blyden Jackson found out that one of Wright's relatives on the father's side had an advanced degree and taught at Southern [University, Baton Rouge, Louisiana]. Yet you are given the impression that his father's side is just a bunch of "dumb niggers."

Wright wasn't really born in Natchez. Fabre found that out, too. Wright was born twenty-five miles from Natchez on a plantation. I found out that he was not really born in Roxie. Wright was born before records were kept in Mississippi. They weren't kept until 1912 on anybody in Mississippi, certainly not on black people before then. All people had then were baptismal records. When I was born records were being kept in Alabama. I had a birth certificate, but Wright was seven years older than I. But there are people down there in Natchez and Roxie who remember the family.

As I said, it was at the Richard Wright symposium at Iowa in '71 that Allison Davis called my attention to Wright's neurotic anger. He talked about the anger that had a realistic basis—the anger that Wright had toward society and toward his family. Then Davis talked about the neurotic anger that Wright could neither understand nor control. He said nobody can tell what the well springs of any man's creativity are. You can only guess. The more I thought about it, being a creative person myself, the more I understood. That's why I selected the title, *Richard Wright: Daemonic Genius*. There are different kinds of geniuses: demonic, intuitive, brooding, and orphic. Perhaps Faulkner had all four. Wright was definitely demonic. It's more than an idea of devils. It's the idea of creativity coming out of anger, madness, out of frustration, rage. Creativity comes out of the madness that borders on lunacy and genius. Allison Davis said that Wright's genius evidently came out of neurotic anger arising from his formative environment, and from the fact that Wright felt his mother didn't really love him. He felt rejected by his mother as well as deserted by his father. This rejection was combined with the cruelty and religious fanaticism within his household.

I talk about the lynchings Wright depicts in his work. There's the poem "Between the World and Me," and the story in *Black Boy* of a man in Memphis being lynched and dismembered. We also know that Aunt Maggie had two husbands killed by white people in Elaine, Arkansas. At the very time and place he's talking about in *Black Boy* there was, in fact, a race riot. One of those uncles [one of Aunt Maggie's husbands] was killed in that riot.

Then Wright wrote "Big Boy Leaves Home," which is a story of a lynching. There's another lynching in *Eight Men.* So he's got three substantial pieces dealing with lynching.

When Wright was working on *12,000,000 Black Voices,* he asked where he could find some real, poor, black people in slums. The answer he got was: "Go home, poor nigger, go home."

When I knew Wright he lived at 3836 Indiana Avenue. They have now torn that part of Chicago down. That was a very bad slum when I knew it in the thirties. I was living then in what was considered to be the nice section, Woodlawn—6337 Evans—out there near Cottage Grove and 63rd Street. Now that is a slum. You talk about depravity! The building in which Wright lived had "La Veta" written over the door. Oh, God, what La Veta was like. I went to see Wright and found him in a room that only had one door. I kept trying to figure out what kind of room it was; there was no window; it was not as big as my bathroom. Afterward, I realized that it was originally built as a closet. He and his brother both were sleeping in it. Don't tell me he wasn't living in abject poverty. I can remember just as clear as I'm sitting here, seeing Wright look in a paper bag and take out a sandwich that was two slices of white bread and a piece of bologna sausage that looked like it was turning green, without mayonnaise, mustard, or anything on it. He would just look at it and throw it over into the wastepaper basket. . . .

The second part of the biography is the period covering the Chicago years when Wright began to sing his broken song. The Chicago years were ones in which he learned to write, and his consciousness was raised. Then came the New York years—the Medusa Head. You know Louise Bogan's poem "The Medusa Head?" It's about the whole idea of psychological frustration. Every time you look at the Medusa's head you turn to stone. The psychological analogy is that you freeze and cease to grow. The New York years were the years in which Wright had success: publication, fame and fortune. But it was also the time he broke with everybody. He had started that in Chicago. Now he had no close friends. People like Baldwin weren't the only ones. I wasn't the only one. Neither was Ellison. He broke with the Communist Party. He broke with his family. He spent nineteen years in the South, ten years in Chicago, ten years in New York, and fourteen years in Paris.

He moved from "New York and the Medusa Head" to Paris where we have the "Twisted Torch and the Political Paradox of Black Nationalism v. Internationalism." Wright's marriage and children were just one part of his expatriation. The break with the Communist Party was another. The Communist Party had been the only life he had that was meaningful after he left the South. Now he was outside of that. He had always cultivated black schol-ars and writers. He always had friendships like the one we had, in Chicago, New York and Paris. No matter what he thought about them, he had them. But they always got to a point when he would cut them off. He could not maintain close, meaningful relationships. It was part of his sense of alien-ation, his lack of trust. As he had said, it was his protective covering from being hurt because he had been so hurt so badly.

The Paris years were the years of the international man; he made an effort to pull together a philosophy that will include black people every-where: Africa, Asia, America, the Caribbean, and South America—Pan-Africanism. He wanted to be the spokesman for black people all over the world. He also wanted to say, "Workers of the world unite" but he could not reconcile black nationalism with "red" internationalism. During the *Présence africaine* conference this dilemma became apparent. He denied what he had said in '37 in "The Blueprint for Negro Writers." He got up at the conference and said he hoped that such dictates were no longer neces-sary. It wasn't that he was saying that we were no longer brothers. As he talked, he alienated his audience by saying that he hoped the black writer was beyond the point of prescriptive writing. The Africans got mad; the West Indians and the black Americans got mad. Every black person there was infuriated, which meant that the very thing he was struggling to accom-plish, he had destroyed: the unity of black brotherhood. He was an outsider again. He would not go to the Rome conference.

Wright was a strange person. He could talk all day or all night. I never kissed him in my life, and we spent hours, days, and weeks together. I can remember only one time, when he came back to Chicago and we just had a brief embrace. I could feel him freeze.

CT: You organized a symposium on black women writers.

MW: The Phillis Wheatley Symposium. I'm not going to do any of that again. That phase of my life is over. I don't have energy for it anymore. I've got to write for the rest of my life, no matter how short or long it is. I've got to write. Teaching was never what I intended to do. Sometimes it might appear as though I have wasted so much of my life, but the classroom wasn't a waste. I enjoyed teaching; I was a good teacher. When I began to lose inter-est and enthusiasm for teaching, I quit. I never just sat there and drew the money, though I taught school to make a living. Moreover, I have never prostituted my writing. I toyed with the idea of being a writer-in-residence. But I don't think I will do it. I realize it's late in the day for me to make a list of priorities, but I must.

Writing is the first thing on my list, and I can't live long enough to write all the books I have in me. The sequel to *Jubilee* starts with Minna marrying in 1877, and ends with Vyry's death. Vyry died a month before I was born. Minna's first child was born in 1878, and that's when the family came to Mississippi. The sequel is the story of Minna and Jim. It's the story of the black church and the black school. It's about black benevolent societies, about jazz and blues. It's about Alabama, Mississippi and Florida.

I have another story which concerns a plot that's just recently become sensational. I haven't worked on it in ten years, though I've done over a hundred pages. It's a folk story entitled "Mother Broyer." It's about a black woman who is a faith healer and a cult leader. Two things have happened that make that story sensational. One is the Jonestown incident; the other concerns Satanic cult activity here in Mississippi. A lot of black people in Mississippi have become involved in it. It breaks up homes, kills people, drives them insane. It's psychosexual stuff, and it frightens me. My mother told me the story about forty years ago. It starts in New Orleans, moves to Los Angeles, Harlem, and ends up on the south side of Chicago, involving Jews, Catholics, and black people. The main character is a girl who starts out as a Catholic, goes to the Holiness Church and then a Pentecostal church, and then ends up in jail in New York.

I would have done for black people what Faulkner did for the South. Wright wanted to do that, and he didn't. In recent years I've had to decide that nothing is as important as my writing. I've had to look at the effect of the Haley business on my audience, but I know I'm still on top where the audience is concerned. I know that anything I write will have an audience waiting to read it. That's why it's so important for me to do what I started out to do and not be sidetracked.

About my autobiography . . . I remember something Lawrence Reddick said to me. He asked whether I was going to tell the whole truth. I said I'm not writing a confession. I don't have to tell anything I don't want to tell. I respect people being honest. Nikki is a very honest person; I don't think I have that kind of honesty. I don't believe in flouting what is contrary to the conventional. In "Being Female, Black, and Free," I said I have never felt like I could just defy convention to the point that I went out there all alone. That's a kind of brazen honesty I don't have.

America has a tendency to praise the rags-to-riches phenomenon, the self-made man image. When you talk about being self-made, that's a bubble I intend to burst with the Richard Wright story. The white man in America, the white world, caters to the black person who didn't go to school. I represent education, family, and background. I represent scholarship. I don't see why I must go out and be an entrepreneur. Everybody has help. Richard Wright didn't just learn all by himself. There's no such thing as "Topsy just grows."

Being classified as a middle-class black woman has been my undoing. I'm considered a black snob. I have to face the fact that I inherited a tradition—I'm a third-generation college graduate. Society doesn't want to recognize that there's this kind of black writer. I'm the Ph.D. black woman. That's horrible. That is to be despised. I didn't know how bad it was until I went back to school [to teaching] and found out.

CT: Has the image of black women in American literature changed in recent years?

MW: I got this unpublished manuscript out for you because it addresses your question on images of black women in black American literature. Let me read some of it for you:

The image of black women in American literature has rarely been a positive and constructive one. White American literature has portrayed the black woman as she is seen in society, exploited because of her sex, her race, and her poverty. The black male writer has largely imitated his white counterparts, seeing all black characters and particularly females as lowest on the socioeconomic scale: as slaves or servants, as menial, marginal persons, evil, disreputable and powerless. The status of women throughout the world is probably higher now than ever before in the history of civilization. Black women have as much status in this regard as white women (who really don't have much either).

All black characters fall into typical and stereotypical patterns. Black people are portrayed in slavery and in segregated situations, equated with animals and having subhuman status: wild, savage, and uncivilized. This, in the face of great African civilizations and cultures, is shocking only if we do not understand why demeaning and dehumanizing roles have been assigned to blacks by whites in the first place. If we understand the underlying philosophy of white racism, and its development as a buttressing agent of slavery and segregation and if we see these social institutions as necessary for the development of Western world capitalism, then we would know why these subhuman roles have been assigned to blacks. But why blacks feel they should imitate such castigation of black characters is harder to answer.

It is necessary as always when approaching Afro-American literature in any form—poetry, prose, fiction, or drama—to give a background of the socioeconomic and political forces and the historical context before proceeding to a literary analysis or synthesis. Then we will have the necessary tools with which to examine the strange phenomena found in American and Afro-American literature. Race is the subject of much of American literature, but race is almost the entire subject of Afro-American literature. Character, setting, action, event, tone, and philosophy all partake of the American myth and ethos of race. This focus may seem particular to the southern literature of whites, but is also characteristic of black literature wherever it is found. There are some blacks who debate this issue, who beg the question of black humanity by seeking to avoid racial subjects and claiming a broader theme of universal subjects. I do not wish to avoid the subject. I think it is a natural point of departure for a black writer. I do not, however, feel comfortable with the kind of treatment black women have received.

The plantation tradition is the source of female characters as the mammy, the faithful retainer, the pickaninny, Little Eva and Topsy, the tragic mulatto, conjure-woman or witch, the sex object, the bitch goddess, the harlot and prostitute and, last but not least, the matriarch. These are typical and stereotypical roles of black women in American fiction, poetry, and drama. Furthermore, black as well as white writers have worked within this tradition. It was on the plantation that the brutalizing of black women was at its greatest. Cooks, maids, wet nurses, forced mistresses and concubines were the most "refined" roles of black slave women. In that system it was "tit for tat and butter for fat." There were a lot of critics who tried to show that the field hand was the real black person, while the one in the house was treated more favorably. (They tried to do that with Vyry in *Jubilee.*) Miscegenation became a trite and hackneyed theme. . . .

Leslie Fiedler in *Love and Death in the American Novel* has made a brilliant study of the equating of black with evil and the black woman as portraying the loose, amoral, immoral harlot or slut, while the white, blue-eyed, blond woman was put on a pedestal and worshipped for her virtue and virginal purity. White was not only all right, but perfectly pure, while blackness and darkness meant evil. . . . John Pendleton Kennedy's *Swallow Barn* and Faulkner's *The Sound and the Fury* certainly had great influence on black writers. W. E. B. Du Bois in his *Dark Princess*— and even Sam Greenlee's *Spook Who Sat by the Door*—tried hard to portray black women with sympathy. James Weldon Johnson wrote one famous novel during the span between Dunbar/Du Bois and the Harlem Renaissance, but in it we see the white woman is again favored over the black woman. Langston Hughes and Arna Bontemps did a little better. . . .

Black men seem better when portraying old women. Ernest Gaines does this exceptionally well. No one can deny that a strong theme in Chester Himes is hatred for the middle-class black woman, whom he believes castrates and destroys her black male lover. Richard Wright does a bad job on women, period; but his black women fare even worse than his white women. Violence in his novels is a pattern, and this violence is frequently wreaked on women. The black woman is, therefore, a stereotype in fiction. Rarely does she achieve humanity, at least in the hands of male writers.

Of course, the positive view of women in Afro-American literature is only portrayed by black women. The earliest novel—*Iola Leroy* by Frances Harper—created a woman who is intelligent, attractive, human, and forceful in her personality. Harper sees black women as she sees herself—having strength of moral character, an indomitable will, perseverance, and a determination to overcome all handicaps and obstacles in her path. Zora Neale Hurston created an immortal love story in *Their Eyes Were Watching God,* and her portrayal of Janie and her love for Tea Cake is recognized by black women as typical of their love for black men. . . . Black women have received such cruel treatment in the literature. Only when the author is a black women does she have half a chance. With poetry it is slightly different. The brown girl was a beautiful subject during the Harlem Renaissance.[2]

I was distracted with *Roots.* I'm not distracted anymore. There's nothing that's going to happen, short of my health, that's going to keep me from my work.

You asked what advice I had to offer young writers. Well, I avoid giving advice because people don't want advice; they want sympathy. They want somebody to bolster and buttress them and say what they're doing is right. And I've found folks will not take your advice if you give it. They have to learn their own way.

I had a lot of people tell me I couldn't write. In fact, very few of my teachers encouraged me to believe that I could write. If I had believed them, I wouldn't still be trying.

1. This interview was published in 1983, before the publication of *Richard Wright: Daemonic Genius* (1989).

2. This unpublished excerpt is from a talk Margaret Walker gave at Purdue and at Texas Southern Universities in the late seventies.

Margaret Walker

Black Woman Writer of the South

JOYCE PETTIS

Margaret Walker is a writer who has never been separated for very long from her southern roots. She is southern not only because of her birth in Alabama but also because of her attitude toward the region and its people, particularly black people. She cherishes the beauty of the physical landscape, but she decries the endemic violence, bigotry, and destruction there. Walker is a black southerner whose ear for the distinctive rhythm of spoken words developed precociously. Her historical conscience was awakened early, its potential coaxed and nurtured. Thus when she began to write professionally, the South and black southerners were integral to her vision and were expressed through themes, imagery, and metaphor. The cadences of southern speech, sermons, and Negro spirituals were already encoded in her mind, awaiting their transformation into art. Her work, therefore, is overtly southern through her focus, attitude, voice, and sense of the past. To classify Walker as southern, however, is not to suggest limiting her vision or her work but to recognize what essentially propels them. Such recognition must extend to her family, for without their nurturing of her young talent and creative imagination, the poet, novelist, teacher, and essayist that Margaret Walker became might never have developed.

Walker's father, originally from the British West Indies, and her mother, a teacher of music, created a home environment that emphasized the rich heritage of black culture and inspired Walker's subsequent scholarship and creativity. She inherited her father's love of books and the spoken word, as she grew up listening to his sermons as well as to narratives of slave life in Georgia told by her maternal great-grandmother, who lived with the family. Walker finished high school in New Orleans, where the family had moved, and completed college studies in 1934 at Northwestern in Evanston, Illinois.

The thirties and the Depression found Walker in Chicago, working on the WPA Writers' Project. She lived outside the South for almost ten years (except for visits) before reestablishing her life there. By this time, however, Walker carried the South within her. Her identity with the ways of her people—with their mannerisms, jokes, songs, tales, loves, and fears—had been well formed through both her home environment and living in southern culture, and these ways constituted a richly complex reservoir from which she would draw the substance of both the poetry and the novel she wanted to write. The poems that she would write censuring the consequences of years of servitude, the notes of realistic protest that would distinguish her voice among other prominent voices of the 1930s, were lying dormant, waiting to be activated. The nucleus of the award-winning novel that she would complete lay preserved in her memory to be nurtured over some thirty years, secured there by a grandmother who had wanted her granddaughter's spiritual growth to be informed by history.

Working with the WPA project in company with other writers, including Richard Wright, provided invaluable experience for Walker. "It was a wonderful time, and I was a very young writer then," Walker has said of those years, "but I remember the comradeship of the people on the project. It seems to me that was the wonderful thing."[1] During the thirties, Walker secured the poetic form she had been working to develop, began seriously trying to place poems in national publications, and wrote most of the poems that comprise *For My People* (1942), the book that established her literary reputation. The volume, including an introduction by Stephen Benét, won the prestigious Yale Younger Poets Prize when Walker was only twenty-seven years of age. Moreover, she became the first black woman so honored in a national literary competition.[2] Clearly, then, Walker is classified among earlier southern literary voices such as Richard Wright, Arna Bontemps, Sterling Brown, Zora Neale Hurston, Eudora Welty, and Katherine Anne Porter.

Walker's inclusion as a member of a new generation of southern women writers, therefore, may be questionable to some scholars. However, her rapport with these writers, the appearance of a novel of middle age focusing on the survival and growth of a southern black woman, her continued productivity, and the foresight that kept her work reactive to emerging social conditions are substantial factors that maintained her classification among this newer generation of southern women writers. Her responsiveness to younger writers was symbolized by *A Poetic Equation* (1974), a spirited and animated colloquy between Nikki Giovanni and Walker, two gregarious poets of different temperaments and ages. Indeed, the book originated from Walker's obvious rapport and bonding with younger and different writers.

The Civil War novel *Jubilee* (1966) and two books of poetry, *Prophets for a New Day* (1970) and *October Journey* (1973), may be seen as the beginning of a second phase of Walker's career, for these publications located her amidst a younger generation of writers, including Maya Angelou, Alice Walker, Sonia Sanchez, Shirley Ann Grau, and Elizabeth Spencer. The publication of the long-anticipated biocritical work *Richard Wright: Daemonic Genius* and a collected edition of poetry, *This Is My Century: New and Collected Poems,* including a previously unpublished group, demonstrated continued literary activity that kept pace with the newer generation. Additionally, *Jubilee*, with its focus on a southern black woman, secured Walker's position on the cutting edge of literary interest generated about black women characters. The poetry of the 1970s, although manifesting kinship with her earlier volume, was also responsive to emergent social conditions brought about by civil rights activities. Thus the tenor of Walker's poetry is consistent with the work of other contemporary poets who are clearly of a different generation.

In considering her relationship to a younger generation of writers, Walker thinks first of age difference: "I recognize that I am a generation apart from them. Their boldness is not exactly what would have been boldness for me. I am sure people thought of me, when I was their age, as a bold new poet, but I am not at all certain that I had their kind of courage or even their kind of boldness."[3] Younger writers, however, have judiciously recognized the value of Walker's work to their own. Sonia Sanchez, for example, credits Walker, along with other writers, for helping to establish the tradition in which she has written: "Before me there was Brown, Walker and Brooks among others. Before them, there were others. Otherwise Sterling would not have been. You don't come out of a vacuum."[4]

Walker contributed to the earlier tradition of protest, realism, and rebellion out of which *Prophets for a New Day* came. In writing *Jubilee*, however, she becomes a primary forger of another tradition, out of which later black historical novels with women at their centers have come, such as Ernest Gaines's *The Autobiography of Miss Jane Pittman,* Sherley Anne Williams's *Dessa Rose,* and Toni Morrison's *Beloved*. Historical fiction structured in the same manner as *Jubilee* is also a vital precursor to complex, nonchronological approaches to African American history such as David Bradley's *The Chaneysville Incident,* John A. Williams's *Captain Blackman,* and Ishmael Reed's parody of the genre, *Flight to Canada. Jubilee* is precedent-setting black historical fiction.

Walker's tasks in the novel are to depict slave culture and Vyry, the protagonist, within a narrative that encompasses slavery, the war years, and Reconstruction. For Walker, the re-creation of slave culture, with its folk beliefs and practices, is the essence of the novel. Therefore, she enhances the folk concept by prefacing each of the fifty-eight chapters with proverbial folk sayings or lines excerpted from spirituals. Moreover, the narrative includes verses of songs sung by Vyry, her guardian, or other slaves; a portion of a sermon and the text of one of Vyry's prayers is printed. Slave children's rhymes, a conjure episode, and a catalog of herbs and their medicinal and cooking purposes are also included. More than physical setting and chronological time anchor this novel in the southern experience of black Americans.

Black historical fiction was a sparsely used genre until the 1960s; only a few black writers had undertaken a depiction of the southern black population during the slavery era and its immediate aftermath.[5] *Jubilee* is the first novel by a black author to depict extensively the slave culture from a daily perspective and to expose the havoc of the Civil War and Reconstruction on the black population. The novel, "a synthesis of folk tradition, imagination, and moral vision," focuses on the practical daily lives and survival of plain men and women instead of chronicling heroic feats of achievers such as Gabriel Prosser or Harriet Tubman.[6] Thus it participates in revisionist social history. Moreover, it has the effect of reinterpreting a crucial period in the black experience, a period too frequently viewed with ignominy and humiliation. Exposing the realities of enslavement, Walker depicts its bitter cruelties for all the groups it touched, but particularly for black women. She reaches beyond enslavement and finds individualistic characters united by their desire for autonomy. Although the outlines of some stereotypes are visible (the extensive cast of characters necessitates that many of them must be types), they are personalized, not repugnant buffoons. Walker reaffirms the nature of the human spirit— even when the body is enslaved—to reject oppression and to effect change. Her confirmation that enslavement did not defeat the human spirit of her heroine, Vyry, is Walker's legacy to later female protagonists of historic fiction, including Miss Jane Pittman, Dessa Rose, and Sethe *(Beloved)*.

Vyry's depiction within the daily working of slave culture is a necessary prerequisite to later fictional representations of enslaved women whose behavior, goals, or activities may be perceived as atypical or exceptional to enslaved women in general. Her characterization essentially balances that of other types of enslaved women and provides the fundamental model upon which they may be structured. She experiences all the pain, degradation, and loss common to slavery—orphaned at age two, victimized by a cruel mistress, denied the privilege of legal marriage to her children's father, offered for public sale, and flogged for attempted escape—but she endures and morally transcends. She is not destroyed by an environment with the capability for absolute destruction of morality and self-esteem. In short, Vyry's endurance, survival, and transcendence signal the potential of these realities for forthcoming portraits of slave women. Walker's depiction of Vyry offers a viable means for reinterpretation of the slave experience through gender.

When Walker committed herself to writing *Jubilee*, she also determined that the book would be realistic rather than romantic. Therefore, she became a historian as well as a novelist, saturating herself in the antebellum, Civil War, and Reconstruction periods through history classes, reading, and research, including southern historical collections and slave narratives. The research eventually extended to over twenty years, sandwiched between other obligations.

Walker has written of the ordeal of researching, writing, and living with *Jubilee* in a booklet titled *How I Wrote* Jubilee (1972). It is a narrative of perspiration and pertinacity in keeping a promise and attaining a goal. Moreover, it exposes the complications common to a woman writer because of gender, employment, marriage, and motherhood. In the years following her master's degree in 1940 from the University of Iowa, Walker accepted a college teaching position in North Carolina, married, and became a mother. In 1949, she and her family moved to Jackson, Mississippi, where she accepted at Jackson State University the teaching position that she retained until retirement. She continued her research through both the Rosenwald (1944) and Ford (1953) Fellowships. Meanwhile, her family grew to include four children. Beset by illness and persistent financial pressures, for a seven-year period (1955–62) Walker wrote and published almost nothing, although she continued research for the novel. In 1961, she returned to the Writers Workshop at the University of Iowa and the next year began work toward completion of a doctorate degree, with *Jubilee* planned as her dissertation. She met degree requirements with the completion of the *Jubilee* manuscript in the spring of 1965.

The publication of *Jubilee* is evidence that Walker survived the "silences" that often plague, limit, or terminate the literary careers of women writers.[7] She has eloquently expressed her awareness of the trials that beset a woman writer in general and black women writers and her own work in particular:

To choose the life of a writer, a black female must arm herself with a fool's courage, foolhardiness, and serious purpose and dedication of the art of writing, strength of will and integrity, because the odds are always against her. . . . Sometimes the only quiet and private place where I could write a sonnet was in the bathroom, because that was the only room where the door could be locked and no one would intrude. I have written mostly at night in my adult life and especially since I have been married, because I was determined not to neglect any member of my family; so I cooked every meal daily, washed dishes and dirty clothes, and I nursed sick babies.[8]

Even while Walker worked on the doctoral degree and *Jubilee,* she responded to the momentous social upheaval of the 1960s and wrote *Prophets for a New Day* (1970), her first book of poems since *For My People.* In structure and style, the poems of the second book are not remarkably different from those of the first. She retains what Blyden Jackson has called the "Whitmanesque" method in stanza formation, and, stylistically, the rhythmic cadence of the black southern minister is apparent.[9] More sonnets are evident in the first volume, however, than in the second. The second book, like the first, derives in large part from Walker's ethnic consciousness and her responsiveness to political changes directly affecting black Americans. The tonal difference between the two volumes primarily reflects the difference of political climate between the 1930s and 1960s. Black people were passive in the 1930s rather than retaliatory, as in the 1960s. "We were apathetic, we were not militant, we were not altogether articulate," Walker has said of her perception of black people in the 1930s, but "in the Sixties Black people became very conscious, very articulate, very militant, very vocal. And all of the consciousness grew, and it has grown and continues to grow in the Seventies."[10]

Walker's voice, however, was loud among those articulating their dissatisfaction with the economic and political life of black Americans in the 1930s. Therefore, several of the poems in *For My People* protest the debilitating stagnancy in the political, social, and economic mobility of black Americans. She observes little in black life about which to write genteel or romantic poetry; thus the poems are characterized by direct, strong language and realistic, accessible images and symbols. Some poems express raw rage at immobility ("How long since 1619 have I been singing spirituals?"), disgust with southern living conditions ("moonlight hovered over ripe haystacks / or stumps of trees, and croppers' rotting shacks / with famine, terror, flood, and plague near by"), and enormity at the struggle still necessary to overcome ("The struggle staggers us / for bread, for pride, for simple dignity"). "We Have Been Believers" sardonically attacks blind faith as a contributor to nonproductivity and stasis. A different attitude, however, is recognized in the final stanza:

> Now the needy no longer weep and pray; the long-suffering arise,
> and our fists bleed against the bars with a strange insistency.

"For My People," widely regarded as Walker's signature poem, contains the strongest demands for absolute change for oppressed black Americans. The nine stanzas or strophes of free verse—marked by parallelism, repetition of phrases, and paradox—are dependent upon the preemptory sentences of the tenth stanza for their completion and meaning. Meaning and form merge perfectly as Walker expertly sets out a panorama of the history of her people. As the speaker in each stanza telescopes a succinct vision of the black experience, the lenses freeze scenes that are representative of the multitextured collage of that experience:

> For my people thronging 47th Street in Chicago and Lenox
> Avenue in New York and Rampart Street in New Orleans,
> lost disinherited dispossessed and happy people filling the
> cabarets and taverns and other people's pockets needing
> bread and shoes and milk . . . (14)

Underlying the diction, absence of punctuation in word series, and the breathless tumbling of verbs and gerunds is the explicit meaning that, from a historical perspective, the frenetic efforts aimed at race "improvement" for the majority of the population have been futile and have resulted in appalling despair and disappointment. Disturbed by the plight of black Americans, the poet urgently speaks to them in this poem, graphically demonstrating that, historically, conditions remain largely unchanged. In eight short, strong, imperative sentences, the last stanza commands change that may have to be wrought through a "bloody peace." Knowing history, Walker also knows its resistance to change. Nothing less than another world and a bloody peace will effect the sweeping changes necessary.

In addition to the poems of protest, several poems communicate the poet's southern ties. "Southern Song," "Sorrow Home," and "Delta" recall "For My People" in their stanza format and use of parallel structures. In content, they recognize the South as home region. "Southern Song" and "Sorrow Home" are arresting in the poet's delicate balance of tension and lyricism. The speaker's love of the southern landscape is suggested by the lush imagery of "Southern Song":

> I want my body bathed again by southern suns. . . . I want to
> rest again in southern fields, in grass and hay and clover
> bloom. (18)

"Sorrow Home," too, communicates the speaker's reminiscence of things distinctly southern—"I want the cotton fields, tobacco and the cane"—and rejects other places:

> I am no hothouse bulb to be reared in steam-heated flats with the
> music of El and subway in my ears, walled in by steel and
> wood and brick far from the sky. (19)

Unfortunately, the beauty of the lyricism and pleasant memories is broken by the intrusiveness of stark reality in each poem:

> I want no mobs to wrench me from my southern rest; no forms
> to take me in the night and burn my shack and make for
> me a nightmare full of oil and flame. ("Southern Song" 18)

Eugenia Collier identifies "Delta" as the poem "that most completely exploits the motif of the South." [11] In this long poem, less lyrical but more assertive than the preceding southern poems, the poet's message is precise: black Americans have lived miserably and labored for others in the Southland but reaped few rewards. However, "there is a new way to be worn and a path to be broken / from the past" (22). The realization crystallizes that the land belongs to its tillers, who "with [their] blood have watered these fields" and have earned the right to possess it.

Although Walker emphasizes the spiritual links between black Americans and the South, she balances these ambivalent poems with others, such as "Dark Blood" and "How Many Silent Centuries Sleep in My Sultry Veins" (in *Prophets for a New Day*), that recognize Africa and the Caribbean as additional ancestral homes.

The ten poems of the middle section of *For My People* reflect the oral and folk traditions of southern black culture. Writing in the tradition of James Weldon Johnson, Sterling Brown, and Zora Neale Hurston in drawing characters and speech from the southern folk tradition, Walker offers ten real-life folk heroes, among them "Bad-Man Stagolee" and "Big John Henry." Written in the "swinging ballad rhyme and meter" that "reveal a finely controlled and well-disciplined narrative technique," [12] these poems offer broadly drawn portraits of men and women from the folk community whose extraordinary lives or abilities inspire awe and pride. One of the most engaging portraits in the series is "Molly Means," a ballad in which a conjure woman turns a young bride into a dog. The husband has the spell reversed on Molly, who subsequently dies. Her meanness, however, survives with her ghost; the ballad tells of the terror that Molly's ghost continues to inspire. These portraits confirm Walker's interest in and affection for her southern roots and her affinity with the folklore of the region.

Only one poem, "Today," suggests that the poet's vision is not totally engaged by the black American experience. Here Walker foresees the imminence of World War II and decries the complacency with which the threat is received. Her fear is that Middle America, "complacently smug in a smug somnolescence" and occupied with petty concerns, is oblivious to the warnings rumbling in Europe. Beginning each stanza with "I sing," she effectively employs irony, for such images as "slum scabs on city faces / scrawny children scarred by bombs and dying of hunger," "wretched human scarecrows strung against lynching stakes," and "cankerous mutiny eating through the nipples of our breasts," images that offer no support for the beauty of song. The poet's hope is that the population will become aware of the imminently destructive situation.

Walker's second volume of poems, obviously akin to her first one in structure and tone, is also conceived with similar unity of design. The poems of *Prophets for a New Day* recognize, applaud, and eulogize those dedicating blood, sweat, and sometimes life to the destruction of racial inequity and injustice. Written in 1963 and called by the author her "civil rights poems," they record the history-making events and attitudes of that period. Only "Elegy" and "Ballad of the Hoppy-Toad" are not inspired by the movement.

The unity of design—with the exception of "Elegy" and "Ballad of the Hoppy-Toad"—is achieved by the development of the title, for the poems extol courageous leadership and the promise of a prophecy fulfilled. Employing her knowledge of the Bible, as she had throughout her career, Walker constructs analogies between prophets of biblical times and old and new leaders in the history of the black experience. Moreover, the analogies are strengthened by her use of diction and imagery reminiscent of the language of the King James version of the Bible as well as the undisguised rhetoric of a black minister in a southern pulpit. "Ballad of the Free" pays homage to earlier advocates of freedom already preserved in history—Nat Turner, Gabriel Prosser, Denmark Vesey, and others like them—while "Street Demonstration" and "Sit-Ins" recognize the countless numbers of jailed civil rights advocates and the unnamed participants of the sit-ins. Martin Luther King Jr., unidentified by name, is surely analogous to Moses leading his people to the promised land in "At the Lincoln Monument in Washington, August 28, 1963." "For Andy Goodman—Michael Schwerner—and James Chaney" recognizes the sacrifice and eulogizes the lives of the three young civil rights workers murdered in Mississippi. Many leaders/prophets are linked with specific southern cities marked by racial unrest; "Micah," for example, evokes the memory of Medgar Evers in Jackson, Mississippi.

The ambivalence that characterizes the poet's response to the South as one of the ancestral homes of black Americans in *For My People* is consistent in *Prophets*. In "Jackson, Mississippi," for example, the tension and violence in the city occasioned by racial unrest, its ugly and seamy side, are juxtaposed with its physical beauty. However, since this city and others like it are repositories of black southern history, black Americans can neither wholly leave it, ignore it, nor love it. Therein lies the ambivalence.

The vital elements of Walker's work—its identity with the South, its historical perspective, folk tradition, and racial themes—remain consistent in *Prophets for a New Day* as well as in the poems of *October Journey* (1973), a brief book (thirty-five pages) of mostly previously published poems. The title poem of the volume is notable for its thematic consistency with earlier ambivalent poems about the South. "October Journey," however, excels those earlier poems in its extravagant imagery of the physical appearance of the Southland in the fall, when the land is awash with warm autumnal colors. As in the earlier poems, landscape and memory change when reality intervenes and displaces the visual scene in the mind of the traveler.

The rigorous depiction of realism in the South and the demand for social, political, and economic changes for black Americans have been consistent characteristics of Walker's work. Her knowledge of tradition and history has constituted fecund sources from which she has extracted material for transformation into art. Additionally, she has located her themes and insistence for change within a humanistic framework and within a tradition accessible to nonacademic as well as academic readers. But more than anything else, Walker has anchored her work in the love and experiences of her people.

Margaret Walker, southern black woman poet and novelist, occupies a unique position in American literary history through her inclusion with two generations of writers. It is a well-earned position, however. Beginning in the 1930s, Walker's work illustrated and confirmed an unquestionable dedication to art, determination to survive as a writer, and a refusal to be defeated by the "silences" that often have stymied women writers' voices. The second phase of her career, beginning with the appearance of *Jubilee*, affirmed her commitment and perseverance. Walker's work survived the pressures that had the potential for silencing her voice. Readers can be grateful that her work will continue to be strong and vibrant among the coming generation of southern women writers.

1. Charles Rowell, "Poetry, History and Humanism: An Interview with Margaret Walker," *Black World* 25 (1975): 15.

2. Richard Barksdale, "Margaret Walker: Folk Orature and Historical Prophecy," in *Black American Poets Between Worlds, 1940–1960,* ed. R. Baxter Miller (Knoxville: University of Tennessee Press, 1986), 106.

3. Rowell 13.

4. Claudia Tate, *Black Women Writers at Work* (New York: Continuum, 1983), 148.

5. I explore reasons for the dearth of historical fiction by African American writers in my dissertation, "The Search for a Usable Past: Black Historical Fiction" (University of North Carolina, Chapel Hill, 1983). Arna Bontemps's *Black Thunder* (1936), the story of Gabriel Prosser's rebellion, is set during the antebellum period but only narrowly recreates the folk culture as appropriate background to the activities of Gabriel Prosser.

6. Minrose Gwin, "Jubilee: The Black Woman's Celebration of Human Community," in *Conjuring: Black Women, Fiction, and Literary Tradition,* ed. Marjorie Pryse and Hortense Spillers (Bloomington: Indiana University Press, 1985), 134.

7. See Tillie Olsen, *Silences* (New York: Delacorte, 1978). The book confronts the relationship between gender oppression and the cessation or absence of writing by women.

8. Quoted in Janet Sternburg, *The Writer on Her Work* (New York: Norton, 1980), 100–101.

9. Blyden Jackson and Louis Rubin, *Black Poetry in America* (Baton Rouge: Louisiana State University Press, 1974), 68.

10. Rowell 9.

11. Eugenia Collier, "Fields Watered with Blood: Myth and Ritual in the Poetry of Margaret Walker," in *Black Women Writers (1950–1980): A Critical Evaluation,* ed. Mari Evans (Garden City NY: Doubleday, Anchor 1984), 503.

12. Barksdale 110.

Down from the Mountaintop

MELISSA WALKER

Margaret Walker's *Jubilee,* in many ways a conventional historical romance, has an interesting history of its own. When Walker was a small child living in Birmingham, Alabama, her born-in-slavery maternal grandmother told endless stories about her own mother's life before, during, and after the Civil War. To fulfill her promise to tell the story of her own great-grandmother, Walker created three generations of women: Hetta, the black mistress of the plantation owner; their daughter Vyry, the protagonist, modeled after the great-grandmother; and her daughter, Minna, the fictional counterpart of Walker's grandmother, who first told the stories.

Walker first began to write down the stories in 1934, when she was still a college student. Years and then decades passed before she completed the novel. While raising a family, attending graduate school, publishing poetry, and teaching English, Walker periodically immersed herself in the history of plantation life, slavery, the Civil War, and Reconstruction. She read histories, slave narratives, diaries, letters, and other personal documents; studied Civil War newspapers, pamphlets, and songs; and traveled to the places her grandparents lived, delving into records of real-estate transfers in the court house in Dawson, Georgia. In the early 1960s, as the Civil War centennial approached, she reported feeling "desperate to finish" the novel. She was more than fifty when she fulfilled her promise in 1966 and published *Jubilee.*

In the winter and spring of 1965, during the same months that civil rights activists were marching in the streets of Selma, Alabama, Walker wrote parts 2 and 3—approximately two-thirds of the novel—in a frenzy of creativity and concentration. The events of those climactic moments of the Civil Rights movement seemed to have informed the novel as a whole and the final part in particular. The Voting Rights Act was passed in August 1965, as Walker was preparing *Jubilee* for the publishers. By ending *Jubilee* in 1870, a period of relative calm, she leaves her characters on the brink of events that would lead to decades, and even another century—two more jubilees—of betrayals and violence. She was close to producing a completed draft at the end of March when Martin Luther King Jr. stood on the steps of the Alabama state capitol, warning that blacks were "still in for a season of suffering" and repeating the words of "The Battle Hymn of the Republic," stressing the song's final lines: "Be jubilant, my feet, our God is marching on. . . . His truth is marching on." Even though she worked at breakneck speed that winter and spring, writing from 7: 00 A.M. to 11:00 P.M. and pushing herself "beyond all physical endurance," Walker surely noted the front-page news from Selma, Montgomery, and Washington D.C.

The almost fifty years from the time her grandmother first told those tales until the publication of *Jubilee* correspond to the period when the foundations of the modern Civil Rights movement were laid: by the National Urban League, formed in 1911 to find ways for blacks to have equal opportunity for housing and employment; by the NAACP, which was founded in 1910 and began organizing in the South in 1917; by the Garvey movement, 1916–23, which glorified racial pride and demonstrated that a mass movement was possible; by the Legal Defense and Education Fund, established in 1939 to finance the court battles that eventually led to *Brown v. Board of Education;* by the Congress of Racial Equality, which staged a number of nonviolent, direct-action protests throughout the forties; by A. Philip Randolph's March on Washington Movement of 1941 and his call in 1943 for mass protests modeled after Gandhi's passive resistance movement in India; and by the lifelong efforts of such individuals as Mary McLeod Bethune, W. E. B. Du Bois, Bayard Rustin, and Ella Baker. During the more than thirty years that Walker was struggling to tell the story of the men and women a century before who longed for freedom and fought to claim it, most of the battles in the war for civil rights were fought.

Jubilee is set in rural southwest Georgia and nearby Alabama communities, the same part of the South associated with the extreme racism that was the target of important campaigns of the Civil Rights movement. Vyry, the protagonist of the novel, is the child of a white plantation owner and a slave woman; the novel recounts her life from her birth around 1834 to a new beginning at the end of the summer of 1870. For some readers, as for some reviewers, *Jubilee* may seem to be little more than a conventional romance, complete with the cliches of the genre: the elaborate entertainments on the plantation, the patriotic lady who runs the plantation and bravely sends her son and her son-in-law off to die in the war she believes is fought to defend her way of life, emotional deathbed scenes, a love triangle in which a woman must choose between the man she loves and the one to whom she owes her life. Hazel Carby has observed that *Jubilee* was "a particular response to the dominant ideologies of the popular imagination embodied in Mitchell's *Gone with the Wind*." But Walker has used the elements of popular romance to create a very different kind of novel, one that celebrates not the Old South but the twentieth-century struggle for civil rights. Her history is not the story of a dead past but of the past as the precondition of the present. As Carby has observed, "Walker's representation of slavery is her philosophy of history, which is to be understood as the necessary prehistory of contemporary society."

Rather than being haunted by the past, Vyry lives in the present, only occasionally looking back from her bustling kitchens to all that she has lost. She moves from one tragedy—and even one beloved husband—to another with some sadness and difficulty, but she is rarely incapacitated by suffering. A celebration—a jubilee—of what Maya Angelou calls "the heroes and sheroes" of the past, this novel does not belabor the most devastating experiences of slavery. Even the horror of Dutton's sexual exploitation of Vyry's mother, Hetta, is mitigated by his visit to her deathbed to comfort her and by his grief when she dies. Only once, after suffering a miscarriage and losing her house in a fire, does Vyry experience despair. Unlike even Scarlett O'Hara, she is never hungry. Though the overseer beats her when she runs away, Vyry is neither raped nor abused by the men in her life. She is more like Faulkner's Dilsey than the heroines of other black women novelists—Sophia in *The Color Purple* or Pilate in *Song of Solomon,* for example.

Concentrating on the conventional aspects of the novel, some critics have ignored its relevance to the mid-1960s. Although *Jubilee* does not highlight the ugliest conditions of slavery, it also does not celebrate the Old South but focuses on the slaves who live on or near the plantation owned by John Morris Dutton, a wealthy white planter who has two children by Salina, his socially prominent wife from Savannah, and some fifteen others by Hetta, the black woman his father gave him when she was still a young girl. Of Hetta's children, only Vyry, her mother's favorite, becomes a part of his life; the others he sells or apparently forgets. Events in this novel about slavery and its aftermath, and even the form of the novel, are directly related to the struggle for civil rights that peaked in the mid-1960s.

Each of the novel's three parts could stand alone as a novella. "Sis Hetta's Child: The Ante-Bellum Years" begins by exploring everyday events of slave life as Hetta is dying in childbirth and ends as Vyry recovers from the beating she endured after attempting to run away. "'Mine eyes have seen the Glory': The Civil War Years" focuses on life in "the big house" during the war, relates the destruction of the white family and degeneration of the slave society, and ends with the closing of the plantation and the departure of the slaves. "'Forty years in the wilderness': Reconstruction and Reaction" begins in 1866 as Vyry and her children leave the plantation with her new husband Innis Brown in search of land, work, and education for the children and ends in 1870 after they have finally found these and other benefits of freedom.

Even in part 1, "The Ante-Bellum Years," the narrative chronicles progress. Vyry, for example, fares better than her totally oppressed mother. As the mistress of John Dutton, who has used her sexually since she was fifteen years old, and the wife of a black man Dutton has forced her to marry, Vyry's mother, Hetta, does not even have the freedom to decide who uses her body. After some fifteen debilitating pregnancies, she dies in childbirth before her thirtieth birthday. Though Dutton exploits his daughter by bringing her to the big house where she serves first as playmate to her own half-sister, then as a kitchen helper, and finally as the family's cook, he does allow her to maintain a relationship with Randall Ware and to raise their children. And he promises to free her—but only after his death.

But progress within slavery is severely limited. To run away with the man she loves, Vyry would have to abandon her children. When Ware begs Vyry to leave with him, her maternal feelings override the desire for freedom. At the end of part 1, after she has made a half-hearted attempt to escape with a small child and a suckling baby, Vyry struggles to regain consciousness after being beaten. She recalls seeing John Dutton standing over her "cursing terrible oaths" (145). This image of a subdued black woman examining her almost mortal wounds and a white man cursing is emblematic of the condition of all subservient people whose freedom is enjoyed at the indulgence of their oppressors. At the end of part 1, Vyry has exhausted the limits of personal freedom within a slave society. Though it is not clear whether Dutton is cursing Vyry for trying to run away or his white workers for beating this woman who is, after all, his own child, the motives for his curse are irrelevant. Within the slave society, Dutton, like all oppressors, will inevitably curse those he oppresses.

Written before the Civil Rights movement's final push for federal legislation, part 2 belongs to that stage in the long struggle for liberation when white supremacy prevailed. When Ware writes to Vyry that there will be a war to free the slaves, she retorts, "A war to set us niggers free? What kind of crazy talk is that?" (166). At this point Vyry sees what Walker herself perhaps saw when she first conceived of the novel: a work in which white people make promises they never keep and black men join the struggle for freedom, leaving women behind with the children.

In part 2, "The Civil War Years," composed in early 1965, Vyry's desire for freedom is replaced by a struggle for survival, as she works to hold together the white family on which she and her children depend. In the course of the war the Dutton family slowly disintegrates: Marse John dies after an injury; his son and son-in-law receive fatal wounds in battle; with the sound of "big Yankee guns" firing in the distance, Miss Salina suffers a deadly stroke; and her daughter, Lillian, sustains a head injury and permanent brain damage when a Yankee soldier rapes her. As the world collapses around her, Vyry determines "to plant some kind of crop," since she has "the younguns to feed"—Miss Lillian's and her own (231).

Scenes in which characters fail to recognize the relationships between their own private experience and sweeping public events surface here and repeatedly in black women's fiction written since *Jubilee*. The limitation of Vyry's exclusive private vision is most conspicuous when Union soldiers come to read the Emancipation Proclamation to the slaves. Preoccupied with feeding the crowd and caring for the children, Vyry does not understand the implications of this momentous public event. And at the end of the war, ignorance of the public arena leads Vyry to lose the man she loves: when Randall Ware does not return immediately, Vyry accepts the protection and eventually the love of Innis Brown, a kind but less compelling man.

In the final scene of part 2, on Christmas day of 1865, Vyry prepares two feasts. She serves "baked fresh ham and candied sweet potatoes and buttered whole okra and corn muffins and pecan pie and elderberry wine" to the white folks in the dining room, while she, Innis, and the children eat "possum with sweet potatoes and collard greens and okra and . . . sweet potato pone" in the kitchen (257). Like the tableau at the end of part 1—a white man standing over a subdued black woman—this scene is emblematic of the nature of race relations at a particular time: two families, each without a father, celebrating Christmas in separate rooms with different meals. Both the structure and the imagery of the fiction are determined by history. The dinner is in a sense both the last of an old way of life and the first of a new; from the perspective of the mid-1960s the alienation of the races began when masters and former slaves first chose to sit down at separate and not-so-equal tables.

In part 3, written during the climactic moments of the southern Civil Rights movement, public attitudes and events increasingly impinge on the lives of the characters as whites engage in violence to limit the freedom of blacks, who in turn struggle to claim the rights promised by freedom—housing, food, employment, education, and involvement in the political process. Having won the battle of "freedom from," they now must fight the battle of "freedom to." When Vyry and Innis set out with her two children, Jim and Minna, their plight is the same as that of "hundreds of thousands of emancipated Negroes" (263). Locating what seems like an ideal spot for farming, Vyry and Innis build a cabin, plant crops, and enjoy a plentiful harvest. But the following spring the river floods their house and fields, and they soon are on the road looking for a new place to settle. In the next three years, Vyry and Innis are cheated, exploited, and terrorized by poor whites who are determined to prevent blacks from owning farms and competing with them for jobs. Light enough to pass for white, Vyry contributes to the family income by selling eggs to white women who do not know she is a mulatto. After Vyry assists one of these women in childbirth, her fortune changes. In need of a midwife, the white families urge Vyry to stay in their community, and the men volunteer to help Innis build a house.

The day of the house-raising is idyllic. The women bring quilts; the men work all day building the new house. Just as she had done that last Christmas on the plantation, Vyry prepares a feast: peaches, dew berries, sweet cream, ham, eggs, fried chicken, biscuits, buttered corn, greens, okra, blackberry pie, and coffee. In striking contrast to that earlier segregated meal, which served as a symbolic vignette at the end of 1865, blacks and whites now sit together and enjoy the food and fellowship. The first half of the summer of 1870 is "fully of halcyon days one dreams and scarcely believes are real" (371). But before long the stresses of unrelenting economic pressures and unending labor begin to take their toll. Innis, frustrated by Jim's laziness, lashes out in anger and beats him brutally.

Randall Ware, meanwhile, very much alive, has delayed his return to private life to attend the First Convention of Colored People in Georgia. Putting his public responsibilities before his private ones, he joins the Georgia Equal Rights Association and determines to take "an active part in the political affairs of his country, town, and state" (270). It is during Ware's delay that Vyry despairs and leaves with Innis. Just as Vyry's exclusively private vision robs her of the power of public action, Ware's public commitments result in the loss of his private world. Had Vyry known about the scramble for political power that followed the war and had she understood Ware's commitment first to freedom and then to power, she might have concluded that he was involved in the struggle and would take care of his private life in due time. On the other hand, if Ware, out of consideration for Vyry's personal needs, had gotten word to her, she would surely have waited for him. But in fact neither finds a way to balance public and private responsibilities.

At first Randall Ware, like Vyry, underestimates the tenacity of racism. As a propertied free black, Ware is a ready target for racist terrorism. When he returns to claim his land and forge, the whites threaten him and demand that he sell them his land. When he refuses, "white-sheeted callers" arrive at his house, throw the bloody body of his journeyman at his feet, beat him, and leave him half-conscious in the woods (327). Defeated and frightened, Ware abandons his plans to play a part in the public arena, and he recognizes that a new war has only just begun: "This is a war of white against black and it's a night war with disguise and closed doors. The first white man you see in the morning could be the very man who beat you within an inch of your life the night before. No, they have begun a reign of terror to put the Negro back in slavery. They will never accept the fact that the South rose up in rebellion against the Union North and the North won the war. They mean to take out all their grudges on us" (333). In certain communities—Selma, Alabama, for example—these words were as appropriate in the mid-1960s as they were a hundred years before. But unlike many of his counterparts in 1965, Ware sees no way for direct political action.

Toward the end of the novel, Ware, hoping that Vyry will come back to him and his son Jim will go away to school, searches out his family. Surprised and shaken by Ware's visit, Vyry soothes her uneasiness by preparing a welcoming feast. Once again, a dinner-table scene is emblematic of the condition of a community, this time the extended black community. At the end of the war Vyry prepared for her two families two meals served at separate, segregated tables; during the brief period after the war when some whites and blacks recognized their mutual dependency, she enjoyed one jointly prepared, integrated meal; now, members of her family, representative of the larger black community, sit down at the table together. Their differences are subsumed in a larger commitment to each other's welfare.

Randall explains that he had run for the state legislature and won but that "white folks couldn't and wouldn't stand for it" (400). Having abandoned his dream of playing a role in the public arena, Ware adopts a different plan for bringing about change. The first step, he argues, is education: "And so far as education is concerned, I tell you it may not be the only way for our people but it is the main way. We have got to be educated before we know our rights and how to fight for them" (404). By putting education—a top priority for many contingents of the modern Civil Rights movement—as the first item on Ware's agenda and by not having him advocate retaliatory violence, Walker established him as a predecessor to some contemporary nonviolent movement leaders; much of his rhetoric, however, is consistent with that of black militants of the mid-1960s. Like many movement activists Ware is uncertain about the best means to achieve his goals.

The differing positions of the characters in this final part of the novel are almost parallel to those of contemporary reformers as Randall, Innis, and Vyry each voice one of three conflicting positions dividing the black community. Randall Ware's views, though sometimes moderate, are more consistent with those of the emerging separatists who by 1966 would take over the leadership of SNCC. Ware argues that blacks will have "to fight and struggle" for "education, land, and the ballot" (396), that the "average white man hates a Negro, always did, and always will," and that "every white man" believes that every black is inferior and should be treated like "a brute animal" (397). Like Malcolm X, he never advocates specific acts of violence, but he does use militant language, equating the struggle to come with the "years of fighting and struggling" that were necessary to end slavery (396). Like SNCC leaders in 1965 who were arguing for the expulsion of whites from the organization, Ware opposes any cooperation with whites and urges a kind of 1870s black power.

Innis Brown, on the other hand, argues that blacks must accommodate to life in a racist society by relinquishing any hopes of equality: "They was a man not so long ago made a speech round here and he says the colored peoples got to forgit about the political vote and tend our farms and raise our families and show the white folks we ain't lazy and ain't stirring up no trouble for nobody, but we is for peace and we's good citizens. . . . I kinda believes like that man" (399).

As a mulatto, Vyry, on the other hand, represents that integrated society dreamed of by Martin Luther King Jr. She insists that all people are capable of good and that being "apart and separated from each other" makes people hate (397). As she sees it, the solution to the racial problem lies in blacks and whites acknowledging their interdependency: "They ain't needing me no worser that I is needing them, that's what. We both needs each other. White folks needs what black folks got just as much as black folks needs what white folks is got, and we's all got to stay here amongst each other and git along, that's what" (402). Each position might be summed up in a single word: separatism, accommodation, and coalition. The novel itself, however, does not validate one view over the other but rather gives each a voice, suggesting that any solution to the problems of racism, if there is to be one, whether in 1870 or 1966, will inevitably evolve from the clash and resolution of such differences and conflicting assumptions on which they are based. As the protagonist of the novel, however, Vyry stands between two extremes, and her advocacy of integration and interdependency, compatible with the position of Martin Luther King Jr., seems to have the greatest weight.

As Vyry, Innis, and Randall sit talking through the night, they all have their say, and the conflicts that divide them, though unresolved, are set aside for the sake of communal goodwill. Walker completed *Jubilee* before the Watts riots in 1965, but her first readers, still reeling from the violence that erupted in August of that year, may have had difficulty imagining how such apparently mutually exclusive positions would ever be reconciled in a jubilee of good feeling.

Jubilee is mostly a story of the 1860s for the 1960s. In 1966, the year that *Jubilee* was published, blacks had begun to enjoy full access to public accommodations, to go to the polls occasionally to elect black officials, and to see the racial barriers fall in public schools and in colleges. The Civil Rights Acts of 1964 and 1965 had given legal sanction to the gains of the struggle, and for a while it seemed that progress would continue. Vyry's condition at the end of *Jubilee* is similar to that of her counterparts a hundred years later. She is not only free from slavery, but she has learned to cope with everyday responsibilities and to enjoy limited but significant privileges of freedom: a home, work, a loving husband, and an education for her children.

The relationship between the post–Civil War period and the modern Civil Rights movement emerges in the final pages of the novel as this family—Vyry, her two husbands, and the children—becomes virtually allegorical, with the three adults each representing a major faction of the black community and the children representing the future. Soon after the war, former slaves were systematically deprived of their civil rights through a series of compromises, legislative acts, and court decisions, culminating in the validation of the separate-but-equal doctrine of *Plessy v. Ferguson* in 1896. While the final events leading to the restoration of these rights were occurring, as Walker completed her novel in 1965, the language and place names associated with those events came forth in the text, connecting the present with the past. Vyry talks of being "free at last" (405) and Ware of having had "a dream" (409). Jim, on his way to Montgomery and then to school in Selma, Alabama, is literally and figuratively beginning a journey that will pass through Montgomery and Selma and culminate in the civil rights legislation of 1964 and 1965. When Jim boards the train—its first stop Montgomery—and the "white trainman" shouts, "Colored up front! White ladies to the rear," he is experiencing the early days of the Jim Crow system that will remain intact for nearly a century (415). The first major battle of the movement was fought over the issue of seating on the city buses of Montgomery, the very city to which Jim is heading.

The final scene of the novel looks both forward and backward. Vyry, simultaneously grieving over her son's departure and waiting expectantly for the birth of another child, goes out into the dying light and looks "over the red-clay hills of her new home" (416). She recalls herself many years before as a little slave child chasing her master's dominicker hen while Aunt Sally calls her back to work in her white master's house, and for a moment she feels "peace in her heart," as her own "flock of white leghorn laying-hens come running" when she calls (416).

The jubilee of Old Testament law mandates the release of slaves from bondage every fifty years. Like history, it suggests caution, for the battle for freedom will have to be fought again and again. Shortly after the close of the Civil War, plans were already underway to reinstitute slavery in the more subtle form of Jim Crow. The next "jubilee," fifty years after the Civil War, came roughly at the time of the First World War, when those African Americans who went to France and survived the war enjoyed some freedom from Jim Crow and came to expect freedom from racism at home. Lynchings and other acts of terror tightened the shackles again as soon as the Great War ended. Just before *Jubilee* was published, some fifty years later, the promised jubilee came forth in the culminating events of the movement. The title, then, may be both a celebration and a warning. While linking the contemporary movement to the past, the novel anticipates the need to adjust to new freedom and prepare for a backlash from threatened whites determined to reestablish the conditions that existed before the Civil Rights movement. Readers in the 1990s are more likely than their 1960s counterparts to recognize the implied warnings and to acknowledge the accuracy of its prophecy.

It seems likely that Margaret Walker, who by her own admission had been writing this book all her life, was able to draw on energy generated by the urgency of the movement itself to bring it to fruition, but perhaps in those heady days she was able to end the novel with a more positive commitment to progress than would have been possible for her later. As the great-granddaughter of a former slave, Walker's own life reflected the progress made possible by those women in the nineteenth century who struggled to create the homes and families that would nurture growth and development. In the spring of 1965—while blacks and whites were confronting each other on the Edmond Pettus bridge in Selma, Klansmen were murdering Civil Rights workers of both races on the back roads of the South, and blacks themselves were gearing up for an internecine struggle—Walker was completing with breakneck speed this book that celebrated progress while calling for reconciliation, cooperation, and commitment to common goals. Before he leaves Vyry at the end of the novel, regretting the loss of his wife and children, Randall Ware observes that they "just got caught in the times" (409). In 1965, James Reeb, Jimmie Lee Jackson, and Viola Liuzzo—all killed during the Selma campaign—were caught in the same stream of history.

Some readers in 1966 were likely to have experienced the novel as a celebration of the linear progress toward racial justice; a generation later, we know that regression is as likely as further progress. Margaret Walker once promised a sequel to *Jubilee*. One wonders what its vision of the state of racial justice would be today, or what future it might project.

Humanism is not a tradition; it is the medium
through which all traditions exist.

—R. BAXTER MILLER

We *are* the historical process.

—MARGARET WALKER

The "Intricate Design" of
Margaret Walker's "Humanism"

Revolution, Vision, History

MINROSE C. GWIN

In the poem "Elegy," written in memory of an admired professor,
Margaret Walker envisions living as the process of weaving a tapestry that becomes "an intricate design" of a "rich pattern" inevitably disrupted and de-
constructed when "fate unties the knot / And snips the thin-worn twine" (lines
28–29).[1] I want to use Walker's own metaphor to comment on the tapestry of
her life's work as a writer; that is, I want to attempt a weaving of my own as
I describe Walker's work as an "intricate design" composed of three connective
threads: first, a series of discursive affirmations of a creative "humanistic" vision; second, her literary texts' subversive disruption of racist ideology—a disruption I see as complexly gendered; and, finally, an emphasis in all of her
writing upon an Afrocentric heritage and vision as powerful sources of deconstruction and reconstruction of American culture. Read together, Walker's
oeuvre, then, may be experienced as an interwoven fabric that paradoxically
becomes what it is through its ability to differ from itself, and to allow its
production of difference to translate into ideology. In Walker's case this is an
ongoing production out of the crossings and recrossings of gender and race

that generate, as Nancy K. Miller says of Arachne's mythical weaving, "a figuration of woman's relation of production to the dominant culture" (272) by spinning textual and intertextual patterns that produce and reproduce a multivalent design of resistance.

Walker's essays, poetry, and fiction each intersect and shape the directions of the other. Together they defy dominant structures of thought, "the master narratives" of culture, as Jean-François Lyotard would call them (64). At the same time, Walker's discursive emphasis upon a "new humanism," her defining and redefining of it throughout her career, inscribes the desire for vision in cultural experience, as her emphasis upon African American heritage reflects the centrality of history to her thinking and writing. From Walker's early poetry of the 1930s and 1940s—the powerful "For My People," for example—to her civil rights poems of the 1960s and her novel *Jubilee*, published in 1966, she writes of the African American experience and what it means to be black and southern. This heritage, which is both enduring and visionary and derives its identity out of the interstice between creative vision and modes of resistance, is at the core of Walker's activism and writing. As Houston A. Baker Jr. more generally suggests in his discussion of the blues as a trope for conversing with the elusive and disruptive texts of African American literature and culture, the Afrocentric vision of Walker's writing seems always in motion—"always becoming, shaping, transforming, displacing" cultural experience (5), always negotiating repressive economies of mastery and dominance through creativity and imaginative dexterity.

Throughout her career, and particularly in the decade of the 1960s, Walker wove her own tapestry out of the threads of revolution, vision, and history—all of which are overlapping and interconnected, but all of which figure their own differing negotiations of the tight spaces of racist oppression. In her life's work as a southern black woman writer, teacher, and public figure, she navigated those spaces in white southern culture and said no to the injustices she found there. At the same time she affirmed a humanistic vision that is generated out of the interweaving of the history of African American experience and what Hélène Cixous would call a woman's "unthink[ing]" of patriarchal history (252), in Walker's case the "unthinking" of racist cultural codes. Walker's texts, then, may be read as an ongoing commentary on and a theoretical model for the ways in which race and gender may be considered together as reflexive, interactive forces for change.

It has become commonplace to say that the idea of the feminine is associated with a kind of "unthinking" and undermining of the dominant male perspectives of Western culture and philosophy. The feminine has been seen as other to such a world, and therefore a subversive and disruptive threat to it. Alice Jardine, for example, explores the idea of the feminine as the process of cultural critique inextricably tied to the uncertainty of modernity and to its poststructuralist loosenings of the cultural underpinnings of patriarchal order, particularly "within a culture experiencing a violent ambivalence toward the father" (47). The specifically revolutionary nature of African American women's situated knowledge of oppression has been widely discussed by Angela Davis, Audre Lorde, Patricia Hill Collins, bell hooks, June Jordan, Barbara Christian, Alice Walker, Patricia Williams, and others. As Collins points out, "Black women's concrete experiences as members of specific race, class, and gender groups as well as our concrete historical situations necessarily play significant roles in our perspectives on the world" (33). Such knowledge grounded in material reality forms the basis of revolutionary thought and action. African American women and their experiential knowledge of oppression produce spaces of disruption in some of Walker's texts. In some, there is also a general sense of feminine presence, perhaps what Jardine might call the *process* of the feminine, that undercuts white patriarchal control. The dislodging of such control was certainly underway in both the Civil War and postwar South of *Jubilee* and in the "New South" of the 1960s, which Walker's civil rights poetry and many of her essays and speeches of that period inscribe. It is significant that Walker completed her novel about a black woman's experience in the nineteenth-century South of violent change at a similar time in southern history—the civil rights struggles of the 1960s—out of which she produced some of her most powerful and disruptive poetry.

At the same time, and into the seventies, Walker continued to redefine a "new humanism" evolving out of African American experience and opposed to "the violent and negative philosophy of white racism" ("The Humanistic Tradition of Afro-American Literature" 852). In an important sense, African American literature emerges, she believes, from this "new humanism" and its "unbroken tradition of humanistic values that did not spring from renaissance Europe, but developed in Asia and Africa before the religious wars of the Middle Ages" (853). This is not a return to classical structures or to "culture as an ultimate value" but, as R. Baxter Miller has suggested, to an enlarged definition of "humanness" (3). As Miller points out, such "humanism" has provocative implications for African American literature and vice versa. Indeed, many works by writers such as Richard Wright and Gwendolyn Brooks have compelled readers "to broaden the definition of humanness" (4) and thus to break down in their own minds cultural ideologies of racism. Through this destructuring, new ethical values emerge and are read back into literature. In this process, Miller points out, humanism thereby becomes "not a tradition" but "the medium through which all traditions exist" (6). In another essay in

Miller's edited collection *Black American Literature and Humanism,* Chester Fontenot likewise suggests that the historical associations of the term *humanism* have given way "to mean any philosophy which recognizes the value and dignity of people, which makes them the measure of all things, or which somehow takes as its theme human nature, its limits, or its interests" (34).

Walker's multiple definitions of humanism, developed over a period of years, synthesize natural, religious, historical, and moral elements. Hers is an organic philosophy of human life that embodies "a recognition that we are part of nature and the historical process, that we are implicit in the dynamic evolving of mankind to ever higher planes of being, that all life must be richly developed in spirit rather than mere matter" ("Humanistic Tradition" 853). At several points in her career, Walker referred to her poetry and fiction as humanistic responses to racism and pointed to African American literature as "a reservoir of black humanism" (854). Writing by African Americans becomes the standard-bearer of the values of "freedom, peace, and human dignity" that evolve out of "a continual awareness of the deepest spiritual meaning for freedom, peace, and human dignity" and from "a people who have had to develop compassion out of suffering and who are passionately tied to all that is earthy, natural, and emotionally free." Such revolutionary ideology, Walker implies, is exactly what Western culture lacks (850–54).

In a 1980 essay entitled "On Being Female, Black, and Free," Walker suggests a connection between the feminine and the natural creative principles of humanism inscribed in African American literature and history. As in most of her discursive statements about culture, her emphasis is upon creativity rather than subversiveness or disruption. "All nature," she writes, reflects the "rhythmic and creative principle of feminism and femininity: the sea, the earth, the air, and all life whether plant or animal" (96). In the same essay Walker suggests that the key to humanism lies in the traditional female sphere and in the woman writer who values that sphere. She sounds much like the domestic feminists of the nineteenth century when she writes: "The traditional and historic role of womankind is ever the role of the healing and annealing hand, whether the outworn modes of nurse and mother, cook, and sweetheart. As a writer these are still her concerns. These are still the stuff about which she writes, the human condition, the human potential, the human destiny" (106).

Vyry Ware of *Jubilee* is such a woman and such a symbol. However, Vyry's humanism is as disruptive as it is creative; *Jubilee,* like Walker's civil rights poetry, both explores and explodes patriarchal spaces of racism and oppression, thereby issuing a resounding "no" to white patriarchal values. At the same time, Walker's narrative may be seen as implicitly positing the feminine as the creative and humanistic response to a repressive system and so becomes, in Walker's words, "a canvas upon which I paint my vision of my world" (*How I Wrote* Jubilee 28). In its very context as a slave narrative, and a female one at that, *Jubilee* poses a disruptive threat to white patriarchy. As a narrative about plantation life, its very discourse is subversive, undercutting the primarily white genre of the plantation novel. In exploring female experience as the space of disruption in the narrative, we may see Vyry herself as not so much a realistic female subject in a realistic novel but as what Jardine would call a "woman-in-effect" who, by her very open-endedness and emphasis on nurturance and community, subverts the dominant culture in *Jubilee,* both the culture of the fictional world Walker creates (the antebellum, Civil War, and Reconstruction South) and that of her real world of a century later—the South of Martin Luther King Jr., Rosa Parks, and Medgar Evers. Certainly this is a black woman's narrative. As Phyllis Klotman has pointed out, it presents history from a black woman's point of view. As is the case with women's slave narratives of the nineteenth and early-twentieth centuries, and as in Walker's own great-grandmother's life upon which the narrative is based, Vyry's life *is* the story, and her movement from slavery through the vicissitudes of war to freedom structures the cultural narrative of the demise of the slavocracy and the emergence of African Americans from bondage. In the last pages of the novel, Vyry's rejection of racial bitterness and her proclamation of Walker's humanism represent immense possibility for a regenerated South—past and present (a possibility still unrealized by the sixties, and even today).

As Vyry lists all of the evils done to her by her former master (her father) and mistress, she also insists that she will not become like those representations of patriarchy: she refuses to hate or to kill. She says, "I'm gwine leave all the evil shameless peoples in the world in the hands of the Good Lawd and I'm gwine teach my childrens to hate nobody, don't care what they does. I ain't gwine teach my childrens hate cause hate ain't nothing but rank poison" (404). Of her mistress, "Big Missy" Salina Dutton, whose cruelties exceeded those of any man, Vyry says, "I closed her eyes in death, and God is my witness, I bears her no ill will" (405). In his classic essay, "Everybody's Protest Novel," James Baldwin might have said that Vyry's gesture of forgiveness comes too easily and that she, like Stowe's Uncle Tom and Richard Wright's Bigger Thomas, "has accepted a theology that denies . . . life" rather than confronting and affirming its complexity (585). Yet, Vyry's act of forgiveness and refusal to hate, by their very force, do not embody a passive acceptance of white cruelty but instead create a space of alterity that disrupts the systems that perpetrate ideologies of cruelty, thus asserting the power of Walker's humanism as a counter to them. Vyry herself exemplifies Collins's assertion that black feminist ideology, because it is born out of experience, "views thought and action as part of the same process" and thereby creates "new relationships between thought and action" (29). This holistic view of thought and action as part of the same process, along with the subversive quality of the black woman in the narrative as a whole, undergirds Vyry's revolutionary assertion of humanistic values in response to a patriarchal culture. Generally, the narrative proffers nurturance and human interconnection as "humanistic" responses to racism.

The disruptiveness of female thought and action in *Jubilee* is immediately obvious. As the narrative opens, Vyry's mother, Sis Hetta, is dying at the age of twenty-nine after having given birth to her fifteenth child. She is the victim of what Angela Davis has called "an institutionalized pattern of rape" that constituted black women's experiences in slavery (23), specifically practiced by her master John Dutton. She dies a bloody, gruesome death, with no treatment or sympathy from the white doctor of the plantation. The description of her birthing is that of disruption, of "tearing . . . flesh in shreds" (5). Yet the narrative also ends with birth and the idea of motherhood. This time disruption is generative and empowering as it moves toward healing racial wounds, when Vyry serves as a midwife to a young white woman and probably saves the baby by calming the woman and showing her how to give birth. This act of common female experience establishes a meaningful interracial community that eventually enables Vyry and her family to live in peace with their white neighbors in the racially torn Reconstruction South. It creates a female space of relatedness that disrupts the rigid hierarchies of race, class, and gender in a South described in William Faulkner's *Absalom, Absalom!* as "a country all divided and fixed and neat with a people living on it all divided and fixed and neat because of what color their skins happened to be and what they happened to own" (221).

In the poem "Epitaph for My Father," contained in the 1973 volume *October Journey,* Walker writes about her own inability to construct boundaries between herself and others, marking that inability as a female characteristic that separates her from her father. The poem reveals her mixed feelings at being unable to define her own consciousness as separate from others:

> If I had been a man
> I might have followed in his every step,
> Had preached from pulpits, found my life as his
> And wandered too, as he, an alien on the earth,
> But female and feline I could not stand
> Alone through love and hate and truth
> And still remain my own. He was himself;
> His own man all his life.

And I belong to all the people I have met,
Am part of them, am molded by the throng
Caught in the tide of compromise, and grown
Chameleon for camouflage. (lines 189–200)

In *Jubilee*, however, human interconnectedness is presented more positively, for example, in Vyry's willingness to nurture her childlike white half-
sister Lillian, who loses what little mind she has in the trauma of the Civil War
years. Vyry's mothering of other women across racial lines, particularly in light
of her early mistreatment by her white mistress, disrupts the production of
racist ideology, similar to the way in which the role reversal between black and
white women would later become the central subversive narrative of Sherley
Anne Williams's 1986 novel *Dessa Rose*. It opens the way for the sweeping scene
near the end of the novel in which blacks and whites work together to help
Vyry and her family build their house and create a meaningful interracial community. In the women's communal quilting, female subjectivity becomes an
open arena of interconnection. Although the quilts, like the women who sew
them, are created in different patterns—Vyry's pomegranates contrasting with
Mrs. Medford's double wedding ring and Mrs. Flake's Star of Texas—together
they constitute the larger pattern of a communal female engagement that
makes difference the fabric and thread of a revolutionary form of production.

Following on the heels of this vision of human community, Vyry's unwillingness to join her former husband Randall Ware in his hatred of whites, her
refusal "to try to beat the white man at his own game with his killing and his
hating" (482), resonates with certain African American historical discourses
(e.g., the "passive resistance" discourse of the Civil Rights movement) and
with certain black feminist theory (e.g., Audre Lorde's often-quoted statement,
"The master's tools will never dismantle the master's house" [110]). It may also
reflect what Carol Gilligan believes is a female response to a moral problem.
Women, as Gilligan's research has shown, perceive the moral problem "as a
problem of care and responsibility in relationships rather than as one of rights
and rules" (73) and thus tend to resolve problems through "a mode of thinking
that is contextual and narrative rather than formal and abstract" (19). Vyry's
refusal to hate echoes Walker's own statements in her conversations with Nikki
Giovanni published in 1974: "My integrity is violated by my own hate, by my
own bitterness, and by my own violence. It isn't what I do to the other fellow
that hurts me so much as what I do to myself when I do something to the other
fellow" (29).

The vision of *Jubilee* and of Walker's activism relies, then, on a willingness
to open one's self to the possibilities of connection and nurturance, to meet

violence and hatred in the most revolutionary way possible—through the extension of self in ever-widening circles that disrupt and subvert racism as ideology, that redefine "humanism" as an expansiveness of spirit—as an awareness of human community. This is a humanistic vision that derives from a profound sense of connection with the continuity of African American heritage and, at the same time, an "unthinking" of history and culture as andro/Eurocentric. I see the disruptiveness of Walker's narrative as being that necessary linkage between history and vision, and the breaking up of cultural codes as paramount to the process of re-vision and regeneration. In this sense, Walker's reconstruction of her great-grandmother's experiences produces a different revolutionary ideology than her civil rights poetry written about the same time. By its very nature, *Jubilee's* vision embodies the necessity to rebel and the willingness to reconcile. As such, it offers the possibility of human community in a flawed world.

This is the same community within which the girl of Walker's civil rights poem "Girl Held Without Bail" negotiates the racism of the "unjust state" in which she lives, creating a female community within the "jail" of injustice:

> I like it here just fine
> And I don't want no bail
> My sister's here
> My mother's here
> And all my girl friends too. (1–5)

A similar poem, "Street Demonstration," beginning with the subtitle "Hurry up Lucille or we won't get / arrested with our group." / (An eight-year-old demonstrator, 1963)," speaks the necessity of both the tearing down and building up of culture: those who are "hoping to be arrested / And hoping to go to jail" may be called upon to fight and die (1–2). But freedom is being created, even through death—even perhaps the death of a girl, for "Liberty is costly / and ROME they say to me / Was not built in one day" (8–10). And so the black girl, surely the most vulnerable individual in a racist and sexist culture, becomes the space of its deconstruction. Yet she can only become this space by becoming part of the inner circle of a humanistic community that is imprisoned within a culture that denies its validity; for this reason she must *"Hurry up"* so as not to miss her *"Chance to go to Jail"* (12–13).

In "Now," black women are depicted primarily as the focus of white racism; a mother becomes "nigger girl, and girlie! / Auntie, Ant, and Granny" (18–19). The white voice of the poem renders black women sexless and powerless by making them young or old:

> My old mammy was a wonder
> and I love those dear old darkies
> who were good and servile nigras
> with their kerchiefed heads and faces
> in their sweet and menial places. (20–24)

African American women thus become the space of white discourse in the poem; but in becoming the sign of that discourse they undercut it to make it show its true racist colors, and thus make it speak against itself. African American womanhood becomes the internal difference of white discourse, the site of its rupture.

"OXFORD Is a Legend" is even more aggressively challenging to a white culture "Where all the by-gone years of chivalry and poetry and crinoline / Are dead" (20–21). The poem confronts white history, the disastrous integration of the University of Mississippi, with its "scholars yelling 'nigger'" (5), and, perhaps more significantly, William Faulkner. The poem refers to Faulkner's infamous statement that he would fight for Mississippi against the United States "even if it meant going out into the street and shooting Negroes" (Peavy 70), a statement he later recanted. Walker's poem directly attacks Faulkner:

> Too bad the old man from Jefferson County
> Died before he saw the fighting in his streets
> Before he had to bear arms for Mississippi
> And shoot the Negroes in the streets. (13–16)

As it tears down racist discourse and racist structures of "the by-gone years," the poem asserts that Oxford is now a legend because of black bravery and the breaking of such structures under the weight of the demand for an expanded humanism that included the James Merediths of the South.

> OXFORD is a legend
> Out of time more than battle place, or a name
> With the figure of one brave and smiling little man
> Smiling that courageous, ironic, bright, grim smile
> Smile of a black American. (22–26)

Just as "Now" creates an African American woman as the sign that forces white discourse to speak (against) itself, so the black man, the historical Meredith, is re-created as the site of disruption in white culture as his "grim smile" demands expansion of that culture's narrow definition of humanness.

The insistence of Walker's civil rights poems upon regeneration in the face of sterility and despair may also be found in "Jackson, Mississippi" and in

"For Gwen, 1969," a poem not published in the *Prophets for a New Day* volume. Both poems link the feminine to Walker's interwoven fabric of humanism and African American history. In "Jackson, Mississippi" Walker's deep affection for her home and her attachment to the South and to her people emerge out of a personal vision of a "City of closed doors and ketchup splattered floors" (2). Her vision of teaching and writing is expressed in images of maternal nurturance. Despite living in a city that destroys the dreams of its black citizenry, a city strewn with the shattering of lives seen in "the birthing stools of grannies long since fled" (35), she also can feel herself empowered by a willingness to extend the boundaries of human community, to nurture those who cry out for it:

> Here are echoes of my laughing children
> And hungry minds of pupils to be fed.
> I give you my brimming heart, Southern City
> For my eyes are full and no tears cry
> And my throat is dusty and dry. (36–40)

"For Gwen, 1969," a tribute to Gwendolyn Brooks included in *October Journey*, depicts the power of an African American woman to inscribe humanism in "black words of fire and blood" (16). Such words connect and empower "the Ebon land" whose people "are her heartbeat" (3, 13). The poem in its entirety mediates history and humanism through the figure of the African American woman:

> The slender, shy, and sensitive young girl
> is woman now,
> Her words a power in the Ebon land.
> Outside her window on the street
> a mass of life moves by.
> Chicago is her city.
> Her heart flowers with its flame—
> old stock yards, new beaches
> all the little store-front churches
> and the bar on the corner.
> Dreamer and seer of tales
> She witnesses rebellion,
> struggle and sweat.
> The people are her heartbeat—
> In their footsteps pulsate daily
> all her black words of fire and blood.

Here it is a black woman's vision that remakes the world and propels African American history toward a re-creative humanism. It is her negotiation of the infinite spaces of difference in language that disrupts culture and speaks the "fire and blood" of a complex commitment to the values of "freedom, peace, and human dignity" as the "highest essence of the human spirit."

In a 1975 interview Walker said that it is "only in terms of humanism that the society can redeem itself" (Rowell 12). In her writings of the decade preceding that statement, we may see the possibility of such redemption as evolving out of those textual threads of revolution, vision, and history. These texts undo themselves even as they weave themselves, for their productivity depends upon the force generated by interactions between these elements of internal difference. In terms of language, Barbara Johnson has defined textual *difference* as that which is always in process, "infinitely deferring the possibility of adding the sum of a text's parts or meanings and reaching a totalized, integrated whole" (4). Difference in the world, as Audre Lorde has pointed out, can be and should be a productive, generative force that is deeply and profoundly connected to language. "For women, then, poetry is not a luxury," Lorde writes. "It is a vital necessity of our existence. It forms the quality of light within which we predicate our hopes and dreams toward survival and change, first made into language, then into idea, then into more tangible action" (37). To move a step further in our conversations with Walker's writings of the 1960s, we may see their generative difference not only in motion *within* their textual and intertextual spaces but as opening *out of* those spaces into the process of creative living, into a productivity created out of difference and one that therefore validates and values difference. And this, I think, is what Margaret Walker means by "humanism."

NOTE

1. Unless indicated otherwise in the text of this essay, all poems cited are from the volume *Prophets for a New Day*. Parenthetical references to the poems are to line numbers.

WORKS CITED

Baker, Houston A., Jr. *Blues Ideology and Afro-American Literature: A Vernacular Theory*. Chicago: University of Chicago Press, 1984.
Baldwin, James. "Everybody's Protest Novel." *Partisan Review* 16 (1949): 578–85.
Cixous, Hélène. "The Laugh of the Medusa." *New French Feminisms: An Anthology*. Ed.

Elaine Marks and Isabelle de Courtivron. Amherst: University of Massachusetts Press, 1980. 245–64.

Collins, Patricia Hill. *Black Feminist Thought: Knowledge, Consciousness, and the Politics of Empowerment.* New York: Routledge, 1991.

Davis, Angela. *Women, Race & Class.* New York: Random House, 1981.

Faulkner, William. *Absalom, Absalom!* New York: Modern Library, 1966.

Fontenot, Chester J., Jr. "Angelic Dance or Tug of War? The Humanistic Implications of Cultural Formalism." In Miller 33–49.

Gilligan, Carol. *In a Different Voice.* Cambridge: Harvard University Press, 1982.

Giovanni, Nikki, and Margaret Walker. *A Poetic Equation: Conversations Between Nikki Giovanni and Margaret Walker.* Washington: Howard University Press, 1974.

Jardine, Alice A. *Gynesis: Configurations of Woman and Modernity.* Ithaca: Cornell University Press, 1985.

Johnson, Barbara. *The Critical Difference: Essays in the Contemporary Rhetoric of Reading.* Baltimore: Johns Hopkins University Press, 1980.

Klotman, Phillis. "'Oh Freedom'—Women and History in Margaret Walker's *Jubilee.*" *Black American Literature Forum* 11.4 (winter 1977): 139–45.

Lorde, Audre. *Sister Outsider.* Trumaneburg NY: Crossing Press, 1984.

Lyotard, Jean-François. *The Postmodern Condition: A Report on Knowledge.* Trans. Geoff Bennington and Brian Massumi. Foreword by Fredric Jameson. Theory and History of Literature Series 10. Minneapolis: University of Minnesota Press, 1984.

Miller, Nancy K. "Arachnologies: The Woman, The Text, and the Critic." *The Poetics of Gender.* Ed. Nancy K. Miller. Gender and Culture Series, ed. Carolyn G. Heilbrun and Nancy K. Miller. New York: Columbia University Press, 1986.

Miller, R. Baxter, ed. *Black American Literature and Humanism.* Lexington: University of Kentucky Press, 1981.

Peavy, Charles D. *Go Slow Now: Faulkner and the Race Question.* Eugene: University of Oregon Press, 1971.

Rowell, Charles. "Poetry, History, and Humanism: An Interview with Margaret Walker." *Black World* 25.2 (1975): 4–17.

Walker, Margaret. *How I Wrote* Jubilee. Chicago: Third World Press, 1972.

———. "The Humanistic Tradition of Afro-American Literature." *American Libraries* 1 (1970): 849–54.

———. *Jubilee.* Boston: Houghton Mifflin, 1966.

———. *October Journey.* Detroit: Broadside, 1973.

———. "On Being Female, Black, and Free." *The Writer on Her Work.* Ed. Janet Sternburg. New York: Norton, 1980.

———. *Prophets for a New Day.* Detroit: Broadside, 1970.

PART TWO

From *For My People*
to *This Is My Century*:
The Poetry of
Margaret Walker

The "Etched Flame" of Margaret Walker

*Literary and Biblical Re-Creation
in Southern History*

R. BAXTER MILLER

Margaret Walker learned about Moses and Aaron from the black American culture into which she was born. As the daughter of a religious scholar, she came of age in the depression of the thirties, and her career, like those of Margaret Danner, Dudley Randall, and Gwendolyn Brooks, has spanned three or four decades. Much of her important work, like theirs, has been unduly neglected, coming as it does between the Harlem Renaissance of the 1920s and the Black Arts Movement of the 1960s. Most indices to literature, black American and American, list only one article on Margaret Walker from 1971 through 1981.[1]

Walker knew the important figures of an older generation, including James Weldon Johnson, Langston Hughes, and Countee Cullen. She heard Marian Anderson and Roland Hayes sing, and she numbered among her acquaintances Zora Neale Hurston, George Washington Carver, and W. E. B. Du Bois. What does the richness of the culture give her? She finds the solemn nobility of religious utterance, the appreciation for the heroic spirit of black folk, and the deep respect for craft.[2] Once she heard from the late Richard Wright that talent does not suffice for literary fame. She took his words to heart and survived to write about his life, his self-hatred, and his paradoxical love for white women.[3] She knew, too, Willard Motley, Fenton Johnson, and Arna Bontemps. Her lifetime represents continuity. From a youthful researcher for Wright during her early days in Chicago, she matured into an inspirational teacher at Jackson State University, where she preserved the spirit of her forerunners, the powerful intellect and the flowing phrase, but she still belongs most with the black poets whose careers span the last forty years. Her strengths are not the same as theirs. Margaret Danner's poetry has a quiet lyricism of peace, a deeply controlled introspection. No one else shows her delicacy of alliteration and her carefully framed patterns. Dudley Randall's success comes from the ballad, whose alternating lines of short and longer rhythms communicate the racial turmoil of the sixties. He profits from a touching and light innocence as well as a plea and longing for the child's inquiring voice.

In *For My People* Walker develops this and other paradigms in three sections, the first two divisions with ten poems each and the last segment with six. The reader experiences initially the tension and potential of the black South; then the folktale of both tragic possibility and comic relief involving the curiosity, trickery, and deceit of men and women alike; finally, the significance of physical and spiritual love in reclaiming the southern land. Walker writes careful antinomies into the visionary poem, the folk secular and the Shakespearean and Petrarchan sonnets. She opposes quest to denial, historical circumstances to imaginative will, and earthly suffering to heavenly bliss. Here poetry purges the southern ground of animosity and injustice that separate black misery from southern song. Her themes are time, infinite human potential, racial equality, vision, blindness, love, and escape, as well as worldly death, drunkenness, gambling, rottenness, and freedom. She pictures the motifs within the frames of toughness and abuse, of fright and gothic terror. Wild arrogance for her speakers often underlies heroism, which is often more imagined than real.

The myth of human immortality expressed in oral tale and in literary artifact transcends death. The imagination evokes atemporal memory, asserts the humanistic self against the fatalistic past, and illustrates, through physical love, the promise of both personal and racial reunification. The achievement is syntactic. Parallelism, elevated rhetoric, simile, and figure of speech abound, but more deeply the serenity of nature creates solemnity. Walker depicts sun, slashing brook, pond, duck, frog, and stream, as well as flock, seed, wood, bark, cotton field, and cane. Still, the knife and gun threaten the pastoral world as, by African conjure, the moral "we" attempts to reconcile the two. As both the participant and observer, Walker creates an ironic distance between history and eternity. The southern experience in the first section and the reclamation in the second part frame the humanity of folk personae Stagolee, John Henry, Kissee Lee, Yalluh Hammuh, and Gus. The book becomes a literary artifact, a "clean house" that imaginatively restructures the Southland.

If Dudley Randall has written "The Ballad of Birmingham" and Gwendolyn Brooks "The Children of the Poor," Walker succeeds with the visionary poem.[4] She does not portray the gray-haired old women who nod and sing out of despair and hope on Sunday morning, but she captures the depths of their suffering. She re-creates their belief that someday black Americans will triumph over fire hoses and biting dogs, once the brutal signs of white oppression in the South. The prophecy contributes to Walker's rhythmical balance and vision, but she controls the emotions. How do we change brutality into social equality? Through sitting down at a lunch counter in the sixties, black students illustrated some divinity and confronted death, just as Christ faced his cross. Walker deepens the portraits by using biblical typology, by discovering historical antitypes, and by creating an apocalyptic fusion.[5] Through the suffering in the Old and New Testaments, the title poem of *For My People* expresses black American victory over deprivation and hatred. The ten stanzas celebrate the endurance of tribulations such as dark murders in Virginia and Mississippi as well as Jim Crowism, ignorance, and poverty. The free form includes the parallelism of verbs and the juxtaposition of the present with the past. Black Americans are "never gaining, ever reaping, never knowing and never understanding."[6] When religion faces reality, the contrast creates powerful reversal:

> For the boys and girls who grew in spite of these things to be man
> and woman, to laugh and dance and sing and play and
> drink their wine and religion and success, to marry their
> playmates and bear children and then die of consumption
> and anemia and lynching.

Through biblical balance, "For My People" sets the white oppressor against the black narrator. Social circumstance opposes racial and imaginative will, and disillusion opposes happiness. Blacks fashion a new world that encompasses many faces and people, "all the adams and eves and their countless generations." From the opening dedication (stanza 1) to the final evocation (stanza 10), the prophet-narrator speaks both as Christ and God. Ages ago, the Lord put his rainbow in the clouds. To the descendants of Noah it signified his promise that the world would never again end in flood. Human violence undermines biblical calm, as the first world repeats itself: "Let a new earth rise.

Let another world be born. Let a bloody peace be written in the sky. Let a second generation full of courage issue forth. . . ."

"We Have Been Believers," a visionary poem, juxtaposes Christianity with African conjure, and the Old Testament with the New, exemplified by St. John, St. Mark, and Revelation. The narrator ("we") represents black builders and singers in the past, for Walker seeks to interpret cultural signs. The theme is black faith, first in Africa and then in America. As the verse shows movement from the past to the present, the ending combines Christianity and humanism. With extensive enjambment, the controlled rhapsody has a long first sentence, followed by indented ones that complete the meaning. The form literally typifies black American struggle. The long line is jolted because an ending is illusory, and the reader renews his perusal just as the black American continues the search for freedom. The narrator suggests the biblical scene in which death breaks the fifth seal (Revelation 6:11). There the prophet sees all the people who, slain in the service of God, wear garments as the narrator describes them.

The authenticating "we" is more focused than either Ellison's in *Invisible Man* or Baldwin's in *Notes of a Native Son*. Their speakers are often educated and upwardly mobile people who move between white and black American worlds. Walker's, on the contrary, are frequently the secular and religious "folk" who share a communal quest. She blends historical sense with biblical implication:

> Neither the slaver's whip nor the lyncher's rope nor the bayonet
> could kill our black belief. In our hunger we beheld the
> welcome table and in our nakedness the glory of a long
> white robe.

The narrator identifies Moloch, a god of cruel sacrifice, and all the people who have died for no just cause. She prepares for the myth that dominates the last three parts of the poem, the miracle that Jesus performed on the eyes of a blind man. After he instructs him to wash them in the pool of Siloam, the man sees clearly (John 9:25). Another allusion suggests the miracle that Christ worked for the afflicted people near the Sea of Galilee. Walker's narrator knows the legend, but awaits the transformation (Mark 7:37). The waiting prepares for an irony phrased in alliteration: "Surely the priests and the preachers and the powers will hear . . . / . . . now that our hands are empty and our hearts too full to pray." This narrator says that such people will send a sign—the biblical image of relief and redemption—but she implies something different. Although her humanism embraces Christianity, she adds militancy and impatience. Her rhetoric illustrates liquid sound, alliteration, and assonance:

We have been believers believing in our burdens and our
    demigods too long. Now the needy no longer weep and
    pray; the long-suffering arise, and our fists bleed against
    the bars with a strange insistency.

The impatience pervades "Delta," which has the unifying type of the twenty-third Psalm. Although the first part (II.1–35) presents the blood, corruption, and depression of the narrator's naturalistic world, the second (II.36–78) illustrates the restorative potential of nature. High mountain, river, orange, cotton, fern, grass, and onion share the promise. Dynamic fertility, the recleansed river (it flowed through swamps in the first part), can clear the southern ground of sickness, rape, starvation, and ignorance. Water gives form to anger, yet thawing sets in. Coupled with liquidity, the loudness of thunder and cannon implies storm; the narrator compares the young girl to spring. Lovingly the speaker envisions vineyards, pastures, orchards, cattle, cotton, tobacco, and cane, "making us men in the fields we have tended / standing defending the land we have rendered rich and abiding and heavy with plenty." Interpreting the meaning of earth can help to bridge the distance between past decay and present maturity when the narrator celebrates the promise:

the long golden grain for bread
and the ripe purple fruit for wine
the hills beyond for peace
and the grass beneath for rest
the music in the wind for us
. . . .
and the circling lines in the sky
for dreams.

Elsewhere a gothic undercurrent and an allusion to Abel and Cain add complexity; so does an allusion to Christ and transubstantiation. Rhetorical power emerges because the harsh tone of the Old Testament threatens the merciful tone of the new one. Loosely plotted, the verse recounts the personal histories of the people in the valley. Still, the symbolic level dominates the literal one, and the poem portrays more deeply the human condition. The narrator profits from the gothicism that has influenced Ann Radcliffe, Charles Brockden Brown, and Edgar Allan Poe. Just as Walker's pictures create the beauty of the African American, they communicate a grace to all who appreciate symmetrical landscapes. The tension in her literary world comes from the romantic legacy of possibility set against denial:

High above us and round about us stand high mountains
rise the towering snow-capped mountains
while we are beaten and broken and bowed
here in this dark valley.

Almost no rhyme scheme exists in the poem, but a predominance of three or four feet gives the impression of a very loose ballad. The fifth stanza of the second part has incremental repetition, as the undertone of Countee Cullen's poem "From the Dark Tower" heightens the deep despair, the paradox of desire and restraint: "We tend the crop and gather the harvest / but not for ourselves do we sweat and starve and spend. . . . / here on this earth we dare not claim." In the penultimate stanza the reader associates myth and history. While the narrator remembers the blacks unrewarded in the southern past, the imagery suggests Christ and transubstantiation. The speaker, however, alludes mainly to Abel slain by Cain (Genesis 4:10): "We with our blood have watered these fields / and they belong to us." Implicitly, the promise of the Psalmist ("Yea though I walk through the valley of the shadow of death") has preceded.

In four quatrains, "Since 1619" strengthens Old Testament prefiguration. Aware of World War II, the narrator illuminates human blindness. She emphasizes the inevitability of death and the deterioration of world peace. With anaphora she repeats the Psalmist:

How many years . . . have I been singing Spirituals?
How long have I been praising God and shouting hallelujahs?
How long have I been hated and hating?
How long have I been living in hell for heaven?

She remembers the Valley of Dry Bones in which the Lord placed the prophet Ezekiel, whom he questioned whether the bones could live. Whereas in the Bible salvation is external and divine, here the transformation comes from within. The poem contrasts moral renewal to the spiritual death during World War II and the pseudocleanliness of middle-class America.

Written in seven stanzas, "Today" has four lines in the first section and three in the second. Initially the poem portrays the ancient muse, the inspiration of all poetry, and later it illustrates poverty, fear, and sickness. Even the portrait of lynching cannot end the narrator's quest for cleanliness. Although Americans face death, they will continue to seek solace through intoxication and sex. The beginning of the poem foreshadows the end, but the directness in the second section supplants the general description in the first one. The middle-class Americans in the first part have no bombing planes or air raids to fear, yet they have masked violence and ethnocentric myth: "viewing weekly 'Wild West Indian and Shooting Sam,' 'Mama Loves Papa,' and 'Gone By the

Breeze!' " Calories, eyemaline, henna rinse, and dental cream image a materialistic nation. With a deeper cleanliness, the speaker advises the reader within an ironic context: "Pray for second sight and the inner ear. Pray for bulwark against poaching patterns of dislocated days; pray for buttressing iron against insidious termite and beetle and locust and flies and lice and moth and rust and mold."

The religious types in the second and third sections of *For My People* rival neither those in the first section nor those in *Prophets for a New Day*. When Walker ignores biblical sources, often she vainly attempts to achieve cultural saturation.[7] Without biblical cadences, her ballads frequently become average, if not monotonous. In "Yalluh Hammuh," a folk poem about the "Bad man," she manages sentimentality, impractical concern, and trickery, as a black woman outsmarts the protagonist and steals his money.

Sometimes the less figurative sonnets are still boring.[8] "Childhood" lacks the condensation and focus to develop well the Petrarchan design. In the octave a young girl remembers workers who used to return home in the afternoons. Even during her maturity, the rags of poverty and the habitual grumbling still color the southern landscape. Despite weaknesses, the poem suggests a biblical analogue well. The apostle Paul writes, "When I was a child, I spake as a child: but when I became a man, I put away childish things" (1 Corinthians 13:11). Walker's sonnet begins coincidentally:

> When I was a child I knew red miners . . .
> I also lived in a low cotton country . . .
> where sentiment and hatred still held sway
> and only bitter land was washed away.

The mature writer seeks now to restore and renew the earth.

In *Prophets for a New Day* Walker illustrates some historical antitypes to the Old Testament. Her forms are the visionary poem, free-verse sonnet, monody,[9] pastoral, and gothic ballad in which she portrays freedom, speech, death, and rebirth. Her major images are fire, water, and wind. When she opposes the figure of marching to the foil of standing, the implied quest becomes metaphorical, for she re-creates the human community in the spiritual wilderness. She looks beneath any typological concern of man's covenant with God, and even the pantheistic parallel of the southerner's covenant with the land, to illuminate man's broken covenant with himself. The human gamut runs from death ("mourning bird") to the potential of poetry ("humming bird"). Hence, poetry re-creates anthropocentric space. The speaker depicts the breadth through dramatic dialogue, sarcasm, and satire. Even the cold stone implies the potential for creative inspiration or Promethean fire. The narrator verbally paints urban corruption in the bitter cold and frozen water. Her portrait images not only the myth of fragmentation and dissolution but the courage necessary to confront and transcend them. Her world is doubly southern. Here the Old South still withstands Northern invasion, but the black South endures both. One attains the mythical building beyond (compare Thomas Wolfe), the human house, through fire. Poetic form is imagined silence. Poetry, both catharsis and purgation, parallels speaking, crying, and weaving. Its center includes geometric space and aesthetic beauty. To portray anthropocentric depth is to clarify the significance of human cleansing.

Although the sonnets and ballads in *For My People* are weak, the typological poems in *Prophets for a New Day* envision universal freedom. But neither Walker nor her reader can remain at visionary heights, for the real world includes the white hood and fiery cross. Even the latter image fails to save the poem "Now," in which the subject is civil rights. Here both images of place and taste imply filth as doors, dark alleys, balconies, and washrooms reinforce moral indignation. The Klan marks "kleagle with a klux / and a fiery burning cross." Yet awkward rhythms have preceded. In shifting from three feet to four, the speaker stumbles: "In the cleaning room and closets / with the washrooms marked 'For Colored Only.'" The ear of "Sit-ins" catches more sharply the translation of the Bible into history. Written in twelve lines of free verse, the lyric depicts the students at North Carolina A & T University, who in 1960 sat down at the counter of a Woolworth's dime store and began the Civil Rights movement. The speaker re-creates southern history. In the shining picture, the reader sees the angel Michael, who drove Adam and Eve from Paradise, but the portrait becomes more secular:

> With courage and faith, convictions and intelligence
> The first to blaze a flaming patch for justice
> And awaken consciences
> Of these stony ones.

The implement that in the Bible and Milton symbolized Paradise Lost becomes a metaphor for Paradise Regained. In viewpoint the narrator gives way to the demonstrators themselves: *"Come, Lord Jesus, Bold Young Galilean / Sit Beside This Counter / Lord with Me."*

As with most of Walker's antitypical poems, "Sit-ins" hardly rivals "Ballad of the Free," one of her finest. The latter work portrays the heroic missions and tragic deaths of slave insurrectionists and excels through consistent rhythm as well as compression of image. At first the verse seems true to the title. Although the design of the typical ballad usually emphasizes a rhythmic contrast between two lines in succession, "Ballad of the Free" stresses a contrast between whole

stanzas. Of the twelve sections that comprise the poem, each of the four quatrains follows a tercet that serves as the refrain. The narrator adds a striking twist
to St. Matthew (19:30; 20:16), in which Peter asks Jesus what will happen to
people who have forsaken everything to follow him. Christ replies that the social
status will be reversed. Although he speaks about the beginning of the apocalypse in which all persons are judged, Walker's narrator foresees the end of
the apocalypse in which all are equal: "The serpent is loosed and the hour
is come."

The refrain balances social history and biblical legend. The first stanza presents Nat Turner, the leader of the slave insurrection in South Hampton, Virginia, during 1831. After the first refrain, the reader recognizes Gabriel Prosser,
who a storm once forced to suspend a slave revolt in Richmond, Virginia. With
a thousand other slaves, Prosser planned an uprising that collapsed in 1800.
Betrayed by fellow bondsmen, he and fifteen others were hanged on October 7
that year. After the first echo of the refrain, Denmark Vesey, who enlisted thousands of blacks for an elaborate slave plot in Charleston, South Carolina, and
the vicinity appears in the fifth stanza. Authorities arrested 131 blacks and four
whites, and when the matter was settled, thirty-seven people were hanged.
Toussaint L'Ouverture, who at the turn of the nineteenth century liberated
Haitian slaves, follows the second echo of the refrain. Shortly afterward an
evocation of John Brown intensifies the balance between history and sound.
With thirteen whites and five blacks, Brown attacked Harper's Ferry on October 16, 1859, and by December 2 of that year, he was also hanged. In the
poem, as in the southern past, the death of the rebel is foreshadowed. Gifted
with humane vision, he wants to change an inegalitarian South. But those who
maintain the status quo will kill, so the hero becomes the martyr.

In order to emphasize Turner as historical paradigm, the narrator ignores
the proper chronology of L'Ouverture, Prosser, Vesey, Turner, and Brown. She
gives little of the historical background but calls upon the names of legend.
What does she achieve, by naming her last hero, if not a symmetry of color?
The ballad that began with black Nat Turner ends with white John Brown,
for if action alone determines a basis for fraternity, racial distinction is in-
significant.

For a central portrait of Turner, the verse moves backward and forward in
both typological and apocalyptic time. As with the narrator of Hughes's "The
Negro Speaks of Rivers," the speaker can comprehend different decades. Because she is outside of time, L'Ouverture and Brown, who come from different
periods, appear to her with equal clarity. Until the eleventh stanza, the biblical
sureness of the refrain has balanced history. The note of prophecy sounds in
the slowness and firmness of racial progress:

> Wars and Rumors of Wars have gone,
> But Freedom's army marches on.
> The heroes' list of dead is long,
> And Freedom still is for the strong.

The narrator recalls Christ (Mark 13:7), who prophesies wars and rumors of war but foretells salvation for endurers. The final refrain interfuses with the fable and history: "The serpent is loosed and the hour is come."

"At the Lincoln Monument in Washington, August 28, 1963" presents analogues to Isaiah, Exodus, Genesis, and Deuteronomy. Written in two stanzas, the poem has forty-four lines. The speaker dramatizes chronicle through biblical myth, racial phenomenology, and Judeo-Christian consciousness. She advances superbly with the participant to the interpreter, but even the latter speaks from behind an aesthetic mask. The poetic vision authenticates the morality of her fable and the biblical analogue. The first stanza has twenty-eight lines, and the second has sixteen. As the speaker recalls the March on Washington, in which more than 250,000 people demonstrated for civil rights, she attributes to Martin Luther King Jr., the leader of the movement, the same rhetorical art she now remembers him by. The analogue is Isaiah: "The grass withereth, the flower fadeth: but the word of our God shall stand for ever" (40:8). Two brothers, according to the fable, led the Israelites out of Egypt.[10] Sentences of varied length complement the juxtaposition of cadences that rise and fall. The narrator names neither King as "Moses" nor King's youthful follower as "Aaron," yet she clarifies a richness of oration and implies the heroic spirit. King, before his death, said that he had been to the mountaintop and that he had seen the Promised Land. But the speaker literarily retraces the paradigm of the line; she distills the love of the listeners who saw him and were inspired: "There they stand . . . / Old man with a dream he has lived to see come true."

Although the first eleven lines of the poem are descriptive, the twelfth combines chronicle and prefiguration. The speaker projects the social present into the mythical past. Her words come from a civil rights song, "We Woke Up One Morning with Our Minds Set On Freedom." The social activist wants the immediate and complete liberation that the rhetorician (speaker and writer) translates into literary symbol: "We woke up one morning in Egypt / And the river ran red with blood . . . / And the houses of death were afraid."

She remembers, too, the story of Jacob, who returns home with his two wives, Leah and Rachel (Genesis 30:25–43). Laban, the father-in-law, gave him speckled cattle, but now the narrator understands that Jacob's "*house* [black America] has grown into a nation. / The slaves break forth from bondage" (emphasis mine). In Old Testament fashion, she cautions against fatigue in the pursuit of liberty. Through heightened style, she becomes a prophet whose medium is eternal language. She has mastered alliteration, assonance, and resonance:

> Write this word upon your hearts
> And mark this message on the doors of your houses
> See that you do not forget
> How this day the Lord has set our faces toward Freedom
> Teach these words to your children
> And see that they do not forget them.

Walker's poetry alludes subtly to King but refers to Malcolm X directly. The verse dedicated to Malcolm portrays him as Christ. Nearly a Petrarchan sonnet, the poem has several lines of four or six feet instead of the expected five-foot line. The comments sound repetitious because they are. As with the earlier sonnet "Childhood," "Malcolm" appears at first to deserve oblivion because here, too, Walker fails to condense and control metrics. Still, the quiet appeal is clear. The Christ story compels rereading. When Malcolm is associated with a dying swan in the octave, the narrator alludes to the Ovidian legend of the beautiful bird that sings just before death.[11] Malcolm takes on Christ's stigmata: "Our blood and water pour from your flowing wounds."

Vivid and noble portraits of crucifixion, another type of martyrdom, give even more vitality to "For Andy Goodman, Michael Schwerner, and James Chaney" (hereafter, "For Andy"), a poem about three civil rights workers murdered in Mississippi on June 21, 1964. The elegy complements seasonal and diurnal cycles through the reaffirmation of human growth and spiritual redemption. Despite the questionable value of martyrdom, sunrise balances sunset, and beautiful leaves partly compensate for human mutilation. In dramatic reversal, Walker's narrator uses the literary technique that distinguishes *Lycidas, Adonais,* and *When Lilacs Last in the Dooryard Bloom'd.*

The flower and the paradigmatic bird (lark, robin, mourning bird, bird of sorrow, bird of death) restore both an epic and elegiac mood. The reader half hears the echo of the goddess Venus who mourns for Adonis, as *mourning* and *morning,* excellent homonyms, signify the cycle and paradox of life.[12] The short rhythm, two feet, and the longer rhythm, three or four, provide the solemn folksiness of a very loose ballad or free verse. With interior rhyme, the musical balance communicates quiet pathos: "They have killed these three. / They have killed them for me." The gentle suggestion of the trinity, the tragic flight of the bird, and the slow but cyclical turning from spring to spring intensify the narrator's sadness and grief.

Just as "For Andy" shows Walker's grace of style, the title poem of *Prophets* illustrates that the Bible prefigures eloquence. As with the earlier poem "Delta," "Prophets" resists paraphrase because it abstractly portrays black American history. The poem has three parts. The first shows that the Word that came to the biblical prophets endures, and the next represents the actual appearance of the ancient vision to new believers. In the third part, the reader moves to a final understanding about tragic death. While the poet marks the recurrence of sacred light, fire, gentleness, and artistic speech, she contrasts white and black, dark and light, age and youth, life and death. Some allusions to Ezekiel and Amos now fuse with others from Ecclesiastes and Isaiah. Amos tells of a prophet-priest of sixth century B.C., a watchman over the Israelites during the exile in Babylon, by the river of Cheber (Ezekiel 1:15–20). As a herdsman from the southern village of Tekoa, Judah, he went to Bethel in Samaria to preach a religion of social justice and righteousness. He attacked economic exploitation and privilege and criticized the priests who stressed ritual above justice. Because Amos is Walker's personal symbol of Martin Luther King Jr., she provides more background about him than about others. The reader knows his name, character, and homeland.

But Walker socially and historically reinvigorates the scriptures. She is no eighteenth-century Jupiter Hammon who rewrites the Bible without any infusion of personal suffering. She feels strongly and personally that the demonstrators in the sixties encapsulate the spirit of the Scriptures: "So today in the pulpits and the jails, / . . . A fearless shepherd speaks at last / To his suffering weary sheep." She implies perseverance even in the face of death, and her speaker blends the images of the New Testament with those from *Beowulf.* Her lines depict the beast, whose

> mark is on the land.
> His horns and his hands and his lips are gory with our blood.
> He is Death and Destruction and Trouble
> And he walks in our houses at noonday
> And devours our defenders at midnight.

The literary word images fear and sacrifice more than immediate redemption. What shadows the fate of the good? The beast

> has crushed them with a stone.
> He drinks our tears for water
> And he drinks our blood for wine;
> He eats our flesh like a ravenous lion

And he drives us out of the city
To be stabbed on a lonely hill.

The same scene relives the crucifixion.

Walker draws heavily upon the Bible for the typological unity. Of the twenty-two poems in *Prophets*, seven of the last nine have biblical names for titles, including "Jeremiah," "Isaiah," "Amos—1963," "Amos (Postscript—1968)," "Joel," "Hosea," and "Micah." A similar problem besets all of them, though to a different extent. The aesthetic response relies on historical sense more than on dramatized language, and passing time will weaken the emotional hold. In "Jeremiah," the narrator is conscious of both the fallen world and the apocalyptic one. She suggests Benjamin Mays, who has been a preacher and educator in Atlanta for over fifty years. Seeking to lift the "curse" from the land, Mays wants to redeem the corrupted city. The mythical denotation of the place—"Atalanta"—inspires the cultural imagination. Once a girl by that name lost a race to Hippomenes, her suitor, because she digressed from her course to pursue golden apples.[13] Yet Walker's poem does more than oppose Mays to urban materialism. Through his articulation (the spoken word), he signifies the artist and the writer. The narrator who recounts the tale is an artist, too, since Walker's speakers and heroes mirror each other. Although Jeremiah appears as a contemporary man, he exists in a halfway house between legend and reality. Despite limitations, the final six lines of the verse combine myth and anaphora, where the speaker compares the imaginative and historical worlds more closely than elsewhere. Once destroyed by fire, Atlanta suggests Babylon, capital first of Babylonia and then of Chaldea on the Euphrates river. As the scene of the biblical Exile, the city represents grandeur and wickedness. The book of Psalms portrays the despair of the Israelites who sat down and wept when they remembered Zion. With an undertone of an old folk ballad, Walker builds a literary vision. While anaphora strengthens solemnity, the voice subsumes both narrator and prophet:

My God we are still here. We are still down here Lord,
Working for a kingdom of Thy Love.
We weep for this city and for this land
We weep for Judah and beloved Jerusalem
O Georgia! "Where shall you stand in the judgment?"

Through the fire, the mark, and the word, "Isaiah" clarifies the typology that leads from "Lincoln Monument," midway through the volume, to "Elegy" at the end. Jeremiah expresses himself in the public forum as well as on television. He resembles Adam Clayton Powell Jr., a major civil rights activist in Harlem during the depression. Powell persuaded many Harlem businesses, including Harlem Hospital, to hire blacks. As Chairman of the Coordinating Committee on Employment, he led a demonstration that forced the World's Fair to adopt a similar policy in 1939. He desegregated many Congressional facilities, Washington restaurants, and theaters. He was the first to propose the withholding of federal funds from projects that showed racial discrimination; he introduced the first legislation to desegregate the armed forces; he established the right of black journalists to sit in the press galleries of the United States House of Representatives and in the Senate. As Chairman of the House Committee on Education and Labor in 1960, he supported forty-eight pieces of legislation on social welfare and later earned a letter of gratitude from President Johnson.

In 1967, however, Powell's House colleagues raised charges of corruption and financial mismanagement against him. In January he was stripped of his chairmanship and barred from the House, pending an investigation. On March 1, 1967, Powell was denied a seat in the House by a vote of 307 to 116, despite the committee's recommendation that he only be censured, fined, and placed at the bottom of the seniority list. On April 11 a special election was held to fill Powell's seat. Powell, who was not campaigning and was on the Island of Bimini, and who could not even come to New York City because of a court judgment against him in a defamation case, received 74 percent of the Harlem vote.[14]

Even more clearly, the "Amos" poems reconfirm Walker's greater metaphor for Martin Luther King Jr. The first of these two verses, twenty lines in length, portrays Amos as a contemporary shepherd who preaches in the depths of Alabama and elsewhere: "Standing in the Shadow of our God / Tending his flocks all over the hills of Albany / And the seething streets of Selma and of bitter Birmingham." As with the first "Amos" poem, "Amos (Postscript, 1968)" is written in free verse. With only ten lines, however, the latter is shorter. King, the prophet of justice, appears through the fluidity and the wholesomeness of the "O" sound:

> From Montgomery to Memphis he marches
> He stands on the threshold of tomorrow
> He breaks the bars of iron and they remove the signs
> He opens the gates of our prisons.

Many of the short poems that follow lack the high quality found in some of Walker's other typological lyrics. "Joel" uses the standard free verse, but the historical allusion is obscure. "Hosea" suffers from the same problem. Is the man Eldridge Cleaver? The letters and the theme of redemption clearly suggest him, but one can never be sure. The legend could better suit the man. The last poem in *Prophets* appropriately benefits from some of Walker's favorite books, such as Ecclesiastes, Isaiah, and the Gospel of John. "Elegy," a verse in two parts, honors the memory of Manford Kuhn, professor and friend. Summer and sunshine give way to winter snow and "frothy wood," since the green harvest must pass. But art forms ironically preserve themselves through fire, and engraving comes from corrosion. Eternity paradoxically depends upon decay. The first section concerns the cycle of nature that continually turns; the second, an elaborate conceit, depicts people as ephemeral artists.

Reading the cultural memory means invoking a classical source probably beyond the conscious intent of either Margaret Walker or her poetic narrator. In the *Metamorphoses*, Philomela and Procne are daughters to Pandion, King of Athens. By marrying Tereus, Procne gives birth to a son, Itys. Five years or so later, asked by his wife to bring her sister from Athens for a visit, the husband imprisons Philomela. So, locked within a "ramshackle building" in the Thracian woods, she becomes the lustful object of his desire. In raping her repeatedly, he cuts out her tongue so she can never tell the tale. He greatly underestimates the truth of literary art:

> She had a loom to work with, and with purple
> On a white background, wove her story in,
> Her story in and out, and when it was finished,
> Gave it to one old woman, with signs and gestures
> To take it to the queen, so it was taken
> Unrolled and understood.
>
> Ovid, *Metamorphoses*, 6.587–92

Whether of weaving or of poetry, the artist expresses in creative forms the historical violation of the sacred body by suffering. Wisdom emerges of purgation by telling the consecrated truth. And it is in the narrative delivery of this great epiphany ("with signs and gestures . . . take it to the queen") that Ovid and Margaret Walker—across the great divide of races and twenty centuries— offer a profound sense of completion: "So it was taken / Unrolled and understood."

Reminiscent of Virgil's *Aeneid*, Shelley's "The Witch of Atlas," and Danner's short lyric, "The Slave and the Iron Lace," Walker's second section, begins:

> Within our house of flesh we weave a web of time
> Both warp and woof within the shuttle's clutch
> In leisure and in haste no less a tapestry
> Rich pattern of our lives.

The gold and scarlet intertwine
Upon our frame of dust an intricate design.

Here are her ablest statement and restatement of the iamb. The "I" sound supports assonance and rhyme, even though the poem is basically free. At first the idea of human transitoriness reinforces Ecclesiastes, which powerfully presents the theme. In a second look, however, we trace the thought to Isaiah (40:7): "The grass withereth, the flower fadeth; because the spirit of the Lord bloweth upon it." But the speaker knows the ensuing verse equally well: "The grass withereth, the flower fadeth; but the *word* of our God shall stand for ever" (40:8; emphasis mine). Poetry, an inspired creation in words, is divine as well. To the extent that Kuhn showed Christlike love and instruction for his students, his spirit transcends mortality. For any who demonstrate similar qualities is the vision any less immortal? To Nicodemus, the Pharisee whom Jesus told to be reborn (John 3:8), the final allusion belongs:

We live again
In children's faces, and the sturdy vine
Of daily influences; the prime
Of teacher, neighbor, student, and friend
All merging on the elusive wind. (33–37)

Patient nobility becomes the poet who has re-created Martin Luther King Jr. as Amos. She has kept the neatly turned phrase of Countee Cullen but replaced the Greek figures of Tantalus and Sisyphus with black students and sit-ins. Beyond the classical poets Pindar and Ovid, for her literary fathers, she reaches back to the nineteenth-century prophets Blake, Byron, Shelley, and Tennyson. Her debt extends no less to Walt Whitman and to Langston Hughes, for her predecessor is any poet who foresees a new paradise and who portrays the coming. As with Hughes, Walker is a romantic. But Hughes had either to subordinate his perspective to history or to ignore history almost completely, and to speak less about events than about personal and racial symbols. Walker, on the contrary, equally combines events and legends but reaffirms the faith of the spirituals. Although her plots sometimes concern murder, her narrators reveal an image of racial freedom and human peace. The best of her imagined South prefigures the future.

NOTES

1. See Paula Giddings, "'A Shoulder Hunched Against a Sharp Concern': Some Themes in the Poetry of Margaret Walker," *Black World* (Dec. 1971), 20–34. Although

it fails to emphasize the importance of literary form, the essay gives a general impression of historical background and literary tradition.

2. See Margaret Walker and Nikki Giovanni, *A Poetic Equation* (Washington DC: Howard University Press, 1974), 56. Through logic Walker has the better of the friendly argument.

3. Charles H. Rowell, "Poetry, History, and Humanism" (Interview), *Black World* 25 (December 1975), 4–17; Arthur P. Davis, "Margaret Walker," in *From the Dark Tower: Afro-American Writers 1900 to 1960* (Washington: Howard University Press, 1974), 180–85.

4. Poems mentioned, other than those by Walker, are available in Dudley Randall, ed., *The Black Poets* (New York: Bantam, 1971).

5. See Joseph Greenborg, *Language Typology* (The Hague: Mouton, 1974); Paul J. Korshin, "The Development of Abstracted Typology in England, 1650–1820," in *Literary Uses of Typology,* ed. Earl Miner (Princeton: Princeton Univ. Press, 1977); Mason I. Lawrance, introduction to *The Figures or Types of the Old Testament* (New York: Johnson, 1969); Roland Bartell, "The Bible in Negro Spirituals," in Lawrance, op. cit.; Sacvan Bercovitch, "Typology in Early American Literature," in *Typology and American Literature* (Amherst: University of Massachusetts Press, 1972); Emory Elliott, "From Father to Son," in Miner, op. cit.; Theodore Ziolkoski, "Some Features of Religious Figuarlism in Twentieth-Century Literature," in Miner, op. cit.; Ursula Brumm, *American Thought and Religious Typology* (New Brunswick: Rutgers University Press, 1970).

6. Primary texts used are Margaret Walker, *For My People* (New Haven: Yale University Press, 1977) and *Prophets for a New Day* (Detroit: Broadside, 1970).

7. See Stephen Henderson, *Understanding the New Black Poetry* (New York: William Morrow, 1973), 62–66.

8. Reviewers disagree about the form in which Walker succeeds most ably. See Elizabeth Drew, *Atlantic* 170 (December 1942), 10; Arna Bontemps, *Christian Science Monitor* (November 14, 1942), 690; Louis Untermeyer, *Yale Review* 32.2 (winter 1943), 370. All discuss *For My People.* Drew praises the experimentation in rhythmical language. Bontemps says that the ballads and sonnets show a folk understanding but comments less about their literary success. The review in *New Republic,* on the contrary, finds the sonnets to be weak but the ballads to be strong. Untermeyer praises Walker's success in winning the prize in the Yale series (a first for a black) but discovers flaws in both the sonnets and ballads.

9. Editor's note. A "monody" refers to a dirge or poem of lament, in which the author expresses her grief for another.

10. See Exodus 4:14–17; 7:8–12; 32:1–6; Numbers 17:1–11; 20:12–29.

11. Ovid, *Metamorphoses* (Baltimore: Penguin Books, 1961), 322.

12. Ovid 244.

13. Ovid 240–44. See the brilliant analysis in W. E. B. Du Bois, *The Souls of Black Folk* (New York: New American Library, 1969), 117–20.

14. Peter M. Bergman and Mort N. Bergman, *The Chronological History of the Negro in America* (New York: New American Library, 1969), 354–55.

Fields Watered with Blood

Myth and Ritual in the Poetry of Margaret Walker

EUGENIA COLLIER

"For my people everywhere . . ." the reader began, and the audience of black folk listened in a profound and waiting silence. We knew the poem. It was ours. The reader continued, his deep voice speaking not only *to* us but *for* us, " . . . singing their slave songs repeatedly: their dirges and their ditties and their blues and jubilees." And as the poem moved on, rhythmically piling on image after image of our lives, making us know again the music wrenched from our slave agony, the religious faith, the toil and confusion and hopelessness, the strength to endure in spite of it all, as the poem went on mirroring our collective selves, we cried out in deep response. We cried out as our fathers had responded to sweating black preachers in numberless cramped little churches, and further back, as our African ancestors had responded to rituals that still, unremembered and unknown, inform our being. And when the resonant voice proclaimed the dawn of a new world, when it called for a race of *men* to "rise and take control," we went wild with ancient joy and new resolve.

Margaret Walker's "For My People" does that.[1] It melts away time and place and unifies black listeners. Its power is as compelling now as it was sixty-odd years ago when it was written, perhaps more so as we have experienced repeat-

98

edly the flood tide and the ebb tide of hope. The source of its power is the reservoir of beliefs, values, and archetypal characters yielded by our collective historical experience. It is this area of our being that defines us, that makes us people, that finds expression *in black art and in no other.*

Make no mistake: what we call the "universal" is grounded in particular group experience. All humans (except, perhaps, an occasional aberrant individual) share such fundamentals as the need for love, an instinct for survival, the inevitability of change, the reality of death. But these fundamentals are meaningless unless they are couched in specific human experience. And there is no person who is not a member of a race, a group, a family of humankind. Nobody exists alone. We are each a part of a specific collective past, to which we respond in a way in which no person outside the group can respond. That is right. This is good.

Margaret Walker has tapped the rich vein of black experience and fashioned that material into art. By "black experience" we refer to the African past, the dispersal of African people into a diaspora, and the centuries-long incubus of oppression. Included is the entire range of human emotion, from despair to joy to triumph. The discussion here will be of Margaret Walker's use of this shared experience in her poetry.

Margaret Walker's signature poem is "For My People." Widely anthologized in black collections and often read at dramatic presentations, it is the work most closely associated with her name. Some years ago, when I was involved in compiling an anthology of ethnic literature for high schools, the editor (white) refused to permit us to include this poem. It was too militant, he said. The man was unutterably wise: the poem thrusts to the heart of black experience and suggests a solution that would topple him and the culture he represents from its position of power. White response to African American literature is often, and for obvious reasons, diametrically opposite to black response; this poem is indeed a case in point.

"For My People" exemplifies Walker's use of black myth and ritual.[2] The poem first evokes the two mechanisms that have ever been a source of strength to black folk: music and religion. But even in the first stanza is implied a need to move beyond historical roles, for the "slave songs" are sung "repeatedly," the god (lower case) to whom the people pray is "unknown," and the people humble themselves to "an unseen power." Then the poem catalogs the rituals of the toil that consumes the life of the people, hopeless toil that never enables one to get ahead and never yields any answers. The stanza jams the heavy tasks together without commas to separate them, making them all into one conglomerate burden: "Washing ironing cooking scrubbing sewing mending hoeing plowing digging planting . . ." The poem rushes by, as indeed life rushes by when one must labor, "never gaining never reaping never known and never understanding."

Walker now changes focus from the general to the specific—to her playmates, who are, by extension, all black children playing the games that teach them their reality—"baptizing and preaching and doctor and jail and soldier and school and mama and cooking and playhouse and concert and store and hair and Miss Choomby and company." She shows us the children growing up to a woeful miseducation in school, which bewilders rather than teaches them, until they discover the overwhelming and bitter truth that they are "black and poor and small and different and nobody cared and nobody wondered and nobody understood." The children grow, however, to manhood and womanhood; they live out their lives until they "die of consumption and anemia and lynching . . ." The poem then returns to the wide angle of "my people" and continues its sweep of black experience, cataloging the troubled times wrought by racism. The form of the first nine stanzas supports their message. Rather than neat little poetic lines, they consist of long, heavily weighted paragraphs inversely indented. The words and phrases cataloging the rituals of trouble are separated by "and . . . and . . . and." There is little punctuation. Each stanza begins with a "for" phrase followed by a series of modifiers. Finally the long sentence, with its burden of actions and conditions, ends with one short, simple clause that leaves the listener gasping: "Let a new earth rise." Five words. Strong words, each one accented. Five words, bearing the burden of nine heavy stanzas, just as black people have long borne the burden of oppression. The final stanza is a reverberating cry for redress. It demands a new beginning. Our music then will be martial music; our peace will be hard-won, but it will be "written in the sky." And after the agony, the people whose misery spawned strength will control our world.

This poem is the hallmark of Margaret Walker's works. It echoes in her subsequent poetry and even in her monumental novel, *Jubilee*. It speaks to us, in our words and rhythms, of our history, and it radiates the promise of our future. It is the quintessential example of myth and ritual shaped by artistic genius.

The volume *For My People* is the fruit of the Chicago years in the 1930s when the young poet found her voice. A lifetime's experience went into the writing of the book: the violent racism of the deep South, her gentle and intelligent parents, her bitter struggle to retain a sense of worth despite the dehumanizing forces of Alabama in the 1920s and 1930s; her disillusionment at discovering that racial prejudice was just as strong in the Midwest, where she went to college, as in the South. After her graduation from Northwestern University in the mid-1930s, she went to Chicago to work at various jobs, including the Federal Writers' Project. There her developing sensitivity was nurtured by her association with young artists and intellectuals, including Richard Wright. She became interested in Marxism and, like many of her contemporaries, saw it as the key to the accomplishment of the dream. After four years she left Chicago to study in the School of Letters of the University of Iowa. The poems in *For My People,* reflecting the thoughts, emotions, and impressions of all these years, were her master's thesis. After receiving her degree, she returned to southern soil, this time to stay.

The South is an ancestral home of black Americans. It is true, of course, that slavery also existed in the North and that black people have lived from the beginning in all sections of this country. But collectively it is the South that is the nucleus of African American culture. It is here that the agony of chattel slavery created the history that is yet to be written. It is the South that has dispersed its culture into the cities of the North. The South is, in a sense, the mythic landscape of black America.

This landscape as portrayed vividly in this first important volume for the South is the psychic as well as the geographic home of Margaret Walker. The children in "For My People" play "in the clay and dust and sand of Alabama." The strong grandmothers in "Lineage" (25), who "touched earth and grain grew," toiled in the wet clay of the South. And the farm in Iowa reminds the poet of her southern home. "My roots are deep in southern life," writes Walker in "Sorrow Home" (19), flooding the poem with sensual images of warm skies and blue water, of the smell of fresh pine and wild onion. "I want my body bathed again by southern suns," she writes in "Southern Song" (18), "my soul reclaimed . . . from southern land." This poem is rich in images of silver corn and ponds with ducks and frogs, of the scent of grass and hay and clover and fresh-turned soil.

Both poems portray what Eleanor Traylor calls the ruined world, the fragmented world of the American South, the ambivalence that ever haunts black people. For the Southland is the "sorrow home, melody beating in my bone and blood!" And the speaker (for us all) demands, "How long will the Klan of hate, the hounds and the chain gangs keep me away from my own?" (19). And the speaker, the collective "I," after portraying the peace and beauty of the Southland, pleads in graphic detail for undisturbed integration of the Self.

The poem that most completely exploits the motif of the South is the long poem "Delta" (20–24). "I am a child of the valley," Walker asserts, and again the "I" is collective. The valley is both literal and symbolic. The images are realistic descriptions of an actual place. But the poem's essence is its symbolic meaning. The valley is, in the beginning, a place of despair, of "mud and muck and misery," hovered over by "damp draughts of mist and fog." Destruction threatens, for "muddy water flows at our shanty door / and leaves stand like a swollen bump on our backyard." Here the sounds are the dissonance of the honky-tonks, the despairing sounds of "the wailing / of a million voices strong." The speaker, in deep despair, demands that her "sorrowing sisters," "lost forgotten men," and a desperate people rise from the valley with a singing that "is ours."

The vision of hope recalls the fact that the generations-long labor of the people has made the valley theirs/ours. The snowcapped mountains tower high above the "beaten and broken and bowed" ones in "this dark valley." On the river, boats take away "cargoes of our need." Meanwhile, our brother is ill, our sister is ravished, our mother is starving. And a deep-seated rebelliousness surfaces from inside our collective self. Oppression increases with the destruction of a sudden storm, and the rape and murder of all we love leaves us "dazed in wonder." From this lowest of all points, when we are threatened with total loss, we realize our love for this place and our right to it, precisely because it is "our blood" that has "watered these fields."

"Delta" encompasses the essence of black myth in America. The valley depicts our traditional position as the most completely oppressed people in America; the mountains, snowcapped, are our aspiration for the fulfillment of America's promise—ever before us but totally beyond our reach. Again, the rituals of toil and despair and regeneration affirm the myth. The message of the poem is that we have bought our stake in this nation with our labor, our torment, and our blood. And nothing, nothing, can separate us from what is ours.

The poems of the South portray one level of the black American ancestral home. Walker is not unaware of the scattered places worldwide that created the African American. "There were bizarre beginnings in old lands for the making of me," she asserts in "Dark Blood" (15). The "me" is both personal and collective as she refers not only to her own immediate ancestry in Jamaica but to the eclectic background of black people—Africa, Asia, Europe, the Caribbean. "There were sugar stands and islands of fern and pearl, palm jungles and stretches of a never-ending sea." She will return "to the tropical lands of my birth, to the coasts of continents and the tiny wharves of island shores" to "stand on mountain tops and gaze on fertile homes below." This return is a psychic journey into the mythic past, a journey necessary for the African American, for only by reuniting with the fragmented self can one become whole. On her return to the place of her physical birth, Walker writes, the "blazing suns of other lands may struggle then to reconcile the pride and pain in me." The poem thus encompasses space and time—continents and islands, antiquity and now. It thrusts deep into the black American self.

In another section of the volume, Walker shows another aspect of our psyche: our folklore. Here the voice is that of the tale teller indigenous to black America, especially the South, who reaches back ultimately to the people who swapped tales around the fire in ancient Africa. Using ballad forms and the language of the grassroots people, Walker spins yarns of folk heroes and heroines: those who, faced with the terrible obstacles that haunt black people's very existence, not only survive but prevail—with style. There are the tough ones: Kissie Lee, who learned by bitter experience that one must fight back and who "died with her boots on switching blades"; Trigger Slim, who vanquished the terror of the railroad workers' mess hall, Two-Gun Buster; and the baddest of them all, Stagolee, who killed a white policeman and eluded the lynch mob. There are the workers: Gus the lineman, who handled his live wire and survived many certain-death accidents only to drown drunk, facedown in a shallow creek; and the most famous worker, John Henry, who "could raise two bales of cotton / with one hand anchored down the steamboat," but who was killed by a ten-pound hammer. There are the lovers: Sweetie Pie, done wrong by her lover Long John Nelson; the Teacher, whose "lust included all / Women ever made"; Yalluh Hammuh, who was defeated by jealous Pick Ankle and his girl friend May; Poppa Chicken, whose very presence on the street made the girls cry, "Lawdy! Lawd!" There are the supernatural elements throughout: Old Molly Means, "Chile of the devil, the dark and sitch," whose ghost still "rides along on a winter breeze"; Stagolee's ghost, which still haunts New Orleans; Big John Henry, whom the witches taught how to conjure. These are all archetypes that recur repeatedly in black American lore and are vital to the culture— mythic characters performing endlessly their rituals of defeat, survival, and triumph.

Contrasting with the ballads are the poems that end the volume: six sonnets. But even here the setting is the mythic landscape, the South of Walker's memory. It is peopled by "red miners" who labor incessantly and hopelessly, "painted whores," pathetic and doomed, and people who are hurt and bewildered, muttering protests against their oppression. The landscape is filled with tree stumps, rotting shacks of sharecroppers, and cold cities with tenements. The form of these poems supports their theme. For the dignified sonnet form, which emerges from a European vision of an orderly universe, substitutes here approximate rhyme rather than true rhyme, indicating that, for these people, the promise has been distorted.

The symbols in the *For My People* poems are elemental: sun, earth, and water. The sun is the primary symbol, appearing repeatedly. The sun is a beneficent force, radiating comfort; it is the source of healing. "I want my body bathed again in southern suns," she writes in "Southern Song," "to lay my hand again upon the clay baked by a southern sun." In "Dark Blood" it is the "blazing suns of other lands" that bring together the scattered ancestry and "reconcile the pride and pain in me." Often the sun force is implied in the many agrarian images of growing grain or seeds planted with the expectation of fulfillment. In "Sorrow Home" the absence of the sun is symbolically significant. Declaring that "I was sired and weaned in a tropic world. . . . Warm skies and gulf blue streams are in my blood," the poet asserts her longing for the sun and the natural things it produces in contrast to the unnatural environment of the city: "I am no hothouse bulb to be reared in steam-heated flats with the music of El and subway in my ears, walled in by steel and wood and brick far from the sky."

The most sustained reference to the sun is the brief poem "People of Unrest," where the speaker gazes "from the pillow" at the sun, the pillow seeming to symbolize lethargy or other conditions that prevent one from knowing one's potential and taking appropriate action. The sun is the "light in shadows"—hope when all seems hopeless. The day grows tall; it is time for action—for self-knowledge, for healing, for positiveness. We should seek joyfully the force that will make us whole and move us to positive action. For our curse of "unrest and sorrow," the sun will provide regeneration.

Earth and water are closely associated with sun. Soil, sun-warmed, is also healing. It is the womb from which springs nourishment for spirit as well as body. The sturdy, singing grandmothers "touched the earth and grain grew." The persona caught in the unnatural environment of the northern city longs for unbroken rest in the fields of southern earth, where corn waves "silver in the sun" ("Southern Song"). We need "earth beneath our feet against the storm" ("Our Need" 57). Water also is a life force, working with earth to produce nourishment and peace. The city-dwelling person longs to "mark the splashing of a brook, a pond with ducks and frogs" ("Southern Song").

But an imbalance between sun, earth, and water produces chaos. The valley, where there is little sun, yields "mud and muck and misery" ("Delta"). The soil there is "red clay from feet of beasts." The red of the clay suggests violence as "my heart bleeds for our fate." There is muddy water at our shanty door, and we are threatened by swollen levees. Rivers are the mode of transportation by which the fruits of our labor are taken from us. In the city, where there are "pavement stones" instead of warm earth and "cold and blustery nights" and rainy days instead of sun, the people shield themselves from nature, brooding and restless, whispering oaths ("Memory" 36).

The symbols of sun, earth, and water arise from racial memory of generations when nature, not Western technology, sustains life. The slave culture was an agrarian culture, and before that the African sun and earth and water in balance kept us living, in imbalance made us struggle against death. Walker uses these symbols in accordance with our history, tapping black myth and ritual.

Something else particularly significant to black people infuses the *For My People* poems: music. In poem after poem music is heard as a life-sustaining force. There are not only the rhythms of the long-paragraph poems and the ballads, but also the repeated references to music. It is music that reflects the emotional tone of many of the poems and often provides an essential metaphor. In "Sorrow Home" the music of the city is dissonant; the persona is plagued by the restless music propelling her toward home. Beneath it all is the melody of the South, the sorrow home, beating in her bone and blood. "Today" is itself a song, singing of the terrible images of a wartime world: "I sing these fragments of living that you may know by these presents that which we feared most has come upon us" (28–29). In two poems Walker defies black tradition. In "For My People," the religious songs are called "dirges," and she demands that they disappear in favor of "martial songs." In "Since 1619" she demands impatiently, "How many years since 1619 have I been singing Spirituals? / How long have I been praising God and shouting hallelujahs?" (26). Music, for Walker, is a medium for communicating her message, as it has been for black people since the beginning of time.

The poems in *For My People* thus emerge from centuries of African American myth and ritual. Tinged with the Marxism that influenced a young poet's thinking at the time, they nevertheless reflect not only the writer's own grounding in black southern tradition but the generations of racial experience that were the ingredients of that tradition. The major dynamic in the book is the tension between the natural beauty of the land and the unnatural horror of racism, the poet's longing for the South but dread of its oppression and violence. The book is a demand for revolution.

The major part of this essay is concerned with these poems because this critic feels that *For My People* is Margaret Walker's most vital contribution to our culture. It is the nucleus that produced her subsequent volumes. Nearly thirty years passed before Walker published another collection of poems. Meanwhile the nation had engaged in wars, declared and undeclared, and black people's fortunes had risen and fallen several times over.

Prophets for a New Day (1970) was the fruit of the upsurge of rebellion of the 1960s; it was published by a major black influence of the times, Dudley Randall's Broadside Press. The poems in this small paperback volume are

Walker's tribute to the people, celebrated and unsung, who contributed their agony and sometimes their lives to freedom.

Here the southern landscape has become the battleground for the struggle for civil and human rights. As in *For My People,* the poet contrasts nature's beauty with the horror of violence and oppression. The elemental symbols of sun, earth, and water have disappeared as the scene shifts to the cities, which are the backdrop for struggle and death. Jackson, Mississippi, where lie "three centuries of my eyes and my brains and my hands," is called "City of tense and stricken faces . . . City of barbed wire stockades." The sun is destructive here, for it "beats down raw fire." The jagged rhythms and uneven rhyme underscore the tension ("Jackson, Mississippi" 12–13). Birmingham, Alabama, is a place where beautiful memories, tinged with fantasy, contrast with the present reality of hatred and death ("Birmingham" 14–15).

The people on the mythic landscape are the heroes of that time. They are the "prophets." Some, like the children who were jailed, will not be remembered individually, but their collective effort is unforgettable history. Others are names whose very mention elicits floods of memories of that bitter time: Malcolm X, Martin Luther King, Medgar Evers, the three slain young civil rights workers. Walker has captured their heroism in poem after poem. She alludes often to specific events—the 1963 march on Washington, Dr. King's ringing speech there, the march on Selma, the dogs and fire hoses and cattle prods used against young and old nonviolent demonstrators, the murder of heroes. The poems are infused with rage, controlled and effective.

One difference from the *For My People* poems is immediately apparent: the biblical references in *Prophets for a New Day.* The early poems, consistent with their Marxist cast, saw religion as an opiate. "Since 1619" demands that "these scales fall away from my eyes" and that "I burst from my kennel an angry mongrel." In another poem from that volume, "We Have Been Believers" (16–17), she damns all black religion, the "black gods from an old land" and the "white gods of a new land," ridiculing the faith of the people and insisting, "We have been believers believing in our burdens and our demigods too long." She demands revolution, which she apparently sees as the antithesis of religion. *Prophets for a New Day,* however, reflects a profound religious faith. The heroes of the sixties are named for the prophets of the Bible: Martin Luther King is Amos, Medgar Evers is Micah, and so on. The people and events of the sixties are paralleled with Biblical characters and occurrences. The title poem makes the parallel clearly. The religious references are important. Whether one espouses the religion in which they are couched is not the issue. For the fact is that black people from ancient Africa to now have always been a spiritual people, believing in an existence beyond the flesh. African art, the music of the slave culture, and the fervor of urban storefront churches affirm the depth of this faith.

Prophets for a New Day, like its predecessor, is grounded in black myth and ritual. It records the generation of the sixties' contribution to the history of bloody struggle against oppression and the soul-deep conviction that we—that all people—are meant by nature to be free.

Another volume, *October Journey,* a collection of poems from 1934 to 1972, was published by Broadside Press three years later. Less impressive than the others, these are a combination of occasional poems and sonnets, using formal diction, that seem artificial and lacking in spontaneity. Here I admit a personal bias: I have never found European structures such as the sonnet, nor poems written for specific occasions, to be sturdy enough vehicles to contain the weight of our centuries-long tragedy and triumph, nor of our vision that stretches from an African past to the future.

"October Journey," the title poem, is an exception. It is a fine work, rivaling the best poetry of our times in its imagery, its emotional appeal, and the way it burrows deep inside the reader. The poem is a journey into the mythic homeland. It begins with a warning fashioned out of folk beliefs, suggesting that for the traveler the "bright blaze" of autumn's rising is to be preferred to heady spring hours or to what might be tempting summer nights; cautioning that broad expanses of water should be avoided during the full moon, and that some kind of protection should be carried. The message is that the finest journeys occur in October. Then follows a series of passionate images of the Southland in October, "when colors gush down mountainsides / and little streams are frightened with a caravan of leaves," and in all the seasons. The description is a collage of form and color and sun-earth-water. The speaker eagerly anticipates the return to the place of so many loving memories; such a return is necessary if one is to be whole. "The train wheels hum, 'I am going home, I am going home, / I am moving toward the South.'" But, as in Walker's other poems, the old ambivalence is there: " . . . my heart fills up with hungry fear." And when she arrives in her homeland, the natural beauty of the place and the warmth of childhood memories are swallowed up in the dreadful reality of the ruined world: the withering of promise, the grief too deep and pervasive to be expressed, the dried blooming, the wasted potential. Again Walker has portrayed brilliantly the profound historical experience of black people, the mythic past that lies just behind our eyes.

Margaret Walker is a profoundly important poet whose works plumb the depth of our racial experience. And our racial experience is a deeply human experience no less universal than that of our oppressors and, in fact, more important. For it takes inhumanity, greed, and technology to be an oppressor;

but it takes all the attributes of godly humanity to survive oppression and to emerge as victorious human beings. Margaret Walker shows us the way. The power of her emotion and poetic craftsmanship transcends ideology and bares the struggle and strength that are integral to our individual and collective selves. Despite the many images of brutality inflicted upon us, Walker's vision from the beginning has been of a people striking back at oppression and emerging triumphant. Despite her avowed abhorrence of violence Walker has ever envisioned revolution.[3] Rapping with Nikki Giovanni, Walker admitted that her feelings about black people and the struggle for freedom were best encompassed in an early poem published in *Prophets for a New Day*, "The Ballad of the Free." This poem unites the old urge toward revolution and the militancy of Christian teachings learned from her minister father. She evokes the champions whose blood colors our history: Nat Turner, Gabriel Prosser, Denmark Vesey, Toussaint L'Ouverture, John Brown. She repeats, in a stirring refrain, words that sing our most intimate racial self. The metaphor is that of a serpent loosed, and echoing Frantz Fanon, Walker prophesied that there is more to come than merely the last being first.

Margaret Walker's poetry has mined the depths of African American racial memory, portraying a history and envisioning a future. Like all artists, she is grounded in a particular time and thus labors under particular limits of conscious perception. Her vision of the African past is fairly dim and romantic, in spite of various individual poems on ancestry. Consciously she sees African Americans as a minority group in the United States of America, the stepchildren, rejected, oppressed, denied, brutalized, and dehumanized by the dominant group.[4] But her poetry emanates from a deeper area of the psyche, one which touches the mythic area of a collective being and reenacts the rituals that define a black collective self. When she was nineteen, Margaret Walker wrote:

> I want to write
> I want to write the songs of my people.
> I want to hear them singing melodies in the dark.
> I want to catch the last floating strains from their sob-torn throats.
> I want to frame their dreams into words; their souls into notes.
> I want to catch their sunshine laughter in a bowl;
> fling dark hands to a darker sky
> and fill them full of stars
> then crush and mix such lights till they become
> a mirrored pool of brilliance in the dawn.[5]

And she has done just that.

1. *For My People* (New Haven: Yale University Press, 1942), 13–14.

2. By myth is meant the wellspring of racial memories to which I have previously alluded. By ritual is meant the actions, gestures, and activities that recur in a culture and overlap with and result from myth.

3. See, for example, her informal conversations with Nikki Giovanni taped in November 1972 and January 1973, published as *A Poetic Equation: Conversations Between Nikki Giovanni and Margaret Walker* (Washington DC: Howard University Press, 1974).

4. See Walker's essay "Willing to Pay the Price" in *Many Shades of Black*, ed. Stanton L. Wormley and Lewis Fenderson (New York: William Morrow, 1969), 119–30.

5. "I Want to Write," first published in *The Crisis*, April 1934, reprinted in *October Journey* (30).

her voice turns the afternoon brown . . .
removing false veils
baptizes us with syllables
woman words.

    —SONIA SANCHEZ, "Poem for Margaret Walker"

"Bolder Measures Crashing Through"

Margaret Walker's Poem of the Century

ELEANOR TRAYLOR

"I want to write," begins the speaker. The half-line, haunting, measures the cadence of another famous line, answers that even as a new sound, another mode, begins a recitation declaring desire and vocation. Tutored, compelling, the recitation, like that of a valediction at commencement, wins its audience through its elocution of the strategies of delight. For as the opening alliterative half-line rejoins the incremental statement of the second, a crescendo of images plays the recitation in cadences of song. More like a psalm than a sonnet, the music of the poem sings a dawn song, the *mutima* of a young and strong and lovely-hearing-sounding voice of a new painter-poet:

> I want to write
> I want to write the songs of a people.
> I want to hear them singing melodies in the dark.
> I want to catch the last floating strains from their sob-torn throats.
> I want to frame their dreams into words; their souls into notes.
> I want to catch their sunshine laughter in a bowl;

fling dark hands to a darker sky
and fill them full of stars
then crush and mix such lights till they become
a mirrored pool of brilliance in the dawn.

Here already sound "the verbal arpeggios, the cascading adjectives, the rhythmic repetitions" (Barksdale 105); the concrete imagery; the fusion of meter;
internal and near rhyme; alliteration and assonance; the privileging of liquids
and labials; the prominence of verbs, second only to nouns, that bear the pro-
sodic signature of Margaret Walker.

From this earlier of her published poems (*The Crisis*, May 1934) to the benediction of "A Poem for Farish Street Green" (27 February 1986), the penultimate poem of *This Is My Century: New and Collected Poems*, Margaret Walker
Alexander mines the depths of heritage: music *(melos)*, memory *(ethos)*, and
community *(epos)*. And it should not surprise us that one of America's most
distinguished and senior Afro-American poets, twelve years before the millennium, delivered for posterity the poem of the century. For each of Margaret
Walker's published volumes, beginning with the famous and award-winning
For My People (Yale University Press 1942), signaled a major poetic event. It is
true that twenty-eight years intervened before the poet published another volume after *For My People* sounded the second phase of modern poetry written
in the United States. For while it interrupted the sound created in the earlier,
modernist phase by poets, on one hand, like Ezra Pound, T. S. Eliot, Amy
Lowell, and Wallace Stevens, and, on another, like Countee Cullen, Claude
McKay, Georgia Douglas Johnson, and the earlier Langston Hughes, *For My
People* stood as the sole book-length publication of Margaret Walker's poetic
voice. But in 1970, when *Prophets for a New Day* entered publication through
Dudley Randall's Broadside Press, we received our singular poetic memorial to
the Civil Rights movement of the mid-1950s through the 1960s. In 1973 *October
Journey* (Broadside Press), a collection of autobiographical and occasional
poems written over Margaret Walker's lifetime, provided the link between the
earlier two volumes and those poems written since and included in *This Is My
Century: New and Collected Poems*. Thus, what may appear to be a discontinu-
ous record is actually the record of a poetic vocation consistently practiced for
over fifty years. But those fifty years become immortal here, not only as the
journey of a Self as it creates the features of its wonderful plenitude but as the
journey of a people and the voice of an age. *This Is My Century* is a poetic
biography of the twentieth century.

« « «

"Yes these are ours." The applause thunders as the senior poet, in black velvet, a ruby necklace luminescent at her throat, stands at the podium. Reading before an audience of hundreds at the Afro-American Historical and Cultural Museum at Philadelphia on the evening of 10 April 1986, Margaret Walker was culminating the Museum's Larry Neal Cultural Series, named for the late young poet-critic-herald of the Black Arts Movement of the 1960s. She was also completing a tour of several cities, presaging the publication of a biography of her late colleague, Richard Wright, and the publication of this historic volume—her collected poems. And she was receiving the unabated applause of a community whose memory she had shaped in language for more than fifty years. As she had said of "The Spirituals" (*Opportunity*, August 1938), so the applause of her audience said of every poem she read:

> Yes these are ours . . . the spirituals . . .
> dark sons of moonless nights, bruised blood of
> crushed and weak. Dig no grave to bury them—
> these our children chained in grief.
>
> Cotton pickers sing your song. Grumblers weed and
> hoe the corn. Let the dirge of miners and
> rebellious stirring road songs keep on ringing.
>
> Mills of oppression grind songs of the poor.
> Heels of the Moguls on necks of the humble
> still click like castanets. And our sorrow
> songs now rise to bolder measures, crashing
> through crescendo into everlasting cadence.

The strength of the voice, the music of the words, animating the images upon the walls of the color-drenched gallery where she read, gave immediate occasion to the thunderous applause. But it was what the music of the words evoked, the strength by which the voice seemed strengthened that moved the outbursts of ovation. It was something that stood beside the poet as she stood. Something remembered. Something re-minded.

« « «

The great mimosa tree, its trunk a seat for lovers or for children playing, shades the Poet's vast backyard, itself a green piazza embroidered here and there with patches of petunia, jasmine, spiderwort. Outlining this, an arbor of trumpet vine meets the tall pines, occasional wisteria, ceremony of magnolia, and the sentinel jactaw oaks that border Margaret Walker Alexander Drive, the street that bears her name. Situated west of Birmingham, Alabama, where she was born and north of the fecund opulence that is New Orleans, where she grew up, the tropical landscape of Jackson, Mississippi, has been, for thirty years, the actual central setting of the life and work of Margaret Walker. And yet, as early as eleven, she had begun to record the life of an imagination whose explorations and experiments would eventually sound the *diapason* of the region where she lives and works.

In those now yellow pages of her day-books, a gift from her father, the young poet begins those experiments suggesting what Stephen Henderson, echoing Richard Wright, has succinctly identified as the particular challenge of the Afro-American poet: "The challenge of the cultural base (the folk and popular roots of Black American poetry); the challenge of the tradition (that of Afro-American and other traditions); and the challenge of the modern world which impacts upon us all" ("Challenge" 1). There in her day-books, Margaret Walker begins her experimental synthesis of time, her synthesis of Afro-American oral and ancient world literature:

> Out from Egypt
> They come
> In droves.
>
> Empty pursued and faint
> And separate from their Women
> and little ones . . .
>
> Three hundred years
> Then once again
> They came forth from Egypt
> As penniless as before
> With the blood of all men in their veins
> Only to become a persecuted mass
> Tormented beyond belief
> And looking up to God in tears they laugh
> A puzzled people.
>
> (unpublished, circa 1930)

And if the syncopated tercets and the strophe approximate the ever-surprising meters of the sublime spirituals, the parallelism of the Exodus text in the King James Version, and the cadence of the folk (and educated) clergy, then the daughter of the professor of biblical literature, philosophy, and ancient religions, Sigismund Constantine Walker of Jamaica Buff Bay, Jamaica, and likewise, the daughter of the music teacher, Marion Dozier, who had also corresponded with Melville Herskovits, was early realizing the inheritance to which her first major critic, Stephen Vincent Benét, saliently alludes. But the day-books of the young girl are also filled with octaves and sextets recalling an inheritance from Petrarch through Wordsworth. Here in her day-books, she plays with Browning monologues and creates Blakean songs. She chants hymns to her "Dark Skinned Brothers" who "Strong and bronzed and smart / Though men have tried to crush their hearts / They've stood the test of time." Among these day-book exercises, she enters her meticulous translations of Goethe, Schiller, and Heine, and for these she wins her first literary citation as the Sunday, 19 June 1932, German daily—*The Philadelphia Gazette*—mentions Fraulein Margaret Walker, student of Dr. Otto Edward Krieger at New Orleans University (now Dillard), for her imaginative translation of Goethe's "Heidenroslein."

But the keyboard exercises through which the poet explores tradition remain only that unless a bolder measure crashes through. And here resides the question of the poet's modernity: the relation of the individual to tradition. By 1912, James Weldon Johnson, in his seminal modern novel, *The Autobiography of an Ex–Coloured Man,* had addressed that question and offered the trenchant response on which twentieth-century poetics turns: "The fact is nothing great or enduring . . . has ever sprung full-fledged from the brain of any master; the best he gives to the world, he gathers from the hearts of the people and runs it through the alembic of his own genius," argued Johnson's narrator. And in 1919, T. S. Eliot was to argue in his famous essay—"Tradition and the Individual Talent"—that "no poet, no artist of any art, has his complete meaning alone," for "his significance . . . is the appreciation of his relation to the dead poets and artists," and that "the historical sense compels a man to write not merely with his own generation in his bones, but with a feeling that the whole of the literature of Europe from Homer and within it the whole of the literature of his own country has a simultaneous existence and composes a simultaneous order." Eliot's argument, made seven years after the publication of Johnson's novel, became canonical. Nevertheless, the "power mode" of Afro-American poetry, as Kenneth Burke has phrased it, surges from the Johnsonian "gathering" even as it generates the Eliotic "historical sense." But the ultimate Afro-American "particularizing," of Stephen Henderson's meaning, occurs as the moment of expansion: when the (each new) poet extends the boundary of language either counter-stating, accessing, or improvising so that tradition is examined and revised. Such a revision is the target of Margaret Walker's poem "Our Need," which is included in the *For My People* poems. Renegotiating the turns and redistributing the rhyme scheme of Claude McKay's famous sonnet, "If We Must Die," Margaret Walker's "Our Need" revised the Eliotic "dead poets" by reencountering the Agamemnon story to which Eliot alludes in his "Sweeney Among the Nightingales." In that poem, the speaker laments Sweeney's ignorance of "the whole of literature . . . from Homer" and his blindness to its "simultaneous existence and order." The counter-statement of the speaker of "Our Need" is this:

> If dead men died abruptly by a blow—
> startled and trapped in today's immediacy,
> having neither moments to speak dazedly
> nor whimper wistfully—how can they know
> or tell us now the way which we should go?
> What price upon their wisdom can we stake
> if ultimately we would live, not break
> beneath a swift and dangerous undertow?
>
> We need a wholeness born of inner strength:
> sharp thinking running through our stream of days,
> having certain courage flame with honest rays
> like slaps of life along the body's length.
> We need the friendly feel of human forms
> and earth beneath our feet against the storms.

"Today's *immediacy*" (my emphasis) buttressed by "the friendly feel of human forms"—the creation of human beings on behalf of human beings—is the large topic of the Walker poetic canon refracted in *This Is My Century*. And "wholeness born of inner strength" (the great gathering) is the huge theme. "Courage [a] flame with honest rays / like slaps of life along the body's length . . . / the birth and rebirth of the cultural body politic / if ultimately we would live, not break / beneath a swift and dangerous undertow" is the great challenge of modernity that Margaret Walker's craft addresses. "Immediacy," like "shoulders hunched against a sharp concern,"[1] is its stress and accent. But tradition, reexamined, is the great unifying "stream" of *This Is My Century: New and Collected Poems*.

Yet before the particularizing leap to freedom of the *For My People* poems, the young poet had played the keyboard exercises of traditional verse until she uncovered the great subject, a traditional one, that she would run through the "alembic" of her own genius and discover in her own song—the *diapason* of her region:

There is a place deep in the dense grown swamp
Secret and mournful of the dying pomp
Of bygone days when red men chanced to rove
On hunts or ceremonies in this grove
Where jasmine blossoms hang in great festoons
Of fragrant blooms while sinuous lagoons
Are close about the feet of cypress trunks.

High overhead in intertwining bunks
Or leafy hammocks stretched from vine to vine
The Redwing plays among the sweet woodbine
Below the white cranes are rustling in the reeds.
And on a marshy bank a heron feeds.
Great cornucopias of Spanish moss
Diaphanously floating wind across
The swinging arches of the live oak trees
While wild purple irises sway in the breeze.
Here Jean LaFitte set up his auction block
Iniquitously selling human stock.

The eight-hundred-line unpublished epic of the horrors of Jean LaFitte, the
Baritarian, as they are represented in the ruined world of Margaret Walker's
actual and mythic South, is told in faithful Keatsian couplets. It is the last faithful keyboard rendering that the day-books record. For at eighteen, now a
senior at Northwestern University where she continues the habit of her day-
books, Margaret Walker writes her story-poem of Jean LaFitte. Yet in that same
year, she crashes through the main traditions of the English Romantics, over-
steps the Victorians, points back at Phillis Wheatley, enters the tradition of
Frances Ellen Watkins Harper, gestures both to the cadence of Claude McKay
and to the images of Langston Hughes in her declaration of independence—
the valediction and commencement—"I Want to Write."[2]

« « «

*The applause having subsided, the senior poet resumes her reading. Standing with
her at the podium of the Afro-American Historical and Cultural Museum at
Philadelphia and floating, diaphanously, through the gallery are ghosts. The
memory of a people stands with her as she stands; the needs and aspirations of
a community sit close about her as she stands; the music of singers, past and
present, plays chorus to her song. Her voice steadies. And, like some cresting tide,
the audience moves to its feet, silent now, as she intones:* Let a new earth rise.
Let another world be born. . . .

There is an echo about her . . .
She stands over centuries as she talks.

   —SONIA SANCHEZ, "Poem for Margaret Walker"

This Is My Century is, on the one hand, a retrospective. On the other, it is the splendid achievement of a grand poetic vision. And to witness both, we will serve our delight if we read with our eyes upon the world within the poems and upon the world without. As retrospective, the collection establishes Margaret Walker's poetic canon. It includes three volumes of poems published between 1942 and 1973: *For My People* (1942), the famous collection whose title poem, first published in the November 1937 issue of Harriet Monroe's *Poetry: A Magazine of Verse,* earned Margaret Walker her signature as poet; *Prophets for a New Day* (1970), the collection that celebrates the Civil Rights movement; and *October Journey* (1973), a collection of autobiographical and occasional poems written between 1934 and 1973. *This Is My Century* also includes thirty poems written between 1968 and 1985, whose *Poem* is the title of the collection; of the thirty, only thirteen have been previously published. One long poem, the dedicatory *For Farish Street Green* (1986), completes the collection.³ And while a record of a lifetime's poetic vocation, the collection is also a poetic biography of the twentieth century refracted through the lens of the poet's community of memory.

Yet as crucial to our historical sense as is its large exploration of time, the genius of this poem of the century is its navigation of space. For the grand design of *This Is My Century* configures a journey even as the music of the poem sounds the range that Dunbar's auditor has taught us: "from the kitchen to the big woods / When Malindy Sings." That range is also graphed in the lyrics of the blues: "from Natchez to Mobile / from Memphis to St. Jo / Wherever the four winds blow." For all that, in the voice that sings us through the great design, we hear even older voices. Stephen Vincent Benét had heard them too when, in his foreword to the poet's first collection, he wrote: "Older voices are mixed with hers" (*FMP* 5). The mixture, as we shall see, conjures the wide vision of the poem while each of the works that shape it figures landmarks of its journey and sounds chords of its wonderful music:

> Speak, heralds of our honored dead
> Proclaim the hero's line.
> Declaim the sculptured and created truths
> from prehistoric time.
>
> Infinitude is bared to finite eyes:
> We see the whirling suns and stars

first fixed and moving space
to shape beginning time . . .

O living man behold
Your destined hands control
the flowered earth ablaze
alive, each golden flower unfold

(*TMC* 2–3)

The singer's *oratorio* wakes centuries into "simultaneous order and existence." For her polyphonic voice is variously lyric, epic, and dramatic as, like
Sundiata's "griot," it replays the memory of humankind. At times, the voice
assumes that of Osiris ("I am Osiris / Lord of the Dead, and Prince of Resurrection" [*TMC* 21]) or Isis (the evoked *anima* of "Delta" [*FMP*]); sometimes it
resounds Virgil, Dante, Chaucer, Milton, Bunyan, Eliot. It is Harriet Tubman
(*OJ* 14), and it intones Frederick Douglass, W. E. B. Du Bois, Marcus Garvey,
Martin Luther King, and El Hajj Malik ("Five Black Men," *TMC* 13–20). The
voice is always "Delta," woman (*FMP* 20); sometimes girl ("I Want to Write,"
OJ 30; "On Youth and Age," *TMC* 29, "On Youth and Age II," *TMC* 40); daughter
("Epitaph for My Father," *OJ* 30); lover ("Black Paramour," *TMC* 23); wife
("Love Song for Alex," *TMC* 55); worker ("Lineage," *FMP* 25); teacher ("Jackson
State," *TMC* 58); mother ("This Is My Century," *TMC* 6); and anima *(passim)*.
And, alternately, it becomes comedienne ("When I was a little girl / the little
girl on Morton's Salt was white / She still is," *TMC* 31); avenger ("I quickly leave
the scene / before they know the deadly role I play," *TMC* 24); sage ("We seek
Paradise / but we will be content / without the mystic ecstasy," *TMC* 54); and
sibyl ("O man, behold your destiny," *TMC* 1).

Still, in William H. McClendon's terms, some music of the poem is
"uniquely situational" (quoted in Henderson, "Music" 4). We hear it creating
"the fusion of the South, my body's song and me" in a "Southern Song"; it
plays through "Dark Blood," "Sorrow Home," and "Delta" in the *For My
People* poems. This music, not only a song of myself but, in concert with the
blues-ballads (part 2 of *For My People*) and similar cadences throughout the
Century poems, measures what Stephen Henderson has called "a reference line
to the historical, cultural, political, and economic forces confronting the Black
community in the West" (Henderson, "Music" 3). That reference occasions
the speaker's epic roll call in the *Poem of the Century* poems: "Satchmo" (Louis
Armstrong), "the Count" (Count Basie), "the Duchess" (Billie Holiday), "the
Queen" (Ella Fitzgerald), and "the Princesses" (Sarah Vaughan and Dinah
Washington). The rhythms of this royalty occasionally punctuate the *Century*
poems. We hear them in the bluesy quintain of "The African Village":

I'll hawk your dreams
Your broken stars of glass
I'll paint your visions
On a rainbow road
That shines across dark starry skies.

And in the folk song—the hoodoo man's warning—in "Black Magic," of *For Farish Street Green:*

But remember when you sell your soul to the devil
Prepare to live in hell!
Black man you know well
Lie down with dogs and get up with fleas
There's a man going round taking names.

Indeed, the particularizing music of the poem is textured as well by the speaker's salute to other poetic voices contemporary with her own. "For Gwen" of *October Journey* is the speaker's tribute to the resplendent achievement of Gwendolyn Brooks's rich contralto voice. As senior to the renowned poet, our speaker reminds us in the opening lines of the poem that "The slender, shy, and sensitive young girl / is woman now." And in the final five syllables of the first line, she scans one famous phrase of the Brooks canon: "Thaumaturgit lass . . ." Similarly, the speaker hails the magnificent tenor of Robert Hayden's voice singing "a multiplicity of Jewelled Words / Taken from the casket of memory / like a magician with legerdemain." And in her line that tributes the poet's wife in "Tribute to Robert Hayden" of the *Century* collection,

Erma spelling the music
The speaker approximates the beat of
Heart Shape in the Dust

she echoes the title of Robert Hayden's first book. Her tributes extend also to Sterling Brown, whose folk ballads she re-sounds, to Melvin Tolson, and to Gwen Dodson. But to her mentor, Langston Hughes, and her father, Sigismund Constantine Walker, she dedicates the beautiful *October Journey.*

The poems of *October Journey* contain some of the most varied music of *This Is My Century.* In them many wonderful birds of the *Century* poem sing: "halcyon," "dove," "phoenix," "Pegasus," "eagle," and "bird of paradise":

O bird of Paradise
bird of the wilderness
Cardinal bird of truth
Now sing the song I love to sing

the song of hope and love
Pride in our past
faith for our future
and hope undimmed by all our ancient fears,
Sing now a paean for this rising man
a prayer breathed on the wings
of shifting wings
that search the world
and bring the storm of change into our land.
Now steady one man's hand
and may the winds of fate
be neither harsh nor rude.
Sing birds of paradise,
bird of the wilderness, now sing!

(*oj* 29)

In *October Journey*, the panegyric and oracular voices of the speaker sing the great "gathering." We hear the music of *Oriki, mutima, mu'allaqa,* and *rajaz* (Serjeant). This music, as the expository voice of Margaret Walker has described, is

> suffused with an emotive content that is humanistic, realistic, and historically tied in tradition to that ancient, oriental world of literature. It is still tied to Black Africa and to everything racially indigenous to Black people and nonwhite cultures everywhere in the world. Nationalistically, it is distinctly different from any national body of European literature. It may sometimes be of necessity Anglo-Saxon or Anglo-American in form, but never in content, in tone, or in philosophy; and always it is permeated with ideas of revolt against artifice, sterility, self-consciousness, contrived morality, and pseudo-natural ethics. (Walker 849–50)

For the traveler through the poetry of *Synthesis, October Journey* is a port. We have left the Whitmanesque anaphora of "Today" in *For My People*, where "I sing of slum scabs on city faces . . . / I sing these fragments of living that you may know," and where such singing recalls, in "Iowa Farmer," the sound of Carl Sandburg even as it disturbs the affirmation of his *The People Yes* in the analecta of the speaker's "Today": "You walking these common neighboring streets . . . / smug in a snug somnolescence." For "the music of El and subway" in *For My People's* "Sorrow Home" transmutes in *October Journey* as fulfillment of the song promised in the former's "Dark Blood."

> Someday I shall go to tropical lands of my birth to the coasts of
> continents and the tiny wharves of island shores. I shall
> roam the Balkans and hot lanes of Africa and Asia.
>
> ("Dark Blood," TMC 8)

In the *Oriki* of *October Journey,* like those of *Prophets for a New Day,* we hear the music of commemoration, of effusion, of community: "Harriet Tubman," "Epitaph for My Father," "Ode on the Occasion of the Inauguration of the Sixth President of Jackson State College," "For Mary McLeod Bethune," "For Paul Laurence Dunbar," and "For Gwen." We hear the poet's *mutima,* the song of heart's desire, "I Want to Write." Her *mu'allaqa,* "October Journey," a reprise of traditional themes, hymns "I," "you," and "we" in a "music" that "sings within my flesh." *October Journey* crescendos as a *rajaz,* "A History From the Dark People," whose couplets chant a coming forth (Serjeant 42–47).

By such a synthesis of sound does the whole poem play the symphony of our immediacy—twelve years before the end of the millennium. But the poem is no *fin-de-siècle* whimper:

> I will not flinch before the holocaust
> for I am a deathless soul
> immortal, black, and free.
>
> (TMC 7)

Rather by its grand design, the poem balances an assessment configured beautifully as a journey (rite), a conjuration, and a prophecy. As journey, it is a *rite de dessounin* or purification ritual:

> I am the lord of passage
> from death to life eternal . . .
> I am the captain of the ship,
> the ferryman, the holder of the helm,
> the charioteers . . .
> I am Osiris,
> Lord of the Dead, and Prince of the Resurrection.
>
> (TMC 22)

and a rite of reclamation:

> I have come through the maze and mystery of living
> to this miraculous place of meaning
> finding all things less than vanity

all values overlaid and blessed . . .
a traveller through this labyrinth
I taste the bitter-sweet waters of Mara
and I look to the glory of the morning of all life.

(*FFG*)

As conjuration, the poem situates us as pilgrims on a journey perilous. And yet our guide, whose stereophonic voice singing through "this labyrinth," leads our safe passage:

Traveller take heed for journeys
undertaken in the dark of the year
Go in the bright blaze of Autumn's equinox
Carry protection against ravages of a
sun-robber, a vandal and a thief

(*OJ* 11)

Finally the poem is prophecy:

The serpent is loosed and the hour is come
The last shall be first and first shall be none
The serpent is loosed and the hour is come.

(*PND* 10)

But the wide wonder of its spatial form is that one may enter the poem at the moment of its glorious summoning, "For My People Everywhere," syncopating the great collective dream:

Let a beauty full of healing and a
strength of final clenching be the pulsing in
our spirits and our blood.

(*FMP* 14)

Or one may enter as it swells to the sublime noumenal music of the "Proem":

O man, behold your destiny
Look on this life and know our future living:
our former lives from these our present days
now melded into one.

(*TMC* 1)

Regardless of the point of entry, one becomes the central *persona* of its encyclical replay of memory.

Words ripen on her mouth like pomegranates.

—SONIA SANCHEZ, "Poem for Margaret Walker"

As a journey of memory, *This Is My Century* reclaims the four matters of Afro-American poetry as *écriture*. Before the publication of "For My People" in 1937, these four matters had become traditional: the matter of Africa, the matter of America, the matter of the South, and the matter of the North. By 1773, the matter of Africa had been inscribed in the poetry of Phillis Wheatley, especially in the dedicatory "To Mycenæs." The African matter expands to embrace the Caribbean (Claude McKay), South America (Robert Hayden), and Europe (Langston Hughes). The matter of America begins with Lucy Terry's "Bars Fight" (circa 1746), not only the first extant poem by a person of African descent in the English colonies but one that establishes a distinctive sign of the Afro-American speaking mask in poetry: that of witness. Moreover, the matter of America expands to include the matter of the New World, adapting and metaphorically re-envisioning Caliban and Prospero in Shakespeare's *The Tempest*. And the matters of South and North configure regions in tropes and in linguistic particularities revealing, for one thing, how formal English is expanded and transmuted by black speech and music idioms. Along the axis of these matters, Margaret Walker's poetry references, mainly, the matter of America. It stands as a port of trade transacting the linguistic yield of what Richard Barksdale has called Southern Black Orature as that transforms the cadences of southern and midwestern American *parole* and formal English. Yet much of her prosody gains resonance from biblical cadence (Miller 120); her experiments with *Oriki* and *rajaz,* as we have noticed, inform her meter; and her allusions range the mythical matter of the African discursive world.

This Is My Century also reclaims the major themes of the pre- and post-industrial world that play about the matters of Negro poetry before 1937: colonialism, mercantilism, slavery, imperialism, racism, and gender chauvinism.[4] And texturing the matters of Africa, America, North, and South before 1937, black poets weave the major ideas affecting the twentieth century that, in Margaret Walker's *Century* poem, become revolution, psychoanalysis, relativity, existentialism, and pan-Africanism.[5]

But the mnemonic rite is the ceremony of the forger-poet. That poet is the shaman-smith, "who is first a worker in iron" (Eliade 25). It is that voice that gathers us together in "We Have Been Believers" as

Now we stand ready for the touch of one fiery iron, for
the cleansing breath of many molten truths, that the eyes

of the blind may see and the ears of the deaf may hear and
the tongues of the people be filled with living fire.

(*FMP* 16)

Here, we have entered the realm of Ogun, the "First Smith" of the Yoruba
pantheon. It is Ogun who plunges through "the abyss of transition" (Soyinka
29), and it is this civilizing smith who becomes "the principal agent in the
spread of myths, rites, and metallurgical mysteries" engendered in the Iron Age
(Eliade 25). Ogun, "master craftsman and artist . . . essence of destruction and
creativity . . . is 'lord of Ifa'. . . . He opens the way to the heart of Ifa's wisdom.
The journey and its directions are at the heart of Ogun's being" (Soyinka 27).
The Ogunic journey leads to the poet's "Delta," the "valley" of the "red clay"
where "We with our blood have watered these fields / and they belong to us."
Here is the region traditionally inhabited, also, by the Sibyls, where "the red
earth [symbolizes] the blood of the Goddess" (Eliade 41). "Here in this valley
of cotton and cane and banana wharves / we labor." It is here that

> Love overwhelms our living with longing
> strengthening flesh and blood within us
> banding the iron of our muscles with anger . . .
> standing defending the land we have rendered
> rich and abiding and heavy with plenty.
>
> (*FMP* 23)

But if we exist, solely, as *homo faber* or as *homo fides*, we are haunted by an
absence that denies the presence of our living. We cannot fully live without the
presence of jubilee (or *jouissance*). For after all, "We are like the sensitive
Spring / Walking valleys like a slim young girl." And in this valley, we hear "the
music in the wind for us." That music is the "winnowing flail" of Margaret
Walker's mimetic voice in poetry.

When in 1937 it overspoke "the intimate tone of voice, the speech of one
person addressing one person," the characteristic style of "the sophisticated
'highbrow' artist" (Auden, qtd. in Spears 86) normally published in *Poetry:
A Magazine of Verse*, "For My People" raised the voice that nationalized Afro-
American poetry as *écriture* and as *orature*.[6] Its martial song transposed the
sound of the Harlem twenties, transmitting the *zeitgeist* of the Chicago thirties.
But the nationalism of the poem and of the Walker canon is properly understood as "a hymn by everyone for everyone"; it is not an anthem, as Jean-Paul
Sartre has put it, summoning "the eternal boulevards with cop . . . disintegrat-
ing Europe." Earlier, Dr. Du Bois had named the antecedents of the song
that "For My People" redounds as "of me and mine" (*Souls of Black Folk* 1901).

And by 1937, "Negro Writers" in Chicago had understood their "national-ism" as feeling "the meaning of the history of their race as though they in one lifetime had lived it themselves throughout all the long centuries" (Wright 47).

In 1942, "For My People" resounded a *traditum* (Shils 12). It also projected a vision of Afro-American poetry as a distinct community of memory. That community of memory becomes the "bizarre beginnings" of this "child of the valley," who creates "the fusion of the South, my body's song and me" in her poetic maiden voyage ("Dark Blood," "Delta," "Southern Song," FMP 15, 18, 20). Only when the fusion of such a Self appears in poetry, a Self infused and empowered by what it understands to be a tradition of speaking Selves, can we define such a particularity as a national poetry or what recent cultural historians have called "a genuine community of memory" (Bellah 152). What Dr. Du Bois, in his assessment of the sorrow songs had called "of me and mine," Robert Bellah has re-called, though unwittingly. His "discovery" de-scribes, as if edited to fit, the achievement of Margaret Walker's canon and, similarly, the continuously developing canon of the literature of Afro-America. The recollection is resonant:

> Communities have a history—in an important sense they are consti-tuted by their past—and for this reason we can speak of a real commu-nity as "a community of memory." In order not to forget that past, a community is involved in retelling its story, its constitutive narrative, and in so doing, it offers examples of the men and women who have embodied and exemplified the meaning of the community. (153)

This observation describes, as though to witness, Margaret Walker's collec-tion of 1970, *Prophets for a New Day*. That collection melds "a collective history and exemplary individuals" that, as the historian observes, "are an important part of the tradition that is so central to a community of memory" (153). Yet, appropriately,

> The stories [that] make up a tradition contain conceptions of character, of what a good person is like, and of the virtues that define such charac-ter. But the stories are not all exemplary, not all about successes and achievements. A genuine community of memory will also tell painful stories of shared suffering that sometimes creates deeper identities than success. . . .
>
> And if the community is completely honest, it will remember stories not only of suffering received but of suffering inflicted—dangerous memories, for they call the community to alter ancient evils. (153)

As we move through the poems collected in *This Is My Century,* we may see with greater clarity the vision they position. And as we hear the song of memory played through the painful story-poems of *For My People* and the poems of exemplary character in *Prophets for a New Day,* the candor of the singer's voice commands our ear as that voice chants the "death in life" story in the superb *October Journey.* For here the culture-bearing poet at the forge signals a definition of Afro-American *ethos* in its southern community, and recites its *paideia* in the glorious "Epitaph for My Father." First the definition:

> He was himself;
> His own man all his life.
> And I belong to all the people I have met
> Am part of them, am molded by the throng
> Caught in the tide of compromise, and grown
> Chameleon for camouflage. Yet I have known
> A noble prince-like man for all my life,
> For he was humble in his dignity
> Composed and calm in every storm of life.
> Harsh poverty could not debase, demean
> His deep integrity. He rose above the fray.

Then, the *paideia:*

> He did not leave a fortune made with gold
> Nor lands and wealth of human hands
> But all the deep recesses of our minds and hearts
> Were filled with plunder from the Ages old:
> The way to greet a stranger and a guest;
> The love to bear a friend and how to pray
> In deep compassion for an enemy;
> The courage and the faith to face all life;
> The willingness to learn new lessons every day;
> Humility and truth and deep integrity—

Ethos is the text of the poet's ritual of recall. Her *Oriki* recreates poet, hero, and choral audience "in a common discursive space" (Vance 382). That song, ministered to all, brings about the conservation of the whole community.

Yet, though commemoration is her conjure, in "Delta,"

> Truth rides upon us
> and makes us restless and wakeful

and full of a hundred unfulfilled dreams of today;
our blood eats through our veins with the terrible destruction
of radium in our bones and rebellion in our brains
and we wish no longer to rest.

The journey of the forger-poet is destiny.

> i swallow
> her whole as she pulls herself up from youth . . .
> her crane-like neck on the edge of the world,
> emphasizing us
> —SONIA SANCHEZ, "Poem for Margaret Walker"

*We seek Paradise / but we will be content without the mystic ecstasy /
to see thy Face and feel the healing touch of fire* ("Dies Irae," TMC 174). The
Ogunic journey is no Edenic quest. It is rather, "a journey from the me to you
and the journey from the you to me." On this journey, "a union of two strange
worlds must meet" ("The Struggle Staggers Us," FMP 58). The gulf between
you and me is the abyss that the forger-poet seeks to bridge. This, then, is a
journey toward reconnection. It requires the rites of communion—"Drink
wine in my memory / and pour water on stones / singing libation songs" (TMC
4)—and its destiny is community, an ever-widening gyre. The stages of the
journey require cleansing rites, "time to wipe away the slime," and burial rites,
"time to end this bloody crime" ("Now," PND 9). But the cleansing must take
place within the deepest reaches of our memories. Memory must evoke the
monster who fouls "clean winds blowing through our living" (PND 23). And
will must destroy its dread ravage. But the evocation and the act of will requires
vision. The poet brings us to the place of revelation. That terrain is vast and
terrible, and what must be discovered can be seen only through the stereopti-
con of the shaman-smith's mirror. For our eyes have been trained to comprehend the thing of dread as a thing without. We know that

> a beast is among us
> His mark is on the land.
> His horns and his hand and his lips are gory with our blood.
> He is War and Famine and Pestilence
> He is Death and Destruction and Trouble.
>
> (PND 23)

And we believe "him" to be an alien self stalking us:

> We have been believers feeding greedy grinning gods, like a
> Moloch demanding our sons and our daughters, our
> strength and our wills and our spirits of pain.
>
> (FMP 16)

We have believed the "beast" to be the hydra-headed impersonal force of history. But we are well reminded that our naturalism may blind us:

Once literary naturalism was progressive because it promised to reveal the pervasive force of systematic or environmental oppression. Later, however, as literary naturalism was "perfected" as a completed version of realism and as a set of technical requirements for narrative, it became repressive instead of liberating. The original relativistic insight of literary naturalism that found human social experience, even history itself, arising from the reciprocating interplay of individual actor and environment became less important than an implied conception of fate that portrayed human beings devastated in their environment and powerless to escape its direction. Expressing a view of all-determining necessity, literary naturalism became reactionary, affirming, "What is" as immutable, even though it might have expressed a tone of regret; mystifying the relationship of the writer and the text through a pretense that a narrative naturalistically conceived finds truth in the same way that objective science does. (Reilly 25–26)

But the truth reflected in the shaman-poet's mirror is of a very different kind. It is of an older order. And in the voice of exposition, the poet explains:

The tradition of Afro-American literature began in the ancient oriental world; in Black Africa, in Egypt some thirty-five hundred years ago with the Collin texts and pyramids and the book of the Dead. [The] literature of Black people, like all people, grew out of the cosmogony and cosmology that developed around the Nile River and not from Greece or Rome at the end of the ancient world, nor in the Middle Ages with the European Renaissance (that grew out of the Renaissance already dead in Asia and Africa), nor with the modern expansion of European man. . . . To what extent the African religion of animism and worship of the Ioa . . . affected and still affects [the culture] of Black Americans . . . no anthropologist really knows. . . . Black America is tied to her ancient African heritage in all her physical and cultural manifestations. . . . The

Black writer, therefore, has a heritage . . . the unbroken tradition of humanistic values [that] developed in Asia and Africa before the religious wars of the Middle Ages. This humanism includes a recognition that we are part of nature, and the historical process that we are implicit in the dynamic evolving of mankind to ever higher planes of being, that all life must be richly developed in spirit, . . . and that one must regard the sacred nature of a brother as one values his own privacy and his own inner sanctity. (Walker 849–54)

« « «

For the traveler who undertakes the Ogunic pilgrimage, time runs backward even as it surges forward in contiguity:

> This is the place of yesteryear's
> forgotten street of dreams . . .
> Oh! Hear the song
> Go whistling down the empty years
> And let the afterglow
> of all my hoped tomorrows
> Fall on my lonely shadow.
>
> (*FFG*)

We enter the chthonic regions even as we travel familiar cities that, lit by the poet's "lamp of truth," shimmer like mythical bolgia or stratospheric plains. We are anointed by the waters of the Euphrates valley or burned by a blazing Mississippi sun; we are harried in "wind-swept streets" of Chicago, and we bask in "Warm skies and gulf-blue streams." We are mired in "mud and muck and misery of lowlands," and "We wake one morning and woods are like a smoldering plain / a glowing cauldron full of jewelled fire / the emerald earth a dragon's eye." We stand upon a precipice trembling as we witness "infinitude . . . bared to finite eyes." From Benin to Montego Bay, where "star apples grow and breadfruit," to Bocas del Toro we travel. Then, by "a mountain road, rain forests, and valleys green and sweet," we enter a "Crystal Palace": "I have walked these streets all over the world." Sometimes on this pilgrim journey, the songs of birds are our compass:

> With the last whippoorwill call of evening
> Settling over mountains
> Dusk dropping down shoulders of red hills
> And red dust of mines . . .

We are in "Birmingham," one *unreal* city on our sojourn in the land of *Prophets for a New Day:*

> And my winging heart flying across the world
> With one bright bird—
> Cardinal flashing through the thicket
> Memories . . .
> Come home again. [my emphasis]

Along the way strewn with "violets pushing through early new spring ground," we descend "Deep in[to] a Mississippi thicket" and hear a disturbance of birds:

> the burned blossoms of the dogwood trees
> Tremble in the Mississippi morning
> the wild call of the Cardinal bird
> Troubles the Mississippi morning
> *I hear the morning singing*
> larks, robins, and the mockingbird
> While the mourning dove
> broods over the meadows . . .
> Bird of death singing in the swamp.
>
> (*PND* 19, my emphasis)

Here the shaman-poet's voice assumes the timbre of the *loa-racine* intoning the *rite de dessounin.* The rite fulfills "the conditions necessary for a proper remission of the divine heritage" (Deren 45). A death ritual, the ceremony releases the Self *(gros-bonange)* from the now defunct matter of body—launching it as an independent spiritual entity into the spiritual universe where it, in turn, becomes "part of the general spiritual heritage of [its] descendants" (Deren 45). Throughout our journey, the cleansing ritual of the winnowing *rite de dessounin* conjugates the rite of reclamation:

> Rich pattern of our lives
> the gold and scarlet intertwine
> Upon our frame of dust an intricate design.
>
> (*PND* 31)

The poet's "intricate design" translates "semantic levels of black culture" (Baker 163) across the ancient and modern, mythical and expository African world of discursive experience. And one sign of the ceremony of *dessounin* is the mirror:

> three faces . . .
> Mirrored in the muddy stream of living . . .

Young and tender like quiet beauty of still water . . .
sensitive as the mimosa leaf . . .

three leaves
Floating in the melted snow
flooding the Spring . . .
. . . the dead ones appear.

(<small>PND</small> 19)

The mirror, appearing on the Ogunic journey, is glossed by Haitian myth as a metaphor of the cosmos:

> The mirror is an x-ray and its vision penetrates matter. . . . The metaphor for the mirror's depth is the cross-roads, the symbol is the cross . . . not only a symbol of the totality of the earth's surface. . . . It is, above all, a figure for the interaction of the horizontal, which is this mortal world, by the vertical plane, the metaphysical axis, which plunges into the mirror. (Deren 34–35)

The poet, reading the images swimming up from the mirror's depth, intones:

Three lives . . .
Turning on the axis of our time . . .
Turning on the wheeling compass
of a decade and a day
the concerns of a century of time
. . . an hourglass of destiny.

(<small>PND</small> 19)

For the metaphysical order of the Ogunic poet's world unites ancestral, living, and yet unborn at every juncture of our immediacy.

And crashing barriers of time
Those dark imprisoned sons
Of all my wild ancestral hosts
Break from their time-locked sea
To make these modern, sensate sons
Immortal men, and free.

(<small>PND</small> 15)

Thus, continuity in the Ogunic world "operates both through the cyclic concept of time and the animist interfusion of all matter and consciousness" (Soyinka 145):

Cycle of life and Spring of early days
With golden summer ripening into Fall
Winter snow blanketing a slumbering seed
of new anemone . . .

This day a normal time
Another hour, another year
of summer fruit and harvest
And of man.

(PND 31)

If "Ogun is best understood in Hellenic values as a totality of the Dionysian,
Apollonian, and Promethean virtues," in the Yoruba discursive universe Ogun,
"the first artist and technician of the forge," evokes "a massive impact of image, concept, ethical doctrine, and sympathy" (Soyinka 141):

Our human hearts become
Old hearthstones of our tribal birth and flame
the hammer and the forge,
the anvil and the fire,
the righteous sparks go wild
like rockets in the sky.
The fireworks overhead
flame red and blue and gold
against one darkened sky. . . .

Gods of compassion rise
In mortal human form
The splendor of your eyes
Streaks lightning in the storm.

(TMC 3)

As "protector of orphans, roof over the homeless, terrible guardian of the
sacred oath, Ogun stands for a transcendental humane but rigidly restorative
justice" (Soyinka 141). We hear it in the magical *We Will* of children's voices
signifying the *Word of Fire* that burns in the land of *Prophets for a New Day*.
And as it sounds throughout that land, the Ogunic voice becomes antitype of
the sixth-, seventh-, and eighth-century prophets transformed by the mirror
at the crossroads: Jeremiah becomes Benjamin Mays; Isaiah becomes Roy
Wilkins; Amos becomes Martin Luther King; Hosea becomes James Farmer;
Joel, John Lewis; and Micah, Medgar Evers. The Ogunic voice is the bearer
of the *Word*. And the *Word* is "the music in the wind for us," "the winnowing flail," "the avenging fire," "the bulwark against poaching patterns of dis-

located days," the "buttressing iron against insidious termite," the "sharp thinking running through our stream of days," the "certain courage flame with honest rays":

> As the Word came to prophets of old
> As the burning bush spoke to Moses
> And the fiery coals cleansed the lips of Isaiah;
> As the wheeling cloud in the sky
> Clothed the message of Ezekiel;
> So the Word of fire burns today
> On the lips of our prophets in an evil age.
>
> (*PND* 22)

On the Ogunic journey, we come to the place of revelation. This is the summit of the journey and its end. Through the hourglass of the crucible at the forge, we arrive at the poet's "Today":

> This is my century
> I saw it grow
> from darkness into dawn

And the mirror at the crossroads discloses a pageant. We see, passing in review, "a heroes' line," "the marching dead," "the tyrants too," "the child [with] prophet's eyes," "cities through the veil," "the living hell," "the Beast," "the shining hills before us": "Sculptured and created Truths." We stand staring, witnessing an ugly face, the id of an age

> in the dark of churches and schools and clubs and societies,
> associations and councils and committees and conventions,
> distressed and disturbed and deceived and devoured by
> money-hungry glory-craving leeches, preyed on by facile
> force of state and fad and novelty, by false prophets and
> holy believers.
>
> (*FMP* 14)

And against the image, the poet rhymes the *ethos* of the blues:

> You can't afford to live or die
> A baby cost too much to buy
> Hospital bed for just one day
> will scare your very death away.
>
> (*TMC* 76)

We are in the briarpatch. Here we have entered the region of transition. For the briarpatch is a kaleidoscopic zone. It is the ground on which imagination challenges the actual, contending for the territory of the real. Terror and glory commingle here, and time backrolls as ever forward it moves. The briarpatch is a place of reckoning.

According to the folktales, reality is a briarpatch inhabited by bumblers and the wise, by those who see and those who do not see, by truth and by the lie. According to the spirituals, reality is the moment when the dungeon of the mind shakes itself and its chains fall off. According to the blues, reality is a play of oppositions between the horrible and the splendid, causing a displacement of both so that a new zone of possibility emerges. According to the narratives of self-emancipated slaves, reality is a moment when neither past nor present are effective in the immediate situation. And therefore navigation, the art of transition, is reality. According to Dr. Du Bois, reality is a rent veil requiring double vision. According to Booker T. Washington, reality is a progenitive institution. According to Claude McKay, reality is a moment when two actions are possible: a backward look of nostalgia or a plunge as into a refining furnace out of which something transformed and strong emerges. According to Langston Hughes, reality is the dance of the spirit. According to Zora Neale Hurston, reality is a mad dog–version of experience that must be revised. According to Richard Wright, reality is a big white fog that must be cleared away. According to Gwendolyn Brooks, reality is a measured spin in the whirlwind. According to James Baldwin, reality is a heretic in the cathedral. According to Ralph Ellison, reality is a dim hole that must be lit by the light of mind and feeling. According to Ishmael Reed, reality is the dross spoofed by the poet's talisman. According to Sonia Sanchez, reality is the hummmmming of our mothers. According to Maya Angelou, reality is our heroes and sheroes. According to Paule Marshall, reality is an irresistible call, compelling a response beyond even our own perceived limits of response. According to Amiri Baraka, reality is the ever-changing same. According to Toni Cade Bambara, reality is an explosion, its fragments merged by the imaginative will. According to Alice Walker, reality is a kiss across the abyss. According to Toni Morrison, reality is the discovery of the beloved (Traylor 44).

It is to this "miraculous place of meaning" that the forger-poet leads us. It is here that the profound act of self–re-creation, the anguished struggle of the Will, is possible. Here, we may choose to connect the "two strange worlds": "the journey from the me to you" and "the journey from the you to me." Yet the Ogunic art of reconnection is not a static text. Rather, like the folk preacher's sermon or the valediction of "the slim young girl" of the Delta, it is a rhythmic motion. Or like the intricate *veve,* the text of the *rite de dessounin,* it prepares the way for the entrance of the spirit. But the grand extratextual improvisational act responsive to the spirit's call depends upon a *rite de possession:* the *mutima* of you and me.

> Hurry up, Lucille, hurry up
> We are going to miss our chance.
> —MARGARET WALKER, "Street Demonstration," *PND* 7

Walker, like many of her forebears and heirs, writes a poetry of reconnection. That poetry is different from what Joseph Riddel, echoing Emerson and Pound, has described as the "project" of an American poetics:

> The "project" of an American poetics . . . has been to invent a machine of its own origins—to invent or re-invent "language," an "Image," where the fiction of Being can be entertained, not as that which has been lost and can be recuperated, but as that which has been invented as a pure fiction so that it can be destroyed, or deconstructed, in the "beginning again." (358)

Rather, the project of an Afro-American poetics appears to be a reconnection of language, the image, to a large anteriority: not for the purpose of discovering origins or essences but in pursuit of a sustaining, even as changing, continuity. The use to which the Afro-American poet has put the image is toward re-membering images of the human and toward shaping "a humanism of the future—one standing in a different relation to the powers of the lower world, the unconscious and the id" (Spears 72). What the Afro-American language of memory attempts, as in the Walker canon, is "a relation bolder, freer, blither, productive of a riper art than any possible in our neurotic, fear-ridden hate-ridden world" (Spears 72).

"Hurry up, Lucille, hurry up . . . / We will sing and . . ." (*PND* 7).

« « «

On that call, our speaker pronounces benediction:

> As I go
> a traveller through this labyrinth
> I taste the bitter-sweet waters of Mara

And I look to the morning of all life.
Amen. I say Amen.

(*FFG*)

1. "Memory," in *For My People* (New Haven: Yale University Press, 1942). (All quotations from the *For My People* poems, hereafter *FMP*, refer to this collection.) Also see Paula Giddings's "'A Shoulder Hunched Against a Sharp Concern': Some Themes in the Poetry of Margaret Walker," *Black World* (Dec. 1971): 20–34, which emphasizes this poem.

2. Richard Barksdale's essay, "Margaret Walker: Folk Orature and Historical Prophecy," details the features of Margaret Walker's oratorical sound, and William Robinson discusses the oratorical poetry of Frances Ellen Watkins Harper. It is interesting to compare Frances Harper's themes in her "Songs for the People" (reprinted in William Robinson, ed., *Early Black American Poets* [Dubuque: Wm. C. Brown, 1969]) with those of Margaret Walker's "I Want to Write" and "For My People."

3. Hereafter, acronyms will cite the discrete collections: *Prophets for a New Day*, PND; *October Journey*, OJ; *This Is My Century: New and Collected Poems*, TMC; and *For Farish Street Green*, FFG.

4. Phillis Wheatley's "To . . . the Earl of Dartmouth" (1773) is the poetic precursor of the Declaration of Independence. Frances Ellen Watkins Harper's "The Slave Auction" (circa 1854) is metaphor of a mercantilism that, since the Iberian decision of the fifteenth century facilitating the voyages of Columbus, weaves a large motif on the tapestry of New World poetry. George Moses Horton's "Hope of Liberty" (1829), Charles Reason's "Freedom" (circa 1842), Frances E. W. Harper's *Poems of Miscellaneous Subjects* (1854), and other poetry of the period sing the "anathemia" of slavery. In poetry from Paul Laurence Dunbar's *Lyrics of Lowly Life* (1896) to Sterling Brown's *Southern Road* (1932), the anatomy of racism receives thorough examination. And Frances Harper, Angelina Grimke ("To Clarissa Scott Delaney"), Ann Spencer ("Letter to My Sister"), and Georgia Douglas Johnson (*The Heart of a Woman* 1918) draw the profile of gender chauvinism.

5. As early as 1899, Dr. Du Bois's "The Smoke King" had insinuated the idea of pan-Africanism into Afro-American poetry. By 1923, Jean Toomer had appropriated the implications of quantum theory as calculus for poetic construction in *Cane*. In his *The Black Christ* (1929), Countee Cullen experiments with psychoanalytic theory; in *Good Morning Revolution* (1932), Langston Hughes examines the implications of Karl Marx; and in his powerful "Between the World and Me" (1935), Richard Wright resounds the haunting line from the Spirituals, "adrift in this wide world alone," a pervasive existential note in black American poetry.

6. By 1845 Frederick Douglass had described the sorrow songs as "revealing at once the highest joy and the deepest sadness . . . the most pathetic sentiment in the most

rapturous tone, and the most rapturous sentiment in the most pathetic tone" (*Narrative* 31). And by 1901 Dr. Du Bois had called these "of me and mine." By 1937 the early songs along with the folk sermons and tales of agrarian southern captivity; the blues and ballads landmarking the Great Migration; and the urban music, ragtime, and (emergent) jazz had been traditionalized both as reference and as poetic diction by Afro-American poets. Yet to the category of *orature* must be added those poems, first written, that, like the spirituals and the blues, crash through the sleep of common memory and wake to resonance the long past, texturing contemporaneity and investing immediacy. By 1937, several such poems, by their popular reception, had supplied a community of memory: Frances Ellen Watkins Harper's "The Slave Auction," Paul Laurence Dunbar's "We Wear the Mask" and "When Malindy Sings," James Weldon Johnson's "The Creation" ("Lift Every Voice and Sing," declared national anthem, had always been song), Claude McKay's "If We Must Die," Countee Cullen's "From the Dark Tower," Langston Hughes's "The Negro Speaks of Rivers," Sterling Brown's "Strong Men," and Robert Hayden's "Runagate." From its publication in 1942, as title poem of the collection that earned Margaret Walker a Master of Arts degree from the Iowa School of Letters at the University of Iowa and also won her the Yale Younger Poet's Award (becoming number forty-one in that series), "For My People" became one of those poems. Moreover, well before 1937, *orature*, in Afro-American poetry, had become distinguished both as practice and as theory. The poetry of Frances E. W. Harper, by 1857, is an example of the practice. James Weldon Johnson's *God's Trombones* (1927) employs it as method, and his preface to that collection writes its theory.

7. Compare my reading of ritual in the poetry of Margaret Walker with that of Eugenia Collier in "Fields Watered with Blood."

WORKS CITED

Baker, Houston. *The Journey Back: Issues in Black Literature and Criticism.* Chicago: University of Chicago Press, 1980.

Barksdale, Richard. "Margaret Walker: Folk Orature and Historical Prophecy." In *Black American Poets Between Worlds 1940–1960.* Ed. R. Baxter Miller. Tennessee Studies in Literature 30. Knoxville: University of Tennessee Press, 1986.

Bellah, Robert, et al. *Habits of the Heart.* New York: Harper, 1985.

Collier, Eugenia. "Fields Watered with Blood: Myth and Ritual in the Poetry of Margaret Walker." In *Black Women Writers (1950–1980): A Critical Evaluation.* Ed. Mari Evans. New York: Doubleday, 1984.

Deren, Maya. *Divine Horsemen: The Voodoo Gods of Haiti.* New York: Dell, 1970.

Eliade, Mircea. *The Forge and the Crucible.* New York: Harper, 1971.

Henderson, Stephen. "Black Poetry: The Continuing Challenge." Melvin Butler Poetry Festival. Southern University, Baton Rouge LA, 30 April 1979 (unpublished lecture).

———. "Music as Metaphor of the Black Experience." WETA Humanities Grant Committee, 11 July 1978 (unpublished lecture).

Miller, Ron Baxter. "The 'Intricate Design' of Margaret Walker." In *Black American Poets Between Worlds 1940–1960*. Ed. R. Baxter Miller. Tennessee Studies in Literature 30. Knoxville: University of Tennessee Press, 1986.

Reilly, John M. "Thinking History in *The Man Who Cried I Am*." *Black American Literary Forum* 21.1–2 (spring–summer 1987): 26–42.

Riddel, Joseph. "Recentering the Image: The 'Project' of 'American' Poetics?" In *Textual Strategies: Perspectives in Post-Structural Criticism*. Ed. Josué V. Harari. Ithaca: Cornell University Press, 1979. 322–58.

Sanchez, Sonia. "Poem for Margaret Walker." In *Homegirls & Handgrenades*. New York: Thunder's Mouth Press, 1984. 60–61.

Sartre, Jean-Paul. "Orphée Noir." Preface to *Anthologie de la nouvelle poésie nègre et malgache de langue française*. Ed. Léopold Sédar Senghor. Paris: Presses Universitaires de France, 1948.

Serjeant, R. B. "Arabic Poetry." In *Princeton Encyclopedia of Poetry and Poetics*. Ed. Alex Preminger. Princeton: Princeton University Press, 1974. 42–47.

Shils, Edward. *Tradition*. Chicago: University of Chicago Press, 1981.

Soyinka, Wole. *Myth, Literature, and the African World*. London: Cambridge University Press, 1976.

Spears, Monroe K. *Dionysus and the City: Modernism in Twentieth-Century Poetry*. New York: Oxford University Press, 1970.

Traylor, Eleanor W. "Toni Cade Bambara's *The Salt Eaters*: A Symposium." *Contributions in Black Studies* 6 (1983–1984): 44–48.

Vance, Eugene. "Roland and the Poetics of Memory." In *Textual Strategies: Perspectives in Post-Structural Criticism*. Ed. Josué V. Harari. Ithaca: Cornell University Press, 1979. 374–403.

Walker, Margaret. "The Humanistic Tradition of Afro-American Literature." *American Libraries* 1 (Oct. 1970): 849–54.

Wright, Richard. "Blueprint for Negro Writers." In *Richard Wright Reader*. Ed. Ellen Wright and Michel Fabre. New York: Harper, 1978.

Folkloric Elements in
Margaret Walker's Poetry

B. DILLA BUCKNER

Much of the work of Margaret Walker has as its base a grounding in the history of black people, for she is the voice of, to, by, for, and about the black race. In addition to being a historian, she is also a folklorist. Her words in *How I Wrote "Jubilee"* add credence: "I always intended *Jubilee* to be a folk novel based on folk materials, folk sayings, folk beliefs, folk-ways." [1] If Walker's description of *Jubilee* is still not enough to substantiate her own folk style— since hers could possibly be biased—James Spears, in an article entitled "Black Folk Elements in Margaret Walker's *Jubilee,*" gives further substantiation of the novel: "Folk culture undergirds it and mirrors the morals, mores, and sociological patterns implicit in the ethos of the novel. The folk songs, the folk speech, the clothing, the food, the folk description of animals and of plants— all these tie the novel to the folk, to the soil." [2] Spears points out example after example of folk elements that pervade the novel, including the fact that each chapter begins with an epigraph excerpted from a traditional folk song; many of these are from spirituals.

Since, quite often, there are misconceptions about the definition of folklore or "fakelore" (a term coined by Richard Dorson in 1950, which means the falsifying of the raw data for capitalistic gain rather than totalitarian conquest),[3] it is necessary to establish some ground rules for exploring folklore in literature. The following three tests can be used to see if an author has used folklore:

1. There must be biographical evidence; we should be able to establish that the author knew of and was part of the oral tradition.
2. From reading the story, we should be able to establish that the author gives an accurate description of the folk group and their customs—in other words, he has observed the group firsthand.
3. We must be able to show that the folk motifs can be found in the Motif Index and that the folk material has had oral circulation before the author included it in his story.[4]

Couple the above three-faceted test set forth by Dorson with a four-part test by Laubach—(1) folklore is oral; (2) folklore is traditional within a certain group; (3) folklore must exist in different versions; and (4) folklore is anonymous—and one readily observes that Walker definitely utilizes the folk tradition in the novel.[5] Generally, the story told in *Jubilee* is by a black and about black life, customs, and mores; the author learns much of the story orally, for her grandmother relays it to Walker as family history; there are any number of anonymous slave stories to provide different versions of similar situations; and many of the customs, "superstitions," and cures are cataloged in the Motif Index. While these are general statements about her longer work of prose, a close examination of any number of Walker's poems reveals just how deeply steeped she is in the folkloric traditions of black people.

"Ballad of the Hoppy-Toad" is an example of Walker's masterful usage of folklore elements. Surface-wise, this poem is about a protagonist's concern about an evil spell cast upon her by "the goopher man" or the "root worker." No reason is given for this act, but the spell is reversed and the caster is ultimately the victim of his own evil deed. On the surface, also, is the tall tale told in ballad form. Structurally, the poem follows most of the conventions of the traditional ballad. Each stanza consists of four lines with four beats or stresses in the first line, three in the second, four in the third, and three in the fourth. The second and fourth lines rhyme; the first and the third do not. Thus, if the word "Ballad" were not included in the title, one could merely scan the poem and identify its form. An example is this stanza:

The góo/pher mán/ was hól/lering   a
"Don't kill/ hat hóp/py-tóad."   b
Sis Á/very/ she sáid/ "Hóney,   c
you boút/ to lóse/ your lóad."   b

The above stanza follows the traditional ballad format, while other lines in some of the stanzas veer from this pattern; the first line of the poem is an example of such a variation (poetic license, perhaps). Yet, the rhyme scheme *abcb* pervades the poem. (It may be necessary to point out that the ballad is one of the most common forms for relaying folk information. Note, for example, "Sir Patrick Spens" or "Barbara Allan.")

Like a number of ballads, also, the "Ballad of the Hoppy-Toad" has many of the properties of a full-blown short story: setting, plot, characters. This story takes place on a Saturday on Market Street, Wherever, U.S.A. While the street may mean some place specific to Walker, her description leads the reader to a vivid description of the southern Saturday marketing day, washing day, and fighting and drinking day. Thus, she gives a time, background, and place for the oncoming story. Her characters, likewise, are well established: the narrator or protagonist, the goopher man or antagonist, and Sis Avery. The rise in action begins with "the night I seen the goopher man / Throw dust around my door," and continues throughout the narrator's seeking Sis Avery's assistance in curtailing the spell. The climax of this dramatic piece is the changing of the horse to a toad with the dénouement being the toad and goopher man dying simultaneously.

In addition to the traits previously listed, the ballad abounds in other folklore elements. There is, for example, the constant mentioning of various animals, and the animal stories are very much a part of folklore tradition. The reader is introduced to the toad, via inference, of course, in the first stanza: "When the Saturday crowd went stomping / Down the Johnny-*jumping* road." In the second stanza, the deacon's daughter is "lurching / Like a drunken alley *goat*"; the "root-worker" is a *dog* that needs to behave; and the charging *horse* is reduced to the ultimate "hoppy-toad." Paula Giddings observes that the animal imagery that Walker uses shows her in-depthness:

> The toad in Nigerian myth was responsible for man's reappearance after death on earth in another form. The horse symbolizes the power to infuse man with the spirit of a god, evil or good, which can completely dominate the soul. In African mythology and belief, evil not only manifests itself in an actual embodiment, but that embodiment has a protean nature.[6]

Another element that authenticates this ballad as folklore is Walker's use of the conjurer or conjurers, when one considers Sis Avery. The use of magic, juju, mojo, voodoo, hoodoo, etc. has long been a part of the black heritage. The user of such magic (a conjurer) has a special place in black history:

> Conjurers could be pictured as exotic Old Testament–type prophets or magicians: "He could turn as green as grass, most, and was just as black as a man could very well be, and his hair covered his neck and he had lizards tied on it. He carried a crooked cane. He would throw it down and pick it up and say something and throw it down and it would wriggle like a snake, and he would pick it up and it would be as stiff as any other cane!"[7]

Historically, while the slave conjurer, for the most part, used his powers to ward off some of his master's abuse, quite often that same power could be used against other slaves. As Lawrence Levine notes, "The power of conjurers to wreak retribution upon slaves when requested to do so by other slaves was believed to be almost unlimited. . . . Other conjurers, of course, could be consulted to reverse these effects."[8] So the conjurer with such great powers becomes highly respected, and this background information is evident in "Ballad of the Hoppy-Toad" when the goopher man or root worker casts a spell on the storyteller and has it reversed by Sis Avery to his disadvantage.

One other significant aspect about the spell-casting episode is the back-and-forth play between good and evil or sacred (good) and profane (evil). The narrator tells the reader that the spell is an "evil note," and hexes usually carry a negative connotation. Yet, the conjurer may use a counter spell to reverse the act only after the narrator has tried the Christian or "right" way via the church and prayer. Giddings notes the same dichotomy and explains it this way: "When Christian prayer failed, goopher hexes had to be used to counter goopher hexes. It was the implementation of traditional beliefs which maintained the moral order of the community. . . . It is reminiscent, for example, of the Haitians who practice Catholicism as their 'official' religion, but use the images and rites of Vodun to regulate their daily lives."[9]

One final observation about the "Ballad" is that it conforms to the Dorson test of folklore in literature: (1) it is definitely an outgrowth of the oral tradition since the story was told to Walker by someone (anonymous) from the North Carolina area; (2) the story teller/narrator gives a very detailed account of the characters, as noted, and their customs (any reader would recognize the description of the typical southern Saturday and Saturday-night episodes); and (3) the fire or prayer to ward off evil spirits, the reversal of spells or duper being duped, and the animal lore are representative folk motifs that can be found in the Motif Index.

Equally as compacted with similar folkloric elements is Walker's "Molly Means." There is good and evil (the innocent bride and evil conjurer); there is the spell casting and its reversal; there is the animal emphasis; and the animals in "Molly Means" are a dog and hog. Yet Molly has all the charm of a snake. Further comparison and contrast of these two works reveals a male goopher man in "Ballad" and a female witch in "Molly Means," with both becoming victims of their own evil doings. Additionally, Walker, in "Molly Means," tells how the witch gets her powers:

> Some say she was born with a veil on her face
> So she could look through unnatchal space
> Through the future and through the past
> And charm or a body or an evil place.

Yet the reader is not privy to such information in the ballad's root worker. This particular idiom of a person's being born with a veil had been cataloged, and the belief is still widespread among the black community; however, it does not always indicate evilness: rather, a child born with a veil (in actuality the placenta) is born for good luck and has the *gift* of being able to see into the future.

There is the lack of religious impetus to counteract the evil spirit in "Molly Means," and the reader gets the implication that religion is replaced by the devout love of the husband for his young bride. As with the religion that does not work in "Ballad," the husband has to contact a conjurer, "who said he could move the spell / and cause the awful thing to dwell / On Molly Means." Details of how the conjurer accomplishes this feat are not as explicit as in "Ballad," but the resulting deaths of the evildoers are evident. While nothing remains of the "Hoppy-Toad," the ghost of Molly Means remains whining, crying, cackling, moaning, and, of course, barking, thus iterating that her demise, too, is somehow affiliated with an animal, more specifically a dog. The return of a person in the form of a ghost or an animal can be found in the Motif Index, although the reasons for returning differ.

Two other folklore elements of note found in "Molly Means" are the use of numbers and the refrain structure. In folklore, especially modern lore, each number represents something in particular. Numbers have been cataloged, and usually the odd numbers (3, 7, 11) used by Walker indicate good luck; but these seem to mean the opposite in "Molly Means": "Imp at three and wench at 'leben / she counted her husbands to the number seben."

The second point of note is that the structure of "Molly Means" is a variation of the traditional folk ballad; some ballads repeat the last line of each stanza, and some repeat a particular refrain. Walker thus makes use of incremented repetition in "Molly Means," which "involves repeating the basic structure of a line but changing it slightly (the increment) in order to move the story forward; sometimes this technique has striking dramatic effects."[10] The first line of the refrain that follows each stanza is basically the same— "O Molly, Molly, Molly Means"—with the exception of stanzas two, three, and six, where the "O" is replaced with "Old." So the balladeer refers to Molly as "old" when describing her evilness, her "black-hand arts," and her death. The first two words of the second line of the refrain are also changed slightly to denote progression: "There goes the ghost of Molly Means"; "Dark is . . ."; Cold is . . ."; "Where is . . ."; "Sharp is . . ."; "This is . . ."; "Lean is . . ." The only time Walker asks a question is before the husband goes in search of the witch, thus suggesting a change in the action of the story.

While "Ballad of the Hoppy-Toad" is structurally much like the traditional ballad, "Molly Means" has more dissimilarities than similarities. It is, however, of the oral tradition, about a particular group of people and their customs and about a specific event. Walker is like the traditional balladeer in "Molly Means" because this poem is more objective; she "reports the news of the day in a very impersonal way" and "refuses to condemn."[11] On the other hand, in the "Ballad," she is author/narrator/protagonist, making judgments about the townspeople and even calling the goopher man a dog. With this subjectivity, too, comes more dialogue, particularly between the narrator and Sis Avery and between Sis Avery and the goopher man.

In further searching for folklore elements in these two works, one must take note of the language that is a part of folk tradition. According to Laubach, "Folk grammar often is nonstandard. . . . Particularly good examples of these usages are double negatives, such as 'I ain't got none,' and double superlatives, such as 'most kindest.'"[12] One can readily see the differences between the more formalized English of "Molly Means," which the author treats more objectively, and the nonstandard English of "Ballad," in which the author/narrator seems to be one and the same. Spears says of Walker on this issue (his reference is to *Jubilee*), "Walker is a dialectologist in the strictest sense of the word, and her use of eye dialect for characterization is both accurate and effective. It captures the essence of black dialect in pronunciation, vocabulary items, and usage and grammar, particularly in syntax."[13] Walker's use of dialect in both of the poems tends to lend credibility to her characters. She employs subject-verb nonagreement: "I knows just what will hex him"; auxiliary verb dropping: "And when the tale begun to spread"; double subject: "What you reckon that there mean"; folk pronunciation: "Chile of the devil, the dark, and sich"

("Chile" for child and "sich" for such); and folk sayings: "Honey, / You bout to lose your load." In her dialectal poems, the influence of Paul Laurence Dunbar is quite obvious.

Charles Rowell asks Walker in an interview whether "Molly Means" came as a result of her New Orleans experience. She answers, "My grandmother told me that story of this witch or this woman who put a spell on this young girl who was just a bride. That is a part of my folk heritage and is not limited to a particular place as the way 'Hoppy-Toad' was told to me in North Carolina. New Orleans has all of the juju and the conjure tradition. I never remembered much of it in New Orleans."[14] So the ghost of Molly Means lives on because ghosts, of course, could be evil as well as benign.

Walker's folk heroes come in different sizes and shapes, and she celebrates the good heroes in *Prophets for a New Day* and the more diversified ones in the second section of *For My People*. Most of her prophets are fighters for civil rights, with special attention being given to Micah and Amos, Medgar Evers, and Martin Luther King. In this collection, she calls on numerous Biblical figures and images to describe her heroes; and if one considers the folklore inherent in the Bible, one need not test any of these poems for elements of lore. Of the poetry in *For My People*, R. Baxter Miller writes, "Without biblical cadences her ballads frequently become average, if not monotonous. In 'Yalluh Hammuh,' a folk poem about the 'Bad Man,' she manages sentimentality, impractical concern, and trickery, as a black woman outsmarts the protagonist and steals his money."[15] Yet, in spite of Miller's observation, the weaker person's overcoming the stronger one (as with Lil Lad and Two-Gun Buster) is definitely in the folk tradition and is easily recognizable as a folk motif. In addition to the local heroes that Walker addresses—such as Poppa Chicken, the pimp, or Kissie Lee, who dies with her boots on—Walker renders more compact versions of national heroes, such as John Henry, who dies with a nine-pound hammer in his hand as opposed to a ten-pound one, and Stagolee, who in her version does not take over hell: rather, "his ghost still walks up and down the shore / Of Old Man River round New Orleans / with her gumbo, rice, and good red beans!"

Whether Walker deals with her heroes as tragic possibilities or comic reliefs, she is always very serious about those who gave their lives to set right an inegalitarian society. When asked about her response to William Styron's *Confessions of Nat Turner,* one can almost visualize the writer's anger in her response: "The racism in that book is the damage that he does to the hero for the black child. Nat Turner represents to Black people, first of all, a preacher, and that is one of our heroes—you see, folk heroes. . . . He [Styron] attacks Nat Turner as a man; he attacks him as a preacher; and he attacks him as a folk hero."[16]

Perhaps it was out of such an attack on Nat Turner that Walker wrote "The Ballad of the Free," which celebrates such insurrectionists as Turner, Vesey, L'Ouverture, and John Brown. These legendary figures, about whom there are written and oral accounts and versions, offer Walker material to describe the heroic missions and tragic deaths of slave insurrectionists. The power of this poem may lie in the balance that Walker finds between historical fact and Biblical imagery. The facts are about the heroes, and the religious images are in the refrain:

> The serpent is loosed and the hour is come
> The last shall be first and the first shall be none
> The serpent is loosed and the hour is come.[17]

Although the above reference can be found in the Bible, it is certainly no accident that Walker uses words that are included in Nat Turner's confessions about a vision dictated to Thomas R. Gray: "And on the 12th of May, 1828, I heard a loud noise in the heavens, and the Spirit instantly appeared to me and said the Serpent was loosened, and Christ had laid down the yoke he had borne for the sins of men, and that I should take it on and fight against the Serpent, for the time was just approaching when the first should be last and the last should be first."[18]

In conclusion, Walker's poetry is definitive proof that she is a poet of the people, her people. The folkways, customs, beliefs, or superstitions embodied in the lines and words of her poetry reveal that she is a folklorist and, indeed, a folk poet.

NOTES

1. Margaret Walker, *How I Wrote* Jubilee (Chicago: Third World Press, 1972), 25.

2. James E. Spears, "Black Folk Elements in Margaret Walker's *Jubilee*," *Mississippi Folklore Register* 14.1 (spring 1980): 13.

3. Richard Dorson, *American Folklore* (Chicago: University of Chicago Press, 1959), 4.

4. David Laubach, *Introduction to Folklore* (Rochelle Park NJ: Hayden Book Co., 1980), 141.

5. Ibid., 2.

6. Paula Giddings, "'A Shoulder Hunched Against a Sharp Concern': Some Themes in the Poetry of Margaret Walker," *Black World*, December 1971, 24.

7. Lawrence Levine, "The Sacred World of Black Slaves," in *Black Culture and Black Consciousness* (New York: Oxford University Press, 1977), 74.

8. Ibid., 78.

9. Giddings 24.

10. Laubach 2.

11. Ibid., 67.

12. Ibid., 100.

13. Spears 14.

14. Charles Rowell, "Poetry, History and Humanism: An Interview with Margaret Walker," *Black World,* December 1975, 9.

15. R. Baxter Miller, "The 'Etched Flame' of Margaret Walker," *Tennessee Studies in Literature* 26 (1981): 163.

16. Rowell 11.

17. Margaret Walker, "Ballad of the Free," in *Prophets for a New Day* (1970), rpt. in *This Is My Century* (Athens: University of Georgia Press, 1989), 60.

18. Levine 77.

Performing Community

Margaret Walker's Use of Poetic "Folk Voice"

TOMEIKO R. ASHFORD

The poetry of Margaret Walker has become a hallmark of African American heritage, authenticating expressive folk idioms and traditions endemic to the culture itself. While many of her poems echo the shared experiences and history of the black race, specific pieces further appropriate and assume the characteristics of a communal folk voice in which those common experiences are shaped into oral narratives. These poems engage in a mythological discourse that institutes familiar cultural markers as symbolic "cues," highlighting conjure and supernatural tales, privileging verbal agility and sagacity, incorporating various linguistic and dialectal patterns, and, ultimately, enjoining readers to act as primary storytellers of the verses. Walker inscribes such compositions as "Molly Means," "Poppa Chicken," "Long John Nelson and Sweetie Pie," "Ballad of the Hoppy-Toad," and "For My People" with particular performative tonalities, making their formal declamation virtually mandatory.[1]

These poems represent two main narrative forms for which Walker's mastery has been noted: the ballad and free verse ("For My People" singularly exemplifies the latter). Arguably, all of the pieces serve as "folk tributes," but their most prominent rhetorical features include inscribed song and speech, devices which render them as oral literature. Hence, the poems are most effective when shared in active participation: Walker intends for them to be, in part, read, sung, spoken, acted, and heard. What results is a "kind of verbal music" and a "magnificently wrought oral poetry."[2] Moreover, the musicality of her work is undeniable. When asked by scholar Jerry Ward Jr. in a 1988 interview how music has informed her art, Walker quips: "I think always that music has been uppermost in my mind, and in all of my thinking and *writing* all my life" (emphasis added).[3] The four ballads (which by the nature of their form are to be sung or recited) and the final free-verse piece illustrate the author's proclivity as a lyrist. Walker employs both song, or "verse," and speech as a means of relaying visions of African American folkways. Although many scholars have invariably analyzed the lingual propensity of the selected poems, the following examinations show how all of the aforementioned literary devices execute impulses of black cultural life.

"Molly Means" belongs to the genre of the "Bad Women Folk Ballads," concerning itself with the characterization and actions of its heroine, Molly Means.[4] The narrator's initial portrayal of her is one of an ugly and, by correlation, evil woman. The opening line, "Old Molly Means was a hag and a witch," attests to this. She is an elderly woman of a downtrodden and corrupt disposition whose own name ("Means"/"mean") signals her heartless and vile temperament. As the narrator continues to establish Molly's personality, he draws on analogies infused with the mechanics and phonetics of the vernacular. A "*chile of the devil*," Molly has "eyes black as *picch*" with the ability to shape-shift into a "wench at *'leben*" all the while being able to "count . . . her husbands to the number *seben*" (emphasis added). The depiction of a "dark" woman with "heavy hair" that hangs "thick in ropes" imbues the ballad with the qualities of a ghost story. The audience learns in the subsequent refrain that Molly Means later becomes a ghost. Noting her ghoulish presence during the rendering of the tale, the narrator remarks, "There goes the ghost of Molly Means."

Walker further reveals Molly's supernatural status, claiming that "she was born with a veil on her face" and, as a result, "could look through unnatural space." The narrator warns that although she could "charm" anybody or anything, she was still to be "despised" for the "evil look in her coal black eyes." The speaker reinforces this notion, reminding us that, "Dark is the ghost of Molly Means." Walker establishes an underlying theme of that which is sinister, gruesome, and feared. Walker builds a narrative climax and provides oral leverage for the tale's dramatic rendering.

Even within the ballad, Walker recognizes the power of oral transmission. Says she,

And when the tale begun to spread
Of evil and of holy dread . . .
The younguns was afraid at night
and the farmers feared their crops would blight. (33)

"The spreading of the tale" implies a word-of-mouth transference of information about the infamous heroine throughout the community. Therefore, the "tale" of Molly Means is dually transmitted to both a fictional and a real audience, allowing Walker's readers to participate in her imaginary world and charging them with the responsibility to pass the story on. Professional storyteller and author Julius Lester agrees with Walker's privileging of her audience's participation in her works. Recognizing the telling of story as an act of individual ownership and self-definition, he notes: "Each person who tells a story molds the story to his tongue and to his mouth, and each listener molds the story to his ear. Thus, the same story, told over and over, is never quite the same."[5] Through such narrative malleability and multiple ownership, we learn that Molly is not just a woman of ill repute. She is also a sorcerer endowed with specific powers to "cast spells and call . . . the dead." Thus, the tale takes on more grandiose proportions and grows more widespread as the townsfolk become enthralled with Molly's adeptness at alleged "black-hand arts."

It is at this point that the ballad takes a metafictive turn. Walker imbeds a mininarrative regarding one instance in which Molly casts a spell on a "young gal-bride" who lives "in the lane just down from Molly's shack." The reader may question Molly's decision to cast a spell on this particular woman. The most obvious explanation of her actions would be that Molly is jealous of her. In the tradition of legendary fables, the author draws a vast distinction between the old, ugly, evil, and presumably unwed Molly and the young, probably beautiful, innocent, and newly married woman. And though Molly's spell leaves the young bride "barking like a dog / And on all fours like a common hog," the bride's husband returns to rescue his distressed damsel.

What is problematic with the scene is that Walker commissions the husband as well as another townsman to completely disable and eradicate Molly. In effect, the author places "man" and "woman as evil being" in direct opposition to one another. Admittedly, Molly does attempt to kill the younger woman and, in all fairness, should probably receive a fitting punishment. Still, the entire community turns against Molly ("[t]he neighbors come and they went away") in favor of the young bride, leaving her to bear a collective wrath alone. Swearing that "he'd break the wicked charms" placed on his wife, the husband goes on a mission of revenge to "turn the spell on Molly's hand" instead.

Walker subsequently allows for Molly's physical demise. When the towns-man meets the grieving and determined husband, he promises that not only could he "move the spell" from the young bride but also that he could "cause the awful thing to dwell / On Molly Means." Vowing to make Molly "bark and bleed / Till she died at the hands of her evil deed," the two men succeed in avenging the hexed young bride. Walker renders a moral tale where evil does not (and, by implication, cannot) triumph over good. It can be argued, still, that good is achieved by equally devious and violent means.

Molly Mean's character, however, remains mythic since she becomes for-ever a part of the community's shared memory. Even after she dies, they can still hear "her holler and whine and cry" as she "rides along on a winter breeze" at night. They remember how she brought "terror to the young and old." She still imparts fear in them, haunting them with her "cackling laugh or her barking cold." A "dark," "cold," "sharp," "lean" ghost, Molly remains an immortalized figure for generations to come. Thus, the community owns the story of Molly Means's fateful encounter with those two men. Yet, it is Walker who ordains its narration. For Walker, Molly Means and her ballad constitute a cultural mythology through which she imparts lessons of virtue bequeathed to her audience—an audience for whom it becomes imperative to recount the tale, an audience licensed to tell the story for themselves. That story, of course, remains a "living, growing, changing thing." [6]

In contrast to the malevolence of Molly Means, the character of the self-titled poem "Poppa Chicken" is a familiar male prototype commonly depicted in both urban and rural black settings. Poppa Chicken is a "figure . . . of real-ism," as Stephen Vincent Benét notes in the foreword to Walker's inaugural book of poetry, drawing his personality from the kaleidoscope portraits of the "fancy men" who would claim ownership of city streets.[7] Walker unfolds the narrative as if the speaker were sitting on a corner relaying a tall tale to a crowd of eager onlookers. Of course, the resulting verse encompasses the nuances of verbal transmission: although Poppa's character is believable, his story is ren-dered with hyperbolic flair.

As in the previous poem, Walker pays special attention to subject develop-ment. Most obviously, she draws analogies between Poppa Chicken's pompous demeanor and the haughty behavior of a rooster since Poppa parades around as if he "own[s] the town." Calling him a "sugah daddy," Walker indicts him for "pimping . . . / All the gals for miles around." Walker portrays Poppa as a pretentious womanizer who "g[i]ve[s] his women hell." Despite the maltreat-ment they receive from him, all the women "on Poppa's time" still revere him and think him "swell."

Unlike Molly Means, for whom being "dark"-complexioned was a curse and a sign of her wicked nature, Poppa's sable hue seems to be an aphrodisiac, making him more sexually desirable and appealing. With a "long and black" face and a "broad" grin, Poppa proudly struts the streets displaying his physical wares. Molly, who is viewed as unattractive by her community, contrasts markedly with Poppa, who is apparently so handsome that he makes all the ladies cry, "Lawdy! Lawd!" The standard of beauty and sexuality that Walker posits in "Molly Means" shifts in the latter poem. Using Molly's black skin and physically aged body to create an evil narrative presence, the author unwittingly desexualizes the heroine and elicits disdain toward her in the former poem. Molly's demise, however deserving, is sanctioned, expected, and, most of all, desired. The mood and tone of "Poppa Chicken" is quite different. In this piece, the hero, who fosters equally immoral and illegal acts of prostitution and violence, is praised for his lewd actions and esteemed for his sexual potency, both of which are augmented because of the mesmerizing and empowering effects of Poppa's dark skin. Even though he initially receives just punishment, Poppa's ultimate triumph over all equalizing forces in the poem (including the law, a jealous boyfriend, age, and sexual impotency) is greatly anticipated and, finally, realized. Unlike Molly Means, he is not killed, nor does he lose his physical attractiveness. Rather, he lives to defy the odds, ensuring narrative longevity.

Walker employs the vernacular in very familiar ways in "Poppa Chicken." She relies more heavily on idiom, dialect, and inscribed dialogue to make the narrative and the characters more believable, realistic, and thus accessible through oration and recitation. Referring to Poppa's women in the colloquial as "gals," Walker relays a sense of girlish naiveté that encourages the women to follow Poppa aimlessly and reverently. When Walker speaks of them as being expected to adhere to Poppa's expectations or "toe his special line," she immediately allows for Poppa's voice, his perspective, to enter, further confirming his chauvinistic and egotistical attitude. He proclaims in high vernacular, "Treat 'em rough and make 'em say / Poppa Chicken's fine!" Walker suggests that Poppa's arrogant subjugation and dismissal of his women and their subsequent acquiescence to him feeds his persona, making him larger than life in many ways and a "bad man/Negro" figure in others.

Poppa affirms his own tough guy image by acquiring devices with which to inflict violence and by involving himself in compromising situations. Somehow, he always survives and triumphs. According to Walker, he "toted guns" and "wore a knife," both types of weapons typically associated with and generally thought to be demonstrative of a man's physical and sexual strength.

Poppa both carries deadly weapons and uses them to defend his macho image. Although he is jailed for having shot a guy, "[H]e [gets] off light," buying "his pardon in [only] a year."

Walker continues to bolster the image of Poppa Chicken as supreme ruler of his territory, all the while creating an indomitable character. Now pardoned and back on the streets with "[g]als around his neck," Papa Chicken has not lost any of his power and influence. It "[h]urt him nary speck," the poem's narrator reports. In fact, his release from jail seems to boost his ego. He smokes "long cigars"—the "[s]pecial Poppa brands," of course—and has diamonds "in his tie" and "[o]n his long black hands." Poppa reaches the status of a deity, unaffected by human frailties:

> Poppa lived without a fear;
> Walked without a rod.
> Poppa cussed the coppers out;
> Talked like he was God. (37)

Clearly, Poppa becomes a memorable and legendary protagonist, one whose story warrants perpetual literary attention.

Just as the "fairer sex" sustains him, so too does a woman cause Poppa's downfall. After having taken "one look" at a "pretty gal" named Rose, he is immediately smitten and goes out to buy her "pretty clothes." Walker finally rebukes his behavior, allowing another male figure to confront him. In a climactic scene, Rose's "man," Joe, catches the two in an embrace and says simply, "Poppa's got to go." At the very least, the author shows us that there are a few moments when Poppa can be vulnerable.

Poppa remains undaunted, however. Even in old age, he is "still hot." Obviously, his sexual virility thrives as he continues "[w]alking round . . . with his gals / [p]imping every day." His "pimp daddy" image persists since the poem makes no intimation of the subject's impending death. Poppa is such a "cool dude"—he is so "bad"—that he "couldn't [possibly] die" (a feat Benét attributes to another one of Walker's unconquerable characters, Gus, the Lineman).[8] In effect, Walker leaves us with the portrait of an ultra-masculine hero whose reputation endures. Transcribing Poppa's life from his "prime" to his old age, she renders the biography of a renowned ladies' man, punctuating it with vernacular peculiarities.

"Long John Nelson and Sweetie Pie" is Walker's treatise on black heterosexual love and the concomitant struggles and fears therein. Allowing for two central subjects in this piece, the author grapples with dichotomized perspectives of "male" and "female" responses to affection. As a result, readers witness how the two lovers relate to each other in the face of sustaining their bond. The poem becomes memorable because of its inscription of convincing conversations and its honest portrayal about the tentative nature of love.

The nicknames of the couple initially establish them as foil characters to one another. John's "moniker," "Long," implies a man who is tall and lean in stature. Sweetie Pie's pet name, however, conjures up images of a rotund woman who probably enjoys eating sweets and pastries. Their names are no coincidence, of course, since Walker makes a direct correlation between those appellations and the characters' dispositions. According to her, "Long John was a mellow fellow / And Sweetie Pie was fat and sweet." Although Walker encourages us to believe that their opposite personalities do indeed attract, she also prepares for a time when their unique behaviors will cause them to be diametrically opposed.

The audience learns that the two become a couple long before the "story" begins. But the narrator does not provide background information regarding how the couple meets and eventually unites. We are told, though, about the moment of their dissolution. Revealing that the two "live . . . together" but remain unmarried, she notes with disdain that "Sweetie cook[s] on the Avenue" while "Long John's loving [i]s all he'd do." This is the first such conflict between the two. The fact that Sweetie works in a physically demanding, service-oriented job makes her a sympathetic character since she seems to be industrious, responsible, and conscientious. Long John's choice to "love" rather than to work makes him despicable and suspect. Sweetie's diligence conflicts with Long John's apparent laziness.

Walker's initial description of John as "mellow" and Sweetie as "sweet" becomes questionable when those traits transform as the relationship grows more volatile. Sweetie, who dutifully "br[ings] [John] his grub" and feeds "him well" every night, changes from a nurturing counterpart to the proverbial "nagging" girlfriend who "would fuss and pick a fight" afterward. John, who allegedly possesses a very calm and cool demeanor, on the other hand, evolves into an extremely violent figure. Supposedly in response to Sweetie's constant nagging, he "beat[s] her" and gives her "hell."

Even more disturbing is the implication that Sweetie provokes his behavior, that she harasses him until he viciously reacts. The love/hate relationship intensifies as she uses several expletives to demonstrate her frustration with him. Says Walker, Sweetie "would cuss and scream, [and] call him black." Walker's colloquial reference to Sweetie's "cursing" tirades illuminates, as in the previous poems, how blackness becomes aligned with that which is undesirable and scorned. In this instance, calling John "black" is the ultimate insult and is employed in conjunction with other demeaning and harsh language. Speaking in dialect to John, Sweetie commands, "Triflin' man git outa my sight." Incongruities in their alliance abound, though. When John leaves at her behest, she "beg[s] him back" and then "love[s] him half the night." Their union is chaotic and their responses to each other are unpredictable as well.

The subsequent stanza exemplifies Walker's artful play with color and image in the poem. Just as black skin is despised, so too is white skin celebrated. When a "yellow gal" rides into town one day, she takes Long John "clean away / [f]rom Sweetie Pie." The strange woman remains identifiable only by her skin color throughout the rest of the poem because it is that which imbues her with the power to "steal" Sweetie's man away from her. The notion of the fair-skinned woman's ability to win the heart of the other's boyfriend immediately pits the two against each other, placing them in competition for John as if he were a prize. This standard of beauty, "the lighter the prettier," particularly in regard to the women, is upheld just as it was in the earlier ballad, "Molly Means." The anonymous woman appears to be even more striking, as the author notes, possessing "coal black hair" and wearing a "bright blue gown." Walker very descriptively depicts her in contrast to Sweetie.

Long John's and Sweetie's personalities change once again as Sweetie diminishes in stature to John. Walker interjects dialogue and otherwise "spoken" narrative to signal their transitions. Using such "semi-speech" to report that Sweetie begs John "to please come back," the author details our heroine's demise. John, in reaction to Sweetie's cries for pity, becomes unmerciful, cold-hearted, and unyielding. He replies simply, "I'm gone to stay." The episode that follows demonstrates one of Walker's standard means of including cultural markers as poetic devices. Sweetie Pie speaks and then breaks out into a blues song:

> Long John, Baby, if you'll come back
> I won't never call you black;
> I'll love you long and love you true
> And I don't care what else you do. (47)

This blues structure provides "a form that is freer and larger than [the] dialect" that Sweetie engages earlier, offering instead one that accommodates her individual experience yet "still hold[s] . . . racial flavor."[9] Through musical narrative, Walker can creatively and sympathetically express Sweetie's heartache while capturing the subtleties of cultural mores. Obviously, her plea for John's return further demeans her as she relinquishes her own desires and, especially, her pride to win him back. Although her promise to discontinue ridiculing his dark skin is admirable, her vow to shower him with long-lasting, devoted, and "true" love—no matter how he treats her—proves that she has little regard for her own emotional needs. Her seeming nonchalant attitude regarding his behavior toward and treatment of her problematizes her sense of self-esteem.

Despite all of her pleading, John leaves Sweetie anyway. As Walker notes, "They're still apart this very day." Their permanent separation seems to be the impetus, however, for John to turn his life around. Having secured a job, he runs off to make a new life with the strange woman who, once the "yellow gal," becomes John's "yellow bride." Thus, the saffron-colored woman succeeds in winning John's heart and in procuring a status that Sweetie never acquires— that of John's wife.

John's increasing stability triggers Sweetie's steady decline. Upon John's departure, she gets "sick and waste[s] away." On the surface, Walker appears to privilege the notion that brown-skinned "fat" girls cannot achieve healthy, loving relationships since Sweetie becomes ultimately a doomed character. We are told that, having finally given up on her prospects for happiness, "Sweetie just up and died." Yet *no one* wins in this star-crossed tale.

After learning of Sweetie's death, John quits his job and leaves his yellow wife. He pines after the lover he once spurned and dismisses the fairer woman who suffers a loveless fate as a result. Walker's portrait of black love in the poem is troubling, to be sure. Still, she offers a powerful and all-too-familiar voiced testament to the uncertainty and insecurity of even the most heartfelt emotions and well-intentioned sentiments. If anything, Walker invites us to take inventory of our own lives and challenges us to reach for a higher, more complete love.

"Ballad of the Hoppy-Toad" is one of Walker's most highly performative poems if for no other reason than that it engages obvious lyrical and narrative qualities that warrant vocalization. Especially exemplary of the tradition of African American folktales, the composition combines humor, conjure and trickster motifs, and common idioms to posit an expressive shared vision. In fact, the piece borders on the fantastic, including detailed imagery and carnivalesque figures as a backdrop. These figures allow Walker to stage "new identities" where she "reclaims . . . [a] subjugated knowledge and [a] historical memory" regarding the workings of a spiritual realm within African American everyday life.[10] The poem foregrounds a familiar Walker theme, the supernatural interaction between "good" and "evil" forces, and emphasizes communal reverence for those powers. In highlighting the people behind those forces, Walker articulates a "radicalized black subjectivit[y]."[11]

The ballad opens with depictions of the absurd, foreshadowing a tale of otherworldly occurrences. To begin, the narrator goes to Market Street (under the pretense of washing clothes) just to witness the spectacle of the "Saturday crowd" as they go "stomping / Down the Johnny-jumping road." Certainly, that crowd does not fail to disappoint the speaker nor the reading/listening audience, for we are graced by the likes of "Sally Jones" who "come[s] running / With a razor at her throat" and by "Deacon's daughter" who is strangely "lurching / Like a drunken alley goat." The fact that such appearances seem habitual—that our narrator knows exactly where they will occur and that he deliberately seeks them out—suggests more than just a haphazard brush with the bizarre. Rather, it allows us, through him, to be spectators of and participants in what Walker indicates is the result of conjuring practices. The images prepare us to accept or, at least, to be party to the plot that is yet to unfold.

Indeed, our unsuspecting narrator receives a visit from Jim, the conjuring "goopher man." In his brilliant use of analogy, the speaker describes his encounter with Jim as "the biggest for my money / And the saddest for my throw"—ostensibly, the most troubling day of his life. The encounter with the goopher man results in a marked warning of "dust" and an "evil note" left on the speaker's doorstep. The image of the conjurer is not scary in the least. We view him rather as an eccentric old man. He is said to have had "a stovepipe hat and coat," a description that likens him to Abraham Lincoln. His portrayal adds to the outlandish and humorous posture of the piece. While Walker privileges the existence of conjuring, she also pokes fun at our personal fears.

As in "Molly Means," Walker counterbalances "evil" with "good." Just as there is a "goopher man," there is also a "goopher woman" working against him. Sis Avery is the first person to whom our speaker runs for help. After reporting the incident to her, he asks for her advice: "Root-worker's out to git me / What you reckon that there mean?" Again our poet employs linguistic patterns to emphasize the local color. By engaging her characters in conversation, Walker reifies the otherwise concealed cultural imperatives of their everyday experiences. Underlying the narrator's question is rather a request—nay, a plea—for the woman's help. Sis Avery assures him that she "knows just what will hex him / And that old goopher sack." The notion that she possesses the ability to cast a spell on the goopher man himself suggests that *she* is a very powerful woman.

Walker juxtaposes folk superstition, black religious practice, and a belief in "root work" to indicate their often simultaneous occurrence in African American folk custom. Using all of these prescribed methods, the speaker exhausts every possible means of getting rid of the goopher man. He "burn[s] . . . candles" and goes "to Church and pray[s]," but all to no avail. The narrator claims that he wishes not for Jim's demise, only for his "peace of mind / And [to] make that dog behave." We soon learn that it is the "good" conjuring that wins out in the end.

Sis Avery emerges as a major supernatural force with which to be reckoned, resulting in the goopher man's diminishing influence and his ultimate annihilation. While "[r]unning through the fields one day," the narrator spies a "[b]ig horse . . . stomping after" him. Sis Avery "grab[s] . . . [the] horse['s] mane" and "holler[s] . . . to that horse to 'Whoa!'" Says she, "I gotcha hoppy-toad." In that instant, Sis Avery takes hold of the strange yet sinister manifestation, the very source of goopher's strength. She single-handedly renames the animal "hoppy-toad," changing it from a mighty and dangerous beast to a meek and harmless amphibian. By shrinking the stallion, she instills fear into the once omnipotent goopher man who, scared for his own life, goes "running down the road."

Avery's next warning to our narrator proves her might and calls into question the equalizing nature of justice at work in the poem. As in "Molly Means," "good" eventually wins out over "evil" but in an equally questionable way. In essence, Sis Avery manipulates Jim's power and uses it to effect his own demise. One could argue that this is a far more morbid outcome than either the narrator originally desires for the conjurer or that Jim, the goopher man, ever intends for his victims. (We have no evidence of Jim's actual murder of anyone—only his haunting and physical torment of them.) Even the narrator holds no ill will toward Jim and openly admits, "Don't want to burn his picture / Don't want to dig his grave." But, Sis Avery obviously means to torture Jim. She plots to do away with him. Turning his horse into one of the lowest and most loathsome forms of living organisms is a scare tactic she uses to show the goopher man just what she could do to him. Here, we see her ego in force as Walker augments her character's influence.

As a consequence, Sis Avery proves to be far more unforgiving than the other two and enforces her own agenda. Revealing her wicked plan to the speaker she confesses, "I'm killing . . . this hoppy-toad / And you'll be rid of Jim." Understanding his fate to be intertwined with the toad's, the goopher man yells for her not to kill the animal. She replies forcefully and in her best idiom, "Honey, / You bout to lose your load." As the toad lay dying, the goopher man lay screaming for her to reverse her spell. The long, climactic, and agony-filled death scene alludes to the ruthlessness of Sis Avery's act and to our author's narrative prowess.

Walker succeeds in creating enthralling drama, delineating character parts that simply beg to be acted out. With one last shake, the hoppy-toad finally dies and the conjurer falls "dying, too." The goopher's last words, "O hoppy-toad," are a pathetic lament for their lives and for their untimely deaths, actuated in the name of revenge. Although the poem sanctions conjuring's downfall in favor of the narrator's fearlessness and safety, it testifies to the reality of a supernaturally endowed community within a larger society. Walker bequeaths to us a conjuring legacy, validating its presence. Out of her tale emerge legendary characters and one mystical yet unforgettable story.

Walker's "For My People" remains the quintessential discourse on the black experience. It has served as the manifesto for a disenfranchised race since its initial publication in *Poetry* magazine in 1937. A truly timeless and now signature piece, the poem is both a record of black history in the United States and a lyrical dedication to those people whose lives determined that history. Perhaps in more ways than all of the previously mentioned compositions, "For My People" calls attention to itself as an oral narrative because of its elegiac treatment of a population's tribulations and victories. In a tripartite examination, the poet-bard celebrates the bittersweet moments of African American life, advises her people against their own vices, and demands a change in world order.

Walker adopts a song motif in the poem, using it to gain metaphorical and structural advantage. Asserting at once that the piece is a devotional for blacks "everywhere singing their slave songs repeatedly," she establishes the *slave song* as a cultural denominator for tenacity in the face of personal danger, for the masking of suffering and sorrow, for the expression of joy, and for an unfailing belief and hope in the future—all qualities she cites as part and parcel of black cultural identity. She demonstrates the dual complexities of a people, singing "their dirges and their ditties and their blues and jubilees." She alludes to a delusive optimism as she witnesses them "praying their prayers nightly to an unknown god, bending their knees humbly to an unseen power." Walker literally chronicles time by moving us from one era to the next, symbolically taking us from the problematic beginnings of slavery, through the years of emancipation, and into the trying decades of Jim Crow and beyond.

The author ardently testifies to the hardships of those years. In a ceaseless enumeration, she confirms the relinquishing of physical, mental, and emotional "strength" in the name of survival. The poignancy of sacrifices are felt as she makes us privy to the back-breaking "washing ironing cooking scrubbing . . . plowing digging planting pruning" that they perform as significant and necessary labors of love. We understand the natural frustration and grow in awe of the discipline and drive of those who, in spite of their circumstances, continue "dragging along never gaining never reaping never knowing and never understanding." Although her people receive few tangible rewards, we are assured that the intrinsic value of their efforts will be felt for generations to come.

Walker shares some fond memories as well. Reminiscing about her own childhood, she makes those intimate moments of affectionate "play" representative of what she deems a communal upbringing: by telling the story of her humble beginnings, she tells everyone's. Recognizing her "playmates in the clay and dust and sand of Alabama backyards," she allows her audience to tap their inner innocence. Images of children "playing baptizing and preaching, and doctor and jail and . . . school and mama and . . . playhouse" litter the stanza. Those visions of "pretend" games impart a sense of naiveté.

As we watch those youngsters evolve, Walker brings the life lessons of the ensuing "cramped bewildered years" to the fore. She gives us a glimpse of systematic racism. It is in school where those adolescents "learn to know the reasons why and the answers to." It is also there that they "discover" their seeming insignificance and invisibility. It is institutional prejudice that teaches them that they are "black and poor and small and different" and that "nobody care[s] and nobody wonder[s] and nobody underst[an]d[s]." Undaunted, those "boys and girls" persevere.

Noting that they "grew in spite of these things to be man and woman," Walker shows the failure of her peers to be an ironic consequence of their happiness. It is true that her people go on "to laugh and dance and sing . . . and drink their . . . success." But, so too do they fall prey to their fruitfulness, become victims of their own pride and of a jealous world. Going about their daily lives, they "marry their playmates and bear children" and then "die of consumption and anemia and lynching." Walker seems to suggest, here, that theirs is a fated reality, despite the strides they make.

The poem's focus then discernibly shifts, panning out to include a more vast black perspective. Turning to the streets of Chicago, New York, and New Orleans for inspiration, it documents those familiar places and spaces the author's broader community inhabits. The blacks who "throng . . . 47th Street . . . and Lenox Avenue . . . and Rampart Street" are happy, we learn. Ironically, they are also "lost disinherited [and] dispossessed." Even though the poet implies that a bifurcated black existence results from the oscillation between life's various joys and pains, Walker adopts a tone of admonition toward her people, showing the inconsistencies of their actions. She chastises them for "filling the . . . taverns and other people's pockets" while "needing bread and shoes." The author reasons, on the other hand, that such behaviors are manifestations of a lack of basic necessities and of the unfulfillment of human desire. Beyond "needing . . . milk and land and money," she asserts a need for "something all our own."

Walker alleges a cause and effect relationship regarding the plight and social status of African Americans: she suggests that white oppression spawns black cultural decay. The "unseen creatures who tower . . . omnisciently and laugh" help to foster a "tied . . . and shackled" people who, admittedly, are also "tangled among [them]selves." Still, she holds her own accountable for their seeming frivolity, chiding them for "losing time being lazy." The poet warns her folk of their shortcomings while understanding that façades of complacency sometimes disguise "quiet desperation." Thus, their tendencies to "sleep . . . when hungry" and "drink . . . when hopeless" function as coping strategies to get them through the hard times.

Walker airs more "dirty laundry" by candidly criticizing black organizational structures. Recalling her earlier description of the generation as "lost," she challenges her contemporaries to cease their "blundering and groping and floundering" in order to forge a better life. She calls for them to cower no more behind "the dark of churches and schools and clubs and / societies," and to no longer be "distressed and . . . deceived" by their own iniquities. Hers is, too, a belligerent cry against and an open attack on bureaucratic and religious machinery that dupe the common citizenry. In essence, she calls for a radical racial awakening.

In that summons, the poet validates social consciousness as having always been the underlying mission of the struggle. Blacks, though "standing [and] staring"—not knowing in which direction to proceed, have fought to carve out a more tenable and hospitable living space. Their attempts "to fashion a world that will hold all the people . . . all the adams and eves and their countless generations" have been grounded on the premise that they are rightful inhabitants of the earth and as such already possess a predestined place in it. Walker contends that their fight concerns itself not with the issue of assimilation, rather it involves a revelation of dignity and humanity.

Finally, the poet reveals her proclamation of justice. With fervor, she announces: "Let a new earth rise. Let another world be born. Let a / bloody peace be written in the sky." She predicts that although a new society will perhaps be achieved through war, racial harmony will be the outcome. Her prophecy requires that her beloved embrace "a beauty full of healing and a strength of final clenching." At the poem's end, the once sad and grief-laden "dirges" of slavery to which Walker alludes in the opening stanza transform into the battle-cries of "martial songs." Realizing the social impact of such cultural combat, she implores a new "race of men," "a second generation full of courage" to "issue forth," ordering them ultimately to "rise and take control."

Walker's uncompromising look into the lives of her people sheds light on and renders understanding of their everyday experiences. She inscribes "For My People" with a collective and thus oral quality, making it representative of the black community as a whole. Perhaps that inscription of a voiced history is what enjoins countless others to consistently render the poem through dramatic speech. Walker herself marveled anecdotally at the poem's popularity as a performance piece. Recognizing the distinctively black oral intricacies of the poem, Richard Barksdale urges that "it must be read aloud; and, in reading it aloud, one must be able to breathe and pause, pause and breathe preacher-style." [12] Yet the poem's widespread appeal should come as no surprise. It is little wonder that a "people loving freedom" would articulate and sustain a composition that embraces an entire race and dares "to sing [their] songs."

As demonstrated by all of the preceding poems, Margaret Walker succeeds in continually deepening our perceptions of heritage through her writing of culture. Her poetry, in turn, breathes life into that heritage, inviting readers to stake personal claims in it. The poetry's inherent participatory inclinations undergird discussions, here, regarding its performability. Positing, most often, cultural notions of "blackness," the poems serve as self-gleaning and insightful enterprises in which all of Walker's various audiences can partake. Walker enlists those individuals to commune with her characters and with the events that mold their existences. Performance theorist Jill Dolan notes in her article, "Geographies of Learning: Theatre Studies, Performance, and the 'Performative,'" that these poems and resulting vocal renderings of them provide "occasions in which as a culture or society, we reflect upon and define ourselves, dramatize our collective myths and history . . . and eventually change in some ways while remaining the same in others." [13] Whether or not one chooses to articulate them, "Molly Means," "Poppa Chicken," "Long John Nelson and Sweetie Pie," "Ballad of the Hoppy-Toad," and "For My People" make available that opportunity. Through them, Margaret Walker captures her community's symbolic quest for expression and liberation. *Her* voice, though quieted now through death, emerges in her work, establishing her as the griot of African American culture and as the champion "for [her] people."

NOTES

1. All of the selected poems, except one, appear in Margaret Walker's first volume of poetry, *For My People* (1942). "Ballad of the Hoppy-Toad" appears in *Prophets for a New Day* (1970).

2. Richard K. Barksdale uses these terms to describe specifically the oral nature of Walker's poem "For My People." I use the terms to refer broadly to that same inherent quality in the works selected for this discussion. Barksdale further demonstrates an apparent orality in the entirety of Walker's corpus. See Richard K. Barksdale, "Margaret Walker: Folk Orature and Historical Prophecy," in *Black American Poets between Worlds*, ed. R. Baxter Miller (Knoxville: University of Tennessee Press, 1986), 106.

3. Jerry W. Ward Jr., "A Writer for Her People: An Interview with Dr. Margaret Walker Alexander," *Mississippi Quarterly: The Journal of Southern Culture* 41.4 (fall 1988): 515–27. The specific quote was taken from page 519.

4. The editors of *Call and Response: The Riverside Anthology of the African American Literary Tradition* categorize this ballad as such because of its heroine's invincible spirit and vast powers. See *Call and Response*, gen. ed. Patricia Liggins Hill (Boston: Houghton Mifflin, 1998), 1101.

5. Julius Lester, *Black Folktales* (New York: Grove Weidenfeld, 1969), viii.

6. Lester viii.

7. Benét categorizes Poppa Chicken as one of the folk-inspired and legendary Walker character types who garners his very own poetic "portrait." See Stephen Vincent Benét, foreword to *For My People*, by Margaret Walker (New Haven: Yale University Press, 1942), 6.

8. Benét 6.

9. James Weldon Johnson, preface to *God's Trombones* (New York: Penguin Group, 1927), 8.

10. bell hooks, "Performance Practice as a Site of Opposition," in *Let's Get It On: The Politics of Black Performance*, ed. Catherine Ugwu (Seattle: Bay Press, 1995), 200.

11. bell hooks contends that performance is a necessary act in recovering fundamental cultural understandings of African American identity; see "Performance Practice," 220.

12. Barksdale 106.

13. Jill Dolan, "Geographies of Learning: Theatre Studies, Performance, and the 'Performative,'" *Theatre Journal* 45.4 (Dec. 1993): 417–41.

The South in Margaret Walker's Poetry

Harbor and Sorrow Home

EKATERINI GEORGOUDAKI

In her July 9, 1986, interview with Lucy Freibert, Walker calls herself "a creature of the South" and a part of its nature: "When we come together I am complete and it is complete because it is a part of me and I am part of it." [1] She also states that in her works she contrasts "the ideal beauty of the land, the ambience of the South, and the horror of its violence and racial conflict," and she expresses the wish "to see the dichotomy closed, the split ended" (56). In her January 24, 1986, interview with Jerry Ward, Walker describes her sense of place and expresses the importance of Mississippi in her writing: "Mississippi is the epicenter of my life. . . . I have spent over half my lifetime now in Jackson, Mississippi. Mississippi spells for me all my roots gathered in one place." [2] Referring to her 1949 arrival in Jackson and her life there, she adds, "I put down roots here; I came to stay here; I looked at Jackson, Mississippi, like a harbor. After going from place to place and literally tossing on the sea of life, I put in at this harbor. And it has sometimes seemed like a dead-end street, that I'm going no farther. This is my place" (516). In the same interview, while talking about her visual imagination, Walker also admits that her "visual per-

164

ceptions began and were shaped by the Southern landscape," and that she has "had the feel of the South in [her] blood" since she was a child (519).

In Walker's comments quoted above, we notice her ambivalent attitude toward the South. On the one hand, she sees herself as an integral part of its natural environment, whose beauty fulfills her emotional, spiritual, and aesthetic needs. On the other hand, her experience of oneness with nature, her sense of security in the South ("harbor"), and her sense of belonging to the South ("roots," "epicenter") are constantly threatened by divisions (racial, class, and economic) in southern society that trap the poet ("dead-end street"). Walker expresses an ambivalent attitude toward the South (and a black person's place in the South) in her poems, employing various features of the southern landscape to serve her thematic, symbolic, and other aesthetic purposes.

Two poems, "Jackson, Mississippi" and "Birmingham," expound upon the ideas she presented in her 1986 interviews.[3] Although Walker in these poems uses a first-person speaker, it should be remembered that Walker's "I" is usually both personal and collective. In "Jackson, Mississippi" Walker defines the black American's paradoxical relationship with the South by presenting Jackson simultaneously as a "harbor" and as a "dead-end street" and "drain" on the speaker's energy. Moreover, she stresses black people's identification with, love for, and fear of the South, by connecting the images of "heart," "blood," "dust of . . . flesh" with "years of toil":

> I give you my heart, Southern City
> For you are my blood and dust of my flesh,
> You are the harbor of my ship of hope,
> The dead-end street of my life,
> And the long washed down drain of my youth's years of toil. (12)

In "Birmingham" Walker imaginatively re-creates the countryside in the Birmingham area. Through vivid and colorful images, she conveys its beauty: the setting sun resting "in a blue blaze of coal fire," the "red dust of mines / Sifting across somber sky," and the "Dusk dropping down shoulders of red hills" (14). In the second section of the poem, images of death replace those of life as the speaker announces that she is dead and buried. The third section affirms the speaker's ties with and love for the southern landscape ("soft warm clay") even in death. Despite the pain ("cross") that the region's "bitter" racial hate has caused her, she still considers the South her home:

> Call me home again to my coffin bed of soft warm clay.
> I cannot bear to rest in frozen wastes

Of a bitter cold and sleeting northern womb.
My life dies best on a southern cross
Carved out of rock with shooting stars to fire
The forge of bitter hate. (14)

In the excerpt quoted above, Walker contrasts black Americans' relationships with the South and the North by juxtaposing the images of "soft warm clay" (South) and "frozen wastes" (North). She thus conveys her concept of the North as a cold and confining place for southern blacks—the "womb" image probably symbolizes the inner cities (black ghettos).

Another kind of visual and thematic contrast, which is more obvious in "Jackson, Mississippi" than in "Birmingham," is the one between the human (urban) and the natural (wild as well as domesticated) world. In "Jackson, Mississippi" Walker juxtaposes the beautiful flowers (zinnias, poppies, petunias, etc.) and the trees decorating Jackson with the city's "closed doors and ketchup splattered floors," "barbed wire stockades," poor black people hauled "in garbage trucks / Fenced in by new white police billies," and "black alleys of filthy rendezvous" (12). What completes the picture of Jackson as an ugly, rotten, fragmented (i.e., a fallen) world is the catalog of nouns and adjectives describing its inhabitants, such as "demagogues," "squealers," "red-necked brothers of Hate Legions," "stooges and flunkeys, pimps and prostitutes, / Barflies and railroad-station freaks" (12).

There are several other poems in which Walker presents cities—southern and northern—as places of material, moral, and spiritual corruption. For example, in "Today" the speaker sings "of slum scabs on city faces, scrawny children scarred by bombs and dying of hunger . . . rotten houses falling on slowly decaying humanity."[4] In "Birmingham, 1963" she recalls the racial hate expressed in the city streets, and she refers to the pain of those confined in its jails and alleys.[5] In "Jackson State, May 15, 1970," she refers to the violence released against a black school, to the senseless wounding and killing of young people (*TMC* 178–79). In "Whores" she focuses on the "painted whores" walking the streets "like whole armies through the nights" and foretells their miserable end: "Perhaps one day they'll all die in the streets" (*FMP* 54). In "Memory" the speaker remembers the "wind-swept streets of cities" where black people, confined in "their squares of hate," are protesting against their poverty (*FMP* 56). In "Jeremiah" she weeps for the corrupted Atlanta while prophesying "the doom of a curse upon the land" and "the downfall on an accursed system" in it (*PND* 23); as Miller points out, the narrator in this poem is "conscious of both the fallen world and the apocalyptic one."[6] In "Disillusion for Flower Children of Long Ago" Walker combines biblical images and themes ("Armageddon," "the damned," "the kingdom" of God, etc.) with natural phenomena (such as tornadoes, whirlwinds, and floods) to prophesy the final damnation of "this City of Dis"—of the South for its iniquity and corruption. She admits her own loss of hope "for freedom, peace, and brotherhood" in the South (*TMC* 167–68).

Four of the seven poems included in *Farish Street* focus on urban nightlife. In "The Crystal Palace" the narrator recalls the elegance of the place where black people enjoyed a game of pool, music, and dancing (*TMC* 202), and in "Black Magic" she remembers the magic performed on Farish Street (207). In "The House of Prayer," however, she expresses her disapproval of black women's prostitution, which she calls "the shame of Farish / Street" (203). In "Small Black World" she again emphasizes black people's moral and spiritual deterioration: "Drunken, stoned, and crazy / slashing stabbing knives and razors cutting throats" (205). Thus, through her speakers' eyes, the poet presents the community of "bloody Farish Street" as a grave: "All our yearning, dreaming, hoping, loving, dying / All our lives are buried here" (205). As Walker admits in her interview with Claudia Tate, *This Is My Century* is "a complete indictment of our present-day society, our whole world. What's wrong with it is money, honey, money."[7]

Walker projects the decay of the human society in the South more effectively in poems in which she deals more openly with the racial problem. One of her major devices is the contrasting of images conveying natural beauty with images presenting human ugliness (physical, political, moral). Walker employs this device, for example, in three of the best-known poems from Walker's first book, *For My People:* "Southern Song," "Sorrow Home," and "Delta."[8] The speaker in "Southern Song" describes her feeling of oneness with the southern sun, with the rain-soaked southern earth. As Eugenia Collier correctly remarks, the sun symbol in "Southern Song" and other poems in *For My People* is associated with comfort, healing, fulfillment, hope, positive action, wholeness, and regeneration (504–5); the earth, womblike and sun-warmed, symbolizes healing and nourishment for spirit and body; and the water is a "life force, working with earth to produce nourishment and peace" (505).[9]

The vivid images in "Southern Song" (sun, land, brook, corn, grass, ducks, frogs, etc.) are employed to appeal to the readers' senses (sight, hearing, touch, and smell). Using a first-person speaker, free verse, long lines, rhythmic repetition, coordinating clauses, cataloging, and other stylistic devices, Walker celebrates the harmony of the individual and collective black self with the southern natural environment.[10] She suggests, however (in images of lynching and burning), that the violence brought by racial hatred threatens this harmony and the wholeness of the self.[11] The poem ends as the speaker asserts her desire to freely enjoy the oneness of the South with her body's "song" and with her individual self:

> I want my careless song to strike no minor key; no fiend to stand
> between my body's southern song—the fusion of the
> South, my body's song and me. (18) [12]

In "Sorrow Home" Walker uses parallels and contrasts to render more vivid black Americans' ambivalence toward the South. The poem's speaker—who asserts that she is part of the southern landscape and also a sower [13]—parallels the natural beauty of the South with that of her ancestral lands, Africa and Jamaica, by combining images of tropical trees and fruit with images of the southern landscape; [14] then she contrasts the natural beauty and fertility of the black homelands (in both Old and New Worlds) with the artificial, new-world city environment ("steam-heated flats," "subway in my ears, walled / in by steel and wood and brick far from the sky" [19]) and its racially fragmented society. She ends with a rhetorical question, thus forcing her readers to share responsibility for the racial violence that destroys black life and property and turns the South into a forbidden paradise, a "sorrow home" for blacks:

> O Southland, sorrow home, melody beating in my bone and
> blood! How long will the Klan of hate, the hounds
> and the chain gangs keep me from my own? (19)

Similarly, in the poem "Dark Blood," Walker's speaker juxtaposes the beauty and plenitude of the "old lands" that made her (images of "sugar sands and islands of fern and pearl, palm jungles and stretches of a never-ending sea," "hot lanes of Africa and Asia," etc. [FMP 15]) with the ugliness and deprivations ("littered streets / and the one-room shacks") of her present "home" (the American South). Additionally, in "Ballad for Phillis Wheatley," Walker contrasts Wheatley's "warm and soft and green" Africa with the cold, icy Boston of pale faces, "men with whips," and the auction block. [15]

In "Delta" Walker likewise compares the South's natural beauty with its social ugliness. The poem opens with the speaker's self-definition: "I am a child of the valley" (20). Although this fertile valley—the Mississippi Delta—looks like an Edenic garden ("cotton and cane and banana," "orange and plantain and cotton," and "wood fern and sour grass and wild onion" grow in it [21]), it's a garden produced and maintained by the hard labor of black farmers ("We with our blood have watered these fields" [23]); it is a garden which is forbidden to black people, for they live under conditions of socioeconomic exploitation and oppression: [16]

> We tend the crop and gather the harvest
> but not for ourselves do we labor,
> not for ourselves do we sweat and starve and spend. (21)[17]

The depiction of the Mississippi Delta as a white paradise and a black hell becomes more dramatic through the use of adjectives that describe its black inhabitants' marginal position and desperate psychological state:[18]

> O valley of my moaning brothers!
> Valley of my sorrowing sisters!
> Valley of lost forgotten men.
> O hunted desperate people
> stricken and silently submissive
> seeking yet sullen ones! (20–21)[19]

The entrapment of black Americans in an unjust socioeconomic system is further stressed through a cluster of mud images: blacks are "bound till death" to the valley (21), stuck in the "mud and muck and misery of lowlands" where "muddy water flows at our shanty door" (20).[20] Seeking comfort in nature, the speaker of the poem observes the "rivulets flow / . . . into one great river" that runs through towns, "swampy thickets," "smoky cities," and "fields of rice and marshes" (20). Yet, unlike the flowing river, her own course of life is fixed, and neither the city lights nor its music can lift the burden of oppression from her psyche:

> My heart bleeds for our fate.
> . . . .
> In cities a thousand red lamps glow,
> but the lights fail to stir me
> and the music cannot lift me
> and my despair only deepens with the wailing
> of a million voices strong. (20)

The only image in the poem which functions as the literal and symbolic opposite to the lowlands inhabited by "beaten and broken" people is that of the high "snow-capped" mountains—the pure, white snow and the sunlight reflected on it are in sharp contrast to the mud and the darkness of the valley (21). The mountains the valley people "dare not claim" (21) represent higher aspirations, the promise of a better life, and freedom from restrictions.[21] Walker ends the poem by reproducing the spectacle of a thunderstorm bursting above the valley in the early spring, to suggest the destructive but also the cleansing effects of rebellion (storm) against oppression ("floods over-whelm us," "a thundering sound in our ears," "the cannons boom in our brains" [22]).

Later in "Delta," the speaker of the poem justifies black people's rising up to claim the land they have cultivated for many generations. When "the storm begins" the valley people are "dazed" and "caught in the downpour," while "danger and death stalk the valley" in the form of "robbers and murderers" who "rape" it and attempt to displace the blacks (23); yet, as the speaker pro-phetically concludes, the uprising will finally be successful:

> Neither earth nor star nor water's host
> can sever us from our life to be
> for we are beyond your reach O mighty winnowing flail!
> infinite and free! (24)

Collier perceptively sums up the essence of the poem and the symbolic meaning of the opposed images of valley/mountain:

> "Delta" encompasses the essence of black myth in America. The valley depicts our traditional position as the most completely oppressed people in America; the mountains, snowcapped, are our aspiration for the ful-fillment of America's promise—ever before us but totally beyond our reach. Again, the rituals of toil and despair and regeneration affirm the myth. The message of the poem is that we have bought our stake in this nation with our labor, our torment, and our blood. And nothing, noth-ing, can separate us from what is ours. (503)

"Delta" is not the only poem in *For My People* that deals with the right of black Americans to reclaim what is rightfully theirs, to rise against injustice, and to create a new order of things. All these themes are present in "For My People," the opening poem of the volume. According to the poem's speaker, the new world that black people will fashion after uprising "will hold all the people, all the faces, all the adams and eves and their countless generations" (*FMP* 14); it will be like the world that emerged from the Deluge.[22] The poem ends with a militant tone, conveying Walker's political/religious/prophetic vi-sion, a vision that guides her later poetry as well:[23]

> Let a new earth rise. Let another world be born. Let a bloody
> peace be written in the sky. Let a second generation full of
> courage issue forth; let a people loving freedom come to
> growth. Let a beauty full of healing and a strength of final
> clenching be the pulsing in our spirits and our blood. Let

the martial songs be written, let the dirges disappear. Let a
race of men now rise and take control. (14)

A characteristic example from her later work *Prophets for a New Day* is the
poem "For Andy Goodman, Michael Schwerner, and James Chaney."[24] Dedicated to the three civil rights workers murdered in Mississippi by the KKK on
June 21, 1964, the poem illustrates how Walker's vision was empowered by the
black revolutionary spirit of the 1960s. Walker presents the three men's deaths
as part of the seasonal cycles and transformations of nature. The three lives are
compared to fallen "golden Autumn leaves" floating on a Mississippi stream
and finally merging with the "surging falls," while spring returns and new
leaves appear on the trees.[25] The images of the fallen leaves and the downward
moving stream suggest the three men's journey from life to death, from individual existence to union with the original source:

> Sunrise and sunset . . .
> Spring rain and winter window pane . . .
> I see the first leaves budding
> The green Spring returning
> I mark the falling
> of golden Autumn leaves
> and three lives floating down the quiet stream
> Till they come to the surging falls. (20)

The final stanzas of the poem celebrate the natural beauty of Mississippi untouched by human evil; they also reveal the speaker's grief over the three men's
premature deaths. As Miller suggests, her sadness and grief are intensified by
"the gentle suggestion of the trinity, the tragic flight of the bird, and the slow
but cyclical turning from spring to spring" (129). Like the "Mississippi bird of
sorrow," the "mourning dove / Bird of death singing in the swamp" (21), the
speaker mourns for the murder of the three freedom fighters.[26] By seeing their
death as part of the eternal natural cycle, however, she is finally able to transcend her pain and affirm her faith in love and life:

> The burned blossoms of the dogwood tree
> tremble in the Mississippi morning
> The wild call of the cardinal bird
> troubles the Mississippi morning
> I hear the morning singing
> larks, robins, and the mockingbird
> while the mourning dove

broods over the meadow
Summer leaf falls never turning brown

Deep in a Mississippi thicket
I hear that mourning dove
Bird of death singing in the swamp
Leaves of death floating in their watery grave

Three faces turn their ears and eyes
sensitive
intense
impassive
to see the solemn sky of summer
to hear the brooding cry
of the mourning dove

Mississippi bird of sorrow
O mourning bird of death
Sing their sorrow
Mourn their pain
And teach us death,
To love and live with them again! (20–21) [27]

"October Journey" is another poem in which Walker associates human movement in time and space with natural cycles and changes. Images of colors; verbs that convey change, growth, and continuity; adverbs that suggest slow motion; metaphors and similes; personifications; as well as the symbolic images of sun, earth, water, and vegetation all make "October Journey" one of Walker's most sensuous and passionate descriptions of the South and its seasonal transformations. The farmers' activities are described as being harmonious with nature:

Travelling southward earth changes from gray rock to green velvet.
Earth changes to red clay
with green grass growing brightly
with saffron skies of evening setting dully
with muddy rivers moving sluggishly.

In the early spring when the peach tree blooms
wearing a veil like a lavender haze
and the pear and plum in their bridal hair
gently snow their petals on earth's grassy bosom below
then the soughing breeze is soothing

and the world seems bathed in tenderness,
but in October
blossoms have long since fallen.
A few red apples hang on leafless boughs;
wind whips bushes briskly.
And where a blue stream sings cautiously
a barren land feeds hungrily.

An evil moon bleeds drops of death.
The earth burns brown.
Grass shrivels and dries to a yellowish mass.
Earth wears a dun-colored dress
like an old woman wooing the sun to be her lover,
be her sweetheart and her husband bound in one.
Farmers heap hay in stacks and bind corn in shocks
against the biting breath of frost. (12)

The speaker's inner journey to the world of her childhood parallels her homeward (i.e., southward) movement on the train. Familiar sights and smells, memories of social events, and mixed feelings emerge from her subconscious:

The train wheels hum, "I am going home, I am going home,
I am moving toward the South."
Soon cypress swamps and muskrat marshes
and black fields touched with cotton will appear.
I dream again of my childhood land
of a neighbor's yard with a redbud tree
the smell of pine for turpentine
an Easter dress, a Christmas eve
and winding roads from the top of a hill.
A music sings within my flesh
I feel the pulse within my throat
my heart fills up with hungry fear
while hills and flatlands stark and staring
before my dark eyes sad and haunting
appear and disappear. (12–13)[28]

By emphasizing the serene beauty of the South in the initial stanzas, Walker arouses the reader's expectations for the speaker's happy return to it. Yet, in the last stanza, she deflates these expectations:

Then when I touch this land again
the promise of a sun-lit hour dies.
The greenness of an apple seems
to dry and rot before my eyes.
The sullen winter rains
are tears of grief I cannot shed.
The windless days are static lives.
The clock runs down
timeless and still.
The days and nights turn hours to years
and water in a gutter marks the circle of another world
hating, resentful, and afraid,
stagnant, and green, and full of slimy things. (13)

The images of decay, stasis, stagnation, and pollution in the last stanza suggest that the evil (racial hatred) lurking in the southern garden of Eden destroys
America's promise of freedom, equal rights, and happiness to all its citizens. It
is obvious in "October Journey" that Walker sees the South as a "sorrow
home" for African Americans. In her poetry Walker exposes the gap between
the ideal and the real South as well as the painful psychic split that the region
has inflicted on black people. Yet, despite its richness of imagination and vision, Walker's poetry is ultimately unable to bridge this gap.

NOTES

1. Lucy M. Freibert, "Southern Song: An Interview with Margaret Walker," *Frontiers*
9.3 (1987), 56.
2. Jerry W. Ward Jr., "A Writer for Her People: An Interview with Dr. Margaret
Walker Alexander," *Mississippi Quarterly* 41.4 (fall 1988), 515.
3. "Jackson, Mississippi" and "Birmingham," in *Prophets for a New Day* (1970; Detroit: Broadside Press, 1989), 12–13, 14. The book title is abbreviated as *PND* in subsequent references.
4. "Today," in *For My People* (1942; Salem NH: Ayer Co., 1987), 28. The book title
appears abbreviated as *FMP* in further citations.
5. "Birmingham, 1963," in *This Is My Century: New and Collected Poems* (Athens:
University of Georgia Press, 1989), 177. In subsequent references the book title is abbreviated as *TMC*.
6. R. Baxter Miller, "The 'Intricate Design' of Margaret Walker: Literary and Biblical
Re-Creation in Southern History," in *Black American Poets Between Worlds, 1940–1960*,

ed. R. Baxter Miller (Knoxville: University of Tennessee Press, 1986), 130; B. Dilla Buckner, "Folkloric Elements in Margaret Walker's Poetry," *CLA Journal* 33.4 (June 1990), 375; and Arthur Davis, *From the Dark Tower* (Washington DC: Howard University Press, 1982), 185, praise Walker's superb use of biblical characters, images, rhythms, etc., in *PND*.

7. See Claudia Tate, ed., *Black Women Writers at Work* (New York: Continuum, 1983), 193. Walker has also written a poem in *TMC* titled "Money, Honey, Money" (186), in which the pursuit of money is presented as people's main concern—the persona reminds the readers of human mortality and the uselessness of money. Another poem in which Walker indicts the artificiality, paranoia, commercialism, and obsession with sex and violence prevailing in modern American society and projected through TV is "The Telly Boob-Tube on the Idiot Box" (*TMC* 180–81).

8. According to Sandi Russell, *Render Me My Song: African American Women Writers from Slavery to the Present* (New York: St. Martin's Press, 1990), 56, *For My People* "chronicles the history of blacks from rural slavery to city tenements," and in it Walker "speaks for all the suffering and joy that blacks have experienced in America." Davis underlines the strong protest elements (139) and the subdued strain of militancy in the book (183). According to Eugenia Collier, "Fields Watered with Blood: Myth and Ritual in the Poetry of Margaret Walker," in *Black Women Writers (1950–1980),* ed. Mari Evans (Garden City NY: Doubleday, Anchor, 1984), 506, the poems in *For My People* "emerge from centuries of African American myth and ritual" and reflect the writer's grounding in the black southern tradition. She calls *For My People* the "nucleus" and "hallmark" of Walker's works and "the quintessential example of myth and ritual shaped by artistic genius" (501).

9. In "People of Unrest" Walker also makes several references to the sun as a source of light, life, and comfort for "the people of unrest and sorrow" (*FMP* 27). Collier traces the three elemental symbols (sun, earth, water) in the racial memory of generations of black Americans, carried from both Africa and the period of slavery, "when nature, not Western technology, sustains life" (505).

10. Walker refers to the Bible as the model for the use of parallelism, cataloging, repetition, and internal rhyme, and to the training she received from her father in the use of rhetoric. In her opinion metaphor, simile, synecdoche, metonymy, and hyperbole are rhetorical devices necessary in poetry writing (Freibert 52).

11. Walker also refers to lynching in "We Have Been Believers" (*FMP* 16); "Today" (*FMP* 28); "Ode on the Occasion of the Inauguration of the Sixth President of Jackson State College," *October Journey* (Detroit: Broadside Press, 1973), 26; and "A Litany of Black History for Black People" (*TMC* 149). *October Journey* appears as *OJ* in subsequent references. Richard K. Barksdale, "Margaret Walker: Folk Orature and Historical Prophecy," in *Black American Poets Between Worlds, 1940–1960,* 115, points out the "contradiction between the South's languorous natural beauty and the ugliness of Black lynched bodies floating in muddy rivers or buried in soggy graves shaded by fragrant magnolias and stately live oaks." He considers "the juxtaposition of floral beauty and bloody violence" the greatest paradox in the South, especially in Mississippi.

12. Asked by Freibert whether there is a connection between the feminist statement "writing from the body" and her own reference to her "body's song" in "Southern Song," Walker explains that in both "Southern Song" and "Sorrow" she says, "in a very sensuous" way, that she is "a creature" of the South. She further explains that when she wrote the poem she was in cold Chicago and neither saw red clay nor grass, hay, and clover in bloom, nor smelt the earth after the rain. She, therefore, felt the need to write about the South (56). Talking to Ward about the influence of the southern landscape on her imagination, Walker refers to the southern climate as the "home" of her "very heart." She also mentions how impressed she was by the "steep hills of red clay" she first saw as a child while travelling on the train from Birmingham to Meridian and back (519).

13. "Lineage" is another poem in which the black woman is presented as sower. Through her persona Walker links her own experience as sower of poems/ideas with the role of her sturdy grandmothers as farmers:

> They followed plows and bent to toil.
> They moved through fields sowing seed.
> They touched earth and grain grew. (FMP 25)

In "Jackson, Mississippi" Walker also defines herself as a poet-sower who has planted her "seeds of dreams and visions and prophecies," and her "fantasies of freedom and of pride" "in the bosom" of Jackson families (PND 12).

14. Collier considers Walker's imaginative return to her ancestral places "a psychic journey into the mythic past" necessary for achieving wholeness by "reuniting with the fragmented self" (503).

15. The poem was added to October Journey when it was reprinted in This Is My Century (122–23).

16. "Childhood" also refers to the material poverty the blacks suffer from despite their hard labor: the "croppers' rotting shacks / with famine, terror, flood, and plague nearby," the "bitter land . . . washed away" in the "low cotton country," as well as to the poverty of the "red miners" coming down "red hills," "dyed with red dust" (FMP 53). "Ex-Slave," on the other hand, focuses on the life of intellectual and artistic poverty imposed on black people (poem added to FMP when reprinted in TMC [14]).

17. "We Have Been Believers" stresses again the racial exploitation and the indebtedness of the American nation to the black farmers' labor: "With our hands have we fed a people and out of our strength have they wrung the necessities of a nation" (FMP 16).

18. Walker creates more hellish images in "Prophets for a New Day," part 3, in which a bloodthirsty beast whose "mark is on the land" becomes the embodiment of black oppression. Barksdale calls it "the beast of racial hatred that roams the land" (116). The beast "devours" black defenders, crushes them "with a stone," drinks their blood "for wine," "cries out against liberty" and "humanity," etc. (PND 23). The poet contrasts its polluting presence with the "dignity of green valleys and high hills / . . . clean winds

blowing through our living" (23). In "Since 1619" there is also a reference to black people "living in hell for heaven," being "hated and hating" (*FMP* 26).

19. In "For My People" Walker also uses a catalog of adjectives that stress black people's oppression: "black and poor and small and different," "lost disinherited dispossessed," "tied and shackled and tangled" among themselves by the "unseen creatures" controlling their lives and laughing, "distressed and disturbed and deceived and devoured by money-hungry glory-craving leeches, preyed on by facile force of state and fad" (13–14).

20. We also find mud images in "For Andy Goodman, Michael Schwerner, and James Chaney." These images convey the social corruption in the South and its "mutilating hatred and . . . fear" that result in the murder of the three Civil Rights workers in Mississippi. The "young" and "tender" faces of the three men are "mirrored in the muddy stream of living," and their lives end in the "miry clay," the "muddy stream," and the "red misery" (*PND* 20).

21. Miller remarks that the second part of the poem (lines 36–78) "illustrates the restorative potential of nature," whose "dynamic fertility, the recleansed river . . . can clear the Southern ground of sickness, rape, starvation, and ignorance" (122).

22. Walker also uses the motif of rising in "Delta": "If only from this valley we might rise with song!" (*FMP* 21) and in "We Have Been Believers": "Now . . . the long-suffering arise, and our fists bleed / against the bars with a strange insistency" (17). In "The Struggle Staggers Us" the persona similarly justifies the necessity of the struggle "for bread, for pride, for simple dignity" (*FMP* 58).

23. Maulana Karenga, *Introduction to Black Studies* (Los Angeles: University of Sankore Press, 1989), 315, considers the poem a praise "to the life, struggle, adaptive vitality, durability, strength and achievement of Blacks," a "call for struggle and a new social order." Collier sees the last stanza as a "reverberating cry for redress" (501). Barksdale traces the roots of "the rhetorical power of the poem . . . the verbal arpeggios, the cascading adjectives, the rhythmic repetitions" in the "preacher-man rhetoric of the Black South" (105). He praises the oral quality of the poem, the ebb and flow of its intonation, and its verbal music as found in folk sermons (106). Davis lists the surge and roll, the rhythms and speech patterns, repetition, alliteration, and imagery among the elements that Walker has borrowed from black folk sermons and transformed into poetic language (181–82).

24. According to Barksdale, *Prophets for a New Day* "stands out as the premier poetic statement of the death-riddled decade of the 1960s" (114). Davis also considers *Prophets for a New Day* the best poems from the Civil Rights movement (185). In his own (185) and in Russell's view (58), the book captures the spirit of the period.

25. Walker celebrates the resurrection of nature and the human spirit every spring in "My Mississippi Spring" (*TMC* 146) through images of trees and flowers (forsythia, dogwood, magnolia, quince, jasmine, etc.).

26. Walker's solitary bird secluded in the swamp and singing mourning songs reminds us of the bird that sings death's carols for his lost mate in Whitman's "Out of

the Cradle Endlessly Rocking," and especially of the solitary thrush hidden in the swamp and singing dirges for Lincoln's murder in "When Lilacs Last in the Dooryard Bloom'd."

27. In the same poem, Walker's speaker defines the three men's killers as "The brutish and the brazen / without brain / without blessing / without beauty" (20).

28. According to Collier, "The poem is a journey into the mythic homeland" (508).

For My People

Notes on Visual Memory and Interpretation

JERRY W. WARD JR.

During the more than fifty years since the initial publication of Margaret Walker's *For My People*, the possibilities for reading and interpreting the texts of the poems have changed substantially. Literary and reading theorists and professional critics have embraced revolutionary definitions of "reading" and "texts," largely in response to changes both in the technologies of representation and in how one might conceptualize the "construction" (representation) of reality in the act of mediating signs. Should one compare, for example, the text of "For My People" in the 1942 Yale edition with its subsequent reprintings in various anthologies, in the 1968 Yale paperback edition, in *This Is My Century: New and Collected Poems* (1989), and in the presentation of the text in the Limited Editions Club version (1993), it is apparent that page arrangement, the size and design of type, and paper texture influence one's reception of the poem. The visual encounter may have a subtle or decisive impact on the decoding of the poem's verbal content; so too may the presence or absence of such paratextual matter as glosses, footnotes, photographs, and drawings have an impact on what we ultimately come to believe is the interpretation of the poem. Moreover, interpretation of "For My People" is complicated by a reader's historicity, by her or his particularized accumulation of knowledge and memories, and by the way the poem's imagery, assertions, articulations of desire for others, and imperatives complement or challenge ideological investments. In light of certain claims that have been made about the hegemony of the visual, it is profitable to speculate briefly on visual memory and interpretation with reference to the book and the poem that share a chartered space in the corpus of African American poetry.[1]

The span of New Critical reading strategies from such figures as I. A. Richards and Cleanth Brooks to postmodern models articulated by Roland Barthes, Wolfgang Iser, Harold Bloom and others provide a fascinating array of tools for interpreting Margaret Walker's poetry, but these should be aligned with the unfinished work of Black Aesthetic inquiry, womanist discourses, the expanding territories of cultural and racial critique, and the humanistic commentaries of Richard Barksdale and R. Baxter Miller.[2] These commentaries provoke special responses from those most likely to be descendants of Walker's people, warranting increased attention to what happens in their memories in reading. There is a need for a revival of interest in "what happens" as it was delineated in Norman N. Holland's *Poems in Persons: An Introduction to the Psychoanalysis of Literature,* with cultural knowledge playing a central role. The wealth of possibilities can be reduced to a paradox: as writing about the reading of texts becomes more interested in public implications, reading poems becomes a privatized responsibility to one's self as reader. In short, seeking to understand *For My People* involves a rich subjective investment, a processing dependent upon individual variables and whether the source of intertwined delight and instruction is accepted as "natural." The paradox by which the public is always the private marks a crossroad at which academic and common readers meet. As meaning-making subjects, both kinds of readers begin to expose how the significance of the book and the poem is influenced by their life histories (which often minimize the importance of their visual repositories).

The final two stanzas of "For My People" might be used to sample what a subjective reading might entail. The road to be taken away from the everyday, the confusion, hypocrisy, and misunderstanding evoked by stanzas one through eight has its beginning in recognition that you are one of the people. This recognition is deepened for readers familiar with the insights of Stephen Henderson's *Understanding the New Black Poetry* (1973). Henderson suggested in his introductory essay for this anthology that theme, structure, and saturation are critical categories in "an arbitrary scheme" (10). For the cultural reading I would test, Henderson's idea of structure (which includes black speech and music as poetic references) is to be held in tandem with his more problematic idea of saturation. Henderson defined saturation, in part, as "the communication of 'Blackness' and fidelity to the observed or intuited truth of the

Black Experience in the United States" (10). To escape metaphysical embarrassments, it is necessary to hold as a possibility (not an essential) that, at some level of reading, analysis of theme and structure and possession or lack of saturation do overlap. Cultural memory, especially its visual components, affects the nature of the overlapping and the significance "For My People" will obtain. If speech and music evoke memories, those memories do not remain abstract; we do not remember without the aid of inner vision or visual thought elicited by the poem (the printed text). The arbitrary comes into free play. For example, the phrase "all the adams and eves and their countless generations" may conjure up for one reader a religious painting of the Loss of Eden or one of the Last Judgment; another reader is drawn to recall an Afrocentric visualizing of the first parents; a third, Coca-Cola's television commercial of all the world singing in perfect harmony. What Walker's wording invites to the visual, interpreting foreground is as varied as the individual reader's memory. Just as readers must select carefully among an excess of motivating factors in literature to get the meaning "right," so too must they select out the most cogent items that occur in visual memory to secure a meaning. In this instance, you know not everything goes better with Coke (especially as the visual image is swiftly displaced by the verbal association of "coke" not with coal but crack and begets another visual image of people "never gaining never reaping" [Walker 13]).

Henderson's analysis marked a watershed moment in Black Aesthetic theory. It opened the space to academic readers who felt limited by prevailing critical prescriptions and needed to liberate themselves into a world that could hold all readings. Nonacademic readers of "For My People" may have been less traumatized about getting it (the interpretation) right; they may have interpreted in terms of vivid racial experiences about which Walker's words were indeed right. The critical intervention Henderson made for "a second generation full of courage" now makes it possible but not easier to speak of visual memory, especially in light of the stance he took against cultural amnesia, a condition from which culturally situated readings of *For My People* protect certain readers and leave others pondering Otherness.[3] Visual memory is unavoidably linked to racialized schema. The validity of giving more attention to the work of visual memory in the processing of literature is strengthened by how habits of cognition are being changed by computer technology.

The displacement of print by electronics has affected how we read quite as strongly as the persuasiveness of critical theory. The attractiveness of hypertext/hypermedia (linking of verbal discourse with visual and aural information) does invite, as George Landow writes in *Hypertext*, the exploration of "multiple reading paths, which shift the balance between reader and writer" (23). Of course, the slower but more complex mind and brain have their own forms of hypertextuality. We have just not applied it in reading as self-consciously as we might. Using visual memories or portions of our human hypertextuality can assist us in becoming more active in the meaning-making process.

As a culturally situated reader responds to individual poems in *For My People*, visual memories from lived experiences, from having viewed photographs, paintings, and drawings, from travel in cities and countries, and from daily visualizing can be willed into play. The poem "For My People" brings to mind a visual catalog: nineteenth-century paintings of "happy" banjo pluckers and dancers around the plantation cabin as well as Henry O. Tanner's "The Banjo Lesson"; twentieth-century photographs of people stomping at the Savoy and laboring in factories and lifting their voices in song to the Lord; visual recollections of streets in Chicago, New Orleans, New York; stored images of one's daily negotiations of others. It would not be strange for the poem "We Have Been Believers" to evoke particularly powerful images of lynchings. "Sorrow Home" may bring to the interpreting foreground a drawing of John Brown embracing a black child on his way to the gallows. "Southern Song" can force a recollection of photographs of ex-slaves that induce awe that an abused people could leave visual evidence that they had so much dignity and fortitude. The visual documentation that memory supplies to the interpretive process can be freely ranging if generated by individuals. But memory can be aided and channeled by another order of visual documentation, the supplements to memory provided by such a book as Roland Freeman's *Margaret Walker's "For My People": A Tribute.*[4]

Walker's 1942 book and Freeman's 1992 photo essay complement one another; Freeman's work is a resource that creates new and interesting tasks for interpretation. Freeman announces that his "photographs are meant to complement the tones, movements, colors, and ethos of the poems in *For My People* while countering the distorted perspectives of African American communities presented on television and in print" (n.p.). The distortion Freeman may have in mind concerns the unbalanced projection in mass media of African Americans as criminals, outlaws in greater and lesser degrees, as objects of entertainment. Three of Freeman's terms (tones, movements, colors) refer at once to the poems and to his black and white photographs, or to features of the photographs that participate dynamically in the interpretive work of his visual essay.

These terms set in motion a dual movement. The interpreter/observer's gaze is like a pendulum swinging between poems and photographs, poems and the additional visual memories evoked by the photography. The aesthetic response bifurcates as the response to the poems themselves is challenged and extended by the different orders of aesthetic response occasioned by the photographs. What occurs can be related to Freeman's fourth term (ethos), which brings to mind culturally specific and historicized values, the very values he bids us see represented in the poems and in his representational commentary on the poems. In that sense, both Walker's poems and Freeman's photo essay must speak to us, in Freeman's words, of beauty and tenacity in African American lives. These photographs reinforce the always present message in *For My People* that the death-orientation imaged in mass media is but one inflated thread in the whole fabric of African American life. The poems and the photographs speak for and to their people and humanity in general. They require exercising our visual powers and memory to make real for ourselves their affirmative properties.

Freeman's book sets forth new work for us as interpreters, for now the photographs, like our individualized visual memories, provoke a more complex engagement with Margaret Walker's poems. The photographs may be "read" and interpreted through the prism of Walker's poems. It is crucial to note that as objects that complement, Freeman's photographs do not lose their status as works of art. Prior to using them to amplify the imagistic and symbolic dimension of Walker's poetry, we attend to the composition, the tonal values, the subject matter, and the continuity and change that the photographs themselves document. The act of reading is heightened by reciprocity, and protocols have to be established that allow the integrity of poems and photographs as works of art to be honored.

Aware that the photographs constitute Freeman's interpretation of the poems in *For My People*, a reader is empowered to use visual documentation in a more organized way. Each photograph can be used rather as we employ critical essays on poetry to confirm or correct our initial impressions of how a poem means. Thus, the pleasure of a less systematic discovery (the pleasure of visual memory) is supplemented.

In the final poem of *For My People*, "The Struggle Staggers Us," two lines are especially germane to the interpretive dynamics under consideration: "There is a journey from the me to you. / There is a journey from the you to me" (58). Substitute for *me* a collection of poems and for *you* the photo essay. The act of interpretation then becomes a struggle that may indeed prove staggering. Interpretation is a back and forth journey between parts and wholes. In this instance, we find ourselves journeying between two texts and among three interpreting minds (Walker, Freeman, the reader). The journey locks us into valuing the reevaluation.

Walker's and Freeman's books, fifty years apart in creation and simultaneous in the demands they can make of us, render the task of reflecting and coming to know all the richer. Recognition that the task exists in our own histories affirms the worth of the undertaking. The main point is that neither reading, use of visual memory, nor interpretation occurs in an aesthetic vacuum, a region that is a combat zone in current critical discussions. What is represented in poetry and photography, these books remind us, cannot be neatly disentangled. The representations are contiguous. Meaning shifts "in a delicate and possibly indeterminable balance between creator, consumer, and occasionally subject. There are no boundaries, no strictly defined limits to meaning" (Edwards 5). Together, the books enable a more creative interpretation of cultural and historical moments. We gain an intensified awareness of dealing with the historicity of poetry and with the function of images as we chart our positions as readers and viewers and reviewers possessed of visual memory.

Whether the visual information comes from free association engendered by the poetic texts, from controlled association necessitated by the presence of the photographs, or from a different level of interpretive activity constituted by Elizabeth Catlett's lithographs in the Limited Editions Club version of "For My People," the reader finds herself or himself witnessing the necessity of art, the necessity in African American cultural space of Margaret Walker's poem and book.[5]

"Memory images," as Rudolph Arnheim asserted, "serve to identify, interpret, and supplement perception," in this case perception activated by the poems (84). Admittedly, visual memory is individualized, particular, defined by primary and secondary images one possesses or comes to possess from external stimuli. Visual memory is limited, too, by habits inculcated in those sectors of American culture or other cultures most familiar to the reader. To be honest, how much or how little comes forth in any given reading is not always predictable. Thus, claims about visual memory and understanding Margaret Walker's *For My People* remain items of speculation, not certainty. Giving them notice in our acts of interpretation secures our rediscovery of the historicity of poetry (its pastness and impact on our sense of the present) and our historical position as readers and viewers, standing always in need of interpretive resources. Increased awareness of how we use visual memory in the interpretation of literature reassures us of the permanence "For My People" has for us in the age of cyberspace.

NOTES

1. An especially useful collection of essays from which one might begin examining the vision-centered paradigm in interpretation of literature is David Michael Levin's

Modernity and the Hegemony of Vision. Some of the ideas about the possibility of using visual memory and visual artifacts in interpreting Margaret Walker's *For My People* are indebted to my reading of David H. Richter's *Falling into Theory: Conflicting Views of Reading Literature,* Elizabeth Edwards's *Anthropology and Photography,* Geneviève Fabre and Robert O'Meally's *History and Memory in African-American Culture,* and Kathleen McCormick's *The Culture of Reading and the Teaching of English.*

2. See Barksdale's "Margaret Walker: Folk Orature and Historical Prophecy," in Miller, *Black American Poets Between Worlds, 1940–1960,* 104–17; and Miller's "The 'Etched Flame' of Margaret Walker: Literary and Biblical Re-Creation in Southern History," in Killens and Ward, *Black Southern Voices,* 591–604.

3. See bell hooks, *Art on My Mind: Visual Politics* for an especially sobering discussion of racial inflections in the use of images.

4. The thirty-nine photographs and textual materials used in Freeman's book surround the poem "For My People." In his afterword, Freeman specifies that the photographs were chosen to "call to mind the special human elements evoked by Walker" and that the pictures also interpret "Walker's imagery and narratives" in the book *For My People* (n.p.).

5. The six lithographs Elizabeth Catlett created for this version of the poem are distributed in the following sequence: Stanza 1, Lithograph 1; Stanzas 2 and 3, Lithograph 2; Stanzas 4 and 5, Lithograph 3; Stanzas 6 and 7, Lithograph 4; Stanzas 8 and 9, Lithograph 5; Stanza 10, Lithograph 6. Catlett's stylized images of males and females and the use of color are exquisitely coordinated with keywords or phrases from the stanzas: singing, praying, dirges, ditties, blues, jubilees, playmates in the clay and dust and sand of Alabama, marrying their playmates, lynching, disinherited, dispossessed, happy, losing time, sleeping, shackled, tangled, all the people, all the faces, adams and eves, generation full of courage, clenching, marital song, rise and take control. The reader's awareness that the lithographs are immediately interpretive occasions a more directed use of visual memory than does the possible arbitrariness of the photographs.

It is not possible to communicate very precisely "what happens" with visual memories in the interpretations unless the reader is physically viewing the photographs and lithographs. The rewards of negotiating among the poem, the photographs, the lithographs, and one's visual memories are enormous. I highly recommend that anyone teaching Walker's poems encourage students to experiment with visual memories and the visual interpretations of Freeman and Catlett. ·

WORKS CITED

Arnheim, Rudolf. *Visual Thinking.* Berkeley: University of California Press, 1969.
Edwards, Elizabeth, ed. *Anthropology and Photography, 1860–1920.* New Haven: Yale University Press, 1992.
Fabre, Geneviève, and Robert O'Meally, eds. *History and Memory in African-American Culture.* New York: Oxford University Press, 1994.

Freeman, Roland L. *Margaret Walker's "For My People": A Tribute.* Jackson: University Press of Mississippi, 1992.

Henderson, Stephen. *Understanding the New Black Poetry: Black Speech and Black Music as Poetic References.* New York: William Morrow, 1973.

Holland, Norman N. *Poems in Persons: An Introduction to the Psychoanalysis of Literature.* New York: Norton, 1975.

hooks, bell. *Art on My Mind: Visual Politics.* New York: The New Press, 1995.

Killens, John Oliver, and Jerry W. Ward Jr., eds. *Black Southern Voices.* New York: Meridian, 1992.

Landow, George P. *Hypertext: The Convergence of Contemporary Critical Theory and Technology.* Baltimore: The Johns Hopkins University Press, 1992.

Levin, David Michael, ed. *Modernity and the Hegemony of Vision.* Berkeley: University of California Press, 1993.

McCormick, Kathleen. *The Culture of Reading and the Teaching of English.* New York: Manchester University Press, 1994.

Miller, R. Baxter, ed. *Black American Poets Between Worlds, 1940–1960.* Knoxville: University of Tennessee Press, 1986.

Richter, David H., ed. *Falling into Theory: Conflicting Views on Reading Literature.* Boston: Bedford Books of St. Martin's Press, 1994.

Walker, Margaret. *For My People.* New Haven: Yale University Press, 1942.

———. *For My People.* New York: The Limited Editions Club, 1992. Lithographs by Elizabeth Catlett.

———. *This Is My Century: New and Collected Poems.* Athens: University of Georgia Press, 1989.

Poet of History, Poet of Vision

A Review of This Is My Century

FLORENCE HOWE

In 1989 at the Graduate School of the City University of New York, Margaret Walker accepted the Feminist Press's annual literary award in honor of her "achievement as poet, novelist, critic and essayist; as teacher and fighter for human rights; and as a spirit of great empathy, compassion and understanding." The citation continued: "You came of age in a world not friendly to women or black people. You helped lead the way towards changing that world. You offer all of us, whatever our race, a vision of possibility. Without diminishing the pain of prejudice, conflict and war, you also see past the suffering and sorrow into a different dimension, into the moments or even the months and years of *Jubilee*." In *This Is My Century: New and Collected Poems*, Walker's spirit blazes through one hundred poems written during the past half-century, the early ones as powerful today as they were when *For My People* won the Yale Younger Poets Prize in 1942.

In a preface to that volume (included in this one), the poet Stephen Vincent Benét praised the early poems for their "straightforwardness, directness, reality," their "controlled intensity of emotion." "Out of deep feeling," he wrote, "Miss Walker has made living and passionate speech" of "deep sincerity . . . at times disquieting." Benét notes Walker's interest "in people"—many of her poems are dramatic monologues in which she catches the tones of unique and memorable "characters"—and he quotes directly three stanzas of the title poem of her first volume, "For My People." This poem, written in 1937, when she was twenty-two (all but one stanza in fifteen minutes, Walker tells us), captures not only that year and the breadlines in Chicago but also the slave songs of the previous century and the "bloody peace" of the rest of this one. The music of that poem rings hauntingly still, "the gone years and the now years and the maybe years":

> For my playmates in the clay and dust and sand of Alabama
>   backyards playing baptizing and preaching and doctor
>   and jail and soldier and school and mama and cooking
>   and playhouse and concert and store and hair and
>   Miss Choomby and company. . . .
> For my people standing staring trying to fashion a better way
>   from confusion, from hypocrisy and misunderstanding,
>   trying to fashion a world that will hold all the people,
>   all the faces, all the adams and eves and their countless
>   generations.

For My People. More than any other poet I can think of, Margaret Walker's first poem in her first volume strikes the note that persists through her half-century of writing poems. Walker herself says she has selected one hundred poems from the thousand she has written through this lifetime, but there are very few poems in this volume that one might call "personal." "Lineage," for example, the poem about "strong" grandmothers at plows, is about *all* the grandmothers, not simply about Walker's own. Only two poems, perhaps, are "personal" lyrics, the mysterious and beautiful "October Journey" that Walker glosses a bit for us in her own preface to this volume, and "Epitaph for My Father," one of my favorites among her long poems.

October, Walker tells us, is the month in which she met her husband, "and after thirty-seven years of our marriage he died in October." But the poem that anticipates both the joy of meeting and the pain of loss was written in 1943 "and expresses," Walker writes, "my emotions at that time."

I found most moving the elegy called "Epitaph for My Father," a poem in which Walker recalls her father's Jamaican roots, the pain of life for him as an immigrant in Jim Crow southern cities. She brings to life not only the family's dynamic (mother's caution about money; father's wanting to be generous), but one hurtful sentence she wishes she had not spoken to him, and a vision of how it might have been, given her view of him, had she been born male, not female:

I might have followed in his every step,
Had preached from pulpits, found my life as his
And wandered too, as he, an alien on the earth,
But female and feline I could not stand
Alone through love and hate and truth
And still remain my own. He was himself;
His own man all his life.
And I belong to all the people I have met;
Am part of them, am molded by the throng
Caught in the tide of compromise, and grown
Chameleon for camouflage. (105)

The image of a woman "grown / Chameleon" for survival in a white patriarchal world might suit many women of Walker's generation and mine. But it is also another way of saying that, if we search for the poet behind the poems in this volume, we need to study the people who fill its pages—from those sturdy grandmothers and their ancestral slaves to the little boy in 1963 who cried, "*Hurry up Lucille or we won't get arrested with our group.*" If we are searching for Margaret Walker, she is telling us, we need to find Phillis Wheatley and Harriet Tubman, Nat Turner and John Brown, Paul Laurence Dunbar and Robert Hayden and perhaps, more surprisingly, Freud, Kierkegaard, Einstein, as well as Du Bois.

When she says she "belong[s] to all the people I have met, / Am part of them, am molded by the throng," she is describing herself as a poet of history. For those who remember the Civil Rights movement of the 1960s, Walker's poems stir memories of the fearless children who ignored threats and attended Freedom Schools, of the sit-ins, of the demonstrations, and of the deaths— Medgar Evers, the children of Birmingham, Andy Goodman, Michael Schwerner and James Chaney, Malcolm X, Martin Luther King. Much of this poetry is inspirational, celebrating, often in elegies, the heroism of people who stood for human—not national or racial—dignity. It is not that Walker ignores race; the poems more often than not speak to "the color line." Rather, she speaks to it and beyond, perhaps because of that visionary quality her poetry has had from the first. Walker is the least sectarian Christian I can name. Steeped, she tells us, not only in the Bible but in the "wisdom literature of the East," she values the lessons of the past, especially when they offer evidence of the human energy for spiritual as well as material survival.

Ultimately, then, as a poet of history, she is a poet of vision, of the flow of past not only into present, but of a reach into the future. The seven new poems called "Farish Street" that close the volume focus with camera-like intensity on the southern street, its shop and people, and, at the same time, recall an ancestral African village, the "Root doctor, Hoodoo man" then and now. And in the final poem of the series, "The Labyrinth of Life," Walker presents herself as "traveler," looking down the road "to the glory of the morning of all life." But the poems that precede this final group remind us of the terrible world still needing mending: "On Police Brutality," "Money, Honey, Money," "Power to the People," "They Have Put Us on Hold," "Inflation Blues"—the titles themselves a litany of troubles for all the have-nots, all the powerless who would have space to live.

In the final poem of this section, "Fanfare, Coda, and Finale," Walker returns to the form of "For My People," only the rhythm is muted, slowed to a dirge:

> I buy bread of bitterness everyday in the markets of the world.
> 　　Peace and plenty are never my share; every day I go hungry.
> 　　Everyday I walk in fear, and no one seems to care. . . .
> Out of my struggle I have sung my song; found hymn and flower
> 　　in field and fort and dungeon cell. Yet now I have constriction
> 　　in my heart where song is born. Such bitterness is eating at
> 　　my vocal chords the bells within me, hushed, refuse to ring.
> 　　Oh lift this weight of brick and stone against my neck, and
> 　　let me sing.

How to conclude? Of all the poems in the collection, the one that speaks to me most personally and urgently today comes from the 1942 volume, which I first read twenty years ago. In 1990, even the title, "The Struggle Staggers Us," overwhelms. For those of us who have lived through three (or more) decades of change know that we are only at the beginning (or at best in the middle) of much more to come. This 1942 poem speaks with immediacy not only to the contemporary women's movement, so interested as it is in "difference," but to a world that needs to solve the problems of poverty if it is ever to have racial and ethnic harmony inside nations and among them.

Walker tells us that being born and dying, like eating, drinking, and sleeping, are "easy hours":

> 　　The struggle staggers us
> 　　for bread, for pride, for simple dignity.
> 　　And this is more than fighting to exist;
> 　　more than revolt and war and human odds.

For persons are involved, individuals and their behavior that cannot be legislated:

> There is a journey from the me to you.
> There is a journey from the you to me.
> A union of the two strange worlds must be.

"Struggle," Walker concludes, "marks our years" of present and future. Amen, Margaret Walker, amen.

PART THREE

Jubilee: Folklore, History, and Vyry's Voice

I am a griot . . . the result of a long tradition. We griots
are depositories of the knowledge of the past. . . .
We are . . . the Memory of mankind.
　　—*The Epic of Sundiata: A Tale of Old Mali*

My grandmothers are full of memories.
　　—MARGARET WALKER, "Lineage"

Music as Theme

The Blues Mode in the Works of Margaret Walker

ELEANOR TRAYLOR

At the Pigfoot, a small nightclub that sits in the cove connecting
northeast Twentieth Street with the wide boulevard that is Rhode Island Avenue just five minutes from sleek, fashionable northwest Washington, D.C., the
bluesman Bill Harris, who is also the proprietor, treks ceremoniously to the
small bandstand shouting,

> Blues ain't noothin'
> Blues ain't noothin'
> Blues ain't noothin'
> but a po' man's heart disease.

The set begins. The drummer and the bassman taking their cue glide into the
bluesman's guitar as the ensemble begins its definition:

> Blues is happy
> Blues is sad
> Sometimes it makes you feel good
> Then again it makes you feel bad . . .
> Blueeeees ain't nothin'

Abruptly, the definition halts; the bluesman leans into the microphone almost whispering, "This is for the children of Atlanta." Then, without instruments (acoustical or electronic, though the bandstand is equipped with both), employing only the mighty, myriad majesty of voice, honed through time by apprenticeship, the bluesman intones, "I am a po' pilgrim of sorrow."

The spiritual combines with the blues and the field holler; they are one. They mix and meld within the same calabash. In the man's voice, a legacy of two centuries of singing, of verse, of tale telling, of ceremony, of ways of making and performing and hearing and seeing and feeling and presenting a view of the world, resounds. Like the perspective of the ancient griot in *The Epic of Sundiata* and like that of the self-emancipated chroniclers of the slave narratives, the insistent *I* of the bluesman's song, the first-person account of experience, defines its being within the context of an implicit *We* that without the *I* would have no meaning, no voice, no address.

"Adrift in this wide world, alone."

The bluesman's song has awakened within me other voices. From thoughts of the children, "I plunge down a well of years."[1] I hear other voices in the bluesman's voice. I hear the voice of Douglass: "They would make the dense old woods for miles around reverberate with their songs. . . . They would compose and sing as they went along. . . . They would sometimes sing the most pathetic sentiment in the most rapturous tone, and the most rapturous sentiment in the most pathetic tone."[2] I hear the voice of Toomer: "An everlasting song, a singing tree, caroling softly."[3] I hear the voice of Wright: "Blues, spirituals, and folk tales recounted from mouth to mouth . . . all these formed the channels through which the racial wisdom flowed."[4] I hear Ellison: "The blues is an art of ambiguity, an assertion of the irrepressibly human over all circumstances whether created by others or by one's own human failing."[5] I hear Baldwin: "The blues sum up the universal challenge, the universal hope, the universal fear. . . . They contain the toughness that manages to make this experience articulate."[6] I hear Zora Hurston: "I, who am borne away to become an orphan, carry my parents with me. . . . So he groaned aloud in the ship and bid his drum and laughed."[7] I hear Langston Hughes: "But softly / As the tune comes from his throat / Trouble / Mellows to a golden note."[8]

The bluesman's song has shifted; he begins to chart a familiar course: "From Natchez to Mobile / From Memphis to St. Joe." And, as he travels that real and mythical highway, calling out its eternal challenge, something very ancient is born anew, resilient and tough; something hugely public becomes acutely personal—in the Pigfoot.

Music as schema or as significant reference distinguishes one major tradition in Afro-American narrative and fiction. The chordal progressions (tonic, subdominant, dominant, tonic) of the sacred and secular songs of the slaves, their lyrical juxtapositions, their arrangement of anguish and exultation, have furnished an index for the writer, should furnish an index for a richer reading of the text. The oracular, evocative, incantatory, elliptical songs of African American oral literature form a base of traditional reference: the blues mode of Afro-American narrative. Those songs have served Afro-American narrators and novelists as an ancestral touchstone. For Equiano and Du Bois, the songs are masks that codify a façade and ensure interior cohesion; for Martin R. Delaney and William Wells Brown, the songs are shapers of sensibility; for Frederick Douglass and James Baldwin, the songs are racial experience; for Langston Hughes, Richard Wright, Arna Bontemps, Maya Angelou, and Amiri Baraka, the songs are the voice of the race; for Jean Toomer, Zora Neale Hurston, Ralph Ellison, Albert Murray, and Ishmael Reed, they are *mythos,* traditional form, or mythopoetic method; and for Toni Cade Bambara and Margaret Walker, they are theory of creation and method of transmission.

Music is the leitmotif of Margaret Walker's *Jubilee.* The celebrant of the novel is a singer. Her songs articulate stages in her life; they amplify its meaning. Through her songs, the personal history of Vyry, Elvira Ware Brown, central dramatic figure, actual maternal great-grandmother of the author, merges with the history of a community, a time, a place, a space—a mythical zone—within the history of world story. Vyry, "adrift" as in a "wide world alone," is a unique wayfarer whose journey, as charted in the bluesman's song, is a series of new beginnings. Her rhythmic movement through experience is not the movement of the ritual tragic hero: she does not topple from the heights of a social order and die in affirmation of a value. Nor does she muddle through the comic hero's bumbling acquiescence to the social norm. Hers is not the movement of the epic conqueror who requires an army. She cannot rid the land of the corruption of the fruitful. Elvira's is no sentimental journey. Neither does her rhythmic progress lead her to the Mount of Sisyphus; her end is not perception through ultimate isolation. Not the existential consummation, her movement through time is a continual process of dissolution, absorption, conversion, and realignment. She locates within her personal experience the public experience of the tribe. She harnesses the dislocations, the rifts, the shards of experience, and makes of them a whole appropriate to the moment. To forge a harmonious coexistence of polarities in experience appropriate to the moment, like the strategy of the bluesman's song whose tale of woe controlled by form invites the world to dance, is the rhythmic motion, the consummation of the model heroine of the blues.[9]

Vyry's history begins in dissolution. "Midnight came and thirteen people waited for death" (13).[10] Among them, attending the death of her mother, Hetta, "the child Vyry stirred in the arms of the old black crone, Mammy Sukey" (13). As we enter the world of *Jubilee* at midnight, we encounter a mourning ceremony suffused in music. It is the music of transition *in tempo large:* "Swing low Sweet Chariot / Coming for to carry me home" (1). We have plunged down a well of years. We have entered the world of the slave quarter twenty years before the Civil War. That world, visible only through memory, is a matter of historical document, yet its meaning is a matter of song, lore, legend, myth, and great story. That world is as familiar as yesterday, as immediate as the present moment, forever new by way of ancestry; and yet its essence is never so palpable as when recalled by the griot's song or tale. The world evoked in *Jubilee* is poised amid polarities as extreme as night and day. It is

> a most unaccessible section of
> Georgia deep in the forest, miles
> from cities and impossible distances
> to travel on foot . . . from the
> live oak trees hung the weird
> gray veils of Spanish moss waving
> wildly in the wind, and trailing
> like gray tresses of an old
> woman's hair lost from the
> head of some ghost in the wilderness. (24)

Lost from the head of some ghost in the wilderness. The image inspires meditation. This wilderness world that we have entered, no Edenic paradise of equity and harmony, no Arcadian bower of simple, rustic joy, harbors some hovering, infusing, engendering spirit. The "ghost" of some antecedent world, its wholeness shattered, resides within the world of *Jubilee.* Here, deep within this womb of wilderness, Hetta, twenty-nine-year-old mother of Vyry and fourteen others—"all single births" (15)—lies dying, shattered by childbirth. Her mourners keep custom outside her cabin: the child Vyry and the old nurse and Brother Ezekiel, the preacher, "you could read and write but the white folks did not know this" (9), and Aunt Sally and Jake and May Liza and Lucy and Grandpa Tom and the others of the quarter. They have heard the screech of "the squinch owl" at twilight; they know it to be the very sign of death. They wait while "the black pot boiled, and the full moon rode the clouds high in the heavens and straight up over their heads" (13). Inside the cabin, John Morris Dutton, master of the Big House, visits Hetta for the last time:

> He remembered how she had looked growing up
> long-legged like a wild colt and
> just that temperamental. She looked
> like some African queen from the Congo. . . .
>   She must have imagined herself,
> he thought . . . among palms and waterfalls
> with gold rings coiled around her neck. (7)

Vyry is one of the fifteen children of John Morris Dutton begotten of Hetta, for "miscegenation was no sin to Marse John. It was an accepted fact of his world" (9). Now Hetta, "the African queen," broken by childbirth, lies dying as her mourners keep custom outside her cabin, awaiting "that changing hour" (14) when Sis Hetta breathes her last. It is Brother Ezekiel, master of word and song, who begins the death chant: "Soon one mornin' / Death come knockin' at my door" (14).

This music of transition moves us toward the primal, the timeless, the cosmic. It seems to tell, like an ancient Yoruba myth, the story of the creation of the world. That story is a tale of dissolution and of realignment like the story told in *Jubilee:*

> Once, there was only the solitary being,
> the primogenitor of God and man *[Orisa-nla],*
> attended only by his slave, Attunda . . . the
> slave rebelled . . . he rolled a huge boulder
> on to the God as he tended his garden on a
> hillside, sent him hurtling into the abyss
> in a thousand and one fragments.[11]

The fragmentation of original wholeness becomes the raw material of creation, each shard of original wholeness containing the essence of *Orisanla,* contained in three Orisha, principles of existence: Obatala, Ogun, and Shango. Within Obatala "is stored those virtues of social and individual accommodation: patience, suffering, peaceableness, all of the imperatives of harmony in the universe." Obatala, one essence of original wholeness, *is the will toward wholeness* without which coherent creation cannot be. In simultaneous opposition and conjunction with Obatala is Ogun, "master craftsman and artist, farmer and warrior, essence of destruction and creativity, a recluse." He is "'Lord of the road' of Ifa [oracle of accumulated racial wisdom]; that is, he opens the way to the heart of Ifa's wisdom, thus representing the knowledge-seeking instinct which sets him apart as the only deity who 'sought the way.'" Ogun—who harnesses "the resources of science to hack a passage through primordial chaos," who dares "the abyss of transition," absorbing the rift between man and God, between wholeness and fragmentation—forges new wholeness. Without Ogun, the conversion of experience into new possibilities of wholeness cannot be. Mediating the *will toward wholeness* and the enabling force of coherence is Shango, "the awesome essence of justice . . . ordeal, and survival." Shango, the anthropomorphic essence of *Orisanla*, "the need to assert the communal will for a harmonious existence," is also the will of God to unite with man and man with God, ending the existential isolation of both. Shango is the spirit of racial renewal, the regenerative force of nature and of man. *Lost from the head of some ghost in the wilderness.* The image, like the songs of the slaves, is a central description of the world of *Jubilee*—a haunted world where ghosts of antecedent worlds, fragmented from a former whole, attend a rite— both macabre and life-sustaining—of dissolution and realignment.[12]

Absorbing disparities of experience in this haunted wilderness—the antebellum South that becomes a battlefield of Civil War and a stage of Reconstruction—the child, Vyry, orphaned of her mother, disinherited of her father, becomes a woman. The story of *Jubilee* is the tale of Vyry's growth, which, like the journey charted in the bluesman's song, is a paradigm of life. "Here in the stillness of the forest . . . cut off from reality and lost in a fantastic world of jungle" (29), Vyry must assimilate two cultural traditions: that of the slave quarter and that of the Big House.

In the slave quarter, Vyry learns that "us colored folks knows what he knows now fore us came here from [*sic*] Africa and that wisdom be your business" (45). She learns, from Brother Ezekiel, "the funny stories about the spider and the cat, the wise donkey and the silly man" (48); she learns the games that the slave children play:

> Las' night, night before,
> twenty-four robbers at my door,
> I got up and let them in,
> Hit 'em on the head with a rolling pin.
> All hid? (44)

She learns, from Mammy Sukey, the midwife, the uses of herbs: poke sallet, barefoot root, cherry root, Jerusalem oats, tansy, red shank, alum stones, Samson snake, Jimson weeds, elderberry, and John the Conqueror (83–84). She learns from the elders of the quarter the mask that language assumes in riddles, in proverbs, in the sayings of the wise: "Talk had feet and could walk and gossip had wings and could fly" (80). And by the time Vyry travels "down the Big Road toward the Big House," her "alto voice . . . still timid and small . . . promised to be as rich and dark as Aunt Sally's" (33). For "Vyry always loved to hear her sing, but the songs often puzzled her before she grew to associate them with Aunt Sally's mood and mind, her anger and resentment that she could voice in no other way. But some of the songs were frightening. They made Vyry want to cry . . . [yet] the melody always poured out sweet and strong" (60). But at the meetings "held deep in the swampy woods . . . at The Rising Glory Church . . . a long way from the Big House . . . there was wonderful and high-spirited singing such as Vyry remembered long afterward . . . and she tried to sing the songs they sang" (37). Moreover, "For a long time Vyry did not understand that these meetings served a double purpose. She enjoyed hearing Brother Ezekiel preach, and most of all she enjoyed joining in the singing. . . . Aunt Sally made her solemnly promise under the terrible threat of never taking her again, never to repeat to anyone what she heard at the Rising Glory Church" (39).

At the Big House, by the time she is ten, Vyry assists Aunt Sally, the plantation cook. She learns "how to put the milk in the crocks, how to separate the heavy cream from the milk, make cottage cheese and clabber, and how to add warm water when you were in a hurry to make the butter come fast" (34). And she learns how to make "beaten biscuits and spoon bread, fried chicken, hot waffles and light bread, light puddings, fruit duffs . . . huckleberry pies, roast turkeys and geese, and the wild game and bird pies" (35). But learning in the Big House is not confined to the kitchen, for "Big Missy . . . loved company and liked nothing better, as Aunt Sally said, than, 'putting on airs' . . . she had been to the manor born and came from the elite of Savannah. Living here in the backwoods of Georgia had been a sore trial" (61). At the galas of the Big House, "Vyry caught snatches of conversation. What she did not hear, the other servants heard and rehashed afterwards in the kitchen and the cabins" (63). The guests "discussed the news and the crops and the weather, their slaves, and the politics of the country, the state, and the nation" (63). In this way, Vyry learns of "those confounded idiots and abolitionists . . . trying to make a different Constitution out of the document written by Jefferson and Hamilton," destroying "our sacred way of life, our agricultural system, [and] classic culture, with the natural divisions of mankind into servile and genteel races" (66).

The Big House, ostensible seat of government in *Jubilee*'s world, is a haunted manor—an apparition of an antecedent world. Like a "feudal medieval castle" lost in time (29), it intrudes upon present time a form inappropriate to the moment. The House of John Morris Dutton, his wife, Salina, his acknowledged heirs, Johnny and Lillian, his unacknowledged heirs, Vyry and fourteen others born of Hetta, is a house divided—torn between contradictions in experience that it cannot absorb. At the Big House, Vyry is silent witness of discussions revealing the major tensions of her time, nineteenth-century America. Those tensions—oppositions between past and present, Europe and Africa, Europe and America, equality and inequality, privilege and serfdom, aristocrat and democrat, Confederacy and Union, nationalism and regionalism, Republicanism and Federalism, conflicting concepts of tradition, conflicting concepts of progress, agrarian economy and industrial corporation, acquisitive economics and inherited wealth—precipitate civil war: the rite of dissolution in the world of *Jubilee*. The Big House is *Lost from the head of some ghost*—an antecedent world no longer useful in time, unable to resolve the play of contrary oppositions—*in the wilderness*.

On the other hand, the quarter, ostensible place of the governed in the world of *Jubilee*, routinely absorbs tensions and invents methods of converting contrary oppositions into new possibilities of wholeness:

> Sometimes I'm tossed and driven, Lord
> Sometimes I don't know what to do
> I've heard of a city called heaven
> I'm tryin' to make it my home. (48)

Sung by Brother Ezekiel, "a singing and preaching man," always alone except when holding meetings not to be revealed at the Big House or by Aunt Sally, whose moods dictate her meanings, the "heaven" of the song is hardly metaphysical. For imagining new possibilities of wholeness *in terram*, which the song implies but masks, is both a tendency and a necessity in the quarter surrounding the Big House of the wilderness. Further, the songs, a consummation of contrary opposites, are both formally and semantically a union of indigenous materials (those native to the articulating sensibility) and foreign influences (those of the Big House). Moreover, the songs, the first utterance of the African Voice in the New World, are also the earliest and sole folkloric and mythopoetic offerings in music and in poetry of the region whose felt life they articulate. In *Jubilee*, the songs of the quarter are objective analogues of Vyry's growth, itself an analogue of the growth of a people cut off from a former whole—"adrift in this wide world alone."

Vyry's movement through time as she absorbs experience impels her to convert experience into new possibilities of wholeness. On one hand, the progressive stages in her life are as *natural* as the movement of the seasons: "Spring was the beginning, like the first blush of a budding rose. Summer was the fulfillment, the ripening of perfect fruit and the opening of the full-blown flower" (89). Thus, as Vyry's girlhood blossoms into womanhood in her sixteenth year, she replaces Aunt Sally as cook in the Big House. Vyry has also learned the meaning of Aunt Sally's songs, which had often puzzled her: "She began to unburden herself as Aunt Sally had by lifting her voice in song. She was surprised to hear the dark rich voice of Aunt Sally come out of her throat" (125). Vyry's language takes on the mask and wit of the masters of word and song in the quarter: "Don't pay no tenshun to what the guinea hen say / cause the guinea hen cackle before she lay" (129). And by the time she is twenty, she has become as fine an herbalist and midwife as was Mammy Sukey. "First make a fire in the kitchen stove and git the house real hot. Put a pot of water in each eye so it'll git hot fast, and build up this fire too . . . just mind you do like I say and we'll be all right" (296).

Vyry extends the experiences of the masters of the quarter, for she, unlike Aunt Sally, outlives the initial bondage of their wilderness world. By the time Vyry is seventeen, she is "troubled with strange emotions. She could not get the black face of the free man out of her mind. She still felt the casual touch of his hand on her arm. Above all she was fascinated with his talk of freedom" (78). Beyond the reach of Mammy Sukey and Aunt Sally and Grandpa Tom but not beyond that of Brother Ezekiel and Lucy and May Liza and Caroline, the fact of freedom—the advent of a new life—is the challenge of Vyry's world: "Now the idea of being free began to take hold of her and to work up and down and pass through her like milk churning to make butter. All day long she thought of nothing but Randall Ware. At night she dreamed confused dreams in which she struggled to be free while something struggled against her to keep her in chains" (79). The *natural* force that moves the womanhood of Vyry is love—the love of Randall Ware, free blacksmith. For Vyry, he is forger of the way to freedom, the Ogun of the abyss of transition.

And yet Vyry's movement through time requires her to confront *tainted nature:* "Bedlam broke loose. Black children screamed and cried; women fainted, but on the faces of some of the men and boys there was an unnatural look, neither human nor sane, a look of pleasurable excitement, a naked look of thrills born of cruel terror" (103–4). There is, in the wilderness world where Vyry comes of age, a *nature hostile* to the cyclic rhythms of human growth; it stunts or maims or kills the fruitful thing:

> He took the whip in his hands. It was a raw-hide coach-whip used to spur the horses. He twirled it up high over his head, and when he came down with it he wrapped it all the way around her body and cut neatly into her breast and across her back all at the same time with one motion while the whip was a-singing in the air. It cut the air and her flesh and cried "Zing" and Vyry saw stars that were red and black and silver, and there were a thousand of those stars in the midnight sky and her head felt as if it would split open and the whip cut her like a red-hot poke iron or a knife that was razor sharp and cut both ways. . . . It hurt so badly

she felt as if her flesh were a single molten flame, and before she could catch her breath and brace herself again, he had wrapped the whip around her the second time. . . . She thought she heard a roaring noise like thunder rumbling and a forest of trees falling in a flood. . . . She was whirling around in a cutting, fiery wind while the fire was burning her flesh like a tormenting fever and she kept sinking down. (143–44)

Sinking down, as though to plunge again through primordial time, there to suffer deluge, disintegration, the fragmentation of worlds, and *rising up,* as though to some insistent morning on creation day, is the distinct rhythm of experience that Vyry's growth, symbolic evolution of a people's growth, controls.

Control is the dominant theme of Margaret Walker's *Jubilee.* Those who inhabit the Big House believe themselves to be in control of the slave quarter. They have elaborately armed themselves to protect their illusion. They crack their whip, drive their patter-rollers, and wrap their minds in layers of willful fancies, hopeless deceptions concerning their powers of control. Thus the Dutton household is unprepared to suffer what the inhabitants of the quarter have confronted in life and raised to art: "Soon one mornin' / Death comes knockin' at my door." The Dutton household does not know the "mystery that only the squinch owl knows"; it does not know the conjure of wringing "cans" from "can'ts" that Granny Ticey knows; it does not know the tricks of Brer Rabbit that Aunt Sally plays each day; it does not know the shrewd double vision of Brer Fox that Caroline and May Liza and Lucy know; it does not know the power of the signifyin' monkey that Brother Ezekiel possesses. It does not recognize in Randall Ware the resolute will of Ogun/Stagolee to reckon with the hard facts of the abyss and not to be overwhelmed by its horrors. It miscalculates the iron determination of the spirit of Shango/John Henry in Innis Brown and Vyry, whose house, made of their own hands, stands after the Big House falls, destroyed by its own illusions—destroyed by its unfounded assumption of control.

Control for the inhabitants of the quarter is not a matter of assumption; nor is it a matter of force if the force is predicated upon illusions of strength. The House of Dutton is a dependent house. Its seeming force depends upon the authentic strength of the slave quarter. But those who inhabit the House of Dutton do not know this:

> They got the judges
> They got the lawyers
> They got the jury-rolls

> They got the laws
> They don't come by ones.
> They got the sheriffs
> They got the deputies
> They don't come by twos.
> They got the shotguns
> They got the rope . . .
> They come by tens.[13]

They are "self-anointed men" who inhabit the House of Dutton; they "dole out freedoms to other men." [14] Assured and arrogant, they are unprepared for and fatefully vulnerable to the unseen, unheard resourcefulness of the quarter.

The "Big Missy" and the "Miss Lillian" who inhabit the House of Dutton are velvet-and-silk-draped Scarlett O'Haras of a world of illusion. They are the glittering queens of a dangerous romance built of fantasy and fancy:

> They got the lippaste
> They got the powder
> They got the crepe de chine
> They got the gold
> They don't come by ones
> They got the papers
> They got the legal deeds
> They own the marriage license
> They got the name
> They don't come by twos.
> They got the carriage whips
> They got the chastity
> They got the Southern charm
> They come by tens.

They dance "the gala cotillions" (62) at great balls in the Big House. The cotillion, resplendent, elaborate, stately, requires adherence to a code, a form, a style rooted in the manners and conventions of an antecedent world—a time and place no longer apropos of the moment. The cotillion is a closed form unsuitable to "the wild profusion of growth" (30) that is life in the wilderness world of *Jubilee*. "Here . . . in this world of half-darkness and half-light . . . one was cut off from reality and lost in a fantastic world of jungle" (29).

Vyry knows, has marveled at, the figure of the cotillion: "There was a gala cotillion planned and an evening soiree after. . . . Vyry kept wondering how she could see and hear the festivities way back in the kitchen. . . . Aunt Sally told her to step outside . . . and stand in the dark under the big oak tree" (62–63). And Vyry has danced the jubas and sung the jubilees of the quarter. Like the jubilees (songs), the jubas (dances), though fragments of original wholeness in an antecedent world, are resembled and shaped from the sounds, the rhythms, the movements of anguish and exultation that characterize the hopscotch, the jerk, the twist, the black bottom, the snakehips, the do-si-do, the cakewalk, the boogie, the slow drag, the Charleston, the bougaloo of life in the wilderness. In the wilderness world of *Jubilee,* control, on the one hand, is an illusion achieved by chain and whip and adherence to transplanted closed forms inappropriate in a new time. It is that illusion that leads to the dissolution of the House of Dutton. On the other hand, the control of experience through adaptation and improvisation leading to the creation and expression of forms appropriate to the exigencies of time is the act of conversion that is the achievement of the quarter. This conversion of experience, by means of absorption, enables Vyry, as a child of the quarter, to translate Old World values into New World uses, to rise from nadirs of anguish to plateaus of exultation, to transpose apprenticeship to mastery.

Even so, in the world of *Jubilee,* the murky wilderness of transition, the endurance of inner and outer dissolution, the absorption of disparities, and even the conversion of experience into new possibilities is insufficient to the achievement of consummate human life. Consummation requires wholeness, and wholeness is no other thing than the balance resident in a human being of all the "imperatives of harmony in the universe." In the fractured world of the slave quarter, deep within the wilderness of the American South, the dreadful terrain of transition where a new sensibility is born, Vyry, the prototypical Afro-American, grows up. That growth is possible only by an act of will arduous enough to expand the dimensions of humanity. That act of will is the message of the spirituals that Vyry sings: "They were climbing the hill that night between nine and ten o'clock. Innis was riding Harry on his back. Vyry was still deep in the mood of the meeting, hearing the singing and the preaching and the stirring testimonies. She could still feel the intense joy of the song she was humming" (314). "The singing and the preaching and the stirring testimonies" are the expressions of the quarter, whose vision of life pierces the dimness of the wilderness world and perceives a clarity that reveals the wilderness to be mere shadow obscuring light:

> Tell me how did you feel when you come out the wilderness
> Come out the wilderness,
> Come out the wilderness,

> Tell me how did you feel when you come out the wilderness
> Leaning on the Lord?

But the vision of the quarter exceeds the terrestrial; it engages the cosmic and discovers the wondrous magnificence of universal wholeness:

> Big wheel run by faith
> Little wheel run by the grace of God
> A wheel in a wheel way in the middle of the air.

Vyry is heir of the sacred tradition of Afro-American blues modality. Not the secular self-emancipated journeyman—defiant, glorious, existential—established in *Narrative of the Life of Frederick Douglas, an American Slave, Written by Himself* (1845), Vyry is the embodiment of the experience of the great group whose toilsome, tragic, and glorious progress through time creates the spiritual sensibility of the race. She becomes the triumphant heroine of that sensibility not mainly because she has experienced the racial order of dissolution, absorption of disparities, and conversion of experience into new possibilities. No, she becomes the racial prototype because she chooses the racial will toward wholeness. That will impels *realignment*—the reshaping of shards of experience into a new whole—appropriate to the moment. The heroic persona of Afro-American sacred tradition incorporated in the mode we call the blues is the persona who chooses the sensibility announced in the traditional songs.

"This lil' light of mine / I'm gonna let it shine."

Or in Vyry's words to her son: "Love stretches your heart and makes you big inside."

At the Pigfoot the bluesman, Bill Harris, begins his ceremonious trek announcing the beginning of the second set. Approaching the bandstand, he shouts— it is a field holler—

> Way down yondah
> By myself
> And I couldn't hear nobody pray.

The bassman and the drummer, taking their cues, join the bluesman's guitar; they swing in three beats from the sacred spiritual to the secular blues: "And every day / Every day I have the blues." And in the crucible of sound measuring the outboundaries of ancestral ground, we listeners are likely to plunge down a well of years discovering meaning hidden in a welter of fragments assuming shape.

The Pigfoot is no more. The tax collector closed its doors a wisp of time ago. Yet passing by, any lonely quiet night, one may hear a sound like someone singing. But the bluesman's craft is portable. He carries it to Lagos, to Madrid, to Bahia, to Hong Kong. His art, ancestral like that of Vyry, is consummate. His achievement, like that of Margaret Walker's *Jubilee*, is permanent.

NOTES

1. A recurrent phrase in Ralph Ellison's *Invisible Man* (New York: Random House, 1952).

2. *Narrative of the Life of Frederick Douglass, an American Slave, Written by Himself, 1845* (New York: American Library, 1968), 31.

3. Jean Toomer, "Song of the Son," *Cane* (1923; New York: Harper & Row, 1969), 21.

4. Richard Wright, "Blueprint for Negro Literature," *Amistad* 2, eds. John A. Williams and Charles F. Harris (New York: Vintage Books, 1971), 6.

5. Ralph Ellison, "Remembering Jimmy," *Shadow and Act* (New York: Random House, 1953), 246.

6. James Baldwin, "The Uses of the Blues," *Playboy*, circa June 1963.

7. Zora Neale Hurston, *Jonah's Gourd Vine* (1934; Philadelphia: Lippincott, 1971), 60.

8. Langston Hughes, "Trumpet Player," *Selected Poems* (New York: Vintage Books, 1974), 114–15.

9. See Albert Murray's *Stomping the Blues* (New York: McGraw-Hill, 1976), 12, and *The Hero and the Blues* (Columbia: University of Missouri Press, 1973), where he uses the terms "confrontation, improvisation, affirmation, and celebration" charting progressions within the ethos of the blues. Other heroic modes in Afro-American story, like the gospel mode of James Baldwin, or the signifyin' mode of Ishmael Reed, or the jazz mode of Toni Cade Bambara, or the fabulous mode of Toni Morrison, are explicated in my study *The Presence of Ancestry: Traditions in Recent Afro-American Fiction*.

10. All quotations from Margaret Walker, *Jubilee* (New York: Houghton Mifflin, Bantam, 1966), will hereafter be acknowledged by page number.

11. Notes 11–19 in Wole Soyinka, *Myth, Literature, and the African World* (New York: Cambridge University Press, 1976), passim.

12. Ibid.

13. Sterling Brown, "Old Lem," "No Hiding Place," in *The Collected Poems of Sterling Brown*, selected by Michael S. Harper (New York: Harper & Row, 1980), 170–71.

14. Oliver Pitcher, "Salute," from *Dust of Silence* in *Beyond the Blues*, ed. Rosey E. Pool (Lympne, Kent: Hand and Flower Press, 1962), 161–62; and in Robert Hayden, ed., *Kaleidoscope: Poems by American Negroes* (New York: Harcourt Brace and World, 1967), 187–88.

I wanted to tell the story that my grandmother had told me, and to
set the record straight where Black people are concerned in terms of
the Civil War, of slavery, segregation and Reconstruction. I believe
that the role of the novelist can be, and largely is for me, the role of
a historian. More people will read fiction than will history, and
history is slanted just as fiction may seem to be. People will learn
about a time and a place through a historical novel.

—MARGARET WALKER, "Poetry, History, and Humanism"

"Oh Freedom"

Women and History in Margaret Walker's Jubilee

PHYLLIS R. KLOTMAN

Women have not always been recognized—nor have they been
seriously considered—as historians. The word itself seems to ring masculine.
At least their genius in the area of oral history has been acknowledged. "Miss
Jane" (from *The Autobiography of Miss Jane Pittman*) is a composite of Ernest
Gaines's aunts and their friends, whose lore he heard in the plantation kitchens
where he spent so much time as a child in Louisiana. Alex Haley heard the
story of "The African" Kunta Kinte from listening to the porch talk of his
grandmother, his aunts Plus, Liz, Till, Viney, and his cousin Georgia.

Some time before Ernest Gaines and Alex Haley set down their recollections
of the oral histories of the black women who had so profoundly influenced
them as artists, Margaret Walker had written into fictive reality the family history told her by her maternal grandmother, Elvira Ware Dozier—daughter of
Vyry of the novel.

The genesis of *Jubilee* was . . . simply and beautifully as a bedtime story
of truth, of black historical truth, repeated time and time again by a
grandmother who refused to forget the painful black past and the
courageous black people who lived it. From the moment of Margaret

Walker's birth until perhaps the very day of her own death, this grand-mother, living within the Walker household, wore the crowns that "All God's" black grandparents wear. Serving both as family historian and family Bible, Elvira Ware Dozier did not amuse the child with stories of a Mother Goose or a Wonderland Alice reproduced on commercially illustrated paper. Rather she inspired the child with the story of Vyry and Randall Ware—a story of black truth.[1]

From 1934 to 1966 Walker researched and wrote *Jubilee*, which, in three years, from September 1966 to October 1969, went into eleven printings. She did a few other things in those years, as women are wont to do: received a B.A. from Northwestern, worked on the WPA Writers' Project in Chicago, com-pleted a master's and later a doctorate at the University of Iowa, published the poem "For My People" and then the book by the same name, married and had four children, and taught at Jackson State University in Mississippi. During those years Walker was also awarded several prestigious fellowships, including one at Yale in 1954.

It is illuminating to examine a novel within the context of the author's pur-pose and methodology when one is privy to such information. According to *How I Wrote* Jubilee, Walker "always intended *Jubilee* to be a folk novel based on folk material: folk sayings, folk belief, folkways. As early as 1948 I was con-ceiving the story in terms of this folklore. I also wanted the book to be realistic and humanistic" (25). It is therefore not particularly meaningful to suggest a comparison, as does the paperback cover of *Jubilee*, with *Gone with the Wind*. Historical romance in latter-day plantation tradition conjures up pictures of tightly girdled, hoop-skirted (white) lilies of the South, sighing and coquetting on broad, shaded verandas, fluttering their eyelids at young, handsome cava-liers sipping mint juleps. Walker's Miss Lillian (and her friends) vaguely re-semble such figures of romance, but her southern belle has to cope with those all-too-human frailties—the result sometimes of overly tight stays—to which genteel ladies were supposed to be immune: "In the midst of a large burst of laughter she [Lillian] suddenly felt a rumble of air bursting loudly from her stomach and she could not refrain from a huge fit of belching."[2] Margaret Walker does not, however, totally reject the comparison:

> I am sometimes amused at the comparison, though there are a number of things alike. I was writing about the backwoods of Georgia, and so was she. I was writing about the same period. So we were dealing with the same time and place, and I find her language is fairly accurate. The difference is, or the distortion is, that she does not distinguish between her cultivated whites and uncultivated whites. She has all the Blacks

speaking one way and all the whites another. That is wrong for the South. But I don't wish to be compared with her turgid expository passages, which would have been better left out of the book. Neither do I have the romantic nostalgia that she has in her book. I am not a romanticist in *Jubilee*. It is a realistic book. . . . In some respects I suppose we could compare superficially the two Margarets—Margaret Mitchell and Margaret Walker. But she was coming out of the front door, and I was coming out of the back door.[3]

Frank Yerby's *The Foxes of Harrow* or *The Vixens* may more properly fit the genre of historical romance, while *Jubilee*, with its "super-structure of facts assembled from word-of-mouth accounts, slave narratives, history books, documents, newspapers" (*How I Wrote* Jubilee 20), has a greater kinship with Arna Bontemps's novel *Black Thunder,* a work of historical fiction published in 1936. A scholar like Walker, Bontemps did meticulous research into authentic court records to recount what was known as "Gabriel's conspiracy," an abortive slave rebellion near Richmond, Virginia, in 1800. Time in *Black Thunder* is much different in *Jubilee* as is the narrative technique, for although the story is essentially Gabriel Prosser's, Bontemps alternates characters to offer multiple views of the rebellion.

Jubilee is definitely Vyry's story; she is at the center of the novel, which begins with the imminent death of her mother, Sis Hetta, in 1839. It ends in 1870 with the news of an impending birth—Vyry's fourth child—some thirty years later. Vyry was born into slavery, the child of a slave woman and her master; this child, Margaret Walker's grandmother, Elvira Ware Dozier, will be born free. Women may not be able to control their destiny, or to record the official events precipitated by those who do, yet they are more than ancillary to the great events that change the direction of history. It is clear that some things could simply not take place without them. As Sojourner Truth said in response to an obstreperous yet ministerial "little man in black," "Whar did your Christ come from? From God and woman. Man had nothing to do with him."[4] Until *Jubilee*, the story of the black woman in the Civil War and in slavery had been told by others; except for the slave narrators who recorded their experiences after manumission or after escape from the "peculiar institution," the perspective, whether of history or of fiction, was almost inevitably white, usually male, and regionally identifiable. In Margaret Walker's dialogue with Nikki Giovanni, recorded in *A Poetic Equation,* Walker stresses the importance of the black woman's perspective: "I'm interested in the black woman in fiction perhaps because I'm a black woman and feel that the black woman's story has not been told, has not been dealt with adequately."[5]

Few slave narratives were written by women. On the whole it was more difficult for women to make their way to freedom alone; the great exception of course is Harriet Tubman, who not only engineered her own escape but in nineteen daring exploits escorted hundreds (some reports put the number at 300) of other slaves to freedom.[6] Women were less mobile. Not only were they required to carry out the master's orders in the field or in the "big house" during the day, but they were often forced to be accessible in order to minister to his nocturnal needs. Vyry's mother, Sis Hetta, was "given" to young master John Dutton when she was "barely more than a pickaninny." She died in her twenty-ninth year, after having given birth to fifteen slave children. Yet in spite of her deathbed agony as the result of another childbirth—and the loss of previous children—Hetta doesn't want to die without seeing her child Vyry, already at the age of two, in the custody of a surrogate mother because of the exigencies of plantation life. The deep concern and attachment slave women had for their children may explain in part why they were less apt to become escapees.[7] Eugene Genovese suggests that those who

headed for freedom in the North, the southern cities, or the swamps— fell into a pattern. At least 80 percent were men between the ages of sixteen and thirty-five. The age profile contains no surprise, but the sex profile does. At least one-third of the runaways belonged to the ranks of the skilled and privileged slaves—those with some education and with some knowledge of the outside world—and women occupied these ranks only as house servants. In view of the physical strength and general assertiveness of the women, their stronger ties to children and family probably account for much of their unwillingness to defect. Many of the young women had children before they had husbands; the young men could more readily fly, for they often had not yet assumed responsibilities toward a woman or children even if they were already fathers.[8]

Vyry is the mother of two children before Randall Ware, their father (with whom she has "jumped the broom"), finally convinces her she must try to make a break for freedom. Until fifteen, when she first meets Randall Ware, freedom is something she associates with miracles: "She tried to imagine what it meant to be free. She had never before entertained the faintest idea or hope of freedom, except some dream or an answer to a prayer, when God would suddenly appear and send a deliverer like Moses, and set free all the people who were in bondage such as she" (94). She is, however, drawn to Randall Ware because he is a free man and because he promises her freedom: "If you would marriage with me, I'd buy your freedom!" (88). Randall Ware is in a highly unique and therefore dangerous position in backwoods Georgia. He runs his own grist mill and smithy built on property in Lee County, Georgia, willed to him by Randall Wheelwright, a Quaker abolitionist, and he is "rich" enough to buy Vyry from her master John Dutton, which he could do legally *if* Dutton would agree:

> She would not be easy to buy. He had ways of learning, however, by the grapevine of the underground railroad whether her master would sell Vyry, who was now his cook in the Big House. He also knew that as a mulatto, by Georgia law she could be free to marry a free man with her master's consent, that is, if she could get that consent. There was also the possibility that she could be smuggled out to freedom. (93)

However, Salina Dutton, the master's wife, is known to hate free Negroes. Vyry "sensed what she did not have to be told: that Big Missy would put up a terrible fight against letting her be sold to a free black man or letting her have freedom in any way" (95), even though she had always hated "white-faced" Vyry, the tangible evidence of her husband's infidelity. In desperation, when she finds that she is pregnant, Vyry goes to John Dutton and asks his permission to marry the man she loves, which he indulgently gives until he hears that she wishes to marry a free man. The ramifications are immediately obvious and Dutton is furious: "When you ask me to let you marry a free-issue nigra you ask me by the law of the state of Georgia to set you, a mulatto woman, free, and that's a mighty lot to ask. There's a big difference between asking to get married and asking to be set free. Why, I never heard of such in all my life!" (144). Like numerous slave masters, John Dutton holds out the promise of manumission in his will, but when Dutton later dies, he is quite mad with the pain of gangrene and all of Vyry's hopes for freedom seem to die with him. Even Randall Ware's abolitionist friend Robert Qualls, acting blind, is unable to buy Vyry when she's put on the auction block, and she remains on the Dutton plantation with her growing family, receiving occasional clandestine visits from Randall Ware.

The position of a free Negro in the antebellum South was tenuous at best, and Randall Ware's covert operations with the abolitionists and the underground railroad finally put his life in great jeopardy. He decides that he can no longer stay in the South, and he urges Vyry to leave the children and escape with him. She wants desperately to go, but she cannot bring herself to leave the children, no matter how convincing Randall Ware is that he will see they are cared for and that they will be reunited in Canada. Vyry has run the gamut of emotions about freedom—from little awareness of its meaning to passionate desire for its fulfillment and finally, after years of promise and frustration, resignation. She loves Randall Ware, but she has not had his experiences, is not literate, does not understand what the underground railroad is and has no confidence that if she leaves her children she will ever see them again. But she does try. She dresses in the clothes that Randall Ware has left her and, disguised as a man, starts for the swamp to meet him, but when the baby Minna begins to cry and wakes up her brother Jim, Vyry takes them along. Needless to say, they do not get to the swamp. Grimes the overseer, the patteroller, and guards take her back to the plantation and she is unmercifully flogged: seventy-five lashes is the penalty for attempted escape, but Vyry is not conscious enough to count them. After three days, when her mind clears and she is able to examine herself, she sees "where one of the lashes had left a loose flap of flesh over her breast like a tuck in a dress. It healed that way" (174).

Walker also records the fact that some slave women did make successful bids for freedom. Lucy, who is branded with an "R" (for runaway) on her face by Grimes after an attempted escape, is able to slip away when the Duttons take their slaves to a Fourth of July celebration at the county courthouse: it is the eightieth anniversary of American independence. The program, a formal affair for the "edification" of planters, poor whites, and Negro slaves, includes music, a sermon by a leading theologian and the ceremonial hanging of two slave women suspected of poisoning their masters. When they return, Lucy is not among them. "Grimes took a posse of men and bloodhounds and went after her. But this time they did not bring her back. She had gone too far, and they could not find a trace" (126).

The story of Harriet Tubman's escape is included in her narrative, but the details of escape are almost as sketchy as the ones that Walker gives about Lucy:

And so without money, and without friends, she started on through un- known regions; walking by night, hiding by day, but always conscious of an invisible pillar of cloud by day, and of fire by night, under the guid- ance of which she journeyed or rested. Without knowing whom to trust, or how near the pursuers might be, she carefully felt her way, and by her native cunning, or by God-given wisdom, she managed to apply to the right people for food, and sometimes for shelter; though often her bed was only the cold ground and her watchers the stars of night.

After many long and weary days of travel, she found that she had passed the magic line, which then divided the land of bondage from the land of freedom.[9]

What remains clear is that most escapes were characterized by a singleness of purpose on the part of a highly motivated individual who usually traveled alone. Harriet Tubman tried to convince two of her brothers to go with her;

they reluctantly agreed but soon turned back "to the known horrors of slavery, and the dread of that which was worse."[10]

Arna Bontemps indicates that Harriet Tubman's narrative, *Scenes in the Life of Harriet Tubman* (1869) by Sarah Bradford, was presented as "out-and-out" autobiography and therefore is a variation of the slave narrative "mold" set by Briton Hammon, John Marrant, and Gustavus Vassa.[11] Frederick Douglass, in his letter of August 29, 1868—which, along with others in the appendix attesting to the authenticity of the facts in Bradford's second edition (*Harriet Tubman, The Moses of Her People*)—seems to suggest (as does Butler A. Jones, who wrote the introduction to the 1961 edition) that the narrative is instead *bio*graphical:

> DEAR HARRIET: I am glad to know that the story of your eventful life
> has been written by a kind lady, and that the same is soon to be
> published. You ask for what you do not need when you call upon me
> for a word of commendation. I need such words from you far more
> than you can need them from me, especially where your superior labors
> and devotion to the cause of the lately enslaved of our land are known
> as I know them.[12]

There is no doubt then that we have the intervention of another person between the actual experience and the printed word; yet the truth of that experience is not in doubt. Many ex-slaves suffered the degradation of the prevailing laws that forbade them to learn to read and write. If they wanted their stories told, they had to use a recorder/biographer, and naturally some of these were better—less obtrusive—than others. Sojourner Truth's narrative is a "told-to" biographical account, published for the author by Olive Gilbert: *Narrative of Sojourner Truth: A Bondswoman of Olden Time, Emancipated by the New York Legislature in the Early Part of the Present Century, with a History of Her Labors and Correspondence* (1850). In the foreword to the 1970 edition, Sterling Stuckey says that the work "as a whole is a rather strange and somewhat unorganized mixture of biography, essays, brief commentaries, and miscellany on Sojourner, rather liberally supported by Sojourner's comments on a multiplicity of subjects. For all the weaknesses of the volume . . . the narrative is a document of great value" (vi). One of the major weaknesses is Olive Gilbert's penchant for sermonizing. A narrative that speaks so powerfully for itself does not need the interjections of woe that she seems unable to resist:

> Such an abominable state of things is silently tolerated, to say the least, by
> slaveholders—deny it who may. And what is that religion that sanctions,

even by its silence, all that is embraced in the *Peculiar Institution?* If there *can* be any thing more diametrically opposed to the religion of Jesus, than the working of this soul-killing system—which is as truly sanctioned by the religion of America as are her ministers and churches—we wish to be shown where it can be found. (23)

Most ex-slave narrators were aware of the intrinsic merit of their cause and felt compelled to share it as best they could for the benefit it would bring to those still in bondage. Ellen Craft helped to mastermind the brilliant escape plan that she and her husband, William, successfully executed, but it was William who wrote the narrative, *Running a Thousand Miles for Freedom; or, The Escape of William and Ellen Craft from Slavery*, published in London in 1860.[13] Whether illiteracy was higher among women than among men is not altogether clear. In *Jubilee* the only blacks who know how to read, write, and cipher are Randall Ware, who is born a free man, and Brother Ezekiel, a slave-preacher who must feign ignorance of the skills it is illegal for him to possess. But women like Aunt Sally hand down, in oral tradition, the history necessary to keep a sense of family alive in young folk like Vyry.

Some narratives *were* written by women: for example, Harriet Jacobs's *Incidents in the Life of a Slave Girl, Written by Herself,* "edited" by L. Maria Child (Boston 1861); Annie L. Burton's *Memories of Childhood's Slavery Days* (Boston 1909); and Elizabeth Keckley's *Behind the Scenes: or, Thirty Years a Slave and Four in the White House, as Mrs. Lincoln's Maid* (1868)—the first "inside the White House" account. And many former slave women have been recorded in collections in various parts of the country, including the Martin Collection in the library of North Carolina College in Durham, where Margaret Walker read them. These are the records not of exceptional women and men—not classics like the narratives of Frederick Douglass, William Wells Brown, Henry Bibb, Gustavus Vassa, Josiah Henson—but of folk experience; they are folk history.[14] These narratives corroborated for Margaret Walker

> the most valuable slave narrative of all, the living account of my great-grandmother which has been transmitted to me by her own daughter. I knew then that I had a precious, almost priceless, living document of my own. There are hundreds of these stories, most of them not written, but many of them are recorded for posterity. These written accounts tell of the brutalizing and de-humanizing practices of human slavery. They recount such atrocities as branding, whipping, killing, and mutilating slaves. . . . [A]ll of them contain crucial information on slavery from the mouth of the slave. (*How I Wrote* Jubilee 18)

Jubilee emerges from the tradition of the slave narrative, and Walker uses the research into this unique African American literary genre to support the oral tradition of the black family out of which the donnée of her novel comes: the life of Vyry, her husbands—Randall Ware and Innis Brown—and her children, handed down by one of those children to the artist who would finally make of the tale a jubilee, a celebration of freedom and restoration. Even though he inadvertently omits the woman writer in this paragraph, Arna Bontemps says of the slave narratives that

> hindsight may yet disclose the extent to which this writing, this impulse, has been influential on subsequent American writing, if not indeed on America's view of itself. Certainly neither Mark Twain nor Herman Melville escaped its influence completely, and writing by black authors from James Weldon Johnson to Richard Wright, Ralph Ellison, and James Baldwin shows a profound indebtedness to this tradition. The standard literary sources and the classics of modern fiction pale in comparison as a source of their strength.[15]

The influence of the slave narrative is obvious in *Jubilee,* not only from the title and Margaret Walker's own testimony, but also from the thematic material and the structure of the novel. "The most obvious themes to be culled from slave narratives," as Darwin Turner suggests, are "courage, love of freedom, and perseverance."[16] Walker's *Jubilee* emphasizes all of these as does the writer's own narrative, *How I Wrote* Jubilee, a book that has its own history of courageous struggle:

1915	Birth of Margaret Walker; death of Vyry in the novel
1934	In the fall, Walker begins writing "her version" of the Civil War at Northwestern
1939–40	At the University of Iowa, Walker begins period of research for *Jubilee*
1942	Contact with Schomburg Collection, Harlem
1944	Receives Rosenwald Fellowship to begin "serious" research
1947	Trip to Dawson, Georgia
1948	Walker blocks out the story: three major periods, with about one hundred incidents (outlines)
1953	Receives Ford Fellowship to complete research
1954	Ford fellow at Yale; writes revised version of *Jubilee* (two hundred pages); lapse in writing for about seven years
1961	Returns to the University of Iowa for a doctorate in English, with her novel as the dissertation

1962	Studies and teaching related to the Ph.D.
1964	In the fall, rewrites and revises two hundred pages of the ante-bellum section
1965	Begins Civil War section in January, completing it in February; completes third section by April 9; works on revisions
1966	Publication of *Jubilee* in September (20)[17]

The tripartite structure of the slave narrative (Bondage, Escape, Freedom—in chronological order) is reflected in the three-part chronological framework of *Jubilee:*

I. Sis Hetta's Child: The Ante-Bellum Years (3–174), ca. 1839–1860

II. "Mine eyes have seen the Glory": The Civil War Years (177–312), 1861–1865

III. "Forty years in the wilderness": Reconstruction and Reaction (315–497), 1866–1870

In the genuine slave narratives as well as the "told-to" accounts, the pattern persists. Generally, greater emphasis was placed on the description of the experience in slavery—the horrors of bondage, brutality, separation of families. Frederick Douglass described the plantation system in detail and also addressed the issue of dehumanization of both slave and master in concrete terms. Examples are given in almost all narratives of gratuitous cruelty; specific incidents are often dramatized, not merely narrated. Evidence of exposure to brutality at a very early age is offered almost offhandedly, sometimes with what may have been unwitting irony. Annie L. Burton, for example, writes of her "care-free childhood days on the plantation" on one page and on the next reports that she and the other slave children were whipped for minor infractions, were given no supper and very little breakfast (one bowl served about fifteen children), had no shoes, and were allowed to observe both the floggings and hangings of adult slaves.[18]

The flight to freedom or Escape section was usually shorter. Douglass eschewed the details of escape. His concern at the time of publication, a concern demonstrated by the vast majority of the pre-1861 slave narratives, was not to expose any workable plan to the eyes of slavemasters or bounty hunters for fear that no other slave would have access to the method. The first twenty-nine chapters of Harriet Jacobs's *Incidents in the Life of a Slave Girl* delineate the harrowing life in bondage of the author, but in only one chapter does she describe her flight to freedom.

Even after successful flight the slave narrator's life was often severely curtailed, because the threat of recapture, especially after the enactment of the Fugitive Slave Law in Massachusetts, was very real. William and Ellen Craft did not feel safe anywhere in America and fled for a time to England; Josiah Henson settled in Canada, as did a number of other escaped slaves. Jacobs fled from New York to New England trying to elude her "master's emissaries" but only felt "free at last" (the title of the last chapter of her book) when her friend Mrs. Bruce purchased her freedom.

What is most interesting about the structure of *Jubilee* is how closely it parallels the experiences of so many slaves in bondage; at the same time it demonstrates how the condition of being female effectively limited the opportunity of many black women to escape to freedom. In part 1, "The Ante-Bellum Years," Walker describes the plantation setting and the slave experience, both physical and emotional, in detail. She also addresses many of the same issues that are included in the Bondage section of the narratives: the question of self-identity, lack of a complete family, confused birthdate, problem of being a mulatto, brutal separation from the mother, little mention of or "lamentation" for the father—the daily struggle against what J. Noel Heermance describes as a calculated dehumanization process.[19] Vyry is two years old as the novel opens; she knows nothing about her mother, and at the time is too young to know anything about grief. The "old crone, Mammy Sukey, was all the mother she had ever known or could remember" (15), and Vyry is deeply grieved when Mammy Sukey soon dies of the plague. Vyry's father is unknown to her—but not to the reader; therefore, she is completely unprepared for the brutal treatment she receives at the hands of Mistress Salina, the wife of Master John, who has fathered other mulatto children. Vyry's link to the past and to her own identity is Aunt Sally, who has taken over the role of surrogate mother.

Part 1 ends with Vyry's attempted escape and recapture, and Randall Ware's presumed escape—he does make his way to the Union Army. But the slave condition continues for Vyry through "The Civil War Years" (part 2). Although John Dutton dies, his slaves are not freed and Big Missy Salina has her last wish: "She would never live to see niggers free and living like white folks" (224). It is 1865 and Vyry is twenty-eight years old before "freedom [would] come to her" (226). The news of emancipation is late in coming to rural southern Georgia, and Walker insists on the reality of experience. Vyry does not attempt another escape nor is she in a hurry to leave Dawson, for Randall Ware has not yet returned, and she's convinced he will. In fact, she waits for him until she has no alternative but to leave with Innis Brown and her children.

Part 3, although unlike the narratives in locale, has some things in common with the genre. Freedom is an unfulfilled promise, whether in the North or in the postwar South. Many narrators expressed shock and dismay to find prejudice and discrimination in the "promised land"; they found some friends and benefactors, but many enemies. Not all northerners were interested in the antislavery cause; many in fact were vociferously opposed. When freedom comes, Vyry and Innis revel in it at first, but when they leave Georgia, bound for Alabama, they find themselves wandering in the wilderness from Abbeville to Troy to Luverne to Greenville rather than reaching Canaan. They are greeted with enmity by the poor whites who have been starving throughout the war years and are certainly not ready to accept black people, whom they blame for their plight. Forty acres and a mule is another promise that seems destined to remain unfulfilled: it is the year of Jubilee, but great disappointment follows. The Klan burns down the house they have built with their hands, and their children are forced to work hard, almost as though slavery still existed.

Because Margaret Walker is recording folk history, she couches the titles of the major sections first in folk, then in historical terms, and she uses folk music and/or folk sayings as epigraphs to each chapter. Sis Hetta's death (part 1, chapter 1) is signaled by lines from the spiritual "Swing low, sweet chariot, / Coming for to carry me home." The title of section 2 is the first line from the "Battle Hymn of the Republic," the music of which was appropriated from the folk tune "John Brown's Body." [20] The final section, "Forty years in the wilderness," reflects not only Walker's own Christian humanism but the strong attachment of the folk to the religious teaching of the Bible. It emphasizes the "leit-motif of the biblical analogy of Hebrews in Egypt with black folk in America" (*How I Wrote* Jubilee 25).

Historical fact and incident are the backdrop for the folk experience that is always of primary importance, as indicated by the fact that the folk reference always takes precedence over the historical. This is not to say, however, that Walker eschews actual historical events or fails to document those that are particularly germane to black history, such as the expulsion of black elected representatives from the Reconstruction legislature in Georgia and the publication of David Walker's *Appeal*.

There are several chapters in part 3 in which Randall Ware's harrowing postwar experiences back in Georgia are juxtaposed with those of Vyry, Innis, and the children in Alabama. While the Klan burns down Vyry and Innis's new home in Troy (chapter 46), forcing them to keep "wandering in the wilderness," Randall Ware is having a concomitant experience in Dawson (chapters 48, "Ku Klux Klan don't like no Koons," and 49, "Keep the niggers from the Polls and we'll return to White Home Rule!"). The Negro soldiers who help Vyry and her family relocate report the election of President Ulysses Grant to

Innis and Vyry, who are far removed from postwar politics; but Randall Ware is shown as characteristically different, more politically engaged. He has not only returned to take up his trade and reclaim his fertile land, he has also become acquainted with Henry McNeil Turner (Randall Ware calls him familiarly Henry Turner), who was *in fact* elected to the first Reconstruction Legislature in Georgia. Bishop Turner had been a chaplain with a commission in the Union Army during the war. During the period of harassment of black people in Georgia, which the novelist describes, Ware is beaten, his helper murdered, and he is forced to sell his prime land to Ed Grimes, former overseer on the Dutton plantation and rising redneck of the new reactionary Georgia. Walker relates the *economic* harassment of Ware to the *political* harassment of the newly elected black legislators: in September of 1868 all Negro legislators were declared ineligible and unceremoniously unseated.[21] Bishop Turner's "farewell" address is one of the masterpieces of nineteenth-century protest oratory. Yet Turner seems convinced at this point in the novel that Congress will investigate the KKK reign of terror and act on the testimony of the victims. Congress has already "thrown Georgia out of the Union again" (397), he says, for expelling the Negro legislators. In fact, the Supreme Court ruled, almost a year later, that the black legislators be reinstated. Randall Ware refuses to be disenfranchised, but he is not convinced that the government can protect "every Negro in the South against all of his White neighbors and their friends" (397). He casts his ballot and, before leaving, responds to Turner's accusation of cowardice: "Right now I'd rather make a good run than a bad stand. I feel like it's better to have folks looking at my back saying 'yonder runs that stinking yellow-bellied coward' than look at my corpse saying 'don't he look natchall?'" (397). Randall Ware is amazingly astute. Although Walker does not pursue the matter of Bishop Turner beyond chapter 49, it is interesting to note that Turner later became completely disenchanted with America and placed his trust in African colonization. Turner was not only drummed out of the legislature, he was also forced out of another position, first Negro postmaster in Georgia, in spite of the fact that he had been a loyal, hardworking Republican, actively campaigning for the party.[22]

Early in the novel (chapter 3, page 49), when Vyry is about ten years old, she begins to learn of the world around her through her (second) surrogate mother, Aunt Sally, the cook at the Big House. Sally is very religious—she and her sons attend Sunday meeting, regularly, for reasons other than mere worship. Brother Ezekiel, who ministers to their souls, is the only slave with extraordinary mobility (and literacy); he is able to feed their hunger for news about the world outside their reach, about abolitionists, the North, freedom, all forbidden subjects, and to warn them of trouble. Aunt Sally is reminded of an earlier troubled time, before Vyry was born:

> And they called on all the God-fearing white folks of Georgy to arrest anybody what they catch with these here papers, like what a man named David Walker had done writ a long time ago, and what they say was stirring up unrestlessness and trouble amongst all us slaves. That was a long time fore you was borned. I wonder what kinda new trouble is us got now? (49)

David Walker's *Appeal* was published in 1829. It was an exhortatory plea to the enslaved to throw off the chains of their oppressors and claim their natural right to freedom, and it caused great consternation throughout the South. Just how far south the *Appeal* was disseminated is difficult to determine. Nat Turner was said to have had a copy in his possession, but that story may be apocryphal. David Walker, in the business of dealing in secondhand clothes, presumably put copies of the *Appeal* in the pockets of the clothes before he sold them. From 1829 until "his strange disappearance sometime in 1830 [Walker] supervised the distribution and reprinting of his booklet, which during the last year of his life went into its third edition." [23]

Aunt Sally is also a fount of genealogical fact about the Dutton family and their slaves; we can place the family, even its economic circumstances, within a general time frame by listening, as Vyry does, to Aunt Sally's rendering of the past. It is history told from the perspective of the women folk who lived it that Margaret Walker has so successfully captured in *Jubilee*.

NOTES

1. Gloria Gayles, "Introduction/Response," in *How I Wrote* Jubilee, by Margaret Walker (Chicago: Third World Press, 1972), 6. Further citations appear in the text.

2. Margaret Walker, *Jubilee* (Boston: Houghton Mifflin, 1966), 109. Further citations from the novel will appear in the text.

3. In Charles A. Rowe, "Poetry, History and Humanism: An Interview with Margaret Walker," *Black World* 25.2 (1975): 10.

4. From an extemporaneous address at a woman's rights convention in Akron, Ohio, in the early 1850s; quoted in Olive Gilbert, *Narrative of Sojourner Truth: A Bondswoman of Olden Times* (1875; rpt. Chicago: Johnson Publishing Co., 1970), 105.

5. *A Poetic Equation: Conversations Between Nikki Giovanni and Margaret Walker* (Washington DC: Howard University Press, 1974), 55. This was said to Giovanni regarding the first creative writing assignment Walker was given by the Writers' Project in Chicago in 1937; it certainly holds true with *Jubilee*.

6. Sarah Bradford, *Harriet Tubman, The Moses of Her People* (1886; rpt. Secaucus NJ: The Citadel Press, 1961), 33.

7. "White southerners, who usually knew better, sometimes pretended that black mothers cared little about children. The whites might have been referring to that stoicism toward the death of an infant which appears in all societies with high infant mortality, especially among the poor. . . . The white women and even the men frequently commented on the grief felt by particular slave parents when they lost a child" (Eugene Genovese, *Roll, Jordan, Roll: The World the Slaves Made* [New York: Random House, 1974], 496). Genovese cites additional evidence: "The sadistic mistress who whipped a slave girl to death fully appreciated the maternal affection of her slaves: she sent for the girl's mother to watch her die" (from Benjamin Drew, *A North-Side View of Slavery: The Refugee; or, The Narratives of Fugitive Slaves in Canada Related by Themselves* [New York: Negro Universities Press, 1968], 259).

8. Genovese, *Roll, Jordan, Roll*, 648–49.

9. Bradford, *Harriet Tubman*, 30–31.

10. Bradford, *Harriet Tubman*, 28. It is not clear just how old these two brothers were at the time. Harriet Tubman, according to Bradford, was about twenty or twenty-five.

11. "The Slave Narrative: An American Genre," in *Great Slave Narratives* (Boston: Beacon Press, 1969), xv.

12. Bradford, *Harriet Tubman*, 134–35.

13. See Phyllis R. Klotman, "The Slave Narrative," in *Another Man Gone* (Port Washington NY: Kennikat Press, 1976), 10–22.

14. "In all the books that you have studied you never studied Negro history have you?" an ex-slave asked an interviewer from Fisk University. "If you want Negro History," he insisted, "you will have to get [it] from somebody who wore the shoe, and by and by from one to the other you will get a book" (Fisk University, *Unwritten History*, 45–46; quoted by Lawrence Levine in *Black Culture and Black Consciousness* [New York: Oxford University Press, 1977], 443–44).

15. Bontemps, "The Slave Narrative," xviii–xix.

16. "Uses of the Antebellum Slave Narratives in Collegiate Courses in Literature," paper presented at MMLA, Nov. 1974, 4.

17. In 1974 Walker seemed distressed about the amount of time she had spent on *Jubilee*. Giovanni's criticism of Paule Marshall for taking five years to write *The Chosen Place, The Timeless People* produced the following dialogue:

WALKER: Well, dear do you realize how long it took me to write *Jubilee*?
GIOVANNI: Yes!
WALKER: Half a lifetime.
GIOVANNI: That's too long!
WALKER: I know it. And it's a waste of time.
GIOVANNI: No, it's not a waste of time.
WALKER: I couldn't—I didn't know how, I had to learn, and every time I put something down it didn't satisfy me. I wrote three hundred pages of that book when I was nineteen years old. I had had the germ of the idea from childhood.

I wanted to write and learn how to write a novel so I could write that story, see? I lived with that story, but when I put down those three hundred pages any fool could see the thing was no good (*A Poetic Equation* 55).

18. *Memories of Childhood's Slavery Days* (Boston: Ross Publishing Co., 1909), 3–6.

19. "Slave Narratives as a Genre," in *William Wells Brown and Clotelle* (Hamden CT: Shoe String Press, 1969), 76–90.

20. "During the close of the year 1861, Mrs. Howe with a party of friends visited Washington. While there she attended a review of the Union troops on the Virginian side of the Potomac and not far from the city. . . . On the ride back to the city the party sang a number of war songs, including 'John Brown's Body.' One of the party remarked that the tune was a grand one, and altogether superior to the words of the song. Mrs. Howe responded to the effect that she would endeavor to write other words that might be sung to this stirring melody. That night . . . 'The Battle Hymn of the Republic' was composed" (Frank Rix, *The Junior Assembly Song Book* [New York: Barnes, 1914], 18).

21. John Hope Franklin, *From Slavery to Freedom: A History of Negro America*, 3rd ed. (New York: Vintage, 1969), 319.

22. Edwin S. Redkey, "Bishop Turner's African Dream," *Journal of American History* 54 (Sept. 1967): 273.

23. Floyd Barbour, ed., *The Black Power Revolt: A Collection of Essays* (Boston: Collier-Macmillan, 1968), 8.

Black Folk Elements in
Margaret Walker's *Jubilee*

JAMES E. SPEARS

Perhaps no other novel depicting the plight and life of southern blacks has made a greater impact on the reading public than has Margaret Walker's *Jubilee*. Alex Haley's *Roots,* both as novel and television serial, has been quite popular, of course; however, it lacks the insight into authentic folkways that *Jubilee* demonstrates. The popular critical reception of *Jubilee* has been extraordinarily positive. As of 1977, it had undergone two hardback and twenty-six paperback printings since its initial publication in 1966.

In essence, *Jubilee* has been proclaimed as a Civil War novel in the reverse tradition of *Gone with the Wind.* It is primarily the story of a search for freedom—chiefly by its main character, Vyry, but symbolically by the black race as a whole. *The New York Times Book Review* says of *Jubilee:* "A heroine to rival Scarlett O'Hara! Daughter of a plantation owner and his favorite black mistress, Vyry was conceived, born, and reared to young womanhood behind the House . . . one of the memorable women of contemporary fiction. In its best episodes, and Vyry, *Jubilee* chronicles the triumph of a free spirit over many kinds of bondages."[1] But is much more than a Civil War novel. *Jubilee* is a folk novel from opening to finish. Folk culture undergirds it and mirrors the morals, mores, and sociological patterns implicit in the ethos of the novel. The folk songs, the folk speech, the clothing, the food, the folk description of animals and of plants—all these tie the novel to the folk, to the soil. It is essentially an agrarian novel from beginning to end.

Structurally, the novel is divided into three parts: "Sis Hetta's Child: The Ante-Bellum Years"; "'Mine eyes have seen the Glory': The Civil War Years"; and "'Forty years in the wilderness': Reconstruction and Reaction." Each chapter begins with an epigraph excerpted from a traditional folk song. Of the fifty-eight chapters, twenty-two begin with spiritual, and thirty-six with secular, epigraphs. These epigraphs help give the novel its basic structural unity. Together with the chapter titles, two of which parallel the bondage of the children of Israel in Egypt, these epigraphs also help to establish the thematic unity of the novel.

Folk songs, particularly Negro spirituals, thus play an important role in the development of *Jubilee*. Bernice Reagon, a black folklorist at the Smithsonian, "has tried to find the story of everyday life of Blacks in Black songs."[2] She comments, "Trace the roots of the songs Black people have sung, and you will find a history no old documents will reveal."[3] She calls the songs "statements of the masses." *Jubilee* is an appropriate affirmation of her thesis. Interestingly enough, the title *Jubilee* itself is drawn from a traditional Negro spiritual whose lyrics signify chronologically a motif in the novel: the anticipated and approaching emancipation of the slaves. Each stanza of this song ends with the refrain, "in the year of Jubilee." Interwoven throughout are numerous other traditional black spirituals that are apropos to the action in each chapter and help give the novel its thematic unity. One of the most salient examples is the title of chapter 26, "Mr. Lincoln Is Our Moses." The symbolic captivity of the American slaves is traced out in part three: "'Forty years in the wilderness': Reconstruction and Reaction." Folk songs are indeed apropos to *Jubilee* and function to help move the narrative.

Folk language, too, plays a major role in the novel. Its usage functions to delineate and lend credibility as characters to the black folk portrayed. In *Jubilee*, characterization depends very much on folk language (Negro dialect) to portray superstitions and folkways, even more so than on character delineation through description and narration. It is noteworthy, parenthetically, that white speakers in most instances use standard literary, not eye, dialect; likewise, Vyry's husband, Randall Ware, a liberated slave, speaks cultivated English. Walker is a dialectologist in the strictest sense of the word, and her use of eye dialect for characterization is both accurate and effective. It captures the essence of black dialect in pronunciation, vocabulary items, usage, and grammar, particularly syntax. An exhaustive study should be made of the novel's language itself, but only a sampling will suffice here.

Subject-verb agreement violations are seen in "Yassah, I *has* a pass," "*Is* you crazy?" "You *liables* to cry," and "Jake gwine (going) to kill you," all of which show typical auxiliary verb dropping in black dialect. "When the new moon come, he be gone" illustrates the now unorthodox subjunctive and the euphemism *gone* for *dead*. "We is been from pillar to post since we seen you last" reflects "to be" verb substitution in auxiliary position for the *have* auxiliary, and *pillar to post* is an old English alliterative form. "I *feels* the same way *bout* vittles (victuals)" indicated an error in subject-verb agreement, and *bout* has undergone prefix dropping.

"You buyed it" and "a big brown bird brung him down the chimney" are examples of analogical verb tense formation. "I ain't nothing but a ignorant field hand *what* you despises" illustrates relative pronoun usage confusion as well as folk article usage. ". . . Bout not letting your *foots* touch ground" is a typical example of pluralization of an already mutated plural noun. "Ain't been no *passel* of time" is an archaic usage. "*Liables* to string me up and *whup me*" as a sentence carries pluralization of the verb instead of the subject which is missing; the auxiliary is also missing, and *whup* (with substitution of back vowel for front vowel) is a general folk pronunciation of *whip*.

"Slip of a lad" is an epithet still in general use among older folk speakers. "You must be *restless in your mind*" is an expression belonging peculiarly to black folk speakers, as is *just plain misery* which is a broad cover term for a spectrum of illnesses. The pronunciation of *Georgy* (Georgia), *Aificky* (Africa), *Floyda* (Florida) and *yestiddy* (yesterday) are in the folk vein. *Honey-boy* as a term of affection is a black folk compound. "It ain't needer one" is illustrative of black folk speakers' substitution of /d/ for the interdental fricative /θ/ or /ʤ/, a sound not found in African languages. The sentence "*colored* folks won't stand for that," carries a well-known euphemism. "Jump the broom" indicates an early Afro-American cultural more in lieu of the traditional Western marriage ceremony. And finally, *caline* (pronounced as /ke/) for the Christian name *Caroline* is an example of vowel mutation and syllable dropping.

No depiction of the black folk would be complete without references to religion, for religion is an integral part of black folk culture. Such references abound in *Jubilee,* and one specific example is the folk sermon by Brother Ezekiel of the Rising Glory Church (38–39). Although it is brief, it is masterfully done in the vein of black folk sermons and worship. It appears in vignette form, but its structure and rhythm make it typically imitative. Based upon the Old Testament story of Moses, Pharaoh's house, and Moses leading the children of Israel out of Egyptian bondage, this story is apropos to the slaves who hear and identify with it. The sermon begins *in medias res* with stichomythic dialogue between the preacher and the congregation, which responds with brief spontaneous liturgical affirmations. Then the preacher gradually builds up to a longer narrative commentary; yet his sentences remain short and simple. Repetitive phrases increase the effect, making sound and sense a dominating rhetorical pattern while yielding desired simplicity.

Superstitions are copious in *Jubilee;* however, they appear primarily at the beginning of the novel—and a few at the end. In the opening pages of the novel, gloom, fear, and death overcast the first episodes; superstitions are, therefore, inevitable. The slave community is intact, and its members function in everyday routine ways; it is during this period that superstitions prevail. However, with the coming of the Civil War, routines are broken, society is disrupted, the slaves uprooted, and social chaos reigns. During this period, superstitions occupy a descendent position. It is not until the end of the novel that Vyry and her family return to the soil and the folklore motif is truly resumed. An enumerative, random list of superstitions and folk medical remedies follows:

1. Screech owl calls signal an approaching death (of a man) (3).
2. Laudanum is used to ease pain (6).
3. A quarter moon that drips blood is an evil omen (5).
4. Tansy tea and red ash, and bathing the mother in hazel root, are administered at childbirth by a granny (midwife) (6).
5. A boiling black pot that emits a hissing sound is an evil omen (not clear from text) (11).
6. Young girls should not let their feet straddle rows in field crops lest the crops shrivel up and die (45).
7. A woman should not let her bare feet touch ground when her "womanhood" is on her (menstruation and pregnancy) (45).
8. A pregnant woman should not touch freshly killed pork lest it ruin (45).
9. Neither should a pregnant woman can (preserve) "green vittles" lest they spoil (45).
10. A doll fetish dressed in clothes of a dead child and streaked with blood brings evil to one under whose doorstep it is buried (56).
11. Laughing too much in the morning brings bad luck before bedtime (59).
12. Tar syrup, horehound, rock candy, and whiskey are remedies for bad colds, whooping cough, and fevers (65).
13. Mullein bath is good to stop swelling in feet and legs and for heart dropsy (84).
14. Barefoot root cooked down, and to which pyo lard and salt are added, makes a salve for rheumatism (84).
15. Apple root is good as a purgative (84).

16. Black halls and cherry root are a good tea to strengthen the appetite (84).
17. Jerusalem oats are good for human worms (84).
18. Samson snake root is good for cramps and "belly" ache (84).
19. Ripe pomegranate hulls and cherry root are a good tea to strengthen the appetite (84).
20. Jimson weed, red-oak bark, or salt and mustard make good poultices (84).
21. Ipecac, ergot, and saltpeter control passionate natures (89).
22. A seriously ill person will die with the coming of a new moon (160).
23. Planting should be done on Good Friday (new moon and spring equinox) (279).
24. The following are used to break fevers: molasses and sulfur powder; quinine; chinaberries; and whiskey (284).
25. It will rain again the next day if it rains while the sun is shining (372).
26. The accidental dropping of a cooking spoon means a visitor is coming (384).

Folk sayings used in a proverbial sense come in for a small share in the novel; however, they are included. Two of the more well-known ones are: "Chilluns (children) are supposed to be seen and not heard" (276), and "An idle brain is the devil's workshop" (278). Another, authentically black, is "I got me a lay-low to catch a meddler, and I'm gwine (going) set with the sick till the poorly gits better" (398).

Jubilee offers profound contrasts between worlds of the aristocrats and the slaves. For the aristocrats, there are emerald brooches, diamond necklaces, sapphire bracelets, and ruby earrings. There are brilliant plum satin, embroidered pink satin rosebuds, bottle-green velvet embroidered with seed pearls and rhinestones. There are soirées and elaborate Christmas festivities, along with attendant delicacies. For the Negro slaves, however, there are blue cotton-linsey shirts, shoeless frostbitten feet wrapped in rags or burlap from ragged croker sacks, and cheap calico and sack clothes, as well as common, staple folk foods. And *Jubilee* is filled with folk accoutrements: gourd dippers, sweet snuff, black iron washpots, rainwater in a barrel for laundry, and lye-potash homemade soap. And for the black folk there are wild fruits, berries, onions, greens, herbs, and roots to add to their diet of corn meal and hog meat, possum, coon chitterlings, liver and lights, and pig's feet.

Many more aspects of *Jubilee* mark it as a folk novel. A typical July 4th folk celebration is portrayed—in conjunction with an execution setting for two women convicted of murder. The folk, field-hands, are gathered for the barbecue and dinner on the grounds. There are cock-fighting, a gander pulling, horsetrading, and homemade fireworks made from saltpeter and black gunpowder. All these latter customs are ones the folk typically enjoy. There are veritable catalogs of birds, of wildflowers, and of wild plants, both edible and medicinal. Included are other folk customs such as hog killing. Folk foods and their cooking are mentioned in an appetizing and encyclopedic manner. Conversation is couched in folk language and concerns folk topics—mainly crops and animals, among other things. In sum, *Jubilee* is a folk novel; the folk backdrop prevails and *Jubilee* is peopled with folk characters engaged in folk activities.

NOTES

1. From the outside cover of the Bantam edition of *Jubilee* (New York: Bantam Books, 1977). All citations are to this edition.
2. "Much Black History Found by Folklorist in Multifaceted Songs of Protest," *Memphis Commercial Appeal,* Sunday, December 25, 1977, sec. C, p. 5.
3. "Much Black History" 5.

My grandmothers were strong.
They followed the plows and bent to toil.
They moved through fields sowing seed.
They touched the earth and grain grew.
They were full of sturdiness and singing.
　　—MARGARET WALKER, "Lineage"

From *Uncle Tom's Cabin* to Vyry's Kitchen

The Black Female Folk Tradition in Margaret Walker's Jubilee

CHARLOTTE GOODMAN

Thanks to the recent efforts of feminist critics, one of America's most important nineteenth-century novels, Harriet Beecher Stowe's neglected and often denigrated *Uncle Tom's Cabin,* has begun to receive the serious critical attention it so richly deserves. Although F. O. Matthiessen devoted only one sentence to *Uncle Tom's Cabin* in his monumental and very influential study of nineteenth-century American literature, *The American Renaissance,* new perspectives on Stowe's novel afforded by such critics as Nina Baym, Elizabeth Ammons, and Jane P. Tompkins have enabled us to appreciate the rhetorical brilliance of this work, which aimed to engage the sympathies of its readers so profoundly that they would be moved to abolish slavery.

A white woman addressing her jeremiad principally to other white women, Stowe beseeched the "mothers of America" to "pity those mothers that are constantly made childless by the American slave trade."[1] Appealing to her readers' maternal sentiments, she effectively dramatized the way in which the patriarchal instruction of slavery threatened the Christian values of nurturing mothers like Mrs. Shelby, Mrs. Byrd, and Rachel Halliday—the true heroines of her narrative. As Elizabeth Ammons has pointed out, through these maternal figures Stowe postulates an alternative system of values to challenge the patriarchal status quo.[2]

Yet, brilliant though it is, *Uncle Tom's Cabin* is nevertheless a novel written by a privileged nineteenth-century white woman to an audience of privileged white women like herself. Although Stowe herself emphasized the historical accuracy of *Uncle Tom's Cabin* both in the novel itself and in the *Key to Uncle Tom's Cabin* that she published subsequently, a twentieth-century reader cannot help but be aware of the significant omissions in Stowe's portrait of the lives of slave women. What is lacking in Stowe's novel is a picture of the black women's own community, of their daily interactions with one another, and of the rich cultural life that flourished in the slave quarters. In part, no doubt, Stowe's failure to depict the life of characters like Eliza and Aunt Chloe in all their particularity and complexity was deliberate, for what Stowe wished to emphasize was the common humanity of all women rather than the cultural differences that distinguished black women from white women. However, as a white woman living in the nineteenth century, Stowe also was not privy to the culture of black women, nor did she have access to the historical documents about the lives of black women that are available to us today. Consequently, if we wish to read a novel that will afford us a perspective on the actual day-to-day experiences of black women under slavery, we must turn to a work other than *Uncle Tom's Cabin*.

One twentieth-century novel that provides a compelling, detailed portrait of the daily lives of black women during the Civil War period is Margaret Walker's *Jubilee*, published by Houghton Mifflin in 1966. The impetus for this historical novel, which took Margaret Walker thirty-two years to write, was her conviction that other fictional narratives about life in the South in the nineteenth century were lacking in verisimilitude because they failed to depict accurately the experience of black women. Believing that "the black woman's story has not been told, has not been dealt with adequately," Margaret Walker set out to depict the lives of black women from a black woman's perspective.[3] Defining *Jubilee* as a "folk novel based on folk material: folk sayings, folk beliefs, folkways," she said that she sought to give her own chronicle "the feel of a fabric of life."[4] Just as Zora Neale Hurston incorporated into her fiction the material she had culled from her anthropological investigations of black culture, so Walker included in *Jubilee* the rich material she had gathered painstakingly during the many years she spent investigating the black oral tradition, historical accounts of slavery, primary documents, and newspapers from the

Civil War era. When Walker was a child, her grandmother Minna had told her stories about her great-grandmother, Elvira Ware Dozier, insisting that these tales about slave life in Georgia were "the naked truth."[5] Explaining the motivation for her own extensive research on life in the South in the nineteenth century, Walker wrote: "What was I trying to prove through this search among the old documents? I was simply determined to substantiate my material, to authenticate the story I had heard from my grandmother's lips. I was using literary documents to undergird the oral tradition."[6]

In a 1980 interview, Walker observed that she had deliberately set out to revise the stereotypical portraits of "the mammy, the faithful retainer, the pickaninny, little Eva and Topsy, the tragic mulatto, the conjure-woman or witch, the sex object, the bitch goddess, the harlot . . . and last but not least, the matriarch" that had appeared in the fiction of other writers.[7] While Walker does not specifically mention *Uncle Tom's Cabin*, the fact that she includes the names of Stowe's little Eva and Topsy among the stereotypes she had set out to revise suggests that one of the important texts that helped to shape her own countertext in *Jubilee* was Stowe's novel. By depicting the history of black women, including their healing arts, their recipes, their crafts, and their oral tradition, Margaret Walker fills in some of the lacunae in Stowe's novel, presenting a comprehensive account of the rich cultural heritage black women have passed down from one generation to the next.

Topsy illustrates what has been omitted in Stowe's novel. When queried about her origins, Topsy replies, "Never was born . . . never had no father nor mother, nor nothin'" (85). With no mother or father and without any ties to a black community of her own, Topsy is adopted by a white family, as are several other black characters in the novel. In contrast to Topsy, however, Walker's protagonist, Vyry, is vitally connected to her own black community, though she too has no parents to protect her. When Vyry is two years old, her mother dies while bearing a child fathered by the owner of the plantation, who is Vyry's father as well. Never acknowledged as kin by her biological father, Vyry is raised by other black women in the slave community.

Stowe's Eliza is also more closely connected to white women like Mrs. Shelby, Mrs. Byrd, and Mrs. Halliday than to black women like herself. Rarely depicting Eliza interacting with the black community, Stowe describes how she is nurtured by Mrs. Shelby and is even married in Mrs. Shelby's parlor rather than in the slave quarters. Instead of having Eliza speak in black dialect, as do the other black characters in *Uncle Tom's Cabin*, Stowe assigns to Eliza speech identical to that of her white owners, emphasizing Eliza's essential similarity to the white women who comprised the intended audience for the novel. Dressed in clothing given to her by her exemplary mistress and carrying with her no language or other signifiers of her black cultural heritage, Eliza does not appear to possess any emblems of her past to transmit to the next generation. In contrast to Eliza, however, Margaret Walker's Vyry speaks the same black dialect as the other slaves, and when she departs from the Duttons' plantation, she carries with her the story of her own past and the artifacts signifying her own black female cultural heritage. Walker depicts Vyry's life not only in the plantation house but in the slave quarters, where Vyry is nurtured by other black women and learns about the traditions of her own people. One of the traditions is the making of cloth. In her introduction to *Jubilee* Walker writes, "I have a true photograph of my own great-grandmother, who is the Vyry of this story. The picture was made approximately one hundred years ago. In it she is wearing a dress of black maline and her shawl is of yellow and red challis. From spinning the thread to weaving the cloth, the garments are entirely her handiwork."[8]

The clothes each character wears symbolize the difference between Stowe's conception of Eliza and Walker's of Vyry. While Eliza is dressed in the "spotted muslin gown" of her benevolent mistress (77), Vyry, demonstrating the skills she has learned from other black women, wears the products of her own handiwork. In addition to wearing the clothes she herself has made, Vyry also carries with her the inscription of her own tragic history: the scars on her back record a brutal whipping she once received when she tried to run away.

A central determiner of Vyry's history is the fact that she is a product of miscegenation. While Stowe makes Eliza a mulatto to emphasize the similarity between her black protagonist and the white Mrs. Shelby, as well as between Eliza and the mothers Stowe addresses in the novel's final chapter, Walker chooses to emphasize instead the negative impact miscegenation had on the relationship between black and white women. Rather than conferring on Vyry special privileges, her light skin and blonde hair cause her to be singled out for special abuse by her mistress, who cannot bear to acknowledge the uncanny resemblance between Vyry and her own daughter. Stowe mentions the issue of miscegenation "en passant" (182), while Walker shows miscegenation to be one of the most central issues in the history of both black and white women in the South.

Jubilee includes numerous signifiers of the black woman's history and culture, linking Vyry to past and future generations of black women. The novel incorporates the tales Vyry recites again and again about her journey from slavery to freedom as well as explicit descriptions of her herbal medicines, her cooking, her needlework, her songs and sayings—all the folk traditions her black female ancestors have passed on to her. As she departs from the plantation, she carries in her wagon iron pots and kettles, a wash pot, skillets, smoothing irons, candle molds and tallow candles, tin plates and cups and dippers of gourd and tin, a china washbowl and pitcher and a slop jar. She had quilts and croker sacks of cotton and feathers for beds and pillows, a precious spinning wheel, lots of potash soap, and most important of all, she had sacks of cracked corn meal, and sacks of seed. She filled the chest with the most valuable keepsakes from the plantation and Big House and tied it on the wagon. (316)

Walker enumerates those items in such detail not only to lend verisimilitude to her novel but also to demonstrate how these material signifiers are passed on from slave to free black women.

Two items in this list are especially significant: a china washbowl and pitcher. In an earlier scene, which depicts the death of Vyry's mother in childbirth, Walker mentions a china washbowl that the black midwife, Granny Ticey, uses to wash the dying woman; subsequently, other black women wash Vyry's bleeding back to remove the salt her cruel captors had poured on it after beating her for trying to run away; later, Vyry herself becomes a nurse to her ailing mistress and her mistress's daughter. As the list of items in Vyry's wagon reveals, the china washbowl and pitcher are two treasured possessions Vyry brings with her to her new community. There she takes on the role of midwife that Granny Ticey had formerly assumed for the slaves on the plantation. By tracing the history of the china washbowl and pitcher, Margaret Walker symbolically portrays how the healing arts are transmitted from black woman to black woman.

Another aspect of a vanishing culture that Walker preserves in her text is the tradition of black folk medicine. She describes, for example, how Vyry learns the lore of herbs and roots from other black women, and later depicts her gathering herbs and roots on her own. When Vyry is accosted by the white foreman, she explains that the mullein she has picked is "for the feets and legs to stop swelling and heart dropsy"; barefoot root is one of the ingredients in a salve for rheumatism; mayapple is good for the bowels; cherry roots strengthen the appetite; pulsey and pomegranate hulls cure diarrhea; and tansy tea, red shank, and hazel roots are effective remedies for "womanhood troubles" (100). Vyry's recitation of this herbal lore enriches the texture of the novel and also records for posterity a part of the black female folk tradition Walker feared was in danger of disappearing.

In addition to revealing how the healing arts are transmitted from one generation to the next, Walker also describes the transmission of other traditional black female arts such as cooking and needlework. In the novel, the older black women on the Dutton plantation instruct the younger ones in the art of food preparation. Showing how Vyry is initiated by another woman into the rites of the kitchen, Walker writes: "Under the watchful eye of Aunt Sally, Vyry learned to churn. The child would watch eagerly and delightedly to see the first pat of butter form around the paddle. Aunt Sally showed her how to put milk in crocks, how to separate the heavy cream from the mill, make cottage cheese and clabber, and how to add warm water when you were in a hurry to make butter come fast" (41). Just as Faulkner's Sam Fathers initiates the young Ike McCaslin into the rites of the hunt, which will signify Ike's entry into adulthood, so Aunt Sally teaches Vyry those skills that will prepare her to assume her role as a black woman.

In *Uncle Tom's Cabin* Stowe depicts the way in which black women feed white people, describing, for example, how Aunt Chloe feeds griddle cakes to Mrs. Shelby's son George when he pays a visit to the slave quarters: "Now Mas'r George, you jest . . . set down now with my old man, and I'll take up de sausages and have de first griddle full of cakes on your plate in no time," Aunt Chloe says, and she proceeds to feed the white boy before she feeds her own sons (69–70). In addition to depicting how black women feed white people, however, Walker also focuses on the way black women feed their own families. Thus Vyry not only learns from Aunt Sally the art of preparing food for the Big House but also the art of stealing food from her mistress's kitchen to supplement her own meager rations. "I ain't cooking nothing I can't eat myself," Aunt Sally proclaims defiantly to Vyry (42). From Aunt Sally and other black women Vyry learns how to prepare the game and edible greens the slaves manage to obtain from the woods and fields. In the text of the novel Walker actually includes descriptions of dishes Vyry learns to cook, such as greens, parboiled and cooked with wild onions and salt meat, and a savory chicken stew. To emphasize the difference between the food black women prepared for their masters and the food they prepared for themselves, Walker mentions that one Christmas during the war Vyry cooked a ham for the Duttons but prepared 'possum and collard greens for her own family's Christmas dinner. One of the traditions black women have passed on from generation to generation, the culinary arts serve as important signifiers of the black female folk culture in *Jubilee*.

Although both Stowe and Margaret Walker celebrate the culinary skills of black women, Walker additionally emphasizes how much arduous labor is involved in the preparation of food. She mentions that house servants like Aunt Sally and Vyry take pride in their skills as cooks and bakers, but she also reveals how bitterly they resent the hard work they must do to prepare elaborate meals for their master's table. Confined in the sweltering kitchen of the plantation house, they perform their endless tasks because they know they will be beaten unless they do so.

Rather than only using food preparation to signify female nurturance, as Harriet Beecher Stowe had done, Walker also notes the way in which slavery had corrupted this activity. Associating food with acts of cruelty, Walker mentions, for example, that Salina Dutton regularly makes the slaves who work in her house ingest ipecac in order to determine whether they have been stealing food from her kitchen. One of the most cruel acts in *Jubilee* takes place in the kitchen: when Vyry accidentally breaks one of her mistress's dishes, Salina Dutton hangs her from a strap in a closet, leaving the terrified child suspended by her hands until she loses consciousness. To signify the devastation members of the Ku Klux Klan cause when they burn down Vyry's new house, Walker also mentions food, observing that all of Vyry's "rows of preserves and canned and pickled goods, jellies and jams" are lost in the fire (386). Black women in *Jubilee* also perform destructive acts connected with the preparation of food. Walker mentions, for example, that two black women poison the food of their master and are later hanged at a public gathering on the Fourth of July. Thus Walker focuses on the culinary arts in *Jubilee* not only to celebrate the nurturing acts of black women but also to dramatize the way in which slavery corrupts basic human values.

Yet another signifier of black female culture in *Jubilee* is needlework. Associating all of her major black female characters with sewing, Walker mentions a quilt in the cabin of Vyry's dying mother that is used to separate the bed from the rest of the room, quilts Aunt Sally hangs over the windows and door to keep out the cold, and quilts that Vyry packs in her wagon when she leaves the plantation. In one of the most joyous scenes in the novel, Vyry and her husband invite their white neighbors to a house raising and quilting bee during which Vyry herself works on a pieced quilt ornamented with pomegranates. Perhaps Walker found the pomegranate to be an appropriate design for Vyry's quilt because the pomegranate originated in Africa and was a fruit whose hull black women used to prepare one of their remedies.

To demonstrate how the art of sewing is passed from mother to daughter, Margaret Walker shows Vyry instructing her daughter Minna in the art of piecing quilts, and Minna gives her brother a gift of a handkerchief that she herself has hemmed. In the beginning of the novel Walker had described how Vyry, as a child, had observed with awe the "high mountain of feather mattresses always . . . covered with a snow-white counterpane" in her mistress's bedroom; by the novel's end, Vyry has triumphantly succeeded in replicating these furnishings in the bedroom of her own house. Minna admires the "high mounds of feather mattresses with the snowy counterpane, crocheted, tasseled, and fringed with white matching shams that Vyry had made for herself" (496). Like the quilts a black mother passes on to her daughter in Alice Walker's widely anthologized short story "Everyday Use," Vyry's needlework is one of the legacies she bequeaths to her daughter Minna.

More important, perhaps, than any other signifier in *Jubilee* are the verbal texts incorporated into the novel. These include female lore about menstruation, cautionary tales about sexual matters, information about pregnancy and childbirth, folk sayings, songs, and passages from the Old Testament. The novel is dedicated to the memory of Walker's grandmothers—her maternal great-grandmother, who is the Vyry of her novel, and her maternal grandmother, who told her the tales upon which the novel is based. Each chapter begins with a folk saying or lines from a song or spiritual, and Walker traces the way in which the oral tradition is passed on from one generation to the next. She depicts, for example the two-year-old Vyry listening to a tune the black preacher is humming as he carries her to her dying mother's bedside, shows her listening raptly to the animal fables another preacher recites, and describes her as she hears his soulful rendition of "I Am a Poor Wayfaring Stranger." The young girl loves Aunt Sally's stories about "who she was and where she came from and what life was like" (43) and is moved by the "mad-mood" songs the sorrowful Aunt Sally sings as she stirs the pot in her mistress's kitchen (71). Walker also shows how the adult Vyry, in turn, tells stories about her past and sings the songs she learned in her youth to her own children.

In one of the scenes that Stowe introduces for comic relief in *Uncle Tom's Cabin,* Aunt Chloe confuses the words *poultry* and *poetry,* using the latter word to refer to the chickens she is about to cut up for chicken pie. As the final paragraphs of *Jubilee* suggest, for Margaret Walker "poultry" *is* "poetry," the daily domestic activities black women perform expressing their creativity. Walker concludes her novel with a description of Minna listening as her mother croons to a huge flock of laying-hens: "Come biddy, biddy, biddy, biddy, / Come chick, chick, chick, chick!" (497). Vyry is surrounded by her "poultry," a symbol of fertility, and Walker reveals that Vyry herself is expecting another child: "I hopes this next child will be a gal. Gal babies don't ever want to leave their maw easy," Vyry says (496). Her words reflect Margaret Walker's own vision of an ongoing women's community—one that will guarantee the survival of the black folk tradition.

It is unfortunate that Margaret Walker's *Jubilee* has received relatively little attention from the critics. As Minrose Gwin pointed out in her discussion of the novel, *Jubilee* is not even mentioned by the male authors of several influential studies of African American literature.[9] Moreover, despite the current interest in fiction by black women, *Jubilee* has been far less frequently discussed even by feminist critics than, for example, the novels of Toni Morrison, Alice Walker, and a number of other contemporary black women writers.[10] Since Walker imitates the conventional linear structure of the traditional slave narrative, perhaps one reason *Jubilee* has received so little critical attention is that it appears to be less innovative than novels like Morrison's *The Bluest Eye* and *Sula* or Alice Walker's *The Color Purple*. In addition, Jubilee does not focus on sexism within the black community as the novels of other contemporary black women writers frequently do.[11] Furthermore, Margaret Walker's espousal of the doctrine of Christian humanism in *Jubilee,* her endorsement of the principles of nonviolence, and her affirmation of the bonds between black and white women may have antagonized the more militant writers of the seventies and eighties. Nevertheless, I would argue that *Jubilee* deserves much more critical attention than it has received to date, for in it Margaret Walker has succeeded in representing what no other American writer has represented with so much skill or authority: a compelling picture of the community of black women during the Civil War period.

If a case can be made for including Harriet Beecher Stowe's *Uncle Tom's Cabin* in the canon of American literature—as indeed it should be—then perhaps Margaret Walker's *Jubilee* should be included in the canon as well. A fine historical novel in its own right, *Jubilee* can also serve as an important countertext to Stowe's *Uncle Tom's Cabin.* Walker's richly imagined and carefully documented representation of the community of black women re-creates a world that is virtually invisible in Stowe's novel, in nineteenth-century male slave narratives, and in better-known twentieth-century historical novels about the experiences of black people in the South during the Civil War period, such as Alex Haley's *Roots* and Ernest Gaines's *Autobiography of Miss Jane Pittman.* Both Harriet Beecher Stowe and Margaret Walker emphasize the bonds between black and white women, but in addition Walker also dramatizes the ways in which women within the black community were vitally connected to one another.[12] Far from crowding too much into *Jubilee,* as one critic has accused her of doing, Walker scrupulously delineates the culture of black women that has been omitted in other works of fiction.[13] Like the preserves and the unfinished quilt in Susan Glaspell's play *Trifles,* the many objects Walker incorporates into her novel and the various aspects of black female culture she depicts are not mere "trifles" but important signifiers of the black female folk tradition. *Jubilee* documents what Alice Walker has called the "creative spark" of those black mothers and grandmothers who might have been poets, novelists, essayists, or short story writers but who expressed their creativity instead in their gardens, in their quilts, and in the stories they told their children.[14] As critics have argued, Stowe's Uncle Tom becomes a black Christ figure; in

Jubilee, whose typology is based on the Old rather than the New Testament, Uncle Tom's female counterpart, Vyry, functions as a black Moses leading her people from bondage to freedom. Like Toni Morrison's *Song of Solomon,* Alice Walker's *The Color Purple,* and Gloria Naylor's *The Women of Brewster Place,* Margaret Walker's *Jubilee* is both a portrait of a memorable black female folk heroine and a celebration of the black female community.

NOTES

1. Harriet Beecher Stowe, *Uncle Tom's Cabin* (New York: Penguin American Library, 1983), 623–24. Further references to this novel appear in parentheses in the text.

2. Elizabeth Ammons, "Heroines in *Uncle Tom's Cabin,*" in *Critical Essays on Harriet Beecher Stowe,* ed. Elizabeth Ammons (Boston: G. K. Hall, 1980), 153.

3. Nikki Giovanni and Margaret Walker, *A Poetic Equation: Conversations Between Nikki Giovanni and Margaret Walker* (Washington: Howard University Press, 1974), 91.

4. Margaret Walker, *How I Wrote* Jubilee (Chicago: Third World Press, 1977), 25, 20; now available in *"How I Wrote Jubilee" and Other Essays on Literature and Life* (New York: Feminist Press, 1990).

5. Ibid., 12.

6. Ibid., 18.

7. Claudia Tate, "Conversation with Margaret Walker," in *Black Women Writers at Work* (New York: Continuum, 1983), 203.

8. Margaret Walker, *Jubilee* (Boston: Houghton Mifflin, 1966), x. Further references to this novel appear in parentheses in the text.

9. See Minrose Gwin, *"Jubilee:* The Black Woman's Celebration of Human Community," in *Conjuring: Black Women, Fiction, and Literary Tradition,* ed. Marjorie Pryse and Hortense J. Spillers (Bloomington: Indiana University Press, 1985), 149 n.9.

10. For a discussion of other novels by black women that also focus on the history and community of black women, see Hortense J. Spillers's afterword to *Conjuring.*

11. See Barbara J. Christian, "Trajectories of Self-Definition: Placing Contemporary Afro-American Women's Fiction," in *Conjuring* 233–48.

12. For a discussion of the bonding between black and white women in *Jubilee,* see Gwin, *Jubilee,* 131–50.

13. Arthur P. Davis, *From the Dark Tower* (Washington DC: Howard University Press, 1974), 184.

14. Alice Walker, *In Search of Our Mother's Gardens* (New York: Harcourt Brace Jovanovich, 1983), 234.

Give us Freedom, Give us Peace
I hear rumbling underground
Bread and Peace and Freedom too
I hear rumbling underground.
—MARGARET WALKER, "I Hear a Rumbling"

"Rumblings" in Folk Traditions Served Southern Style

JACQUELINE MILLER CARMICHAEL

Because *Jubilee* is saturated with various aspects of folk culture—
the songs, sayings, customs, food, medicinal remedies, and language—Barbara
Christian in *Black Women Novelists* (1980) expresses the opinion that at times
Walker's novel is reminiscent of those of Zora Neale Hurston. In "Toward a
Black Feminist Criticism," Barbara Smith lauds Zora Neale Hurston, Margaret
Walker, Toni Morrison, and Alice Walker for incorporating the traditional
black female activities of root working and conjuring, herbal medicine, and
midwifery into the fabric of their stories. According to Smith, "The fabrics of
their stories is not mere coincidence nor is their use of specifically Black female
language to express their own and their characters' thoughts accidental."[1]

In *How I Wrote* Jubilee (1972), Margaret Walker says that she always intended *Jubilee* to be a "folk novel" based on folk material: folk sayings, folk
beliefs, folkways. Walker recalls that as early as 1948, she was conceiving the
story in terms of this folklore. In the 1973 interview with Charles H. Rowell,
she explains how she was consciously or unconsciously influenced by the folk
tradition. She attributes a great deal of her interest in the folk tradition in
Jubilee and in her poetry to the works of Zora Neale Hurston, Paul Laurence
Dunbar, Langston Hughes, and Sterling Brown. As a child, of course, she was

241

taken by the folk tradition as she listened to her grandmother's stories and as she read folktales, but then she was, in the best sense, one of the folk herself. When in college and graduate school, she became a self-conscious artist, like many writers before and since, and she had to discover the peculiar value of her past. Walker recalls that it was "in Iowa in the late Thirties I began to write a great deal in the folk tradition. I realized that *Jubilee* needed to be a folk story."[2] In the 1966 reviews of her novel, many of the critics said that Walker was "singing a folk song."

In Ladell Payne's *Black Novelists and the Southern Literary Tradition* (1981), he writes that "both literatures of the black and white writers who grew up in the South clearly draw upon a folk culture, grow out of evangelical Protestantism, and rely on oral narrative devices; both literatures emphasize a sense locus, stress the importance of family, are concerned about the relationship between man and history, and dwell on an individual's search for identity at a time of social chaos; finally, at their best, both literatures deal honestly with black-white relationships." Payne calls his study "a representative rather than comprehensive one," and he chooses five black novelists and their colleagues whose careers span the time from Reconstruction to the present: Charles W. Chesnutt, James Weldon Johnson, Jean Toomer, Richard Wright, and Ralph Ellison.[3]

H. Nigel Thomas, in *From Folklore to Fiction: A Study of Folk Heroes and Rituals in the Black American Novel* (1988), discusses Margaret Walker, Richard Wright, Ralph Ellison, James Baldwin, and Paule Marshall in a chapter called "Rituals: Enlarging the Perspective." Thomas argues that "Walker and Wright should be examined together, if only because they influenced each other and were products of similar forces, although they produced 'radically different' fiction." In his analysis, Thomas notes that Wright saw "folklore that embodies the black man's hopes and struggle for freedom as the central focus for the creative black artist. Walker, on the other hand, is in the tradition of Hughes, Bontemps, and Ellison, who use folklore in their fiction to reveal the psychology of black American survival." He observes that the world Walker creates in *Jubilee* is one that the slaves and ex-slaves order with their religion and folklore. "With the atrocities of slavery and the Reconstruction framing the world of the characters," he states, "Walker's rituals for the triumph over pain emerge quite forcefully. They are linked essentially to religion, which in turn is linked to a struggle for freedom."[4]

In *Black American Literature* (1973), Roger Whitlow affirms that the slave narrative is not the only model for Margaret Walker. He offers that in the black folk tradition, one counts exaggerated tales of humor, the blues, spirituals, work songs, legendary-men stories, and slave and animal tales. He further offers that out of the black folk tradition has come a large and sophisticated body of written expression, from the poetry of Paul Laurence Dunbar and the short stories of Charles W. Chesnutt to the poetic novels of Jean Toomer and Zora Neale Hurston to the novels, short stories, and poetry of Langston Hughes, Claude McKay, and others. Whitlow places Margaret Walker in this tradition.[5]

In *Jubilee*, Walker includes sermons and prayers, rhymes and conjuring, in her catalog of folklore genres; she even builds a log cabin. The novel incorporates the tales that Vyry recites again and again about her journey from slavery to freedom, as well as explicit descriptions of her herbal medicines, cooking, needlework, songs, and sayings—all the folk traditions that her female ancestors have passed on to her. In a comparative analysis of Zora Neale Hurston and Margaret Walker, Charlotte Goodman concludes, "Just as Hurston incorporated into her fiction the material she culled from her anthropological investigations of black culture, so Walker included in *Jubilee* the rich material she had gathered painstakingly during the many years she spent investigating the black oral tradition, historical accounts of slavery, primary documents, and newspapers from the Civil War."[6] Goodman maintains that beyond the ordinary materials of folklife, *Jubilee* includes numerous signifiers of the black woman's history and culture, linking Vyry to past and future generations of black women.

For those literary critics whose aim is to establish the relationship of a given work, like *Jubilee*, to folk tradition, Richard Dorson offers three principal kinds of evidence. In "The Identification of Folklore in American Literature," he suggests that "the critic examine the author's biographical evidence to determine whether there was direct contact with oral lore." He compares and contrasts the experiences of Hawthorne, Joel Chandler Harris, and Longfellow. Of the three writers, he credits the stories of Harris as being most closely linked to Negro folklore, cited in the comparative notes of collectors. Dorson offers "internal evidence in the literary composition that indicates direct familiarity of the author with folklore." He cites Rowland Robinson's *Uncle Lisha's Shop*, George S. Wasson's *Cap'n Simeon's Store*, and Julia Peterkin's novels about Gullah Negro life as classic examples. Finally, Dorson suggests that "the critic must present corroborative evidence to supplement his proofs from biographical and internal evidence."[7] Here he does a comparative analysis of Rowland Robinson's use of New England traditions and Paul Green's use of North Carolina oral traditions. Dorson's point in all of this is to suggest to literary critics a reasonable and clearer method of identifying the presence of folklore in literature.

In *Fiction and Folklore: The Novels of Toni Morrison* (1991), Trudier Harris theorizes that "the basic pattern of dichotomizing literature and folklore is not only held in the writers' conscious incorporation of these materials but also in how the critics analyze and evaluate them." She recognizes Richard Dorson, Neil R. Grobman, and Sandra K. D. Stahl as folklore scholars of the 1970s who made determined efforts to raise the level of the discussion of folklore in literature and to generate theories about the requirements for studying both of these distinctly different genres. Harris's review of the most relevant criticism reveals that the study of folklore in literature "inherently perpetuates a dichotomous approach to the topic, a superimposition of the literary process of creation on the folk tendency toward oral forms. The folkloristic material is always treated as a wart on the face of the literature."[8] Again Harris recognizes a few scholars who are expanding on this pattern and are arguing for reversals of influence, "from the folk to belles lettres." Houston A. Baker Jr. and Henry Louis Gates Jr. assert that "traditional oral forms, especially the blues and the trickster, provide the basis for theorizing about African-American literature in its 'construction and its intertextuality.'"[9] Harris concludes that both arguments have some merit for interpreting folk concepts in the literature.

Margaret Walker catalogs her research on folklife and folk culture to corroborate the folk stories that her grandmother told her. Walker the teacher and scholar depended a great deal on the recorded folklore in libraries and archives throughout the country. Zora Neale Hurston the anthropologist says she was glad when somebody (Franz Boas) told her, "You may go and collect Negro folk-lore." Hurston writes that this was not a new experience for her, because she had known about Brer Rabbit's capers and what the Squinch Owl says from the housetop.[10] These two writers of the twentieth century, Hurston and Walker, collected their folklore differently but applied the folk traditions equally effectively in their literary work.

Margaret Walker opens her novel *Jubilee* with a folk belief. A screech owl is hovering over Hetta's cabin, and the message is that when the screech owl calls, someone will die, usually a man. Walker reverses this folk belief to forewarn the death of Hetta, Vyry's mother. Newbell Niles Puckett traces the belief that the hooting of the owl signifies death to both Europe and Africa. Puckett's research shows that "this almost universal superstition is doubtless due to the nocturnal habits of the bird and his strange half-human cry, and possibly represents a remnant of the belief of the Middle Ages that such birds were evil spirits coming to devour the souls of the dying." He records that, "considering the double source, it is no small wonder that the hooting of the owl is regarded by the Negro as a death omen."[11] According to collected southern lore, especially in *The Frank C. Brown Collection of North Carolina Folklore,* there are various versions of the screech owl belief. Inevitably, however, the superstition focuses mainly on sickness and death.

One of Walker's minor characters, Granny Ticey, the midwife and "conjuring woman," receives her message of Hetta's death through a quarter moon dripping blood. So when Jake comes to get her to deliver Hetta's baby, Granny Ticey does not want to go because she knows "nothing is right." In a more demonstrative conjuring episode, one of the slave driver Grimes's children dies, and a week later his pregnant wife miscarries. Grimes's suspicions are confirmed when his dog digs up a fetish buried under his doorstep. Big Missy's reaction to Grimes's claim is that she never would have thought he was superstitious. "No, ma'am, I ain't, but these niggers is up to something awful. . . . This kind of stuff ain't nothing but evil witchcraft and black magic. . . . This here is hoodoo" (*Jubilee* 56).

"The fact that conjure seldom worked on whites, or the fact that whites did not believe in it, gave its cultural uniqueness a corresponding practical liability," explains Eric J. Sundquist in *The Hammers of Creation: Folk Culture in Modern African-American Fiction* (1992). Sundquist writes that "many slaves believed that conjure could influence their masters' lives and their own treatment as slaves, but usually the effects were felt directly by blacks themselves." He concludes that "despite the fact that conjure did not pose a direct threat to the plantation regime and seldom made any changes on the balance of power in the slaves' favor, it did form a hidden semiotic code and system of belief that operated secretly, set apart from the white command of slaveholding." [12]

Charles Chesnutt's *The Conjure Woman* (1899) abounds with beliefs and practices in keeping with voodoo, black magic, and superstition. His major conjurers, Aunt Peggy and Uncle Jube, practically determine the fate of the characters around them. In *Long Black Song: Essays in Black American Literature and Culture* (1973), Houston A. Baker Jr. writes that "Chesnutt seems to make a conscious attempt to evoke the sinister mysteriousness of conjure tales, and his carefully delineated narrator, Uncle Julius, is a storyteller in the best tradition of black expression." [13] Besides Granny Ticey, Walker does not identify the conjurer or magician or a specific type of "black art"; she simply writes revealingly and convincingly of yet another folk superstition.

James E. Spears notes that superstitions are copious in *Jubilee:* "The superstitions occur more frequently at the beginning of the novel." Spears attributes this "to the antebellum period when the slave community is intact, and it is in this context that superstitions prevail." He further observes, "During the Civil War, superstitions take a declining position as routines are broken, society is disrupted, and the slaves are uprooted." [14] While searching for a permanent home and farmland in their "forty years in the wilderness," Vyry and her family return to the soil and the folklore resumes.

One way that Walker maintains the continuity of her slave narrative—in what Phyllis Klotman calls a "tripartite structure"—is by selecting an appropriate array of epigraphs to introduce each chapter. Spears also points out that "folk songs, religious and secular, are indeed apropos to Walker's development of *Jubilee*. Of the fifty-eight chapters, twenty-two begin with spirituals and thirty-six with secular song epigraphs, which help to give the novel its basic structural and thematic unity." [15]

Walker begins part 1 of *Jubilee* with the epigraph "Swing low, sweet chariot / Coming for to carry me home." The mood is somber: Vyry's mother is dying. "Mine eyes have seen the glory of the coming of the Lord," the introductory epigraph to part 2, dramatizes emancipation and the rise and fall of the South and the Dutton plantation. Walker's epigraph for part 3 heralds a new freedom and a different and arduous struggle for survival: "I am bound for the promised land / I am bound for the promised land / Oh, who will come and go with me / I am bound for the promised land." Klotman writes that "what is most interesting about the structure of *Jubilee* is how closely it parallels the experiences of so many slaves in bondage, as well as demonstrates how the condition of being female effectively limited the opportunity of many black women to escape to freedom." [16]

Although Vyry is just a child, she has learned how to escape the burden of her long days of work in the kitchen and Big Missy's physical abuse when she goes with Aunt Sally to the Rising Glory Baptist Church. Vyry looks forward to singing spirituals and listening to Brother Ezekiel sing, "I am a poor wayfaring stranger / I'm tossed in this wide world alone / No hope have I for tomorrow / I'm trying to make heaven my home" (*Jubilee* 48). Walker conveys to the reader a genuine, dignified, and universal cry for freedom in the singing of the spirituals. The songs are comforting and intuitively subversive: "Steal Away," "I Got Shoes," "I'm Going to Sit at the Welcome Table," "Religion Is a Fortune I Really Do Believe," and "The Old Sheep Knows the Road but the Young Lambs Must Find the Way" (*Jubilee* 37–38).

Eric J. Sundquist, in *To Wake the Nations* (1993), reconfirms the historical notion that "Steal Away" was a thinly coded song used to announce secret religious services or secular celebrations. Nat Turner and Harriet Tubman, among others, used the spiritual to organize slave resistance and escapes. Miles Mark Fisher has suggested, and many agree, that Nat Turner is the author of "Steal Away." But regardless of its authorship, Sundquist observes that "the lyrics of the spiritual do represent an angry God who is without question a projection of the slave's ardent will to freedom." [17]

Walker continues to show the effectiveness of singing spirituals in the powerful and resonant voice of Aunt Sally. Later in her slave narrative, Walker chooses Vyry to carry on Aunt Sally's oral tradition. The songs often puzzle

Vyry, before she grows to associate them with Aunt Sally's mood and mind, with the anger and resentment that she could voice in no other way. When Aunt Sally is deeply troubled, she opens her mouth and raises a real wailing song over her cooking:

> I been buked and I been scorned,
> Lord, I been buked and I been scorned,
> Lord, I been buked and I been scorned,
> I been talked about sho's you borned.
>
> (*Jubilee* 60)

Some of Aunt Sally's songs are frightening, and they make Vyry want to cry. She does not like to hear Aunt Sally sing,

> Before this time another year,
> I may be dead and gone.
> Be in some lonesome graveyard bed,
> O, Lord have mercy, Lord, how long?
>
> (*Jubilee* 60)

Lydia Parrish, in *Slave Songs of the Georgia Sea Islands* (1942), posits the view that "few people realize that the slaves, like their African cousins, sang on every possible occasion." [18] J. Mason Brewer writes, in *American Negro Folklore* (1968), "The ritual reflects the Negro slave's characteristic philosophy—that heaven was his home and the world only a temporary abode." Brewer says, "This other-worldly view of life helped him endure the hardships and trials of slavery cheerfully, even optimistically." [19] John Lovell Jr. extends this notion in *Black Song: The Forge and the Flame* (1986). Lovell purports that "spirituals dealt with all manifestations of life. The songs were religious and spiritual because they tried, with inspired artistry, to pose the root questions of life, of before life, and of beyond life." [20] Bernice Reagon, folklorist at the Smithsonian, comments, "Trace the roots of the songs black people have sung, and you will find a history no old documents will reveal." Reagon appropriately calls the songs "statements of the masses." [21]

It is some time before Vyry learns that the congregating of the "masses" on big meeting nights at Rising Glory serves a dual role. By listening to the sermons and participating in the singing, the slaves escape for a while the suffering and brutality inflicted on them. They also listen intently to Brother Ezekiel's sermons for information on safe routes to the Underground Railroad. Vyry remembers that Brother Ezekiel's favorite sermon was the Exodus story.

While recording and theorizing about his personal experiences, in *The Souls of Black Folk* (1903), W. E. B. Du Bois says, "The Preacher is the most unique personality developed by the Negro on American soil." Du Bois defines a preacher as a leader, a politician, an orator, a "boss," an intriguer, an idealist.[22] Cultural historian Lawrence W. Levine observes cogently in *Black Culture and Black Consciousness: Afro-American Folk Thought from Slavery to Freedom* (1977) that "the challenge before the preacher-as-creator was to invite his spatially immobile community to join him in creating a new world by transcending the narrow confines of the one in which they were forced to live. They extended the boundaries backward until it fused with the world of the Old Testament, and upward until it became one with the world beyond."[23] In *The Sermon and the African American Literary Imagination* (1994), Dolan Hubbard describes the language of the preacher as the motivating force. He writes, "Through his magnificently oral poetry, the unlettered and semiliterate preacher, in taking Jesus from *there* to *here* and moving the people from *here* to *there,* moves the spirit of the people beyond the boundary of hierarchical social order to the creation of new forms of human consciousness."[24]

With the pictures in the prose as well as in the poetry, and with some rhythm and some music, Walker wrote the sermons both for Brother Ezekiel and the white minister who preaches at the Fourth of July hanging. Walker admitted in the Bonetti interview that she did not remember whether she had read sermons by white preachers at that time. "I may have read one," she says, "but I don't think I modeled it after anybody. I took what I figured was basically his belief and worked with that."[25] Walker's sermons by the black preacher and the white were intended for specific audiences, and she used her language to intensify the meaning and the message.

Raven I. McDavid argues that "despite the tendency to dichotomize between folk speech and the speech of the educated, there seems no justification for it in the American situation." McDavid elaborates, "Many of us are multidialectal in our speech, switching from one code to another as the situation demands."[26] Walker demonstrates such a diversity in *Jubilee* without necessarily calling attention to differences in folk speech or condescending to it. She simply lets the characters, for the most part, speak the language they speak.

Cleanth Brooks asserts in one of his lectures, "The Language of the Gentry and the Folk," published in *The Language of the American South* (1985), that the strength of even the most formal southern writers stems from their knowledge of and rapport with the language spoken by the unlettered. "Most of our writers," Brooks maintains, "have in fact recognized the colloquial and even dialectal aspects for what they are: dialects of great vitality and power, dialects capable of eloquence and even of a kind of folk poetry."[27] Brooks believes that the best southern writers have never held in contempt the speech of the folk or used it only for comic effects. Whether this view is generally shared by literary critics or not, Brooks's assertion does seem applicable to Margaret Walker. Her effective handling of black and white dialects in *Jubilee* reflects simply her knowledge of the folk about whom she is writing. Joyce Pettis writes that "Walker is a black Southerner, whose ear for the distinctive rhythm of spoken words developed early. . . . The cadences of Southern speech, sermons, and Negro spirituals were already encoded in her mind, awaiting their transformation into art." [28]

Walker's folk-inspired prayers are also in keeping with her knowledge of the folk and folklife. In the Bonetti interview, Walker states that she made up most of those prayers. She relates with humor that Vyry's prayer in the woods was originally two or three pages long. The lady with whom Walker lived in Iowa, Miss Hovey, said, "Oh, you know that prayer is too long. I know you said colored folks pray a long time like that, but you got to cut that prayer; that prayer won't last." [29] Walker says she left the prayer in until her editor at Houghton Mifflin saw it. Her response was the same as Miss Hovey's: the prayer was too long. Although Walker thought she had a beautiful prayer, she reduced it to half a paragraph, retaining the essence of what she thought Vyry should be saying: "Lawd, God-a-mighty, I come down here this morning to tell you I done reached the end of my rope, and I wants you to take a-hold. I done come to the bottom of the well, Lord, and my well full of water done run clean dry. . . . We can't go on like this no longer, Lord. We can't keep on a-fighting, and a-fussing, and a-cussing, and a-hating like this, Lord" (*Jubilee* 381).

Walker's prayer provides Vyry the time and the space to release her bottled-up emotions. Jim, Vyry's son, is threatening to kill Innis, and, at the moment, even she feels capable of killing Innis Brown. In a transition from sorrow to epiphany, Walker concludes the prayer with Vyry's "I wants to thank You, Jesus, for moving the stone!" (*Jubilee* 381).

James E. Spears, in "Black Folk Elements in Margaret Walker's *Jubilee*," asserts that "folk language plays a major role in the novel." Spears argues that "its usage functions to delineate and lends credibility as characters to the Black folk portrayed." He recognizes Walker as a dialectologist and claims that "her use of dialect for characterization is both accurate and effective. It captures the essence of black dialect in pronunciation, vocabulary items, and usage and grammar, particularly in syntax." [30] J. L. Dillard, author of *Black English: Its History and Usage in the United States* (1972), points to syntax as the area in which the analysis of black English is most revealing. "In the system of its verbs, Black English reveals the greatest difference from white American dialects—as from British dialects—and the closest resemblance to its pidgin and creole ancestors and relatives." [31] Michael B. Montgomery and Guy Bailey, in their introduction to *Language Variety in the South* (1986), point to Dillard as being the most prolific scholar to follow the lead of William A. Stewart, sociolinguist. Both Stewart and Dillard concentrate most of their research on sociohistorical factors, which they believe make the creole hypothesis the most logical explanation for present-day distinctive black speech. Both scholars, state Montgomery and Bailey, contend that "the Plantation Creole was a development of a pidgin that originated not in the United States but in West Africa, that before the Civil War there was a great deal of diversity in black speech, and that there was one lifestyle and dialect for the vast majority of the slaves." [32]

In James E. Spears's brief investigation and sampling of Margaret Walker's *Jubilee*, he observes that "an exhaustive study could be made of the novel's language itself." His own study of the language in *Jubilee* shows violations of subject and verb agreement as in "Yassah, I has a pass," "Is you crazy," and "I wants to see." "You liables to cry" and "Jake gwine to kill you" show auxiliary verbs dropping in black dialect. Spears cites "When the new moon come, he be gone" as an example of the unorthodox subjunctive and the euphemism *gone* for *dead*. "We is been from pillar to post since we seen you last" reflects *to be* verb substitution in the auxiliary position for the *have* auxiliary.[33] According to William A. Stewart's unpublished essay, "On the Uses of Negro Dialect in the Teaching of Reading," *be* is used with adjectives and the *in* (-ing) form of verbs to indicate an extended or repeated state of action, for example, "He be busy." According to Stewart's analysis, the absence of this *be* usually indicates that the state or action is immediate or momentary, as in "He busy." Therefore, Stewart concludes that *be* and *is* are inflectional variants of the same verb.[34] Spears's language analysis from *Jubilee* tends to support Stewart's theory.

Walker uses the language, in its variations and with its implications, to further the exploration and demonstration of folklore genres in her novel. From the spiritual healing that emanates from and through her sermons and prayers, Walker turns to and generously supplies folk medical remedies in *Jubilee*. She connects folk medicine to the land in the herbs and spices that Vyry gathers for cooking and healing. Under the tutelage of Aunt Sally, Vyry learns to identify and use practically every herb in the woods adjacent to the Dutton plantation. Her knowledge of herbs and roots astounds Grimes, as he listens to her detailed explanation of each. The scene is less than cordial, however, for Grimes and a "patter-roller"—one who helps the slave driver, in this case, Grimes, to keep an eye on the slaves and to search for runaways—are suspicious of Vyry's presence in the woods on a Sunday afternoon. Grimes speaks first:

"What you doing here by yourself in the swamp woods, Vyry, and what you want with them weeds?"

"Them ain't no weeds, Mister Grimes. Them is greens to cook to eat, and yerbs and roots to cure all kinds of miseries what ails you."

The patter-roller said, "Tell us what you may call 'em and what you makes from them." (*Jubilee* 83)

As the faces of Grimes and the patter-roller remain expressionless and a dog sits panting at their feet, Vyry moves unswayed through her monologue:

Now that there is mullein. I takes mullein and pinetop and salt and I does different nother things with different ones. Mullein bath is good for the feets and legs to stop swelling and heart dropsy. I also uses it for teas. This here is barefoot root. I cooks it down and adds pyo [pure] lard and salt and makes a salve for the rheumatiz. Mayapple root is good to work the bowels and black halls and cherry root makes a good tea to strengthen the appetite. Them there is Jerusalem oats for worms. (*Jubilee* 83–84)

Once Vyry finishes her "lecture" on folk medicine, she turns to the men and declares with a great deal of personal pride, "Now gentlemen, that's what I does with my weeds!" Grimes queries her once again: "You sure you ain't got no pizen in there, has you?" With childlike innocence but also a profound wisdom that belies her age, Vyry says, "Nossah, I ain't fooling with no pizen. Course I can't tell what's pizen from what ain't pizen. I just knows the good roots. I ain't never knowed the bad ones" (*Jubilee* 84). Vyry's diplomatic answer wins her a fleeting moment of freedom.

Walker writes of folk medicine in *Jubilee* as tried and true remedies. Newbell Niles Puckett allows that "true it is that some of these remedies are of real medicinal value, but such are not clearly distinguished by the rural Negroes from the quite useless charms, mingled in with the curative herb itself "jes' ter make sho' of the desired result." Puckett refers to folk remedies as "a mixture of herbs and hoodoo constituting Afro-American medicine."[35] Vance Randolph quotes an Ozark mountain folk herbalist as saying, "God Almighty never put us here without a remedy for every ailment."[36] David J. Hufford believes that such a statement illustrates a link between a belief in the efficacy of herbal remedies and a belief in divine mercy.[37]

Folklorist Don Yoder identifies natural folk medicine and "magico-religious" folk medicine as two essential varieties or branches of the same field. He explains that natural folk medicine represents one of man's earliest reactions to his natural environment and involves the seeking of cures in the herbs, plants, minerals, and animal substances of nature. "Magico-religious folk medicine is sometimes called 'occult' folk medicine, which attempts to use charms, holy words, and holy actions to cure disease." Yoder continues, "Folk medicine, like folklore, has outgrown its strict identification with peasant cultures. Its clientele is drawn from a wide variety of groups and individuals."[38] Walker applies this notion in *Jubilee* by linking the folk healing traditions to the folk attitudes of a particular ethnic group and by offering a plethora of folk cures.

She also offers her folk characters traditional celebrations, to interrupt their daily lives and to give them brief respites and limited merriment. Anthropologist Robert Jerome Smith comments, "Most, if not all, of the societies of the world periodically set aside portions of time for celebration." He adds that "these are the moments of special significance to the group or community. They may be moments of transition, from one season to another or from one stage of life to another."[39] For Vyry and the other slaves in *Jubilee*, the traditional celebration of the Fourth of July is a day when they are subjected to hypocrisy. Eugene D. Genovese describes the Fourth of July as an occasion for a big barbecue and the gathering of slaves from various plantations. According to Genovese, "The Fourth has unusual characteristics, for it often gives the slaves access to political speeches not suited to their condition." He cites words and phrases like "'freedom,' 'independence,' 'revolution,' and 'death to tyrants' that did not escape the slaves' ears."[40]

In Frederick Douglass's "The Meaning of the Fourth of July and the Negro," he raises some pertinent questions about the celebration and answers them unequivocally:

> What, to the American slave, is your 4th of July? I answer: a day that reveals to him, more than all other days in the year, the gross injustice and cruelty to which he is the constant victim. To him, your celebration is a sham; your boasted liberty, an unholy license; your national greatness, swelling vanity; your sounds of rejoicing are empty and heartless; your denunciation of tyrants, brass-fronted impudence; your shouts of liberty and equality, hollow mockery; your prayers and hymns, your sermons and thanksgivings with all your religious parade and solemnity are, to him, mere bombast, fraud, deception, impiety, and hypocrisy—a thin veil to cover up crimes which would disgrace a nation of savages.[41]

Walker's setting for the Fourth of July celebration in *Jubilee* appears antiphonal in rhetoric and style to Douglass's discourse. Her judge presides and delivers his speech on the eightieth anniversary of the birth of a great country. The eminent theologian preaches a sermon and addresses three groups: the planters who were masters of black slaves, the slaves themselves, and the awful sinners guilty of the terrible sin of murder. Vyry listens and compares the folk sermons of Brother Ezekiel with the ones she hears on this occasion.

Christmas on the plantation is portrayed as a happier time for the slaves. According to John Hope Franklin and Alfred W. Moss Jr., this is accurate. The authors explain that "at the end of the cultivation period came a considerable reduction of duties. The slaves had an opportunity either to work for themselves or to engage in some kind of recreation. Fortunately for most, the Christmas season brings a complete suspension of work, except the bare essentials such as cooking and washing, and for one week both town and plantation slaves have a period of merrymaking." [42]

No doubt with tongue in cheek, Eugene D. Genovese observes that even the harshest masters usually provided a three-day holiday at Christmas, and they generally gave all their slaves Christmas presents, to the happy cries of "Christmas gif'!" [43] Harnett T. Kane discusses the growth of the southern Christmas as a tradition. "All through the region," he writes, "but particularly in the coastal section—it crystallized, during the antebellum period, into a set of customs which, despite variations here and there, followed a generally similar pattern." [44] Sterling Stuckey observes that "the slaves took advantage of Christmas in North America to revive African cultural expression along somewhat similar lines, since in Africa exchanges of gifts at reunions of family and friends were not uncommon. . . . Exchanges of gifts among slaves were often accompanied by gifts from the master." [45]

Indeed, as Walker dramatizes in *Jubilee,* Christmas is the best time of the year for Marster John Dutton's slaves. Harvesting the crops and preparing for the holidays lifts the load and cares of their bondage. "Jubilee," writes Harnett T. Kane, "if only a limited one, was coming." [46] On Christmas morning in *Jubilee,* there is always a warm and congenial relationship between the big house and the slave quarters. It is a tradition for the slaves to huddle in front of the mansion as Marster John stands on the veranda and thanks them for being good slaves. He then tells them the meaning of Christmas, orders whiskey and rum for everyone, and hands out gifts of candy, oranges, snuff, and tobacco. Following the ceremony, Marster John, his family, and guests go inside for the traditional breakfast. The slaves return to their cabins for a season of rest and with the certainty of food to eat. Vyry is a house servant; therefore, she works as hard on Christmas as on any other day. This year her heart is not in the cooking and celebrating. She has bread on this day, but her heart aches for freedom and for peace.

Perhaps in the deeper recesses of her heart, Vyry is able to retrieve those few days when she was able to romp and play games with the plantation children and Miss Lillian. Walker's introduction of children's folklore is significant as Vyry changes from a child to a child laborer. John H. McDowell suggests that "children's folklore is a species of children's play, but the two categories are not coterminous." He suggests that "what happens is that the play motive common to all forms of children's folklore produces a sense of make-believe."[47] Robert A. Georges suggests that "play is a form of expressive behavior common among all human beings and manifested overtly in all cultures."[48] Georges offers several characteristics of play: it is voluntary, it is nonproductive in a tangible sense, and it is separated from reality in time and space.

The folk games in *Jubilee* are mainly games of physical action, in which the children run, jump, hop, and hide. Vyry, Miss Lillian, and the slave children in the quarters laugh and romp their way through "Hold up the gates as high as the sky / Let King George's horses pass by." They join in other games of physical action: "Steal, Miz Liza" and "Las' night, night before / Twenty-four robbers at my door / I got up and let them in / Hit 'em on the head with a rolling pin / All hid?" In Missy Lillian's favorite game, "Here comes a gentleman just from Spain / To court, to court, your daughter Jane," she is chosen to be the pretty maiden and the fairest in the land. "Baptize Peter, baptize Paul / Baptize yeller gal, head and all" is Vyry's favorite game because she looks forward to the real baptizing by Brother Ezekiel (*Jubilee* 43–44).

"Most slave children," John Hope Franklin and Alfred W. Moss Jr. remind us, "had the run of the plantation and played with the white children in and out of the 'big house,' in and out of the cabins, and through the yards without any inhibitions." But, of course, when the Negroes became of "useful" age, which in Vyry's case was very early, the playing was practically over. Franklin and Moss say that "when they reached the social age, the interracial playing was over altogether, and they settled down to the existence that was the inevitable lot of the slave."[49] Walker vividly illustrates this in one of Big Missy's infrequent trips to the slave quarters. The children are playing games when Big Missy snatches Miss Lillian away. "You come home, you hear me. You're a young lady and you getting too big to play with niggers" (*Jubilee* 44). After this incident, Vyry loses interest and the games are no longer fun, even when the children play her favorite game.

Storytelling is another diversion that Walker provides for Vyry. Folklorists analyze storytelling as folk narrative that encompasses "all genres of oral literature in prose." "The form, contents, and function of the stories belonging to different genres are always variable," offers Linda Dégh. She explains that genres may vary according to cultures or within the same culture. "Rooted in their social environment, stories are extremely sensitive to group and individual attitudes."[50] In *Jubilee*, Aunt Sally entertains Vyry with her slave narrative, which, we imagine, is reminiscent of that of Margaret Walker's grandmother.

Another of Vyry's favorite storytellers is Brother Ezekiel. He soothes her fears, quotes Bible verses to her, and tells her fable-like stories about the spider and the cat, the wise donkey and the silly man. Harold Courlander states that "black oral literature contains elements of humor, irony, criticism and poetry that, in a literary sense, are uniquely expressed. It observes, it comments, it narrates; it ranges from humorous nonsense to profound and moving reflections on the human experience."[51]

With Walker's extensive research and her personal interest in telling her maternal grandmother's story, she makes a literary transition from oral folklore to physical folklife, what Richard Dorson calls "material culture." Dorson postulates that "how men and women in tradition-oriented societies build their homes, make their clothes, prepare their food, farm and fish, process the earth's bounty, fashion their tools and implements, and design their furniture and utensils are questions that should concern those who study material folk culture."[52] Walker's description of material folk culture in *Jubilee* runs the gamut from folk architecture to costumes to arts and crafts to food. She plies her writing craft well as she narrates or gives her characters the occasion to share their particular folklife skills without her comment.

For Walker's portrayal of folk housing, which Jan Brunvand states is the most basic aspect of traditional material culture, she has Vyry describe Aunt Sally's cabin. The cabin is bare and rough, Vyry says, and it has peepholes in the top of the roof where she looks up at the stars. When it rains, she and Aunt Sally set out cans and pots to catch the water. The open fireplace is their source of heat and their cookstove. Their cabin, which is typical of housing in the slave quarters, has one rough, shuttered window and a door. In John Michael Vlach's *Back of the Big House: The Architecture of Plantation Slavery* (1993), he draws on Frederick Law Olmsted's fieldwork to substantiate his claim that slave quarters were only one-room structures. Vlach reports that "by the 1850s, Olmsted found these minimal buildings in use all across the South."[53] In his general observation of houses built for slaves, Olmsted writes that "except for the chimney, I should have conjectured that it had been built for a powderhouse, or perhaps an ice-house—never for an animal to sleep in."[54] Eugene D. Genovese observes that "most slaveholders felt that their slaves lived decently in comparison to most of the world's peasants and workers."[55]

But Vyry and her family do seek a more decent form of housing as they move off the plantation and up the Chattahoochee River and west to Alabama to claim their space and build their first home. Innis and Vyry, co-architects and builders, measure off a space approximately twenty-five or thirty feet square, roll logs for the walls, and chink them with mud. For the building of the chimney, they mix pine needles and sticks with mud and pebbles. Then they thatch the roof with boughs of pine and oak, carve out openings for windows, and make a floor of hard clay covered with pine straw and rushes and leaves. Innis adds the finishing touches by building a loft at the top, where Vyry can store things and the children can have ample space for sleeping (*Jubilee* 267). This cabin is indeed larger and better built than was Aunt Sally's cabin.

Later in *Jubilee,* Vyry and her family build their second house. This time the floor plan calls for four rooms with a wide hall running through the center of the house. This wide center hall serves as another big room, with two rooms opening into it on each side. The front and back doors also open into the hall. Finally, the floor plan includes front and back porches. George W. McDaniel, in *Hearth and Home: Preserving a People's Culture* (1982), contends that "the houses freedmen built after the Civil War are probably the most telling evidence that slaves built houses." He writes, "In a world of severely limited opportunities, constructing these buildings gave free blacks and slaves an important measure of self-esteem."[56]

Folk architecture is put on hold in *Jubilee* momentarily, as Vyry experiences a healing of sorts and a rebuilding of her self-esteem. While Vyry is recovering, Innis begins collecting and storing building materials on their deeded property. On the first day that both blacks and whites band together for a traditional house and barn raising, Innis proudly tells Vyry of his preparation. According to W. E. B. Du Bois, "by far the most pressing problem" of freed slaves was land, which was "absolutely fundamental and essential to any real emancipation of the slaves."[57] Du Bois maintains that the "great impulse toward better housing" came from these successful black landowners.[58] Historically, many of them had learned to construct houses during their days in slavery. Not only had they built their own cabins, but they had also been taught building trades for the construction of antebellum mansions.

Bridging the gap between folk architecture and academic architecture in *Jubilee,* Walker focuses on the interior of the big house. On Vyry's first visit there, she stands in awe of the dark coolness and the noble richness of the lavish furnishings. She observes the great oaken bed whose headboard nearly touches the ceiling in Big Missy's room, and the high mountain of feather mattresses covered with a snow-white counterpane. There is a tester bed with a canopy of sprigged pink and white cotton in Miss Lillian's room. Marster John's and young Marster Johnny's rooms have massive dark furniture with silk upholstery in dark greens and reds and blues. Vyry goes from room to room, tiptoeing in awe and not daring to touch all the wonderful things she sees. Then, when she thinks about it, she wonders why she does not feel happy about coming to the big house to stay (*Jubilee* 17). Vyry's stay in the big house is short-lived, but her work in the adjacent kitchen seems like an eternity.

Kenneth Severens, in his discussion of architecture in the South, writes that it is fairly common knowledge that the picturesque antebellum plantation house emerged from mid-nineteenth-century romanticism, and occasionally it adhered strictly to the Greek Revival style. Severens theorizes that this classicism was thoroughly imbued with romanticism, with the notion that "every new planter was a Southern aristocrat, and the appeal of Greek architecture served to disguise their humble origins and gave them an appearance of root-edness."[59] *In The Mind of the South* (1941), Wilbur J. Cash argues that "most planters were simply successful farmers who through energy, acumen, and good fortune had surpassed their middle-class peers."[60] Severens maintains that "the construction of a great plantation house was not an inevitable development, but rather an act of will, whose aim was the establishment of a sense of place."[61]

In Vlach's *Back of the Big House,* the architectural analysis moves away from the slave owners' homes to those places claimed by their slaves. Vlach asserts that "black presence has been generally ignored in architectural histories written about the South" and that "the need to focus on African-Americans is altogether necessary." He theorizes that "before a revised portrayal of southern architecture can be presented to correct this deficit, black contributions to the built environment must be ascertained. Both Big House and slave quarter, although they were distinct places, were still elements of the single landscape—one helped to define the other." He explains, "Back of and beyond the Big House was a world of work dominated by black people who knew it intimately, and they gave to it, by thought and deed, their own definition of place."[62] Walker renders a similar sense of place in her fictional plantation of "divided houses."

As Vyry makes her trek from the big house to Aunt Sally's cabin, she is grateful for the clothes she is wearing. John Hope Franklin and Alfred W. Moss Jr. offer this explanation of folk clothing. "The average slave wore what was generally called 'Negro clothes,' which consisted of jeans, linseys, kerseys, and osnaburgs for men and calico and homespun fabrics for the women." They continue, "On some plantations, Negro women spun and wove the cloth out of which they made their dresses. As far as shoes were concerned, they were called 'Negro Brogans.'"[63]

Vyry is quite comfortable in her long calico and linsey dress, with an extra apron of blue gingham check and a shawl to throw over her head and around her shoulders. Not only is she wearing shoes, she is also wearing stockings. She recalls that it is usually November when Grimes buys shoes for the field hands, and some of them are already suffering with frostbitten feet before they receive shoes. Many wrap their feet in rags or tear burlap from ragged croker sacks. Vyry remembers that there is hardly a winter when someone does not lose a toe (*Jubilee* 50). Franklin and Moss confirm that "shoes for the slaves were not provided except for the winter months," and "no article of clothing called forth so much complaint as the shoes. Despite their complaints, no more clothing was furnished than was absolutely necessary." According to Franklin and Moss, "the planters reasoned that perhaps slaves needed ample food in order to work efficiently, but they saw little connection between clothing and work." [64]

Walker provides other detailed descriptions of folk clothing in several scenes where Vyry is the observer. At the Fourth of July celebration, Vyry notices that the white women dress in huge bell-bottomed and hoop-ringed skirts and close-fitting bonnets. The slaves, of course, are barefooted and wear their usual homespun and linsey, straw hats, or red head rags. Tagging along with the women are barefooted children wearing ragged shifts. For social events in the big house, Walker is as specific about white material culture as she is about that of the slaves, especially with regard to clothing. Big Missy buys three dresses for one dinner party because she simply cannot make up her mind. "Why, this can decide our social future for the rest of our natural born lives," Big Missy rationalizes (*Jubilee* 62).

Walker does not take the reader through the selection process for Miss Lillian's wedding dress as she does for Big Missy's "choice outfit" that can make or break Marster John's political campaign. Walker simply describes the dress as imported embroidered white silk with a beautiful lace veil. Vyry notices at these formal functions in the big house that even Sam, the carriage driver, is dressed differently. He is all spruced up in a black swallowtail coat with a scarlet vest and gold buttons. George W. McDaniel, in *Hearth and Home: Preserving a People's Culture*, writes that clothes served to identify the higher station of house servants. McDaniel offers this account: "The table was waited on by Uncle Billie, dressed in a uniform, decorated with brass buttons, braid, and a fancy vest, his hands encased in white gloves." [65] At least for Sam in Walker's *Jubilee* and for Uncle Billie in McDaniel's narrative, their costumes are not theirs to choose.

Don Yoder defines folk costume or folk dress, used synonymously, as the "dialect of dress." He fosters the premise that folk costume is "the visible, outward badge of folk-group identity, worn consciously to express that identity. In every case the costume is distinct and identifiable; it identifies the wearer to the outside world as well as to his own community; it is prescribed by the community and its form is dictated by the community's tradition." He theorizes that when costumes are viewed as wholes and set against their functional background in the overall life of the folk community, the focus shifts from the origin of the costume to the basic social and psychological significance of costume in the folk-cultural matrix. Summarizing his theory, Yoder states that "folk costume is one of the symbols of the folk community and one of the variables of a culture."[66] Vyry is aware of the vast differences between the folk costumes in the big house and those in the quarters. Thinking in the humanistic spirit of Walker, she is saddened by the feasting in one folk community while the other suffers.

Charlotte Goodman, in her essay "From Uncle Tom's Cabin to Vyry's Kitchen," writes, "Walker depicts Vyry's life not only in the plantation house but in the Slave Quarters where Vyry is nurtured by other black women and learns about the traditions of her people. One of these is the making of cloth."[67] To support her observation, Goodman refers to Walker's acknowledgments in *Jubilee,* where she describes the dress her great-grandmother is wearing. Walker writes that "from spinning the thread to weaving the cloth, the garments are entirely her handiwork." Eugene D. Genovese believes that "slave craftsmen made a special contribution to Afro-American culture." He writes, "The work of these first-rate craftsmen represented an organic combination of practical needs with the aesthetic they brought to America from Africa. West African culture did not separate art . . . from practical life."[68] Neither does Walker separate Vyry's knowledge of arts and crafts from her life in the kitchen and, eventually, life in her own home.

When Vyry is not doing her chores in the kitchen or for Big Missy, she observes the women plying their crafts. In preparation for a wedding and a war, black and white women mutually engage in work sessions that include spinning, weaving, and sewing. Vyry learns well. By the time the war reaches the Dutton plantation and Vyry is left to run the place, she is spinning and weaving clothes for the children. Out of sheer desperation, Vyry makes soap from kitchen grease and wood ashes, and from a year's supply of tallow she makes candles. After the war, when freedom comes and Vyry and her family move into their first home in Alabama, she makes featherbeds, rag rugs and dolls, and quilts. John Michael Vlach contends that "even though the end results might seem simple and modest, the processes of plying a craft are very complex." Vlach writes, "A craftsman's work is related directly to his social context, immediate ecology, historical period, and economic circumstances as well as his personal training, development of skill, and expression of talent."[69]

Demonstrations of such skills and talents are created by Walker as she provides a colorful and exciting quilt-making scene for the women while the men are building Vyry's third and permanent home in Alabama. Seeing the house built is enough excitement, but Vyry fairly bursts with pride and interest in the quilts. There are six quilts, and each housewife has a different pattern. Vyry's consists of pomegranates, with deep orange fruit and green stems and leaves, on a white background. Warren E. Roberts acknowledges the patchwork quilt as the most popular of several kinds of quilting. According to Roberts, the patchwork quilt involves patterns of pieces of cloth of different colors and sizes sewn together. Roberts says that "not only is the technique of quilting traditional, but designs of great variety, often with colorful names, were also passed from one quilter to the next." [70]

In Susan Roach's essay "The Kinship Quilt: An Ethnographic Semiotic Analysis of a Quilting Bee," there is concern that folklorists are not turning out any substantial body of quilting scholarship. Roach argues that "the dearth of articles on quiltmaking in folklore journals indicates this neglect." [71] John Michael Vlach shares the same concern. Vlach says that "of the recent books on quilting, almost no attention is paid to the creators of a great art form; the concentration is on 'how-to' descriptions." [72] Bell hooks says, "When art museums display the artistic achievement of American quiltmakers, often representation at such shows suggests that white women were the only group truly dedicated to the art of quiltmaking." She argues that black women's quilts are portrayed as exceptions. Usually there is only one, and the card identifies the quiltmaker as an "anonymous black woman." [73] Although bell hooks is beginning to see some effort on the part of art historians to document traditions of black female quiltmakers, she mourns that her grandmother is not among those named and honored.

Walker's women characters are not the only ones engaged in arts and crafts. Randall Ware works as a blacksmith on the plantation and in his own shop. In John Michael Vlach's *By the Work of Their Hands: Studies in Afro-American Folklife* (1991), he recognizes that historically, "the blacksmith was the pivotal craftsman of his community; all the other skills in some manner depended on his efforts." Vlach outlines the immense dependency of the community on the blacksmith: "The woodworkers could not do anything unless the smith made or at least sharpened their tools; the cook depended on the andirons that facilitated the efficient burning of the logs in the hearth; all the tasks of a plantation could be halted if the horses needed shoes, a wagon wheel needed a rim, the plow needed mending." Vlach concludes, "The blacksmith's leadership in the crafts gave him the elevated status that accompanied financial success and made him a likely leader in the social realm of the slave community." [74]

Randall Ware is a black man of many talents. Vyry reminisces about a cradle Ware made when their son, Jim, was born. But she marvels at Innis's craftsmanship. For the furnishings in their first home, he makes chair bottoms with cane and corn husks and a fine trestle table of oak. One of his specialties is taking the hides of animals and making shoes or rugs, as he does with the hide of the black panther in Walker's dissertation version of *Jubilee*. In a more intimate context, Innis makes Jim a game out of a jar. He paints a face on the inside of the lid and makes indentations for the eyes, nose, and mouth. He fills the jar with dried peas that drop into the indentations. The gift is meant to cheer Jim while he is recovering from malaria. Since Minna, Jim's sister, is recuperating from the same malady, Vyry makes her a rag doll with shoe-button eyes. Later Vyry teaches Minna, in the folk tradition, how to do needlework. Minna's first handiwork is a handkerchief, which she gives as a going-away gift to her brother, Jim. Thus, we sense Walker's conscientious efforts to connect the folk beliefs and customs to the arts and crafts in *Jubilee*, in what John Michael Vlach calls "an expression of distinct ethnic heritage." [75]

Walker further demonstrates her folk connections in her treatment of folk foods. Whether the cooks are preparing food for the folk in the big house or for those in the slave quarters, every morsel is meticulously prepared and arranged for consumption. Walker's own experience as a cook and her personal pride in writing creatively about foods lend credence to the appetizing and encyclopedic manner in which she records Aunt Sally's and Vyry's culinary arts. Maryemma Graham, a former student of Walker's at Northwestern University and an author in her own right, says of Walker: "Her two favorite places were in the classroom, where she gave remarkable lectures on Afro American literature and history, freely sharing personal anecdotes and memories of every black writer whose works we read, and her kitchen, where she talked intermittently while cleaning and cooking fresh collards or preparing her own special version of Louisiana gumbo." [76]

In James E. Spears's essay "Favorite Southern Negro Folk Recipes," he writes that "every ethnic group's culinary arts are a basic element of their culture." Spears contends that "this is equally apropos of the Southern Negro, whose culinary arts have deeper roots in an agrarian sub-culture." According to Spears, "Most of the perennially popular Negro folk dishes are derived from a plantation source." [77] Bob Jeffries colors this argument with the premise that "all soul food is Southern, but not all Southern food is soul." Jeffries observes that "to begin with, soul food is honest; it is easy to cook but does not adapt well to 'let's-get-out-of-the-kitchen-fast' shortcuts." He continues, "Soul food cooking is an example of how really good Southern Negro cooks cooked with what they had available to them." Jeffries further contends that "soul food, like jazz, was created in the South by American Negroes. . . . What makes soul food unique—and more indigenous to this country than any other so-called American cooking style—is that it was created and evolved almost without European influence."[78]

In a salute to the chief cook in the big house, Eugene D. Genovese observes that the high praise of southern cooking has usually been lavished on "Ole Missus." Genovese argues that the truth is that "Ole Mammy," or merely "the cook," usually ran the kitchen with an iron hand and had learned what she knew from generations of black predecessors. "What Missus knew," states Genovese, "she usually learned from her cook, not vice versa."[79] In *Jubilee,* Big Missy rules the big house and the servants, but it is Aunt Sally, the best cook in Lee County and in the state of Georgia, who rules the kitchen. Walker's emphasis on Aunt Sally's kitchen and the tools she uses coincides with Jan Brunvand's theory. Brunvand recommends that "the study of folk foods should include the entire process of traditional food handling and consumption: kitchens and cookware; seasoning and serving; food preparation and preservation."[80]

Anthropologist Tony L. Whitehead reports that in his food-related research of African Americans in the South over a period of six years, he used "the Cultural Systems Paradigm (CSP) to identify several categories of activities: acquisition, preparation, preservation, distribution, and consumption." Whitehead explains that "according to accounts of early southern foodways, African-Americans made the greatest contribution in food preparation. The slave cook was generally known as the primary food preparer for the slaves and the planters."[81]

John Edgerton writes in *Southern Food: At Home, on the Road, in History* (1987), "The kitchen was one of the few places where their [slave cooks'] imagination and skill could have free rein and full expression, and there they often excelled."[82] Whitehead credits the cook with creating "spicy" flavored foods, since she was expected to turn the "lowly food items" given to the slaves into the "culinary masterpieces" that are now defined as southern cooking.[83]

And it is as an apprentice that Vyry joins master cook Aunt Sally in whipping up mouth-watering food in *Jubilee.* With one month to prepare for a big political party hosted by Marster John at the big house, Aunt Sally cooks turkey, roast pig, mutton, fried chicken, and guinea hen. She makes an abundance of baked hams, geese, and wild game. Then she selects jars of snapbeans and butterbeans, corn, okra, tomatoes, artichokes, chowchow, and hot mustard pickles for the vegetables. Walker continues her litany of distinctively southern foods as Aunt Sally prepares spoon bread, biscuits, waffles, corn sticks, muffins, light bread, and buckwheats for breakfast. With these she serves walnuts, tomato conserve, and marmalade made of lemons and oranges. Aunt Sally complains at night that her feet hurt, and she and Vyry hardly feel like eating the hot buttered biscuit and damson plum preserves that she has wrapped in a rag and stuck in her bosom (*Jubilee* 62–63).

Often "tired, weary, and worn," Aunt Sally does not neglect to pass on to Vyry the traditions she brought to the big house. Vyry is well prepared when it comes time to replace Aunt Sally as chief cook. She prepares food for the Dutton household, special celebrations, and social events, and she is in charge of preparing dinner for the field hands. But her specialty is Christmas dinner. Actually, she makes two different kinds of dinners. For the family in the big house, Vyry cooks quail, pheasant, turkeys, ducks, venison, fruitcakes, and puddings. In the slave quarters, Vyry and the other families cook possum, coon, and roasted sweet potatoes.

Genovese writes that "the slave recipe that has come down to us most prominently is for opossum—significantly, a food they obtained for themselves." Solomon Northup, who had lived as a free man in the North before being kidnapped into slavery, gives this account: "The flesh of the coon is palatable, but verily there is nothing in all butcherdom so delicious as a roasted 'possum." [84] It is worth noting that opossum was so available because it could be hunted successfully without a weapon. Referring to the reminiscences in the WPA Federal Writers' Project Slave Narrative Collection, Charles W. Joyner observes that "whenever a former slave speaks of good times in slavery, seldom does he leave food out of the picture." Joyner cautions here that he does not mean to run the risk of romanticizing slavery, but the records indicate "such joys as slavery allowed were centered around food and actually found in the food itself, creating a desire deeper than hunger for that kind of food." Joyner concludes, "This food that symbolized so much to the slave earned a genuine love, which is so very well expressed in the narratives." [85]

Walker's slave narrative continues as Vyry remembers her last Christmas in the big house, unlike all of the previous Christmases. She is now the overseer of the plantation, harvester of the crops, preparer of the food, and caretaker of her own family and of Miss Lillian's. Vyry refuses to let this daunt her usual zest for preparing a Christmas dinner. With the help of Innis Brown, she cooks a feast of rabbits, squirrels, an opossum, a coon, pork, beef, and chicken. For desserts, she makes cakes, pies, egg custards, sweet potato custards, pecan and syrup pies.

Vyry's menu for her first Christmas in Alabama contrasts with that of her last Christmas in Georgia, but the feast is by no means less delectable and filling. She continues to make Christmas a happy time. From their butchered hog she makes sausage, liver pudding, crackling bread, chitterlings, and souse meat. She salts and sugar-cures the hams, shoulders, and middlings with molasses. When the family moves on to Luverne, Alabama, Vyry prepares a similar meal, but for this celebration she makes molasses candy and teaches the children how to pull the taffy. Indeed, Walker makes Vyry an ideal preparer of folk foods, committed to carrying on the tradition that Aunt Sally, especially, taught her.

This tradition continues, as Tony L. Whitehead reports in "Soul Food Versus Southern Foodways." Whitehead says that "the emergence of the idea of soul food during the intense cultural revitalization of African-Americans in the 1960s suggested an exclusive ethnic dietary system." According to Whitehead, "Not only does soul food refer to the content of the Southern African-American diet, but it also refers to the preparation styles. Pork remains a favorite soul food meat, there are still various uses of corn and sweet potatoes in the soul food diet, many older African-Americans include squirrel, rabbit, 'possum, and deer in the soul food menu, and traditionally, African-Americans in the South favor foods prepared with high contents of sugar and salt." Whitehead points out that "the content, ethnic origin, preparation styles, and differential consumption of food are less important to our understanding of a cultural group's foodways than is the 'meaning' of such foodways to these groups." [86]

Walker celebrates this tradition with a flare as Vyry entertains those families who have come to help build the new house. As soon as the families arrive, she serves coffee, bowls of fresh peaches and dewberries with pitchers of sweet cream and milk. And for those who had not already eaten breakfast, she fries ham and eggs and bakes pans of hot biscuits. At noon the men and women stop work, and Vyry serves fried chicken, buttered ears of corn, turnip greens, okra, biscuits, blueberry pie, and coffee. Later, in this house built by neighbors of goodwill, Vyry prepares yet another special meal for the return of Randall Ware. In a rare mood for the usually humble Vyry, she brings out the finest treasures from her chest and from the plantation: a real linen tablecloth, silver, and china dishes. She places a bowl of flowers on the table and sets out fried chicken, pies, candied sweet potatoes, okra, lima beans, ham, biscuits, cornbread, and elderberry wine for Randall Ware. In this scene Vyry gets the opportunity to do what she calls "show[ing] off" her family, home, and culinary arts. She has poured out her excitement, pride, and love in the folk foods.

In the folk traditions recorded in *Jubilee*, Walker elevates folklore to a higher plane in literature. H. Nigel Thomas recognizes that "Walker's forte is not in the creation of new techniques; she merely borrows those techniques that are already present." [87] Joyce Pettis observes, "More than anything else, Walker anchors *Jubilee* in the love and experience of her people." [88] Much of the power and success of *Jubilee* must be attributed to Margaret Walker's abilities as an

African American novelist who immerses herself in black folk culture and incorporates a variety of its expressions into her work. Her novel represents the artistic use of folklore, for she is conscious of folklore and adept and comprehensive in her use of it. Her incorporation of it goes beyond contributing to the physical setting or historical accuracy; it grounds this novel in the southern experience of African Americans.

NOTES

1. Barbara Smith, "Toward a Black Feminist Criticism," in Angelyn Mitchell, ed., *Within the Circle: An Anthology of African American Literary Criticism from the Harlem Renaissance to the Present* (Durham: Duke University Press, 1994), 416–17.

2. Quoted in Charles H. Rowell, "Poetry, History and Humanism: An Interview with Margaret Walker," *Black World*, December 1975, 6–7.

3. Ladell Payne, *Black Novelists and the Southern Literary Tradition* (Athens: University of Georgia Press, 1981), 6–7.

4. H. Nigel Thomas, *From Folklore to Fiction: A Study of Folk Heroes and Rituals in the Black American Novel* (Westport CT: Greenwood, 1988) 137–38, 140.

5. Roger Whitlow, *Black American Literature: A Critical History of the Major Periods, Movements, Themes, Works, and Authors* (Chicago: Nelson Hall, 1973), 11.

6. Charlotte Goodman, "From Uncle Tom's Cabin to Vyry's Kitchen: The Black Female Folk Tradition in Margaret Walker's *Jubilee*," in Florence Howe, ed., *Tradition and the Talents of Women* (Urbana: University of Illinois Press, 1991), 327, 331.

7. Richard M. Dorson, "The Identification of Folklore in American Literature," *Journal of American Folklore* 70 (1957): 5, 7–8.

8. Trudier Harris, *Fiction and Folklore: The Novels of Toni Morrison* (Knoxville: University of Tennessee Press, 1991), 9.

9. Quoted in Trudier Harris, *Fiction and Folklore* 9.

10. In Cheryl A. Wall, ed., *Zora Neale Hurston: Folklore, Memoirs, and Other Writings* (New York: Penguin, 1995), 9.

11. Newbell Niles Puckett, *Folk Beliefs of the Southern Negro* (New York: Negro Universities Press, 1926), 482.

12. Eric J. Sundquist, *The Hammers of Creation: Folk Culture in Modern African-American Fiction* (Athens: University of Georgia Press, 1992), 123.

13. Houston A. Baker Jr., *Long Black Song: Essays in Black American Literature and Culture* (Charlottesville: University Press of Virginia, 1973), 38–39.

14. James E. Spears, "Black Folk Elements in Margaret Walker's *Jubilee*," *Mississippi Folklore Register* 14.1 (1980): 16.

15. Spears, "Black Folk Elements," 14.

16. Phyllis R. Klotman, "'Oh Freedom'—Women and History in Margaret Walker's *Jubilee*," *Black American Literature Forum* 11.4 (1977): 143.

17. Eric J. Sundquist, *To Wake the Nations: Race in the Making of American Literature* (Cambridge: Harvard University Press, Belknap, 1993), 511–12.

18. Lydia Parrish, *Slave Songs of the Georgia Sea Islands* (New York: Creative Age, 1942), xv.

19. J. Mason Brewer, ed., *American Negro Folklore* (New York: New York Times Book Co., Quadrangle, 1968), 146.

20. John Lovell Jr., *Black Song: The Forge and the Flame* (New York: Paragon, 1986), 17.

21. Quoted in Spears, "Black Folk Elements," 14.

22. W. E. B. Du Bois, *The Souls of Black Folk* (Chicago: McClurg, 1903), 141.

23. Lawrence W. Levine, *Black Culture and Black Consciousness: Afro-American Folk Thought from Slavery to Freedom* (New York: Oxford University Press, 1977), 32–33.

24. Dolan Hubbard, *The Sermon and the African American Literary Imagination* (Columbia: University of Missouri Press, 1994), 5.

25. Kay Bonetti, *An Interview with Margaret Walker* (Columbia: American Audio Prose Library, 1991).

26. Raven I. McDavid, "Folk Speech," in Tristram Potter Coffin, ed., *Our Living Traditions: An Introduction to American Folklore* (New York: Basic Books, 1968), 232.

27. In Cleanth Brooks, *The Language of the American South* (Athens: University of Georgia Press, 1985), 17. Professor Brooks gave three lectures that pay special tribute to the language itself.

28. Joyce Pettis, "Margaret Walker: Black Woman Writer of the South," in Tonette Bond Inge, ed., *Southern Women Writers* (Tuscaloosa: University of Alabama Press, 1990), 9.

29. Bonetti, *Interview with Margaret Walker*.

30. Spears, "Black Folk Elements," 14–15.

31. J. L. Dillard, *Black English: Its History and Usage in the United States* (New York: Random House, 1972), 40.

32. Michael B. Montgomery and Guy Bailey, eds., *Language Variety in the South: Perspectives in Black and White* (Tuscaloosa: University of Alabama Press, 1986), 10–11.

33. Spears, "Black Folk Elements," 15.

34. In Eugene D. Genovese, *Roll, Jordan, Roll: The World the Slaves Made* (New York: Pantheon, 1974), 436.

35. Puckett, *Folk Beliefs,* 358.

36. Quoted in David J. Hufford, "Folk Healers," in Richard M. Dorson, ed., *Handbook of American Folklore* (Bloomington: Indiana University Press, 1983), 307.

37. Hufford, "Folk Healers," 307.

38. Don Yoder, "Folk Medicine," in Richard M. Dorson, ed., *Folklore and Folklife* (Chicago: University of Chicago Press, 1972), 192.

39. Robert Jerome Smith, "Festivals and Celebrations," in Dorson, *Folklore and Folklife,* 159.

40. Genovese, *Roll, Jordan, Roll,* 577.

41. Quoted in Ramon A. Gutiérrez and Geneviève Fabre, eds., *Feasts and Celebrations*

in North American Ethnic Communities (Albuquerque: University of New Mexico Press, 1995), 34–35.

42. John Hope Franklin and Alfred W. Moss Jr., *From Slavery to Freedom: A History of Negro Americans* (New York: McGraw-Hill, 1988), 123.

43. Genovese, *Roll, Jordan, Roll,* 573.

44. Harnett T. Kane, *The Southern Christmas Book* (New York: McKay, 1958), 63.

45. Sterling Stuckey, *Slave Culture: Nationalist Theory and the Foundations of Black America* (New York: Oxford University Press, 1987), 69–70.

46. Kane, *Southern Christmas Book,* 64.

47. John H. McDowell, "Children's Folklore," in Richard M. Dorson, ed., *Handbook of American Folklore* (Bloomington: Indiana University Press, 1983), 314.

48. Robert A. Georges, "Recreations and Games," in Dorson, *Folklore and Folklife,* 173.

49. Franklin and Moss, *From Slavery to Freedom,* 123.

50. Linda Dégh, "Folk Narrative, in Dorson, *Folklore and Folklife,* 58–59.

51. Harold Courlander, *A Treasury of Afro-American Folklore* (New York: Crown, 1976), 256–57.

52. Richard M. Dorson, introduction to *Folklore and Folklife* (Chicago: University of Chicago Press, 1972), 2–3.

53. John Michael Vlach, *Back of the Big House: The Architecture of Plantation Slavery* (Chapel Hill: University of North Carolina Press, 1993), 155.

54. Quoted in Vlach, *Back of the Big House,* 156.

55. Genovese, *Roll, Jordan, Roll,* 526.

56. George W. McDaniel, *Hearth and Home: Preserving a People's Culture* (Philadelphia: Temple University Press, 1982), 48–50.

57. W. E. B. Du Bois, *Black Construction: An Essay Toward a History of the Part Which Black Folk Played in the Attempt to Reconstruct Democracy in America, 1860–1880* (Philadelphia: Saifer, 1935), 601.

58. W. E. B. Du Bois, "The Problem of Housing the Negro: The Home of the Country Freedman," *Southern Workman,* September 1901, 536; cited in McDaniel 193.

59. Kenneth Severens, *Southern Architecture* (New York: Dutton, 1981), 43–44.

60. Wilbur J. Cash, *The Mind of the South* (New York: Knopf, 1941), 109.

61. Severens, *Southern Architecture,* 3.

62. Vlach, *Back of the Big House,* xiv, 1.

63. Franklin and Moss, *From Slavery to Freedom,* 120.

64. Franklin and Moss, *From Slavery to Freedom,* 120–21.

65. McDaniel, *Hearth and Home,* 115.

66. Don Yoder, "Folk Costume," in Dorson, *Folklore and Folklife,* 295–96, 302.

67. Goodman, "From Uncle Tom's Cabin," 331.

68. Genovese, *Roll, Jordan, Roll,* 394–95.

69. John Michael Vlach, "Folk Craftsmen," in Dorson, *Handbook of American Folklore,* 301.

70. Warren E. Roberts, "Folk Crafts," in Dorson, *Folklore and Folklife,* 250.

71. Susan Roach, "The Kinship Quilt: An Ethnographic Semiotic Analysis of a Quilting Bee," in Rosan A. Jordan and Susan J. Kalcik, eds., *Women's Folklore, Women's Culture* (Philadelphia: University of Pennsylvania Press, 1985), 54.

72. Vlach, "Folk Craftsmen," 304.

73. bell hooks, *Yearning: Race, Gender, and Cultural Politics* (Boston: South End Press, 1990), 115.

74. John Michael Vlach, *By the Work of Their Hands: Studies in Afro-American Folklife* (Charlottesville: University Press of Virginia, 1991), 92–93.

75. Vlach, "Folk Craftsmen," 301.

76. In Walker, introduction to *"How I Wrote Jubilee" and Other Essays on Life and Literature*, viii.

77. James E. Spears, "Favorite Southern Negro Folk Recipes," *Kentucky Folklore Record* 16.1 (1970): 1.

78. Bob Jeffries, *Soul Food Cookbook* (New York: Bobbs-Merrill, 1969), vii, ix.

79. Genovese, *Roll, Jordan, Roll,* 540–41.

80. Jan Harold Brunvand, *The Study of American Folklore: An Introduction* (New York: Norton, 1986), 454.

81. Tony L. Whitehead, "In Search of Soul Food and Meaning: Culture, Food, and Health," in Hans A. Baer and Yvonne Jones, eds., *African Americans in the South: Issues of Race, Class, and Gender* (Athens: University of Georgia Press, 1992), 97.

82. John Edgerton, *Southern Food: At Home, on the Road, in History* (New York: Knopf, 1987), 15–16. Referenced in Whitehead 103–4.

83. Whitehead, "In Search of Soul Food," 104.

84. In Genovese, *Roll, Jordan, Roll,* 546. See also Solomon Northup, *Twelve Years a Slave: Narrative of Solomon Northup* (New York: Miller, Orton and Mulligan, 1853), 201.

85. Charles W. Joyner, "Soul Food and the Sambo Stereotype: Foodlore from the WPA Federal Writers' Project Slave Narrative Collection," *Keystone Folklore Quarterly* 16.4 (1971): 177.

86. Whitehead, "In Search of Soul Food," 98–99.

87. Thomas, *From Folklore to Fiction,* 140.

88. Pettis, "Margaret Walker," 18.

The Use of Spaces in Margaret Walker's *Jubilee*

HIROKO SATO

Jubilee (1966), Margaret Walker's first and only novel, is a complex book despite its seeming simplicity. The story is developed chronologically: the book is divided into three parts that deal, respectively, with the antebellum years, the Civil War, and the Reconstruction period in the South. The plot revolves around the central figure of the slave girl Vyry; her growth, both physical and mental, during that turbulent period in the history of the South is closely followed. In this respect, the novel can be regarded as a typical bildungsroman. However, Walker places the protagonist in a curious position. She is a slave, but her father, John Dutton, is the wealthy owner of a plantation in central Georgia: hence, he is both her father and the master. This dual relationship enables Walker to present not only the lives of the slaves on the Dutton plantation but also those of the Dutton family—including their friends and neighbors, who live through the South of slavery, secession, the Civil War, defeat, reconstruction and decline—while writing about Vyry's life from her childhood to her middle age in the 1870s. To supply the social and historical backgrounds, Walker freely uses oral slave narratives, newspaper articles, and political documents of that time as well as her personal memories of her great-grandmother, who served as a model for Vyry. This attempt has invited certain criticisms; for example, "Many readers have found its story line too enmeshed in the details of slave life uncovered by [her] research."[1]

The result, however, is something beyond the story of an individual: the Dutton family, with their friends, neighbors, and slaves, can be regarded as a microcosm of the South at that time. Cause and effect, the sequence of southern experiences, are clearly indicated in the course of the novel. Certainly Walker shares with white southern writers such as William Faulkner and Eudora Welty what Allan Tate has called "the peculiar historical consciousness," thus creating "a literature conscious of the past in the present." The sole, yet very significant, difference is obvious: she is black. This novel is thus an examination of the southern social institution, its sense of values and its ways of life, from the reverse side. However, the message at the end of the novel is not simply "black humanism as an answer to America's racial conflicts."[2] It seems to me that Walker's main concern in the novel is with the power structure in society. Like many of the nineteenth-century female novelists who created socially and legally powerless heroines, Walker asks, "What is power and where it is located?" Through depicting the life of a slave girl who is likewise oppressed and deprived, Walker is trying to find a new kind of power, one that reverses the prevailing sense of values. However, Walker clearly differs from nineteenth-century women writers. While women of the previous century were satisfied to find a place for their heroines in the "woman's sphere," in the kitchen and by the hearth, Walker's point is that outside influences restrict the heroine. Walker uses the concept of space to show this process of reversal and the extent and limits of Vyry's liberation.

In the novel, all the characters can be categorized under the following eight headings, which make four pairs of opposing concepts: white-black, rich-poor, male-female, and literate-illiterate. Each of these categories characterizes the space in which the people of each group are able to move. Space in this case means not only physical and geographical space but also social, psychological, and intellectual space. Naturally, the first member of each pair has power; hence, such characters have a positive attitude toward life. For example, John Dutton, who possesses four positive qualities (white, rich, male, and literate), travels widely outside of his plantation, often out of the state, for political, social, and sometimes amorous purposes, while his wife's movements are largely restricted to the neighborhood of the plantation. When Salina, his wife, threatens to go back to her family in Savannah in protest against her husband's infidelity, she finds that she can do so only by losing her status as the wife of John Dutton and the mother of his children. Even among the blacks, Brother Zeke the preacher and Randall Ware, a "free-issue Negro," both literate, are well immersed in the happenings of the world. They know quite well about the abolitionist movement in the North, for instance, and what "freedom" means, and they can fake their "passes" so that they are able to move in relative freedom.

At the beginning of the novel, Vyry belongs to all of the negative groups; she is black, female, poor, and illiterate. This state is symbolically illustrated by the four series of small, dark spaces used in the first three chapters of the book. Certainly, "dark" and "small" indicate the restricted state in which Vyry was placed, but Walker's intention in placing Vyry in these spaces deserves careful consideration.

The first of the three is the small, dark cabin of her mother, Hetta. Hetta is dying of toxemia after having borne her master, John Dutton, fifteen mulatto children by the age of twenty-nine. Vyry, the last child of their relationship, is identified as "Sis Hetta's child," which also serves as the title of this part of the book. Her father is her master and owner. At the beginning of the novel Vyry is taken to the cabin to say a final goodbye to her dying mother. When she is brought out of the stifling room, it is like being delivered out of the womb of a dying mother: the birth of a motherless child into the world.

By contrast, in the second chapter Vyry is seven and is taken into the Big House, the domain of John Dutton's wife, Salina, as a housemaid. Salina hates Vyry from the very beginning because, with her white skin, gray eyes, and curly, soft, brown hair, she looks just like Vyry's half-sister Lillian, Dutton's daughter by Salina. In fact, Salina's friends mortify her by pointing out the similarities between the two children and calling them "twins." Lillian is Vyry's "twin" in appearance but the opposite in social status: she is consistently shown as a typical southern belle who lives in whiteness and light, the incarnation of innocence and protection.

The second dark space is the closet in the Big House where Salina hangs Vyry by her thumbs as a punishment for breaking a china plate. From this dark closet she is taken out by John Dutton, who rushes to rescue her from the "death faint." However, he is not motivated by paternal love; his reason for the act is that "she'll be . . . worth much as a slave" when she is older.[3] The few hours Vyry spends in this dark, small space in the Big House constitute a quasi-death experience. Salina, who could be a surrogate mother to her half-white stepdaughter, instead vows to kill "her and all other yellow bastards like her" (30). Salina is like a Jungian "Great Mother" who devours her children.[4]

After this incident, John Dutton takes Vyry out of Salina's way and places her under the care of Aunt Sally, longtime cook of the Dutton plantation. Vyry is expected to spend the daytime in the kitchen while continuing to spend the night in Aunt Sally's cabin. This kitchen of the Big House is a curious place.

Typically situated between the mansion and the Negro quarters, it is separated from the Big House by a few yards of boardwalk. This region is seemingly dominated by Salina, who checks the stock of food carefully out of fear of theft by the blacks. However, the one who really works in the kitchen is Sally, who provides nourishment to the white family. In that sense, black and white women compete for dominance of this space.

The third dark place is the small, dark cabin where Sally and Vyry stay at night. Sally takes loving care of the child as if she were "a mother hen clucking over one biddy" (35). Sally feeds Vyry with abundant food stolen from the kitchen of the Big House. "At night when they closed that door it was like going off into another world that was grand and good" (35). Contrary to the dark closet of the Big House, this dark womblike cabin, with its "shuttered window and door," is where love and nourishment are provided for Vyry. This small space is where a surrogate mother-child relationship is established. This embryonic period is the time in which Vyry models herself after Aunt Sally—the cook of the house, who gives her a warm quasi-home built mainly on the mother-child relationship. While she is under the protection of Aunt Sally, Vyry comes to learn two of the most essential things in her life. One is, as we have seen, the importance of warm human relationships through her life with Aunt Sally. The other is the necessity of freedom for the black people. Vyry loved to attend the "Big Meeting" of the Rising Glory Baptist Church conducted by one of the important figures in the novel, Brother Ezekiel (Zeke). The meeting or "invisible church" service is held deep in the swamps under the cover of the darkness of night. Zeke tells the Negroes gathered there that they are "human beings with a right to freedom" (38). Although Vyry is too young to grasp the meaning of Zeke's words clearly, she is still attracted by Zeke's preaching on Moses and "the story of his leading the children of Israel out of Egypt, out of the House of Bondage, to a vision of the Promised Land" (38). This story sounds very attractive to Vyry but is also misleading, for it implies movement in geographically as well as psychologically wider spaces. At this time, though, the sphere of activities of black people is restricted within the boundaries of the plantation. Though some of the slaves like Aunt Sally, who came to Georgia from South Carolina and who is, later in the novel, sold and sent to New Orleans, have made geographically long trips, they are undertaken not of their own will but are forced on them by white people. Moreover, the story of Moses is misleading in the sense that somebody else will lead her out of bondage to freedom. This idea serves as a mental block in Vyry's growth for a long time.

Around 1851, when Vyry is about fifteen, "mutual distrust hung in the air between blacks and whites" (70). There are rumors of black cooks poisoning their masters. Salina becomes suspicious of Sally and instigates her husband to sell her. Vyry is deeply distressed by the idea of separation: "Vyry found herself shaking like a leaf in a whirlwind. Salt tears were running in her mouth and her short, sharp finger nails were digging in the palms of her hands. Suddenly she decided she would go with Aunt Sally, and just then Big Missy slapped her so hard she saw stars and when she saw straight again Aunt Sally was gone" (71). Vyry's quasi-home with Sally is broken, and she is left alone in the world. At this point, we have to note that the only humane relationship Vyry has had with other human beings has been with Aunt Sally. This one is a mother-child (daughter) relationship in which the father does not play any significant role; this affects the development of Vyry's later life. Her life with Aunt Sally leaves an indelible mark on Vyry. However, this incident can be interpreted as a fight between Salina and Sally over the dominance of the kitchen, the vital space of the plantation. Ironically, though, Salina, the winner, is forced to place Vyry in Sally's place out of necessity.

After they sell Sally, the best cook in Lee County, John Dutton and Salina hire other black cooks one after another: none is satisfactory. "Vyry took her place in the emergency. Thus began her life as the cook in the Big House. She always dated the time back to Aunt Sally's going away. Vyry knew the work thoroughly, having been accustomed to the kitchen from childhood. . . . She cooked exactly like Aunt Sally" (72). John Dutton, taking pity on the heavy responsibilities that fall on young Vyry's shoulders, says that the work will be too much for her. Hearing these words, Salina perversely decides Vyry should be the chief cook of the house. Thus Vyry inherits Aunt Sally's working and living space—the kitchen and the cabin—and becomes the provider of nourishment for the Dutton family.

This process mentioned above is very interesting. Vyry is born, dies, and then is born again in a very short period of time. She loses her natural mother, is denied by a stepmother through a deathlike experience, is adopted by a surrogate mother and placed again in a kind of womblike protected state, then experiences another birth, the recognition of the role she is expected to play in society. If regarded from a sociological point of view, Vyry's experience so far symbolizes the process of growth for black people of the time. Her real birth comes through the pain caused by Salina's slapping.

With her establishment as the cook of the plantation, her relationship with Randall Ware, the free-issue Negro of the village, starts. The owner of a smithy and mill, he is said to have money. He is literate and well informed about the abolitionist movement in the North. Though his "animal magnetism" attracts Vyry, "above all she was fascinated with his talk of freedom, of buying her freedom, of making her free to marriage with him" (78). At this moment he seems to be "a deliverer like Moses" (79). In a dream, she sees a beautiful door named "Freedom." Randall is standing by with a golden key "promising to open the door" (79). However, this dream of Ware as a deliverer and a leader to freedom is just a mockery. Even though, with the help of a white friend, he tries every means to buy Vyry's freedom from John Dutton, his effort is fruitless in the face of the malicious social institution of slavery. In Ware's case, his wealth, literacy, and maleness are powerless because he is black.

When she is pregnant, Vyry in her desperation goes to John Dutton and asks him to allow her to marry Randall Ware, the free-issue Negro. This means asking Dutton to set her free, so that their child will be free also. Though he is in the benevolent mood of Christmastime, Vyry's request makes him furious, because it is asking him to give up a perfectly healthy slave. He shouts at her, "I own you, and I own your unborn child" (120). Vyry's desperate cry, "Marster, does you think it's a sin for me to want to be free?" (120) is skillfully turned into the condescending counter-question, "Who would take care of you, feed you, and clothe you . . . and protect you?" (120). After this experience Vyry no longer shares Ware's hope that he can buy their freedom. "She expected nothing" from him (125). At this stage, her idea of freedom is that it is something that other people will give her. She is passively waiting for her own and her child's deliverance from this state.

When her first child is born, the boy is called "Vyry's Jim," just as she herself has been called Hetta's child. (Their second child is a girl, Minna.) Though she is able to establish a family life in her cabin with her children, the children's father Ware can join them only briefly in the night. A satisfactory family life is thus denied to her. Ware, feeling imminent danger to him as a free man, asks her to escape to the North with him, but they fail. When her only way to escape is to leave their children, Vyry cannot do so. Consequently, though Ware escapes, Vyry is caught and whipped seventy-five times, leaving ugly indelible scars on her beautiful body. This incident obviously shows Vyry's love toward her children, but at the same time it shows that she cannot imagine any mode of life other than the one she experienced with Aunt Sally. She is restricted physically and mentally.

As we have seen, Vyry's state in the first part of the book is at the bottom of the world. As a poor, illiterate black woman, she is restricted in every sense of the word. Being a slave, she is deprived of her personal freedom, her living quarters are restricted, her mental development is thwarted by being kept in ignorance and illiterate, and her only true means of self-expression is singing. In the world where "De white man is de ruler of everything," every means to attain happiness is out of her reach.[5] Even in the kitchen, where women are supposed to express their happiness by providing food for their families, Vyry is unhappy, because that sphere is not really her own, dominated as it is by Salina. At this stage she is indifferent and unsympathetic to the sufferings of the slaves around her. She minds "her own business," a sign of her mental and emotional blockade. When Lillian marries, for instance, the wedding day is "not a happy one for her" (96). After preparing fancy food for everyone's satisfaction, the only feeling she feels is fatigue and unhappiness, for this is forced labor. Here we notice that even the happiness of the woman's sphere is denied to this black woman.

Now we have to examine the lives of the privileged in order to see how free they are by contrast. Walker juxtaposes Lillian with Vyry so that the differences between these two become clear. However, before we examine Lillian herself, we should understand the life of her mother, Salina. She is a strong woman who dominates the Dutton plantation. Her husband is away from the plantation most of the time, for he is busy as a member of the Georgia Legislature. Salina runs the plantation with the help of the overseer, Grimes. Although both are women, she is the opposite of Vyry. Salina has money, the freedom to move around, and education. She is well informed of political and social happenings, peruses newspapers, and is articulate in expressing her opinions. However, even she has her own limitations. At the beginning of the novel, for instance, John Dutton muses upon his relationship with his wife beside Hetta's death bed. Hetta had been his "toy" in his teens, but when he married the aristocratic, Savannah-born Salina, he imagined he would henceforth have a happy, fulfilled married life with his wife. However, after having borne him two children, Johnny and Lillian, "Salina made him understand that sex, to her mind, was only a necessary evil for the sake of procreation" (9). She informed him that "her duty as a wife had ended" (9). Therefore he resumed his relationship with Hetta. When Salina found out about this relationship, she "pitched a lovely tantrum" (9). She threatened to go back to her mother's home. John Dutton's reaction to this emotional outburst was typical of a southern gentleman. He told her she could go home and that he would provide for her all her life, but that she had to leave the children behind. Her subsequent acceptance of the relationship with Hetta was an indication to her husband that "she relented." For John Dutton "miscegenation was no sin" (9). He could not understand "where Salina had been given such romantic notions, and how her loving parents had kept the facts of life from her" (9). This incident shows how rigidly they are restricted in their emotional and physical relationships. Certainly, Salina is haunted by the romantic notion of chivalric love, typical of a southern belle, and John Dutton tends toward self-indulgent debauchery.

Salina realizes that her husband has the legal right to deprive her of her children, but she can do nothing to combat his mistreatment except to take a strong hold on the life of the plantation. She takes as her domain the restricted area of the Big House and makes it a hellish place not only for the slaves but also for the members of her own family and herself. The chief victims are her two children. Both of them are brought up according to her romantic notions of southern society. Johnny goes to West Point to be trained as a "knight." He says to a school friend, "I'm itching for adventure, excitement, anything but the boring life of these backwoods saddled with a wife and responsibility." An army officer "is in the genuine southern tradition of a gentleman" (87).

This rigidity blinds him from seeing the reality of the South at the outbreak of the war. Lillian, on the other hand, is brought up as a real southern belle. She seems not to have her own mind. When she was very little, she depended on Vyry in their play. When older, every single thing in her life is decided by her mother. This protectiveness thwarts her mental development. Though she is endowed with a sweet nature, she cannot face the harsh reality of life and is unable to take any decisive act to protect herself and her family. Throughout the first part of the book, therefore, none of the characters are truly free. They remain restricted, either physically, mentally, or both. In the second section I would like to see how the restricted conditions of these characters affect their attitude toward the war.

In 1861, on the eve of the Civil War, John Dutton dies. A few hours before his death he tells Vyry, "Think I forgot what I told you? I promised to set you free when I die, didn't I? Got it in my will, right here!" (161). However, he does not forget to add, "But I ain't dead yet!" These words are just a mockery because Salina never makes it clear whether or not this is actually written in his will, and Vyry's state as a slave remains the same after his death. "He had taunted her with the promise of her freedom" (165).

Her hope for freedom again soars when she receives a note from the North. Though she cannot read, she knows the note is from Ware. She imagines that he has found some means to set her and the children free. However, this hope soon collapses when Brother Ezekiel reads the note to her. Ware only tells her to wait for him until the war is over. Vyry feels that "the door to freedom was still closed in her face and she didn't know the magic password to open the door" (166). The development of the book from now on concerns how she finds the "magic password" to freedom.

Walker devotes as much attention to white people's reactions to the war as on black people's activities. Johnny comes home to join the Confederate army. The rigid attitude of Salina and Johnny is clearly indicated in the following conversation:

Johnny said, "It's not written they'll fight long. They don't have the fighting spirit, and that shows they are cowards."

But Miss Lillian was terribly distressed. "First papa, and then this! Oh, Kevin, you don't have to go, do you?"

Johnny's lips curled as he looked at her. "What kind of southerner are you? Is that your patriotism?"

Lillian wept and said, "But I don't *feel* patriotic."

"Nonsense," said their mother, "we will all do our patriotic duty and fight for the Cause however we are called upon to serve." (165)

Johnny and his mother are blindfolded by their notion of southern tradition; they cannot see the reality of war. Despite their learning and seemingly well-informed state, indicated by the newspaper articles Walker abundantly cites in this section, only Kevin, Lillian's husband, knows that "it is a life and death matter and a lot of people are going to be killed without reason. Almost anybody who goes into battle is sure to be killed." In answer to these words, Johnny says, "It is a game, and you learn to play the game according to the rules. Your first rule is to learn to protect yourself while you advance the Cause of your side and at the same time kill the enemy" (171). Johnny decided to join the cavalry because it is "aristocratic." His preparation to join the army, the details of the making of his uniforms, and his choice of horses are described minutely, as if it were in preparation for a wedding. Before he leaves the plantation he makes a heroic speech in front of all the slaves and promises that he will set them free when the war ends in victory.

However, both Johnny and Kevin come home mortally wounded. Their deaths are a terrible blow to Salina and Lillian, though Salina still does not try to see the reality and to see how the defeat will affect southern life. During the war, she spends most of her time reading newspapers and political propagandistic documents that distribute false information to people; she desperately clings to these ideals. She contributes labor by sending her able-bodied slaves out to work in an ammunition factory. Those slaves, though, either run away or are wounded by the deteriorated working conditions in the factory. Thus Salina suffers a heavy loss of her workforce. Toward the end of the war, she goes to the banker Barrow and tells him to turn all the Dutton wealth into bonds and stocks and cotton investments in order to support the Confederate cause. Barrow, who foresees Confederate defeat in the near future, advises against this. However, Salina is so adamant in her determination, her single-mindedness makes Barrow blush for his "practical ideas." Certainly Salina immolates herself and the fate of the Dutton family with the collapse of the southern society. On August 6, 1864, when the cannoning of the Northern army was heard even at the plantation, Salina has a stroke, and on the next day, when the noise ceased, the sign of defeat, Salina dies, leaving Lillian with her two young children. "But Big Missy Salina would surely have her last wish. She would never live to see niggers free and living like white folks" (224).

With the death of Salina, the removal of the causes of her oppression, Vyry's attitude toward life undergoes a drastic change. Now it is Lillian, her white counterpart, who is helpless. She spends her days sitting silently in a dreamy state, barely responding to other people's approach. "Miss Lillian was wilted in spirit and energy and she almost made no effort to do anything" (230). On the other hand, Vyry takes the whole responsibility of running the plantation. Despite the opposition of the slaves remaining on the plantation, Vyry bakes and cooks delicacies for her own and Lillian's children at Christmastime of that year, 1864. She feels that to keep the household together and give children a feeling of warm family comfort is her duty. When the next spring comes Vyry decides to plant some vegetables. She insists, "We got to eat . . . and we got the younguns to feed. Leastwise Miss Lillian got hern, and I got mine" (231).

> Vyry took the initiative, and to the amazement of the whole household she set the plow in the field and made more than a dozen long furrows in one day. . . . The first green shoots were in the fields by the middle of May and Vyry looked at their "crop" with pride and pleasure. Life on the plantation was no longer pure drudgery, with every hour one of hard driving labor. Things were not so hard but an almost deserted farm with no men was not easy either. (232)

This pleasure of working for the benefit of her own children and her white relatives is a new feeling for Vyry, along with her sense of responsibility for keeping the household going. Now she moves freely between the Big House and her own cabin. This spatial liberation corresponds to Vyry's mental liberation.

Then comes the political emancipation of the slaves in 1865. At the Dutton plantation a group of Northern soldiers come in May and read the proclamation in front of the remaining slaves: "Vyry caught snatches of the long document as the man's voice droned on, 'Shall be . . . forever free,' and she was caught up in a reverie hearing that magic word. Could it be possible that the golden door of freedom had at last swung open?" (234). Certainly, Vyry is now free socially and politically, and this emancipation brings mental freedom. However, Vyry's understanding of the word is deeper than that of most of the Negroes. They believe that freedom means that they don't have to work anymore. Vyry's son asks her, "We're free ain't we? We ain't got to stay here and work no more is we?" (238). Vyry answers him, "Yes, son, we's free and we ain't got to stay, but being free doesn't mean we ain't gotta work, and anyhow I promise your daddy I'd wait here for him" (238). However, most Negroes think that freedom means that they are allowed to do anything they want. They follow Northern soldiers and ransack the plantation houses they pass on their exodus to Alabama. They have not yet come to understand the responsibility that comes with freedom. Perhaps their homeless and unstable state of life is an indication of their undeveloped mental state.

The Big House, which had been the citadel of Salina's strong egocentric will, is now powerless to protect Lillian. In the evening, when all the slaves of the plantation are proclaimed free and only Vyry and her children are left on the plantation with Lillian and her children, the house is invaded by Northern soldiers and Negroes, who not only destroy almost all the fine furniture of the house but also attack Lillian. The brutal act leaves her insane for the rest of her life. As the doctor says, "The honor of this house is dead this morning" (243). The destroyed house is a symbol of the fall of the southern tradition.

It should also be noted that at the end of their lives all the members of the white Dutton family come to be immobilized and so restricted to the house. John Dutton is confined to bed for months; Johnny, Kevin, and Salina are physically ill or wounded and confined to bed before their deaths; and Lillian, in her insanity, stays immobile for the rest of her life. While the Negroes gain the power to move freely, the white people lose that power and are restricted within small spaces. Here we have a reversal of the power structure.

Vyry is also attacked near her cabin but is saved by Innis Brown, who has come with the soldiers in the morning but has not left with them, being attracted by Vyry's children, Jim and Minna. Brown, who has been a field slave all his life, has had a dream. "He dreamed of a farm of his own, a place further west with a team of mules, with a house for a family, and a cotton crop of his own" (247). He just stays on the plantation, helping Vyry. During the fall of 1865, Vyry takes the whole responsibility of supporting two families, her own and Lillian's. She waits patiently for Ware's return, believing his words that he will come to fetch her and the children when the war is over, despite the news brought by one of the former slaves of the plantation that Ware was seriously ill when Atlanta fell. Innis insists that Vyry be his wife and move with him to the West. Vyry waits until Christmas of 1865. When Ware still has not come back, and Lillian is placed under the care of her relatives, she consents to marry Innis. Thereafter, their new life is "typical of hundreds of thousands of emancipated Negroes" (264).

In the third part, Vyry and her family are in Alabama, moving westward. Here black people have the freedom to move around, at least legally, though hostile feelings toward them are still prevalent among the white people. The main theme of this part is conveyed by the imagery of houses. Walker places great importance on the house as the place where the human self is formed. In this part Vyry and Innis live in four houses. The first one they build on a secluded river bottom near the Georgia-Alabama border. This is a log partitionless cabin they build by themselves. While they live there, they avoid contact with white neighbors and keep to themselves in fear of the threat to their newfound happiness. However, this house is washed away by the high water caused by a heavy rain. Also, though this house is their own, a house located outside a community cannot be called a real house for development of the self.

The second house is the one they rent from the owner of the land they sharecrop. Because they are illiterate, they are cheated in their contract. When they realize that they have become deeply in debt through the malicious manipulations of the contract by the white man, they flee from the house. The third house they again build by themselves. This is a beautiful house with glass windows and four rooms along a wide hall. Vyry and children are "willing to help Paw build the new house" (307). This is a house built in cooperation with the family. The house is divided into rooms, which indicates personal evolution. As Gaston Bachelard says in *The Poetics of Space*, human beings need a small, secluded space to dream in, where we can enrich our inner lives, while larger spaces, such as the community and nature, give the sense of liberation.[6] Healthy human life needs both. The third house is also isolated from the community, and it is destroyed by a fire set by members of the Ku Klux Klan.

These trials through water and fire seem to be sent by God for the final phase of Vyry's development. Throughout the time she was living in these three houses, "Vyry was as happy as a child with a new toy" (294). These houses were good shelters for the family. However, they were isolated places. Vyry, Innis, and their children shrank from contact with white people; hence, they were very reticent in their communication as well as among themselves. We can see they were still in an undeveloped, infantile state.

After the fire, Vyry is depressed for quite a while. Again she is in a small, dark place mentally, waiting for another birth. Though they find a beautiful location for another house, Vyry asks Innis to wait, saying, "We ain't ready to build" (358). When she finally decides to build another house, Vyry first does three things she has never done before. First she travels to the town of Georgiana to visit the Porters, the relatives who are taking care of Lillian. They are grateful to Vyry for what she did for their niece, and they are sympathetic to the black people, as they had never owned slaves. One purpose of the visit is to make sure that Lillian and her children are well taken care of. Lillian, immobile in a rocking chair on the porch, talks to herself rapidly in a high, childish treble, "'I'm not crazy—I know who I am. . . .' [She is] wearing the old, out-of-date clothes she had before the war" (343). Lillian's growth stopped in the antebellum days, and through the contrast with Lillian, her "twin," Vyry's emergence is clearly shown in the scene. Vyry is now the protector of Lillian.

Vyry's second and main purpose on the visit is to ask the Porters to help her secure the legal possession of the land on which they are going to build a house. We are surprised by Vyry's positive attitude and articulateness. Vyry, who has been very reticent to other people, even to her two husbands, is now explaining to the white people the situation they are in and how she feels about it.

The second thing she does is to go among the white people of the nearby town of Greenville in order to know their feelings toward black people. She is trying to know about the community in which they are going to live. Of course, her light skin enables her to pass as a white, but now she openly admits that she is black. While she is walking along a street, a young woman calls for help. She is about to give birth and nobody is around to help her. Vyry acts as a "granny" in this situation. When this woman, Betty-Alice, expresses her fear of black people and some distorted and wrong ideas about black people, Vyry tells her that she herself is "colored" and how such mistaken ideas about black people hurt her. Through the intervention of this white woman's family, who are grateful for Vyry's service in the emergency, the white community of the town decide to accept Vyry and her family as useful members. As a result, the fourth house is built by the help of many white people of the community. It should be noted that while the men are building, the women of the community make quilts, the often-used symbol of cooperation.

This last house, built through the friendship and cooperation of the whole community, is the first of their houses that really deserves to be called one. How Vyry has arrived at her personal maturity with the construction of the house is shown in the scene when Randall Ware suddenly comes to see Vyry and their children. When taunted by Ware that she had been proud because she was the master's bastard, Vyry stands naked before the two men, Innis and Ware, to show the terrible scars on her back caused by the whipping. This is the first time even Innis has seen the scars. She also tells of her past suffering. Vyry now accepts her past, and through it wholly grasps her identity. Vyry's establishment of her self and the completion of the house are in a way united. Vyry comes to realize that the key to the freedom she has long coveted is within herself. She no longer blindly agrees with Randall Ware's fixed ideas, like the "average white man hates a Negro, always did and always will" (397). She can say in reply, "I believes in God and I believes in trying to love and help everybody" (406).

With the completion of the house in the community, Vyry's self-development comes to an end. However, Walker does not bring the novel to an ordered and well-balanced end. In the last chapter, Jim is going away with his father, Randall Ware, to be educated in Selma, while the girl, Minna, is staying home with Vyry, though Minna herself fervently wants to get an education. Minna is trying to convince herself to stay by saying, "I can't leave Maw" (414). At the end of the book, though, Minna dives into yet another small, dark space under a bed and cries "her heart out" (416).

Vyry's own sense of satisfaction is shown in the very last scene in the book: calling her own chickens to come home to roost. This scene recalls her life with Aunt Sally and their mother-daughter relationship. She feels contentment, for Jim is to get the education she has for so long wanted to give to him, while Minna is staying with her. The basic relationship of mother-daughter remains intact. However, the small, dark space Minna is hiding in suggests the womblike space Vyry herself has been placed in many times. The implication is that for Minna there must be a similar journey and evolution—the search for the self and her own way of life.

Having Vyry move from Negro cabins to the kitchen of the plantation and then, after the exodus to Alabama, to a series of small, isolated houses until finally she obtains a house in a community, Walker skillfully manipulates space in order to indicate not only Vyry's own development but also the history of black people as a whole. Perhaps Walker's message is that the true liberation of black people comes only through the acceptance of the series of symbolic spaces from their own past, and yet the future is something unknown, for which the younger generation has to continue its own search.

NOTES

1. Richard A. Long and Eugenia W. Collier, eds., *Afro-American Writing: An Anthology of Prose and Poetry* (University Park: The Pennsylvania State University Press, 1985), 436.

2. Minrose C. Gwin, *Black and White Women of the Old South: The Peculiar Sisterhood in American Literature* (Knoxville: University of Tennessee Press, 1985), 168.

3. Margaret Walker, *Jubilee* (New York: Bantam Books, 1967), 31. Subsequent references will be designated parenthetically.

4. Gwin, 159.

5. Zora Neale Hurston, *Their Eyes Were Watching God* (Philadelphia: Lippincott, 1937), 29.

6. Gaston Bachelard, *The Poetics of Space* (Boston: Beacon, 1969), 9–10.

The Violation of Voice

Revising the Slave Narrative

AMY LEVIN

Why are so many contemporary African American women writing novels that appear to be slave narratives? Examples of this genre include Toni Morrison's *Beloved*, Sherley Anne Williams's *Dessa Rose*, J. California Cooper's *Family*, and Margaret Walker's *Jubilee*. These novels are set in part or in their entirety in pre–Civil War America; moreover, they follow conventions of slave narratives, including acts of rape or other forms of physical violence committed against the heroine.

Certainly, the antebellum period has a hold on writers' imaginations, and it is also critically important as a time in which European conventions inserted themselves into African culture. This circumstance is encoded in many novels, including *Beloved* and *Jubilee*, in acts of rape or violence against women. The results are narrative discontinuities that indicate attempts to suppress voice; as one of the characters in Alice Walker's *Temple of My Familiar* comments, "If you tear out the tongue of another, you have a tongue in your hand the rest of your life. You are responsible, therefore, for all that person might have said" (310). Not only do these novels show the deleterious effects of violence, but they also emphasize the importance of testifying to the cruelty of slavery and keeping its memory alive.

More important, in linking issues concerning voice, violence, and genre, these texts contribute to the dialogue on the role of gender in African American cultural production. Black women writers turn repeatedly to writing about slavery because the topic allows them to focus on themes of power, identity, family, and authenticity. These themes gain rich inflections before a variety of audiences as they find expression in their play across the gendered human body that is the heroine's, as well as across the body of language that is the text.

Recent works about slavery by African American women attempt to redress the double violations of rhetoric and representation. They signify on the conventions of nineteenth-century sentimental novels as well as on the slave narratives that manipulate those conventions. Margaret Walker's *Jubilee* is an important example of such a novel, and it prepares for more contemporary works by Morrison and Cooper. Its pivotal position in the tradition of African American women's writing is due in part to its subtle reappropriation of a genre.

If Harriet Jacobs in *Incidents in the Life of a Slave Girl* insists on her own piety to win the audience's approval, Walker presents Vyry, her heroine, as a devoted Christian. Several critics have commented on Christian humanism as an essential theme of the text (see, for instance, Gwin 147–48), but Walker's novel is more complicated than that. She exposes and resists the violence imposed by white literary conventions and social mores through her use of African and African American folk elements. Many of these African elements manifest themselves as ruptures in the otherwise realistic surface of the narrative. For instance, Walker interrupts an early chapter of the novel for a reminiscence by the slave master Dutton, who is also Vyry's father. This memory, which is irrelevant to the plot, concerns a "coon" hunting expedition. Suddenly, Dutton and his father face an uncanny apparition, "a very large and glittering rooster. He appeared to be all of two feet high. . . . But his eyes were fantastic. They looked like the eyes of a human being. He was wide-eyed and unblinking, and stared back at them unruffled, calm, and steadily" (28). The hunters confront the judgmental eyes of this unnaturally large rooster, an animal that has symbolic and ceremonial significance in many African societies. And although the slaves accompanying the hunters immediately agree that it is neither a 'possum, coon, chicken, or rooster, the white hunters cannot acknowledge this eruption of the supernatural. Dutton's father calls off his hunt; similarly, his son retreats from the memory to contemplate the land. But the rooster remains in the text, as well as in Dutton's memory, as a mark of the culture southern whites would destroy.

Other Africanisms in the text involve rituals and knowledge from which whites are excluded. Eleanor Traylor notes that the novel's opening resembles Yoruba mythology and asserts that "the 'ghost' of some antecedent world, its wholeness shattered, resides within the world of *Jubilee*" (514–15). Vyry's anticipation of her baptism illustrates how remnants of African life are embedded within plantation culture, for her immersion in water invokes not only Christian tradition but also the initiations of many West African women's societies. African beliefs surface again when Grimes, the overseer, loses a daughter. Shortly thereafter, he finds a fetish under his steps: "The face, which had been buried in the soft clay, had been painted chalk white and marked to resemble his little girl as much as if her picture had been painted." Even though his employers tell him to ignore the doll, Grimes is dejected, because, "I reckon I can't fight this kind of stuff" (56). He responds by treating the slaves even more cruelly than before.

When Vyry enters puberty, Aunt Sally explains, "Us colored folks knows what we knows now fore us come here from Affiky and that wisdom be your business with your womanhood: bout not letting your foots touch ground barefooted when your womanhood is on you" (45). This admonition genders Africanisms, rendering the female body a site of resistance to white culture.

While these discontinuities consist of brief appearances of an endangered but still powerful African voice, a second kind of rupture may be found in the text as well. In contrast to Jacobs, Walker provides explicit descriptions of violence and sexual violations, looking away only *after* she has rendered them in detail. In doing so, she finds names and words for the events that occur daily on the plantation, revealing how much violence is part of the southern definition of black womanhood. At the same time, she manages to re-create scenes of tremendous pain without rendering them titillating or sexually suggestive.

The first part of the novel records the heroine's education at the Big House through a series of violent acts. The violence, which escalates as the narrative progresses, is primarily directed at young slave women. Significantly, the three male victims in this section are elderly men who are unable to participate in the field labor that defines manhood on the Dutton plantation (and the most virile black male in this section, Randall Ware, is a free man). For the women, pain is often inflicted by the mistress or overseer in a moment of rage or jealousy. Initially, Vyry is slapped (25), a chamber pot is emptied on her (26), she is hung by her wrists in a closet until she loses consciousness (26), and she witnesses her half-sister's branding, her own body "tightening like a drum" (95). Later, two women are hung for murder, the gallows rope cutting into their necks (103), and Vyry herself is whipped viciously (145). As a result of these incidents, the black female body becomes prominent and highly visible in the text as the site of much of the action. Moreover, scarred, branded, or destroyed, it remains marked by the violence of southern culture, a record or text of the slave's life.

Each of these episodes or clusters of episodes is followed by a break in the narrative or a change in direction. This shift is often marked by physical space, extra blank lines within the chapter, the closing of a chapter, or the end of a section of the book. For instance, after Vyry loses consciousness in the closet, Walker jumps two weeks to discuss the master's progress in local elections (this is the section that is interrupted by the appearance of the rooster). After Lucy is branded, Walker jumps to the preparations for the wedding of Vyry's other half-sister, Lillian, the master's daughter. And after Vyry herself is whipped for an attempted escape, the first part of the novel ends, and Walker shifts to the death of Master Dutton.

The link between breaks in the surface of the female body and interruptions in the flow of the narrative is as deliberate as it is effective. When Walker shifts from violent actions to events among the Duttons, she indicates the casualness with which whites pass from the pain they inflict on others to events within their own lives. Within the discourse of slavery, the cruel slave mistress can perceive herself a good Christian, but Walker's depiction of her callous hypocrisy exposes what southern rhetoric obscures. Furthermore, by shifting directions suddenly, Walker draws attention to the way conventions of narrative continuity flatten individual events. The violence in her work is emphasized and rendered even more horrifying by the abrupt contrasts.

The breaks and visible gaps themselves are markers of silence, of pain that is unspoken because it is inexpressible. It is as if whenever European culture intrudes on the black female body, its prejudices do as well, and the narrator can no longer gaze at it or speak of it. Blackness, which has been so prominent, becomes virtually invisible.

Indeed, Vyry's self is damaged and dominated. But her voice does not disappear altogether—it remains present in the spirituals she sings incessantly, whose content alludes to events in her life. If there is "always a slender undercurrent of a nameless fear" for Vyry, she can "unburden herself as Aunt Sally [one of the women who raised her] had by lifting her voice in song. . . . She was surprised to discover how much she enjoyed singing and what a relief she felt when she sang" (125). Singing, Vyry feels connected to Aunt Sally and the past, and she can express her condition not only through the words of the spirituals, which reveal a yearning after freedom, but also in dance and music, which are derived from African rituals (Traylor 522). Thus popular culture becomes a repository for the African voice when it is threatened by European culture.

The exploration of the relationship between voice and violence shifts in the second section of the novel. This part of the text reverses the first; while the opening traces the imposition of southern white culture on black bodies, this section tracks the disintegration of plantation culture through a series of violent events involving whites. First, the slave owner falls off his horse, and his eventual death contributes to the decline of the plantation. His son and son-in-law are killed in the Civil War. During Sherman's march through Georgia, his wife suffers a stroke, which, significantly, deprives her of the power of speech and proves fatal. A final violent event involves Lillian, Dutton's daughter and Vyry's white half-sister. A Union soldier attacks and rapes Lillian, hitting her in the head so that she never recovers her sanity.

These depictions of violence involving whites are a departure from the conventions of the slave novel, one which redresses some of the imbalances in representation. Whereas Jacobs emphasizes the way white women are protected and shielded, Walker does not privilege slave mistresses or their daughters. The attack on Lillian is ironic because Vyry is rescued in a similar situation.

Walker also overturns the stereotype of the vengeful black found in white popular culture. In *Jubilee* the violence against whites is either accidental or inflicted by other whites. Instead of perpetrating violence, blacks attempt to protect and nurse whites. The attack on Lillian by a white man comments implicitly on the myth of black male violence reinforced so strongly by the film *Birth of a Nation.*

Moreover, the assault is a crucial element in Walker's exploration of the relationship between naming and violence. While slave punishment and abuse is graphically depicted in earlier sections of the novel, the rape of Lillian is never named, and readers must infer its occurrence from Walker's observation that Lillian's dress is torn. Lillian is speechless, unable to describe the events, and the doctor comments, "The honor of this house is dead this morning" (243). Then the scene shifts to a conversation between Vyry and Innis Brown, but not before the doctor speaks to Vyry "like he talking to Big Missy" (243).

This reversal is a radical move on Walker's part. Instead of showing the sexual violation of the enslaved heroine, she shows a white woman who is physically attacked and victimized by the nineteenth-century rhetoric of femininity as well. Lillian's madness is presented as a helpless retreat from difficult circumstances, its unspoken cause another discontinuity in the text, one which Walker never renders explicit. Vyry's black half-sister, Lucy, has been branded and marked for life with an "R" for runaway. What is intended as a badge of shame is transformed by Lucy into a mark of defiance, an accusation. But the body of Lillian, Lucy's white counterpart, is not inscribed with an "R" for rape. Because the source of her pain is never acknowledged, she cannot respond to it or overcome it.

With the silencing of Lillian, the Duttons all but drop out of the action, as Vyry's family travels about the South seeking a modest living and freedom from persecution. Like many of the wise women and conjurers in African societies, Vyry becomes a midwife. Her choice of occupation as a black woman birthing white children is another expression of the complicated and problematic interrelationships of white and black cultural (re)production. Furthermore, the text remains punctuated by Vyry's singing, which expresses her emotions—joy, fear, sadness.

In the last section of the novel, Walker turns her focus specifically to violence against black men. Vyry's first husband, Randall Ware, is nearly killed by Klan members, who force him to sell his successful mill. Her son Jim is beaten by her second husband, who resents Jim's laziness. News of this beating precipitates Ware's search for his family. As a result of these and other events, both Jim and Randall become emblems of anger. The rhetoric of the white South has turned more strongly against black men now that there is no economic benefit to be gained from rape and black reproduction, but the men are not silenced.

Indeed, Ware is especially vocal in asking Vyry to choose between her husbands. Her decision to stay with Brown offers a critique of the two-suitor convention of the courtship novel and revises the nineteenth-century slave narrative as well. In courtship novels, the heroine loses or rejects one suitor, only to marry someone who is more admirable and socially acceptable. The heroine's choice establishes her identity and concludes the novel. In Jacobs's narrative, the ex-slave comments self-consciously on how her story differs from romances: "Reader, my story ends in freedom; not in the usual way, with marriage" (201). Walker offers a third alternative. Vyry has no control over her separation from her first lover, and that match is not sanctioned by white society. She does choose a second lover after she is freed; her very ability to make such a choice becomes an expression of her liberation.

In revising this plot element, Walker is able to signify on both black and white conventions. This manipulation of conventions recurs in more recent works about slavery, including *Beloved*. But more importantly, Vyry's choice is significant within Walker's study of the relationship of voice and violence. In announcing her decision to remain with her second husband, Vyry begins a prolonged diatribe, her most extended speech in the novel, about her experience and her feelings toward whites. She seeks to defend herself against Randall Ware's charges that she has compromised the race by serving as a midwife to white women. In the midst of this speech, she bares her back so both men can see her scars for the first time. It is scarcely credible that Innis Brown, who has fathered several of Vyry's children, would be unaware of the scars; it seems rather that, at this point, Walker is referring to psychic scars as well as physical ones. Thus, Vyry turns violence to rhetorical use.

The baring of Vyry's back and her accompanying verbal self-assertion are linked by more than coincidence. If earlier acts of violence against Vyry are accompanied by the imposition of white culture on the African body and by narrative discontinuity, from this point on the narrative flows smoothly to its conclusion.

This episode signals a different kind of continuity as well. For the first time, Vyry's body is bared by choice. Although serious scars remain, her wounds have healed, and, concomitantly, she has been able to form a family. And it is because of this that she chooses Brown, for "here was the first time I had ever seed a colored family what looked like they was a loving wholeness together, a family what slavery hadn't never broke nor killed. I just couldn't leave there" (408). Rather than compromising the race, Vyry chooses to continue it.

The final emphasis on continuity is associated with the reemergence of a distinctively African American voice. Earlier narrative discontinuities, which are linked to ruptures in the African American female body, are markers of the imposition of southern white culture. But at the end of her novel, Walker is able to demonstrate that the African voice is not lost. Its existence is evident in the closing scene, which might be out of an African compound as well as an American farm, as Vyry tends her chickens, calling them home, to her home, to roost.

WORKS CITED

Cooper, J. California. *Family.* New York: Anchor Doubleday, 1991.

Gwin, Minrose C. "*Jubilee:* The Black Woman's Celebration of Human Community." In *Conjuring: Black Women, Fiction, and Literary Tradition.* Ed. Hortense Spillers. Bloomington: Indiana University Press, 1985. 132–50.

Jacobs, Harriet. *Incidents in the Life of a Slave Girl.* Ed. Jean Fagan Yellin. Cambridge: Harvard University Press, 1987.

Morrison, Toni. *Beloved.* New York: Plume, 1988.

Traylor, Eleanor. "Music as Theme: The Blues Mode in the Works of Margaret Walker." In *Black Women Writers (1950–1980): A Critical Evaluation.* Ed. Mari Evans. New York: Doubleday, Anchor, 1984. 511–24.

Walker, Alice. *The Temple of My Familiar.* New York: Pocket Books, 1989.

Walker, Margaret. *Jubilee.* New York: Bantam, 1967.

Williams, Sherley Anne. *Dessa Rose.* New York: Berkley, 1987.

Jubilee, or Setting the Record Straight

ESIM ERDIM

A concern and a preoccupation with history have always been one of the distinctive characteristics of southern literature. C. H. Holman calls this the South's Hegelian passion for historical process and explains the southerner's attraction to history as a search for meaning. According to Holman, the southerner is dedicated to the Hegelian concept of history because it is in Hegel's thought that history can be seen "as a process, a vast systematic movement toward some at best recognizable goal." [1]

Ralph Ellison, the well-known African American writer, sees this involvement with history as an integral part of African American literature, too. C. Vann Woodward quotes him as having declared, "The Negro American consciousness is not a product (as so often seems to be true of so many other American groups) of a will to historical forgetfulness." [2] Why does the southerner or the African American need to go into the past and decipher its meaning? Why does this specifically historical mode of imagination that doesn't seem to be as important to other Americans have such an appeal to these two groups? C. H. Holman gives us certain reasons for the white southerner's preoccupation with history. One reason has to do with the agrarian nature of southern society, which inevitably results in a kind of "golden-age primitivism." Also, the South, he writes, was trying to find some kind of justification in history for its "peculiar institution." [3] In other words, this was a nostalgic search to understand what went wrong with a society that was "better." What about the African American who is trying to understand his past—a past very different from the white man's, full of suffering, pain, and injustice?

In his book *The Journey Back,* Houston Baker Jr. uses a phrase he borrows from Kenneth Burke to define the African American's quest for meaning in the past. The phrase is "terms for order." Within the African American context, it signifies a quest for a world view that will take black history into account by seeking to give a coherent shape or form to events that happened in the past. Ralph Ellison has expressed the poignancy of this need with the following words:

> Here in the United States we have had a political system which wouldn't allow me to tell my story officially. . . . This record exists in oral form and it constitutes the internal history of values by which my people lived even as they were being forced to accommodate themselves to those forces and arrangements of society that were sanctioned by official history. The result has imposed upon Negroes a high sensitivity of the ironies of historical writing and created a profound skepticism concerning the validity of most reports on what the past was like.[4]

Therefore, the black man had to write his own history and had to create his own meaning out of the welter of events. During an interview, Margaret Walker explained her motive in similar terms: "I wanted . . . to set the record straight where Black people are concerned in terms of the Civil War, of slavery, segregation and Reconstruction."[5]

The search for meaning is the age-old search of humanity confronted with chaos. However, what makes the predicament of the African American and the search for "terms for order" particularly urgent and significant is the confrontation with the absurdity of the human condition, not in the abstract but in the concrete.[6] Being persecuted by a most arbitrary and incomprehensible authority was the everyday reality of the African American during enslavement and the enforced transformation from a human being into property or a commodity in the eyes of others. Thus, it is the threat of destruction or total annihilation that accompanies all encounters with this chaos directly and not just through the imagination. What Michael Cooke has to say about this confrontation throws light not only on African American Literature in general but also on *Jubilee* in particular and the almost unfathomable nature of the humanism expressed by Vyry in the novel. According to Cooke, this confrontation with chaos "took the form of hothouse virtuosity and detachment (if not revulsion) from the human in the White literature of the twentieth century," whereas in African American literature it "took the form of centering upon the possibilities of the human and an emergent sense of intimacy predicated on the human." Cooke goes on to say that this was "an undertaking to reincarnate and reinvest with value the culture's lost sense of being and belonging."[7]

Cooke's analysis sees the reincarnation of cultural values and the sense of intimacy as interdependent processes that were closely linked together in African American thought. It is interesting to note that he chooses to illustrate this development by reference to W. E. B. Du Bois's thought, who was one of three men Margaret Walker has acknowledged as having had a profound influence on her.[8] Du Bois believed that the art of concealment that the African American had developed as a strategy for survival could be turned into a positive attitude by self-knowledge, and by self-knowledge is meant knowledge of one's origins and culture.

Jubilee is one black writer's imaginary journey into the very real chaos of slavery and her triumphant emergence, miraculously and mysteriously, as a human being. Margaret Walker knew the story of Vyry, which she had "inherited" from her grandmother to be

> a precious, almost priceless, living document. Long before *Jubilee* had a name, I was living with it and imagining its reality. Its genesis coincides with my childhood, its development grows out of a welter of raw experiences and careful research, and its final form emerged exactly one hundred years after its major events took place. . . . I have been involved with writing this story . . . and even if [it] were never considered an artistic or commercial success I would still be happy just to have finished it.[9]

Hayden White, who concluded that the demand for closure in the historical story is a demand for moral meaning, seems to be very much in keeping with what literary critics approaching the text from the linguistic point of view have arrived at in their discussions of text as discourse. Roger Fowler, among others, is one of the most ardent supporters of this view. In his book of essays, *Literature as Social Discourse,* he undertakes to show how a seemingly objective narrator voices "prejudices of a precisely historic culture." As a matter of fact, he posits that there should be no difference between "historical" and "fictional" discourse when looked at from the reader's perspective. "My discussion will tend to suggest . . . that 'history' and 'fiction' are both corpora of narrative writings to which the same principles of textual structure apply, though they occupy different positions in traditional Western culture and enjoy different valuations and study perspectives."[10]

This view of historical discourse is not only close to Hayden White's concept of history but also seems to suggest that this is what Margaret Walker had in mind when she said in an interview, "I believe the role of the novelist can be, and largely is for me, the role of a historian. More people will read fiction than will history, and history is slanted just as fiction may seem to be." [11] She also seems to voice the same concern that White talks about when he discusses narrativization of historical events in terms of providing narrative closures. She confesses that years before she finished the book she knew where it would end: "For the first time I clearly envisioned the development of a folk novel and prepared an outline of incidents and general chapter headings. I knew that the center of my story was Vyry and that the book should end with Randall Ware's return." [12] While talking with Nikki Giovanni, Margaret Walker tells her how the first version ended with Vyry's death at age eighty and how someone's comments made her realize that the story "ends when Randall Ware comes back." [13] It seems that the concern with narrative closure was definitely one of the primary structural principles and therefore should be taken into consideration when trying to determine the ideological focus of her novel, *Jubilee.*

Her comments also suggest that another structural factor should be significant in determining the ideological focus. While the first structural principle has to do with the linear arrangement of events, this second one has more to do with what traditionally has been called "centered or central consciousness" in literary criticism. Margaret Walker tells us that she consciously avoided choosing a historical figure as the protagonist in her fictive world. It was from Georg Lukács's book, *The Historical Novel,* where she learned how to use this perspective of "dealing with characters looking up from the bottom rather than down from the top; and for an understanding of Abraham Lincoln as a world historical figure who was always a minor character seen through the mind of major characters." [14] Ralph Ellison's warning against the dangers of using history in fiction is especially relevant on this issue. When asked to talk about the uses of history in fiction, he said, "There is a *problem* about recreating historical figures. . . . Don't appropriate names. Don't move into the historian's arena because you can only be slaughtered there." [15] Margaret Walker seems to have been very much aware of Ellison's advice.

However, the choice of Vyry, a common slave woman, as "the central consciousness" in the novel has raised questions about the artistic authenticity of the narrative. This is one of the main structural problems of the novel and it is the one fault Barbara Christian finds with the novel.[16] According to her, Vyry's point of view and the authorial voice never seem to merge, and this disrupts the unity of the novel. Since slaves were forbidden to read and write, there was no way they could understand what was going on during the Civil War years. Therefore, it would lack artistic unity to have Vyry tell the story. Her criticism seems just when the traditional "central consciousness" approach is employed. However, I am going to try to suggest another approach, from a perspective recently developed by critics who emphasize the discursive aspect of narrative, to bring an interpretation that seems to be more in keeping with what Margaret Walker had in mind. This approach allows us to note that the novel is not first-person narration and that there are other voices in the narrative involved in telling the story, which create ironic tensions that enrich the meaning rather than disrupt the unity. As I shall try to show, the basic tension is between the narrator's and Vyry's voice and, rather than obscuring the intentions of the writer, brings the theme into clearer focus.

The novel employs a third-person narration that is "impersonal," thus the "implied author" and the narrator have become merged into one.[17] The narrator exhibits all the characteristic features of "omniscience," which are familiarity with the characters' innermost thoughts and feelings, knowledge of past, present, and future, presence in situations where characters are supposed to be unaccompanied, and knowledge of what happens in several places at the same time. However, the narrator is not "objective." As the writers of *Style in Fiction* warn us, this is an impossible task. Recent theories of narrative reveal that "messages are, by their very nature, communicated by an addresser to an addressee."[18] Every word has some associations, be it emotive, moral, or ideological. Fowler dismisses the idea of an "objective" narrator with the following statement: "The practical impossibility of authorial silence has been fully argued by Booth in a literary-critical context." Thus, "every text is a discourse, an act of language by an implicit author who has definite designs on an identifiable implied reader."[19]

It is true that the narrator in *Jubilee* goes into Vyry's mind and reveals her thoughts and feelings much more than anyone else's, but we don't necessarily always look at events through Vyry's point of view. There are other minds, very different from Vyry's, that the narrator chooses to go into, and what is more, as I tried to point out earlier, the narrator is far from being "objective." I shall try to reveal the ideological orientation of the narrator by looking at certain linguistic features in the text, making use of suggestions outlined by Short and Leech in *Style in Fiction*.

Even before we learn anything about Vyry and her total bafflement by what she is confronted with, the narrator starts communicating to the reader the disillusionment of the broken promise and the resultant tone of irony from the very first sentence in the book: "The hot spring day was ending with the promise of a long and miserable night" (3). The "collocative clash" caused by bringing together a word like "promise," which has positive connotations, and the phrase "a long and miserable night" creates an ironic stance that will define the semantic pattern of the first section of the novel. As the story develops and the narrator goes into the minds of the characters, this same negative stance of unfulfilled promise and irony becomes more and more pronounced. Caline's thoughts as she helplessly hovers over Hetta's dying body are particularly expressive of this negative attitude: "Slaves were better off, like herself, when they had no children to be sold away, to die, and to keep on having till they killed you, like Hetta was dying now" (4).

The underlying irony and the unfulfilled promise expressed by the authorial *voice* extend not only to the situation in which the slaves find themselves but also to the predicament of the whites. Marse John comes home, dreaming about his land and feeling exulted in its beauty and fertility, only to find six newly dug graves and hear about the horrors of the plague. The same pattern seems to run through the lives of all the other characters. Big Missy suffers from having been terribly disappointed in her marriage. Even the overseer, Grimes, is discontented and unhappy because he's poor and his "nigger-loving" master gives him no credit for his efforts to subdue and control the slaves.

In terms of how the linear arrangement of the episodes prepares the reader for formulating certain attitudes toward what is happening, it is also significant to note the way certain chapters are put together in the first section. For instance, chapter 10 is composed of two main incidents that bring together the branding of Lucy and Miss Lillian's marriage. The next chapter brings together the Fourth of July celebrations with the hanging of two black women accused of having poisoned their masters.

Another important narrative strategy that deserves consideration in terms of establishing the tone of the narrator is the way the characters are identified or described. When speaking of Marse John, the narrator observes, "Marse John was forty years of age and slowly settling into a man of serious purpose" (18). Or when talking about Big Missy, the narrator takes care to note that "One of her major problems was making sure she had the appropriate jewelry for each of the evening costumes" (62). The description of Grimes, the overseer, leaves no doubt in the mind of the reader as to how the narrator feels about him: "Grimes was a short thick-set man, his shoulders big and round like a barrel and his heavy thighs like the broad flanks of a big boar with short, stocky legs and short but powerful arms. His watery eyes were as small as pig's eyes" (21). The attitude of the narrator to Grimes is also reflected by the choice of using free indirect discourse rather than a narrative report of thought. The possibilities of ironic treatment increase when the characters' own idiomatic expressions are reported:

Grimes did not think this was exactly right, but then what can you expect from a nigger-loving man like Dutton when it comes to treating poor white people right. (22)

Sometimes it seems like a fact for certain that niggers is the work of the devil, and cursed by God. They is evil, and they is ignorant, and the blacker they is the more evil. (23)

Grimes thus reveals his own ignorance, stupidity, selfishness and wicked thoughts.

Still another very important element is the discursive aspect of the communication between the characters in the novel. How the slaves communicate among themselves and how this is different from the way masters and slaves communicate is central to the theme of the novel, since Vyry's development as a human being should be seen within the limits set by this discursive pattern. It is obvious that the communicative situation between blacks and whites is one of deliberate noncommunication from the very first chapter. Hetta is dying, and Granny Ticey knows it is mainly because the doctor was two days late in coming. However, "Granny Ticey said nothing. Her lips were tight and her eyes were hard and angry in an otherwise set face. But she was thinking all she dared not say" (6). It is also significant to note that Lucy gets branded because she is caught when speaking her mind.

The consistent undermining of the communicative act only strengthens the tone of disillusionment and irony that the narrator has been expressing throughout the first section. Houston A. Baker describes the attitude of the narrator in traditional slave narratives as one of a "straightforward 'chronicle of horrors' with an undercurrent of subtle, dry and ironic humour which provides comic detachment."[20] This description seems to fit the tone of the narrator in *Jubilee*. However, there's a distinctly different attitude or voice in the novel, that of Vyry's, which slowly develops against this background of horror and irony. The novel gains momentum as the tension between the two voices increases. The final scene, in which Vyry and Randall Ware express opposing views about what the black attitude to whites should be, is the culmination of this tension, because it is Randall Ware who adopts the narrator's tone and argues against Vyry till he is subdued by the prophetic wisdom of what she has to say.

At the beginning, Vyry is just as silent and noncommunicative as the other slaves. What is most significant about this first phase of her experience is its utter absurdity. She is directly confronted with the soul-killing and destructive force of the chaos of slavery. There seems to be no logic or meaning in her universe, and Mammy Sukey knows this as she takes her to the Big House: "Ain't make a speck of difference nohow. Politeness and cleanness and sweet ways ain't make no difference nohow. She gone stomp her and tromp her and beat her and mighty nigh kill her anyhow" (17). It is Aunt Sally's stories that begin to give some kind of meaning or order to her universe by telling her about herself, who she is, why she is there, and why Big Missy hates her so. She also learns the art of concealment from Aunt Sally, who steals food from her master's kitchen or pretends not to know anything about the meetings of the Rising Glory Church, where slaves make plans to run away.

In the first section of the book, Vyry becomes more and more silent as one scene of horror follows another. She even lies to Grimes when he stops to question her about the weeds she has been gathering. When Vyry tries to communicate with her white master and father for the first time in order to ask for her freedom, the attempt ends in silence and withdrawal: "Vyry said nothing, but she thought many things about freedom that she did not say. What she thought was tied with what she felt, and what moved through her heart was without words" (127). The chapter that comes after the refusal of her freedom is appropriately entitled "Freedom Is a Secret Word I Dare Not Say," and when Randall Ware tries to talk to her about the abolitionists, she replies, "Talk don't get you nowhere" (129). This silent and hopeless phase of her life ends with the whipping that leaves her physically and mentally scarred. After the whipping she is like one who has come back from the dead.

The second section starts with a more blatant form of irony on the part of the narrator, in which the deaths of Marse John, Big Missy, the young Marster, and Lillian's husband, Kevin, are symbolic of what is happening to whites in the South. The gap between the narrator's attitude and that of Vyry begins to form after the death of Big Missy, because Vyry is developing a distinctly different stance from the narrator and becoming somewhat compassionate in her attitude toward the fate of the white family while the narrator seems to think that they are getting what they deserve.

A parallel between Marse John's mental and physical states is obviously intended by the narrator when Marse John is made to speak in the following manner: "The Bible is a witness to the benefits of slavery. The Church defends our system and the Constitution protects it. I don't see where they have a *leg* to stand on, but I wish I were out of this bed" (157; italics mine). The narrator reveals his attitude further by making comments on statements or feelings expressed by the characters. Marse John shouts at Vyry from his sick bed, "You ain't free till I die, and I ain't dead yet!" "That night he died," comments the narrator. The same kind of commentary is employed when Big Missy dies: "But Big Missy Salina would surely have her last wish. She would never live to see niggers free and living like white folks" (224). The narrator seems to think it is an end that befits her even though Vyry "bears her no ill will."

The death of Kevin is especially significant in understanding the attitude of the narrator. Kevin goes to war because he has to; he does not share the southern plantation owners' views on slavery, yet he is part of this society and has to share its fate. That Kevin is surprised by "the look of hatred on the black man's face" as the black man stabs him shows how oblivious he was to the injustice around him. Lillian is guilty of the same attitude, and her fate is an ironic statement on her previous state of irresponsible and thoughtless behavior.

Vyry's stance, however, is surprisingly compassionate, understanding, and forgiving. She still doesn't speak her mind for a while, but this time it is out of compassion rather than fear of punishment. For instance, she refrains from telling Lillian how silly her worries sound and tries to comfort her by seeming to sympathize with her: "Vyry looked at Miss Lillian and wondered if she expected Big Missy to rise out of her grave, but instead of speaking her thoughts she muttered, 'I reckon she would turn over in her grave if she thought the Yankees would ever walk in this house'" (229).

The nature of this communicative act not only reveals the difference between the worlds in which the two half-sisters have been living but also brings Vyry's compassionate, unvengeful attitude into the foreground. Lillian is still living in the antebellum South, worrying about her dead mother's reaction to Yankee soldiers plundering the house, and Vyry chooses to humor her. This marks a very important change in the discursive situation of the book, thus causing the tension between the narrator's and Vyry's voice to increase. It is only in Vyry's case that the nature of the communication between whites and blacks shows a shift toward a more positive and constructive approach. Her attitude is so positive and constructive that it even brings about a change in the doctor's attitude. When the doctor comes to examine Lillian after what the Yankee soldiers have done to her, he speaks to Vyry in a tone that surprises her because this is the first time a white person has addressed her in that tone: "*He talk like he talking to Big Missy, and not me, the nigger, Vyry*" (243). The importance of this change in the communicative situation between blacks and whites is duly emphasized in the book by the use of italics. There are not many italicized sentences or phrases in the book, and the fact that this is one of them indicates the pivotal role it plays in the novel as a whole.

In the final section, Vyry's voice develops to such an extent that she is totally in control of the communicative situation. She lies to the poor white family not as a survival tactic but to help them in their struggle for survival and to give them an excuse to share her family's food without loss of dignity. Later, when she helps the white girl Betty-Alice deliver her baby, she openly tells her that she is black and that "nigger mens is got no tails" as her husband has told her. In this section she also makes the first of her speeches, telling Betty-Alice's parents what she's been through as faithfully as she can since leaving the plantation. The white family is deeply moved by her words and is ready to help her family build their house after the fire.

At the end of the novel, after having survived the flood and the fire, Vyry finds herself in a situation in which she can reveal her thoughts and reveal them in such a way as to utter prophetic wisdom. Even she is surprised at how her words can create understanding and harmony among people who find themselves in a position of clashing interests, if not hostile relations. Vyry is finally free to know her mind and to express it, but before she speaks the narrator takes us into her mind and reminds us that memories make her speak the way she does. It may be difficult to understand how Vyry not only retains but even perfects her humanity, but again, as Cooke puts it, this development "veers off into mystery" and is also closely linked with the reincarnation of cultural origins.[21] It is in Vyry where the two elements of humanity and awareness of cultural origins merge. Her assertion of human values is always linked with her awareness of what she has suffered. When Innis Brown whips Jim for not having taken proper care of the sow, Vyry is deeply disturbed and goes into the woods to pray. Before she can pray, however, she tries to put her thoughts and feelings into a perspective that will enable her to understand the significance of what has happened, because this is the first time members of her own family have turned against each other:

> But all that confusion in her house went back to something in her life that she thought she had forever escaped. It brought back all the violence and killing on the plantation when Grimes was driving and beating the field hands to death. . . . Must she stand by and watch this same terrible hatred and violence destroy everything and everybody she loved and held most dear? (380)

This time she has the choice *not* to stand by and she doesn't. Yet, the message of love and forgiveness she finally decides to convey to Jim makes sense only because it comes from one who has been whipped and knows what it means. She describes the experience of hate in such terms that Jim cannot feel bitter any more: "Now when you hates, you shrinks up inside and gets littler and you squeezes your heart tight and you stays so mad with peoples you feel sick all the time like you needs the doctor" (383). Her words to Jim are a preparation for what is going to come later when she defies Randall Ware's words of bitterness and hatred by baring her back and showing her scars as she declares, "I honestly believes that if airy one of them peoples what treated me like dirt when I was a slave would come to my door in the morning hungry, I would feed them" (406). The narrator may not agree with her but he knows her mind and stands in awe of the humanity she becomes a symbol of: "She was, in that night, a spark of light that was neither of the earth nor September air, but eternal fire. . . . She was only a living sign and mark of all the best that any human being could hope to become" (407).

Vyry's voice is a mature voice expressing an attempt to find some meaning in the past, and when we look at the associations more closely we realize that the meaning she has found is directly related to her strong religious orientation. Vyry enters the novel on Brother Ezekiel's shoulders, who later comforts Hetta, her mother, with the following words: "Lead her through this wilderness of sin and tribulation. Give her grace to stand by the river of Jordan and cross her over to hear Gabe blow that horn" (11). As Vyry's voice develops, the religious references increase so that her perspective becomes more and more definable. In the third section, the parallel between the fate of the Hebrews under Pharaoh and the fate of the black man in the South becomes specifically relevant in revealing the position of Vyry and her vision of history. This section is appropriately entitled "Forty years in the wilderness"—a direct reference to the forty years Moses kept the Hebrews in the wilderness before letting them cross the river to the Promised Land. It was during those years that the Hebrews learned to be children of God and what the meaning of their "chosenness" was. Zora Neale Hurston, in her book *Moses, Man of the Mountain*, makes this argument one of the major themes of her book. Vyry comes to see the significance of what happened in similar terms and can rejoice after so much pain and suffering because she sees some meaning or destiny working itself out through her life of deprivation: "I knows we got to wander a while in the wilderness just like the children of Israel done under Moses, but when the battle is over we shall wear a crown" (405). It is she who sees and recognizes this pattern repeated in history. The song "Jubilee," which is quoted on the flyleaf of the book and from which the book gets its name, describes the kind of movement that this historical process involves: "Every *round* goes higher, higher / to the year of *Jubilee*" (italics mine). The process that this vision of history embodies is both repetitious and progressive since each cycle brings the goal nearer.

That narrative closure in the novel is achieved by a cyclical move is more evidence in support of this vision of history. The last scene in the novel is of Vyry feeding her chickens and remembering that other time when, during slavery, she was involved in similar activity on Baptist Hill near the Big House but under very different conditions and with very different feelings in her heart: "Now, with a peace in her heart she could not express, she watched her huge flock of white leghorn laying-hens come running when she called. This time she was feeding her own chickens and calling them home to roost" (416). It is also significant that the novel starts with a dying woman who has just given birth to a dead baby and ends with another pregnant woman in good health and free to plan a better world for her unborn child.

The re-envisioning of the story of the Israelites in the story of the African American is a "repetition with a difference." Critics have commented on the richness of the element of folklore in the novel, but what makes *Jubilee* unique is the merging of the folk with the religious perspective. It seems that Margaret Walker agrees with Richard Wright in that she has tried to discover "the forms of things unknown,"[22] giving them a form and meaning by retelling and re-envisioning the experiences of her race within the framework of a parallel experience of another race—yet somehow she makes it her own with the strong element of folklore. On "the darkest day of her life when Aunt Sally is being sent to the auction block, Vyry hears Aunt Sally say, 'Oh, Lord, when is you gwine send us that Moses? . . . Oh, Lord, how long is we gotta pray?'" (71). This instance is an excellent example of how the religious and folk perspectives complement and complete each other. Ralph Ellison's view of folklore as essential for survival seems to give ardent support to the validity of such an approach: "It describes those boundaries of feeling, thought and action which that particular group has found to be the limitation of the human condition. It projects this wisdom in symbols which express the group's will to survive; it embodies those values by which the group lives and dies."[23] The spiritual perspective is what gives Vyry the strength and the will to survive, and the practical wisdom of her folk makes such survival possible. It is no wonder that Margaret Walker called her novel "a folk sermon" during a talk she gave at the University of Mississippi.

The action of the novel should be seen as the development of the tension created between the narrator's ironical tone and Vyry's vision of acceptance and understanding. To see the novel in these terms redeems it from the status of an "everybody's protest novel" as James Baldwin would define it. In her discussion of *Jubilee,* Minrose Gwin makes the observation that Vyry's forgiveness and acceptance may not seem to be the result of "a fullness of consciousness which would make such a gesture psychologically dynamic."[24] In the absence of such development, it is easy to dismiss Vyry's gesture of love as a simple solution to a complex problem and accuse the writer of shying away from deeper and more painful conflicts. Gwin's answer to this charge is to take into consideration the fact that the novel was written by a black woman who chose to portray her great-grandmother's struggle for survival in these terms: "It is not so much Vyry's gesture itself which is significant, but Walker's association of this loving black woman and her simple act of forgiveness with the black writer's complex commitment to the humanistic values of 'freedom, peace, and human dignity.'"[25] However, I feel that such an argument cannot make Vyry, the character, psychologically credible: unless she is, she fails to convince the reader of her "reality." On the other hand, to see her assertions as juxtaposed against the ironic stance of the narrator would place her vision against a background that defines the limits and the possibilities of her plight. Vyry's voice sings loud and clear at the end, drowning all other voices in its strength and beauty, just like the spirituals Aunt Sally taught her to sing in times of joy as well as in times of trouble. However, while reading the novel the reader is constantly reminded by the narrator that one had to have the faith Vyry had in order to survive the dehumanizing effects of slavery. This is a positive statement, the negative implication of which would be to make the reader speculate on what would happen to a human being who did not have the extraordinary strength of faith and the powerful sense of folk values that Vyry had.

NOTES

1. Hugh Holman, *The Immoderate Past: The Southern Writer and History* (Athens: University of Georgia Press, 1977), 4.

2. C. Vann Woodward, "The Uses of History in Fiction," *The Southern Literary Journal* 1.2 (spring 1969): 60.

3. Holman, *The Immoderate Past*, 10–11.

4. Woodward, "The Uses of History," 69.

5. Phillis Klotman, "'Oh Freedom'—Women and History in Margaret Walker's *Jubilee*," *Black American Literature Forum* 11 (winter 1977): 139.

6. Michael G. Cooke, *Afro-American Literature in the Twentieth Century* (New Haven and London: Yale University Press, 1984), 6.

7. Ibid., 5.

8. John Griffin Jones, *Mississippi Writers Talking II* (Jackson: University Press of Mississippi, 1983), 136.

9. Margaret Walker, *How I Wrote* Jubilee (Chicago: Third World Press, 1972), 12.

10. Roger Fowler, *Literature as Social Discourse: The Practice of Linguistic Criticism* (Bloomington: Indiana University Press, 1981), 108.

11. Klotman, "'Oh Freedom,'" 139.

12. Walker, *How I Wrote* Jubilee, 27.

13. Nikki Giovanni and Margaret Walker, *A Poetic Equation: Conversations Between Nikki Giovanni and Margaret Walker* (Washington DC: Howard University Press, 1974), 56.

14. Walker, *How I Wrote* Jubilee, 27.

15. Woodward, "The Uses of History," 87–88.

16. Barbara Christian, *Black Women Novelists: The Development of a Tradition,* (Westport CT: Greenwood Press, 1980), 71.

17. Geoffrey N. Leech and Michael H. Short, *Style in Fiction: A Linguistic Introduction to English Fictional Prose* (London and New York: Longman, 1981), 266.

18. Ibid., 268.

19. Fowler, *Literature as Social Discourse,* 112; Fowler, *Linguistics and the Novel* (London: Methuen, 1977), 42.

20. Houston A. Baker Jr., *The Long Black Song: Essays in Black American Literature and Culture* (Charlottesville: University Press of Virginia, 1972), 74.

21. Cooke, *Afro-American Literature,* 41.

22. Richard Wright, "The Literature of the Negro in the United States," in *White Man Listen!* (New York: Doubleday, 1964), 83.

23. Ralph Ellison, *Shadow and Act* (New York: Random House, 1972), 172.

24. Minrose C. Gwin, *Black and White Women of the Old South: The Peculiar Sisterhood in American Literature* (Knoxville: University of Tennessee Press, 1985), 156.

25. Ibid., 168.

The Black Woman as Mulatto

A Personal Response to the Character of Vyry

MICHELLE CLIFF

I possess two copies of Margaret Walker's novel, *Jubilee:* the original clothbound edition (1966), and a later paperback edition (1977). On their front covers—amid a bird, the sun, words from a spiritual, overseer, house slave, and a Civil War charge—two female images predominate, of a visibly black woman. Each portrait is intended to illustrate Vyry—depicted as she is never described by the author. Turning to the back of the jacket of the clothbound edition, one finds another image, a photograph of the *real* Vyry—a sternly beautiful woman, light-to-passing; in her high-necked dress, with her straight part and drawn-back hair, she reminds me of my own grandmother, born in the same century as Vyry.

What do these female images convey? Together? Apart? What do they tell us of history, honesty, invisibility, values, in this culture where the visual has such power? Where does the half-breed, light-skin mulatto fall?

Is it significant that the woman on the cover of the paperback is darker, with a broader nose, wider mouth than the woman on the jacket of the cloth edition? Just asking.

As a young woman, reading was my main activity. I sought myself in books;

304

I sought escape. I remember traveling from *A* to *Z* through the fiction stacks of the small public library in my neighborhood. Figurative covers were the norm then and before, particularly on works of fiction. I sometimes studied these covers, if the author was not familiar to me, to see if the book in hand was worth including in the weekly ration of six—plus two magazines.

The front cover of Lillian Smith's *Strange Fruit* was collapsed into a black background, drawing in thin white lines, of a live oak draped by Spanish moss. Oak blocking the great house, rickety cabins alongside. "Southern trees bear a strange fruit," Billie Holiday sang, and Lillian Smith described it. Harper Lee's *To Kill a Mockingbird*—again a tree, the only image, bright green leaves, newly unfolded; a hanging tree? or the tree where Boo Radley hid his treasures? Ann Petry's *The Street*, a stylized portrait of a black woman, looking more like a big-band singer than like Lutie Johnson, gripped in poverty with her nine-year-old son. Nonnie, Scout, Lutie—I guess I most closely resembled Scout, the tomboy girl of *To Kill a Mockingbird* who broke the rules—but she was white, and in Alabama, so the likeness was limited.

Lying on my bed, or on the grass in the backyard, or sitting on the fire escape, when we lived over a drugstore, my forefinger holding my place, looking, again studying the covers of books, believing more often than not that these images meant something, were connected to the theme of the book, the characters as the writer envisioned them. A naive belief—powerful nonetheless. Reading a book, immersing oneself in a "story," is a complex process, of course—trying to shut out the world, while the world is exercising its influence—birdsong, a parent's voice, traffic noise, the smell of cooking, the book itself. I can bring back some of these books, the images on their covers, the surroundings of the act of reading, the time of year, weather, time of day, my age, the feel of the material of which the book was made, an arm falling asleep, the smell of the paper. These things came to me as I studied the covers of the two copies of Margaret Walker's novel, bearing a heroine who has no physical resemblance to Vyry, for Vyry held her blackness inside—at least that blackness visible to the untrained eye.

"Sandy hair . . . gray-blue eyes . . . milk-white skin . . ." —these words describe Margaret Walker's magnificent heroine. Mulatto. Slave. Woman of honor. The woman who was Margaret Walker's great-grandmother, who reminds me of my own grandmother. My grandmother was not born in slavery—but her grandmother was. In Jamaica, some years before freedom in 1835.

Do I take issue with the images the publishers selected because I approach Vyry's physical description? And, like her, the invisible in me is counter to the visible?

Yes; of course.

Mulatto, as the word has come down to us, is a term charged by myth and formed by a false sense of history. *Mulatto* may embrace—at one time—the clandestine, inauthentic, secret, devious, tragic, promiscuous, subversive, confused, irrational. The word refers to an identity, born in the historical and literary imagination of white America; the actual mulatto, the person who carries the black and the white, is found elsewhere. One might say *everywhere,* since there are precious few pure-black African Americans in this country, and many more light-skinned, *pass*-able people than white America would care to admit.

The word *mulatto* has come to us as a hologram—much as the word *nigger* represents a hologram, a three-dimensional image, in white minds, wrought from fear, loathing, a false sense of history. Both *mulatto* and *nigger,* and the mythic beings they represent, have also had an effect on the black imagination in America. They, and their qualities, traipse through some works of black American fiction—but not through others.

Nella Larsen, for example, in *Quicksand* (1928), attempts to show the very real jeopardy and confusion that may come from being of dual heritage, race, in a society that wants to dichotomize everyone, everything. She is in her novel as critical of the dominant white world as of the black subculture she knew. The protagonist in *Quicksand,* Helga Crane, is a light-skinned mulatto, whose fate is tragic but who is not a "tragic mulatto" in the mythic sense. She defies that simple stereotype. Her tragedy stems not from the fact that her veins hold black blood, her cells contain black nuclei, her DNA spiral is tinged—whatever. Her tragedy comes from the inability of the world outside to appreciate her complexity, and her own inability to combat that world. She is a divided soul, estranged from the blackness in her as a source of strength. Her father, her black parent, has deserted her; she has not known a black community in childhood. She drifts. Her female line is white—and that is a crucial difference from most mulatto characters.

Another mulatto heroine comes to mind: Janie Starks, in Zora Neale Hurston's *Their Eyes Were Watching God* (1937). The novel is Janie's telling of her story to her best friend, Phoebe, another black woman. The story takes Janie through the rejection of herself as a "masterpiece" because of her "good" hair and light skin, through her development and deepening as a black woman. It is clear in Hurston's vision that Janie would not be able to find her strength were it not for a black community of which she is part, for the teachings of her grandmother, and for the central relationship she has with Teacake, a black/black man, with whom "her soul crawled out of its hiding place." Unlike Helga Crane, moving between worlds with no real community, Janie inhabits a black world, and within that world she expands herself into fullness. She is, I think, the predecessor to the fictional Vyry, while the actual Vyry was her ancestor.

Writers like Larsen and Hurston, and other black Americans, have been able to swing closer to the truth of *mulatto* than white writers, describing the actual experience of black/white people in American history, the *idea* of blackness in all its complexity.

The first white American novel in which a mulatto character of significance appears is James Fenimore Cooper's *The Last of the Mohicans* (1826). The character portrayed in Cooper's novel is repeated throughout nineteenth-century white American fiction and beyond, the stereotype hardening somewhat during the period of the so-called Negrophobe novelists. Like the most common apparition of the mulatto, Cora Munro in Cooper's novel is female; she is the offspring of a black slavewoman and a white man. Her white half-sister embodies purity, as Cora embodies passion, and her mixed blood, or rather the dark aspect of her blood, the cause of any characteristic or behavior that might be judged improper, uninhibited, unfeminine.

The early version of the mulatto as written by Cooper and others, by reason of her origins, exists apart, dwells in the half-light. She may, like Jane Eyre's opposite, Bertha Rochester, ultimately lose her mind.

The light-skinned mulatto woman was a common feature of many white abolitionist novels of the period 1845–65. Here the portrait was intended to be more sympathetic, yet it was also stuck in white solipsism. Often the light-skinned woman was shown as a white mind, or soul, trapped in a colored body. Her white mind understood the wrong of slavery, for she was possessed of an innate sense of justice. The message to the overwhelmingly white reading audience is clear: isn't a system that enslaves people who look white, and think white, terribly wrong? Maybe the writer was aware that he or she was creating pure propaganda; maybe the writer was unable to rouse compassion for a black/black character.[1]

In these abolitionist novels, the mulatto woman is always the daughter of a white male aristocrat, carrying his intelligence, taste, "breeding," into enforced servitude. Too often this is her tragedy; she is a woman of quality, a princess on a bed of peas. Jean Fagan Yellin has observed about Harriet Beecher Stowe that "[h]er color scheme is rigid. Black people are inevitably subservient; mulattoes . . . combine the sensitivity of their black mothers with the strength of their white fathers."[2]

Through such a formula, I have to wonder: would the mulatto abhor slavery were it not for her father, and also her master, the slaveholder? It is her white mind that indicates to her something is wrong: the daughter of a slaveholder should not be a slave. In this way, the light-skinned woman created by Stowe and other abolitionist writers is the child both of white supremacy and of male supremacy. Her female side, her black side, the side of her *suited to servitude,* a liability to her freedom.

Speaking of the work of Frances E. W. Harper, a black abolitionist and feminist, Barbara Christian states: "One of the main themes of *Iola LeRoy, or Shadows Uplifted* is the horror of slavery as visited upon the most effective heroine of the antebellum abolitionist novel, the beautiful, refined, Christian octoroon."[3] The character of Iola LeRoy takes the light-skinned woman a step further. She is the daughter of a union between a New Orleans plantation owner and his light-skinned wife, educated by him and freed by him from servitude. Her children do not know this fact about their mother and are reared white. Iola is sent to New England to the finest schools; she is wealthy, refined, and a defender of the peculiar institution, despite her education, her qualities—or because of them.

Christian continues:

> It is only when she is cast into the dark condition of slavery that she changes her opinion. Undoubtedly many white women could identify with the beautiful woman who looked as white as they did, who was certainly more wealthy and privileged than they were, and who, despite all this, is instantly pummeled into the pit of servitude only because she has a few drops of black blood in her veins. . . .
>
> Iola is no loose black woman, nor is she coarse or loud, and therefore being a woman of high Christian morals, the novel insists, she does not deserve the brutal, immoral treatment that is part of the tradition of slavery.[4]

Iola, during the course of the novel, becomes a spokeswoman for her people, exemplifying, as Christian astutely observed, "the rise of a black middle class headed by mulattoes who feel the grave responsibility of defining for the black race what is best for it."[5] One of the most destructive things to dog the black race in the twentieth century has been the belief in a talented tenth, which can be traced right back to the light-skinned heroine, her moral imperative, and the mind of her white father.

It does good to remember that while Harriet Beecher Stowe was birthing Eliza and Frances E. W. Harper was envisioning the trials and tribulations of Iola LeRoy, Margaret Walker's great-grandmother, Elvira Dutton Ware Brown, was striving in Georgia, living according to a moral imperative that, as Walker makes clear in *Jubilee,* she learned in the slave quarters, not the great house, from the black people who were her teachers—especially Aunt Sally.

I return to Vyry, with her sandy hair, milk-white skin, gray-blue eyes. She is close in description to Ellen Craft, runaway slave, heroic mulatto, who passed into the free states disguised as an old white man, traveling with her equally heroic husband, William Craft, a visibly black man, as her manservant, her slave. The two, using money William had saved when moonlighting as a hotel waiter, journeyed from Macon, Georgia, to Philadelphia. At Ellen's suggestion they traveled first-class. The irony here is terrific; one might say that Ellen Craft went free disguised as her father. She was the *real* woman upon whom William Wells Brown partly based his character Clotelle, in his novel *Clotelle, or The President's Daughter* (1853), the first black American novel of which we know.

The histories of Ellen Craft and Elvira Brown are parallel in some respects. Both women were the daughters of a plantation master and a female slave. Both were in the service of their half-sisters. Both married dark men who pressed them to escape; like Ellen, Vyry prepared to make her break disguised as a man. Ellen had no children at the time of her escape; in fact, she decided to go with William for fear, and with almost certainty, that if she had a child in slavery, that child would be sold away from her. It was a common practice. Vyry had two children at the time she agreed to run to freedom with her husband Randall Ware, their father. She refused to leave her babies behind; she was their protector—without her she was convinced Big Missy would sell them downriver, and she, Vyry, would never see them again. Against Randall's urging, Vyry sets out with Minna and Jim, is caught on the run and is whipped within an inch of her life. The similarity between Ellen and Vyry with regard to motherhood lies in their love of and devotion to their children—Vyry's already born, Ellen's as yet unborn. Were Vyry childless at the time of her escape, her story might more closely parallel that of Ellen Craft. But she was left to tend her children within slavery and not birth them in freedom. When a child was born dead, "There was no grief within her nor tears to shed. That was one who would never be a slave" (125).

Both women had a genius for survival. Ellen was illiterate, as was Vyry. As Ellen planned her disguise, she decided to carry her right arm in a sling, to avoid having to sign her name to hotel registers, and passes for her slave, William. Vyry's genius abounds in *Jubilee,* feeding, planting, finding sustenance for the community of the plantation that becomes dependent on her. Both Vyry and Ellen, living in the South after freedom, were burned out by the Klan—both realized the limits of abolition.[6]

Ellen and Vyry were born into the institution of slavery. Their white skin, light eyes, straight hair—their so-called white appearances—were meaningless on the plantation, in the quarters, except as a clue to parentage. The only advantage each gained was to be employed in the great house rather than in the field, but given the ill treatment Vyry received at the hands of Big Missy, wife of her father, one questions whether advantage is the proper word. I think especially of both Ellen and Vyry working for their half-sisters. A peculiar closeness grew between Miss Lillian and Vyry; they were, as Margaret Walker writes, as twins—with one extraordinary difference.

The rape of slave women, the sexual use of slave women by white men, whether master, patteroller, or overseer was casual, common. It was out of this violence that each of these light-skinned women was born. They were not born by error into an institution they would find abominable because of their white fathers; they were conceived into an abominable institution that fixed the condition in which their lives would be lived out. Slavery ordained the possibilities of certain people, no matter the color of their skin.

Some escaped. Very few from as far south as Georgia. Most runaways came from the border states—Maryland, Virginia, for example. Most light-skinned slaves lived as Vyry lived. It was only later, after freedom, that the light-skinned black became feared, because he or she might flow into the white domain and practice deceit, endangering the domain by "passing." Under slavery, this was rarely possible, with the extreme exception of Ellen Craft disguised as a white man, reverting to her identity as a black woman as soon as she was safe. The experiences of Ellen Craft and Elvira Brown make plain the dissonance between the antebellum light-skinned heroine of books and the antebellum light-skinned heroine in life.

In Margaret Walker's record of Vyry's life that is *Jubilee*, another aspect of that dissonance is clear: the fact that Vyry received her education, strength, ability to love, from the slaves among whom she lived, particularly, as I mentioned above, Aunt Sally. Barbara Christian has noted about Vyry: "Vyry is a mulatta who does not view herself as caught between two worlds. She is a black woman."[7] One of the reasons *Jubilee* has such a historical and political acuteness is because of Walker's ability to show that Vyry, or another light-skinned mulatta, born into slavery, could only be a black woman. Whether she is a black woman who survives, or one who perishes under the institution and its aftermath, is the question.

Vyry abhors slavery because she observes its laws and customs from the inside; she sees around her the consequences of its brute cruelty—on the branded face of Lucy, at the Fourth of July picnic where two female slaves are hanged, on her own breast where a flap of skin "like a tuck in a dress" is a constant reminder of her whipping. Vyry understands both the sudden violence of the slave system and its mundane, day-by-day attempts to wear away the human spirit—which may result in a young boy who "was just another slave who had been kicked around like a dog all his life, from one plantation to another, from pillar to post, until now he acted more like a dumb, driven animal than a human being"—as Vyry observes (90).

It is Aunt Sally who gives Vyry the tools of a black woman's survival and resistance under slavery, which enable her to grow to wholeness. Aunt Sally is a major character in *Jubilee,* even though she exits from Vyry's life early on, when she is sold away from the plantation; this is Vyry's third experience of deep loss. She has lost her mother, Sis Hetta, and she has lost Mammy Sukey, who became a mother to her. With the loss of Aunt Sally, Vyry's heart is close to breaking.

Aunt Sally represents the obverse of the Mammy stereotype found in highly romanticized novels like *Gone with the Wind* (1936). In that novel, Mammy is the familiar stock character: the subservient female house slave. Aunt Sally will have none of this; she is subversive. Part of Margaret Walker's genius in creating Aunt Sally is in placing a revolutionary's mind and soul in the common type of the Mammy. Like Betye Saar's construction, *The Liberation of Aunt Jemima*—the primary form of which is a Mammy cookie jar armed with a rifle and a pistol—Margaret Walker's character turns the mythic Mammy around.[8] Aunt Sally is large-bosomed, round, and wears a headrag; she is capable of great kindness, but also superb fury. With her fine sense of what is just directing her behavior, Aunt Sally stretches the parameters of the institution.

Through reading about the lives of slave women, their widespread resistance—often undramatic—it becomes clear that Aunt Sally, a product of Margaret Walker's imagination but also years of historical research, is a far more realistic portrait of the slave woman—the house slave exercising her modicum of power for the benefit of her people—than the eager-to-please, love-those-white-folks, vulgar version of *Gone with the Wind* and other novels, which make of slavery a benign institution, miring it in a complex of historical disremembering.

It is of course essential to remember that the Mammy stereotype is a white fantasy. This can be difficult, particularly since for both black and white people the visual image of her is as portrayed by actresses like Hattie McDaniel, for example, in the film of *Gone with the Wind.* If you find yourself envisioning the Mammy Hattie McDaniel cinching Vivien Leigh's eighteen-inch waist, envision also the actress Hattie McDaniel at the Academy Awards dinner in 1940, where she had to occupy a separate table.

Aunt Sally rescues Vyry from the great house and Big Missy's tyranny and takes her into her own cabin. She teaches Vyry history, the history of the slaves as she, Aunt Sally, has lived it. She takes Vyry to moonlit meetings where Vyry hears about abolitionism and learns about resistance. Aunt Sally teaches Vyry about shooting stars, herbs, wild things, the theft of food from the great house, womanhood. She teaches her the joy of subversive acts within the condition of oppression; she teaches her to listen to the conversation of white men over brandy and cigars for news of the world outside, after the white women have retired. Aunt Sally gives Vyry access under her tutelage to the slave culture, a culture in which she has a home. Vyry inherits Aunt Sally's position as cook to the great house, grounded in her education.

Glancing through a study of black American writing by a black scholar, I was interested, and angered, to note his condemnation of Vyry as a "Tom" plain and simple. The scholar spoke almost in the voice of Randall Ware, who upon his reunion with Vyry very late in the novel refers to her as a "white folks' nigger," a "good and faithful nigger." He goes so far as to term all mulattoes "good niggers," implying their deliberate creation by the white plantation master to render black people docile and white-loving. "I still say you've got white man's blood in you. . . . You got his color and his blood and you got his religion, too, so your mind is divided between black and white. I know you can't help it. He made you that way" (402).

That black scholar, whose name I cannot recall, was not alone in his judgment of Vyry. Why isn't she angrier? readers ask. Why does she see to Miss Lillian's safety before leaving the plantation with Innis Brown and her two children? How can she not hate white people? Doesn't her tolerance suggest a loyalty to the white part of her?

The crucial thing that separates Randall Ware and Vyry is not the fact that he is a black/black man and she a white/black woman. What separates these two people and forms their different responses to the world are the experience of freedom, on Randall's part, and the experience of slavery, on Vyry's part.

It would be absurd, and simplistic, to conclude that Vyry is a completely noble character, brave and good and forgiving, untouched by the circumstances of her birth and her history as a slave. Just as it is absurd to suggest her refusal to hate all white people comes from the fact that she is the master's daughter. As the flap of skin over her breast and the network of welts on her back remind her of her attempt to break free, so her light skin, hair, eyes remind her of her birth into the violence of slavery, her mother's life, the lives of other slave women.

Randall Ware's conclusion about mulatto slaves—the "good and faithful nigger" who respects whiteness and rejects blackness—is a conclusion reached entirely from the outside, and not from his own experience, and so is limited.

Randall is also speaking out of his suspicion that Vyry chose to remain on the plantation rather than escape north with him, choosing servitude to white folks rather than freedom.

Walker describes Vyry at Marse John's funeral: "Her condition was peculiar; her color was a badge of shame and her children, like herself, were bound in servitude to the household of John Morris Dutton. He did not prevent the guards from whipping her, he would not give her permission to marry, and now in stone-cold death she knew he had taunted her with the promise of freedom" (165). These few sentences encapsulate Vyry's experience as a white/black slave. She may, somewhere in her soul, have held out the hope that the master might free her, but overall she knows she is a slave—no more, no less:

> You done called me a white folk's nigger and throwed up my color in my face cause my daddy was a white man. He wasn't no father to me, he was just my Marster. I got my color cause this here is the way God made me. I ain't had nothing to do with my looking white no more'n you had nothing to do with your looking black. Big Missy was mighty mean to me from the first day I went in the Big House as a slave to work. She emptied Miss Lillian's pee-pot in my face. She hung me up by my thumbs. She slapped me and she kicked me; she cussed me and she worked me like I was a dog. They stripped me naked and put me on the auction block for sale. And worstest of all they kept me ignorant so's I can't read and write my name, but I closed her eyes in death, and God is my witness, I bears her no ill will. (405)

Vyry's struggle to love, rather than hate, to bear no ill will against her persecutors, ends in triumph, I believe, over those who would dehumanize her.

NOTES

1. For a history of mulatto characters in American fiction, see Judith R. Berzon, *Neither White Nor Black* (New York: NYU Press, 1978), 53ff., especially.

2. Jean Fagan Yellin, *The Intricate Knot: Black Figures in American Literature: 1776–1863* (New York: NYU Press, 1972), 136a.

3. Barbara Christian, *Black Women Novelists: The Development of a Tradition, 1892–1976* (Westport CT: Greenwood Press, 1980), 25–26.

4. Ibid., 26. See also Frances E. W. Harper, *Iola LeRoy, or Shadows Uplifted* (Boston: James H. Earle, 1892).

5. Christian 29.

6. For the story of Ellen Craft, see *We Are Your Sisters: Black Women in the Nineteenth*

Century, ed. Dorothy Sterling (New York: Norton, 1984), 62–64; and *Dictionary of American Negro Biography,* ed. Rayford W. Logan and Michael R. Winston (New York: Norton, 1982), 139–40.

7. Christian 71.

8. For a more complete analysis of the Mammy figure, and a discussion of Saar's construction, see Michelle Cliff, "Object into Subject: Thoughts on Black Women Artists," in *Heresies* 15.

The university is a social institution with a social function, and in this community of scholars social theory is of no value without practice [and] application. To preach one text and practice another is neither expedient nor wise. The university must accept the challenge of contemporary society and respond as best it can to *every segment* of that society.

—MARGARET WALKER, "Revolution and the University," 1969.

Epilogue: "To Capture a Vision Fair"

Margaret Walker and the Predicament of the African American Woman Intellectual

DEBORAH ELIZABETH WHALEY

In Margaret Walker's 1992 address to the Alpha Kappa Alpha Sorority (AKA) in New Orleans, she spoke of the ongoing work of African American women intellectuals in culture and public life. Walker reminded her sorority sisters, the majority of whom hold degrees from institutions of higher learning, that the work of the African American woman intellectual should ideally be to "share the fair vision, the vision we have captured and rendered in service to all [hu]mankind."[1]

Walker's passing on 30 November 1998 was as great a personal loss to her family, loved ones, students, colleagues, and mentors as it was to the academic, social, political, and service organizations of which she was a part. And yet Walker's life should be a lesson; it should encourage reflection on the role that African American women have had and continue to play in the awareness of scholarly and social ethics within and outside of the academy. Walker realized the profound capabilities in the articulation of cultural production within the academy and the necessity for a political consciousness and contribution to the African American and larger public sphere. Indeed, Walker reminded her sorority sisters of this in the same speech when she argued that "our mission . . . as college women of ability and integrity is . . . [to see that] wherever an unfortunate one is suffering, we are called to succor her. Our sisterhood is part of a world family." [2] Walker's commitment to gender and racial plight as demonstrated in her lifelong affiliation with the AKAS was but one outlet for the articulation of her vision.

What makes Walker's work so appealing for many scholars and activists is in the way it realized the "fair vision" of her academic life, which she combined successfully with her writing and social service. The responses to her work by scholars represented in this anthology, as well as Walker's own explication of her work and life in *On Being Female, Black, and Free*, bring to the forefront the dual role that many African American women intellectuals bear.[3] Walker, keenly aware of and committed to the subject positions she simultaneously occupied as a female and African American, reminds us of the attendant capabilities and limits of life within the academy. When Walker proclaimed "This Is My Century," she seemed to represent the sites demarcating the boundaries between academic work and social service. There was, for her, implicit power in the production of knowledge as a force unifying these two seemingly disparate worlds. This fair vision, of course, is not easily captured or maintained.

Cultural and feminist critic Ann DuCille's essay "The Occult of True Black Womanhood" shows how the attainment of such a dream or "vision" often translates into a nightmare in the everyday lives of African American women. "Within the modern academy, racial and gender alterity has become a hot commodity that has claimed black women as its principal signifier," she argues.[4] Of course, this is not entirely a bad thing, as more African American women writers in the tradition of Margaret Walker gain visibility for their professional and extraprofessional work. It is good because it recognizes African American women's writing as making an important intervention inside the academy and in the larger society, too.

Walker's work brought a critical view to culture, life, and politics, creating a humanistic resonance extending beyond the confines of the African American community as we have come to know it. Many academics and nonacademics, as the essays in this volume prove, are affected by Walker's prophetic and gleaning poetry, prose, and cultural criticism.

Yet the "bad thing" about the commodification of African American women writers in general is that the intrinsic prescriptive characteristics and healing capabilities of our work, perhaps symbolized best by the seminal *For My People*, at times become lost in the academic frenzy. As DuCille writes, one of the dangers of standing at the *intersection* of gender, race, and class, as so many African American female literary and cultural critics do, is the "likelihood of being run over by oncoming traffic."[5] Put another way, the contributions to scholarly and public agendas are exercised only to be minimized and appropriated for ends other than that which they were initially intended: to heal, inspire, and bear witness to the contours of being African American and female. The second danger in this commodification, of course, is that in the quest to do it all and out of the responsibility we feel toward our multiple communities, we become exhausted. African American women, as Zora Neale Hurston's writings suggest, become "mules" upon which we carry the weight of our difference.[6] Nevertheless, African American women's writings often reconcile and negotiate our subject positions with our everyday social relations in the way we write of the burdens we bear.

The essays in this volume critically engage Walker's work and are often indicative of the various cultural negotiations deriving from gender, race, culture, nation, and class that her work represents. Margaret Walker the woman, African American, poet, activist, academic, wife, and mother—as well as the diversity of African American expressive culture—are at the center of analysis here. In the wake of Walker's passing we hope to have honored her life achievements or, as bell hooks might say, "her writing life."[7] Walker's dedication to the betterment of her "people"—as seen in her poetry, critical essays on culture, and advocacy and support of black institutions—demands recognition and requires critical reflection. Margaret Walker's multiple contributions also leave African American women intellectuals and the larger academic community with the obligation to "capture the fair vision," that is, to realize the impact our writing and our actions may have on the larger social structure and to use this realization to the ends that Walker so poignantly cried out for in her work. In doing this, we may then begin to think through and act upon ways to cultivate our shared *fields watered with blood.*

NOTES

1. Margaret Walker, "Revolution and the University," in *On Being Female, Black, and Free: Essays by Margaret Walker, 1932–1992,* ed. Maryemma Graham (Knoxville: University of Tennessee Press, 1997), 223.

2. "To Capture a Vision Fair," address to the Alpha Kappa Sorority at the 55th Boule in New Orleans, Louisiana, 1992 (collection of Maryemma Graham).

3. Ibid.

4. Maryemma Graham, ed., *On Being Female, Black, and Free: Essays by Margaret Walker, 1932–1992* (Knoxville: University of Tennessee Press, 1997).

4. Ann DuCille, "The Occult of True Black Womanhood," in *Skin Trade* (Cambridge: Harvard University Press, 1996), 83.

5. Ibid.

6. See, for example, Zora Neale Hurston, *Mules and Men* (New York: HarperCollins, 1990).

7. This phrase borrowed from bell hooks, *Wounds of Passion: A Writing Life* (New York: Henry Holt, 1998).

Selected Bibliography of Works by and about Margaret Walker

COMPILED BY

BERNICE L. BELL AND ROBERT A. HARRIS

BIOGRAPHY

Baraka, Amiri. "Margaret Walker Alexander." *The Nation* 268.1 (1999): 32.

Bardolph, Richard. *The Negro Vanguard.* New York: Rinehart, 1953.

Baytop, Adrianne. "Margaret Walker." In *American Women Writers.* Ed. Lina Mainiero and Langdon Lynn Faust. New York: Ungar, 1982. 315–16.

Beech, Hannah. "Milestones." *Time International* 152.23 (1998): 13.

Bell, Bernice. "Bernice Bell Remembers Margaret Walker, the Teacher, Scholar, and Friend: An Interview." In *Trumpeting a Fiery Sound: History and Folklore in Margaret Walker's "Jubilee",* by Jacqueline Miller Carmichael. Athens: University of Georgia Press, 1998. 125–32.

Black Family (January–February 1982): 28–29.

Block, Maxine, ed. *Current Biography: Who's News and Why.* 1944; New York: H. W. Wilson Company, 1971.

Bonetti, Kay. *The Missouri Review* 15.1 (1992): 112–31.

Buckner, Dilla. "Spirituality, Sexuality and Creativity: A Conversation with Margaret Walker." In *My Soul Is a Witness: African American Women's Spirituality.* Ed. Gloria Wade-Gayles. Boston: Beacon, 1995.

Campbell, Jane. "Margaret Walker." In *African American Writers.* Ed. Valerie Smith, Lea Baechler, and A. Walton Litz. New York: Scribner's, 1991. 459–71.

Campbell, Ruth. *Postscripts.* Mississippi Educational Television, 1983.

"Dr. Margaret Walker Alexander, Noted Poet and Author, Succumbs in Chicago." *Jet* 95.3 (1998): 17.

Emanuel, James A. "Margaret Walker." In *Contemporary Novelists.* Ed. James Vinson. New York: St. Martin's, 1982. 662–63.

"Margaret Walker." *Current Biography* 60.6 (1999): 62.

Miller, R. Baxter. "To a Place Blessed: For Margaret Walker." *African American Review* 33.1 (1999): 5.

Simanga, Michael. *Black Nation* 2.1 (1982): 11–14.

BOOKS AND RECORDINGS BY MARGARET WALKER
(in chronological order)

For My People. New Haven: Yale University Press, 1942. Reprint, New York: Arno Press, 1968.

Jubilee. Boston: Houghton Mifflin, 1966.

Prophets for a New Day. Detroit: Broadside Press, 1970.

How I Wrote Jubilee. Chicago: Third World Press, 1972.

October Journey. Detroit: Broadside Press, 1973.

Profiles of Black Achievement. Sound filmstrip. Prod. Guidance Associates, 1973.

(Giovanni, Nikki, and Margaret Walker.) *A Poetic Equation: Conversations Between Nikki Giovanni and Margaret Walker.* Washington DC: Howard University Press, 1974.

Margaret Walker Reads Langston Hughes, Paul Laurence Dunbar, and James Weldon Johnson. Smithsonian Folkways Recordings, 1975.

Margaret Walker Reads Margaret Walker and Langston Hughes. Smithsonian Folkways Recordings, 1975.

Poetry of Margaret Walker Read by Margaret Walker. Smithsonian Folkways Recordings, 1975.

For Farish Street. Jackson: Jackson Arts Alliance, 1986.

Richard Wright: Daemonic Genius. New York: Warner, 1989.

This Is My Century: New and Collected Poems. Athens: University of Georgia Press, 1989.

"How I Wrote Jubilee" and Other Essays on Life and Literature. Ed. Maryemma Graham. New York: Feminist Press, 1990.

On Being Female, Black, and Free: Essays by Margaret Walker, 1932–1992. Ed. Maryemma Graham. Knoxville: University of Tennessee Press, 1997.

INTERVIEWS WITH MARGARET WALKER
(in chronological order)

Interview by Frank Hains. *"Jubilee:* Fabric of Life as the Author Knows It: An Interview with Margaret Walker." *Jackson Daily News,* 16 Sept. 1966, 4.

Interview by Charles A. Rowell. "Poetry, History, and Humanism: An Interview with Margaret Walker." *Black World* 25.2 (1975): 4–17.

Interview by Phanuel Egejuru and Robert Elliot Fox. "An Interview with Margaret Walker." *Callaloo: A Black South Journal of Arts and Letters* 6 (1979): 29–35.

Interview by John Griffin Jones. "An Interview with Margaret Walker Alexander." *Mississippi Writers Talking* 2 (1982): 121–46.

Interview by Claudia Tate. "Margaret Walker." In *Black Women Writers at Work.* New York: Continuum, 1983.

Interview by Lucy M. Freibert. "Southern Song: An Interview with Margaret Walker." *Frontiers: A Journal of Women Studies* 9.3 (1987): 50–56.

Interview by Jerry W. Ward Jr. "A Writer for Her People: An Interview with Dr. Margaret Walker Alexander." *Mississippi Quarterly* 41 (1988): 515–27.

Book Break: Interviews with Illinois Authors. Sound recording. Sony Corporation, 1989.

Interview by Charlie Rose. *Night Watch.* CBS, 1989.

Interview by Alferdteen Harrison. "Looking Back: A Conversation with Margaret Walker." In *"For My People": A Tribute.* Jackson: University Press of Mississippi, 1992.

"Interview with John Grisham, Shelby Foote, and Margaret Walker." WAPT Television, Jackson, Mississippi, 1992.

Interview by Maryemma Graham. "The Fusion of Ideas: An Interview with Margaret Walker Alexander." *African American Review* 27 (1993): 279–86.

Interview by Patricia Greirson. "An Interview with Dr. Margaret Alexander Walker on Tennessee Williams." *Mississippi Quarterly* 48.4 (1995): 587–88.

Interview by Jacqueline M. Carmichael. "Margaret Walker's Reflections and Celebrations: An Interview." In *Trumpeting a Fiery Sound: History and Folklore in Margaret Walker's "Jubilee".* Athens: University of Georgia Press, 1998. 103–32.

Interview by Joanne V. Gabbin. "An Interview with Margaret Walker." In *The Furious Flowering of African American Poetry.* Charlotte: University Press of Virginia, 1999.

MARGARET WALKER'S POETRY IN ANTHOLOGIES

"Ballad for Phillis Wheatley." *Ebony Magazine* 29 (1974): 96.

"Ballad for Phillis Wheatley." *Jackson State Review* 6.1 (1974): 96.

"The Ballad of the Free." In *Understanding the New Black Poetry: Black Speech and Black Music as Poetic References,* by Stephen Henderson. New York: William Morrow, 1973. 166.

"Ballad of the Hoppy-Toad." In *New Black Voices: An Anthology of Contemporary Afro-American Literature.* Ed. with an introduction and biographical notes by Abraham Chapman. New York: Mentor Books, 1972. 203.

"Ballad of the Hoppy-Toad." In *Understanding the New Black Poetry: Black Speech and Black Music as Poetic References,* by Stephen Henderson. New York: William Morrow, 1973. 161.

"Ballad of the Hoppy-Toad." In *How Does a Poem Mean?* 2nd ed. Ed. John Ciardi and Miller Williams. Atlanta: Houghton Mifflin, 1975. 43–44.

"Ballad of the Hoppy-Toad." In *The Forerunners: Black Poets in America.* Ed. Woodie King Jr. Washington DC: Howard University Press, 1975. 107–9.

"Ballad of the Hoppy-Toad." In *Black Sister: Poetry by Black American Women, 1746–1980.* Ed. Erlene Stetson. Bloomington: Indiana University Press, 1981.

"Ballad of the Hoppy-Toad." In *The Heath Anthology of American Literature.* 3rd ed. Ed. Paul Lauter. Boston: Houghton Mifflin, 1998. 1972–74.

"Big John Henry." In *Words in Flight: An Introduction to Poetry.* Ed. Richard Abcarian. Belmont CA: Wadsworth, 1972. 233–34.

"Birmingham." In *An Anthology of Mississippi Writers*. Ed. Noel E. Polk. Jackson MS: University of Mississippi Press. 363–64.

"Birmingham." In *The Poetry of Black America: Anthology of the Twentieth Century*. Ed. Arnold Adoff. New York: Harper & Row, 1973. 149–50.

"Birmingham, 1963." In *Afro-American Writing Today: An Anniversary Issue of the Southern Review*. Ed. James Olney. Baton Rouge: LSU Press, 1985. 242.

"Birmingham, 1963." *The Southern Review* 21.3 (1985): 829.

"Black Paramour." In *Afro-American Writing Today: An Anniversary Issue of the Southern Review*. Ed. James Olney. Baton Rouge: LSU Press, 1985. 241.

"Black Paramour." *The Southern Review* 21.3 (1985): 828.

"Childhood." In *Black and Unknown Bards: A Collection of Negro Poetry*. Kent OH: Hand & Flower Press, 1963. 39.

"Childhood." In *The Sonnet: An Anthology*. New York: Washington Square Press, 1965. 345.

"Childhood." In *Famous American Negro Poets*. Ed. Charlemae Rollins. New York: Dodd, Mead, and Company, 1965. 81–82.

"Childhood." In *Kaleidoscope: Poems by American Negro Poets*. Ed. Robert Hayden. New York: Harcourt, Brace & World, 1967. 145.

"Childhood." In *Black Out Loud: An Anthology of Modern Poems by Black Americans*. Ed. Arnold Adoff. New York: Macmillan, 1969. 73.

"Childhood." In *Afro-American Writing: An Anthology of Prose and Poetry*. Ed. Richard A. Long and Eugenia W. Collier. New York: NYU Press, 1972. 522.

"Childhood." In *By a Woman Writt: Literature From Six Centuries by and about Women*. Ed. Joan Goulianos. New York: Bobbs-Merrill, 1973. 339.

"Childhood." In *The Poetry of Black America: Anthology of the Twentieth Century*. Ed. Arnold Adoff. New York: Harper & Row, 1973. 148.

"Childhood." In *United States in Literature*. Ed. James E. Miller et al. Glenview IL: Scott, Foresman, 1974.

"Childhood." In *I Hear My Sisters Saying: Poems by Twentieth-Century Women*. New York: Thomas Y. Crowell, 1976. 4.

"Childhood." In *The Penguin Book of Women Poets*. Ed. Carol Cosman, Joan Keefe, and Kathleen Weaver. New York: Viking Press, 1979. 346.

"Childhood." In *Women Poets of the World*. Ed. Joanna Barkier and Diedre Lashgari. New York: Macmillan, 1983. 375.

"The Crystal Palace." In *The Heath Anthology of American Literature*. 3rd ed. Ed. Paul Lauter. Boston: Houghton Mifflin, 1998. 1975.

"Dark Blood." *Opportunity: Journal of Negro Life* 16.6 (1938): 171.

"Dark Blood." In *Black and Unknown Bards: A Collection of Negro Poetry*. Kent OH: Hand & Flower Press, 1963. 41–42.

"Dark Blood." In *By a Woman Writt: Literature From Six Centuries by and about Women*. Ed. Joan Goulianos. New York: Bobbs-Merrill, 1973. 335–36.

"Dark Blood." In *The World Split Open: Four Centuries of Women Poets in England*

and America, 1552–1950. Ed. Louise Bernikow. New York: Vintage Books, 1974. 326–27.

"Dark Men Speak to the Earth." *Negro Story* (1944): 9.

"Daydream." *Crisis* 41.5 (1934): 129.

"Dear Are the Names That Charmed Me in My Youth." *The Virginia Quarterly* 31.2 (1955): 264.

"Ex-Slave." *Opportunity: Journal of Negro Life* 16.11 (1938): 330.

"Fanfare, Coda and Finale." In *Confirmation: An Anthology of African American Women.* Ed. Amiri Baraka. New York: William Morrow, 1983. 372–73.

"Five Black Men." In *Confirmation: An Anthology of African American Women.* Ed. Amiri Baraka. New York: William Morrow, 1983. 363–68.

"For Andy Goodman—Michael Schwerner—And James Chaney." In *A Broadside Treasury.* Ed. Gwendolyn Brooks. Detroit: Broadside Press, 1971. 152–54.

"For Andy Goodman—Michael Schwerner—And James Chaney." In *The Black Poets: A New Anthology.* Ed. Randall Dudley. New York: Bantam Books, 1971. 158–60.

"For Gwen, 1969." In *To Gwen with Love: An Anthology Dedicated to Gwendolyn Brooks.* Ed. Patricia L. Brown, Don L. Lee, and Francis Ward. Chicago: Johnson Publishing Co., 1971. 95.

"For Gwen, 1969." In *Third Woman: Minority Writers of the U.S.* Ed. Dexter Fisher. Boston: Houghton Mifflin, 1980. 249–50.

"For Malcolm X." In *Black Poetry: A Supplement to Anthologies Which Exclude Black Poets.* Ed. Dudley Randall. Detroit: Broadside Press, 1969. 20.

"For Malcolm X." In *For Malcolm: Poems on the Life and Death of Malcolm X.* Ed. Dudley Randall and Margaret G. Burroughs. Detroit: Broadside Press, 1969. 32–33.

"For Malcolm X." In *Black Insights: Significant Literature by Black Americans—1760 to the Present.* Ed. Nick Aaron Ford. Waltham MA: Xerox College Publishing, 1971. 98.

"For Malcolm X." In *The Black Poets: A New Anthology.* Ed. Dudley Randall. New York: Bantam Books, 1971. 157.

"For Malcolm X." In *The Poetry of Black America: Anthology of the Twentieth Century.* Ed. Arnold Adoff. New York: Harper & Row, 1973. 150.

"For Malcolm X." In *Understanding the New Black Poetry: Black Speech and Black Music as Poetic References,* by Stephen Henderson. New York: William Morrow, 1973. 165.

"For Malcolm X." In *Keeping the Faith: Writings by Contemporary Black American Women.* Ed. Pat Crutchfield Exum. Greenwich CT: Fawcett Publications, 1974. 117–18.

"For Malcolm X." In *Celebrations: A New Anthology of Black American Poetry.* Ed. Arnold Adoff. Chicago: Follett, 1977. 181–82.

"For Malcolm X." In *The Heath Guide to Literature.* Ed. David Bergman. Lexington MA: D.C. Heath and Company, 1992. 576.

"For Mary McLeod Bethune." In *Poetry of the Negro, 1746–1949.* Ed. Langston Hughes and Arna Bontemps. Garden City NY: Doubleday, 1949. 188.

"For Mary McLeod Bethune." In *Famous American Negro Poets.* Ed. Charlemae Rollins. New York: Dodd, Mead, 1965. 83.

"For Mary McLeod Bethune." In *Poetry of the Negro, 1746–1970*. Ed. Langston Hughes and Arna Bontemps. Garden City NY: Doubleday, 1970. 326.

"For Mary McLeod Bethune." In *You Better Believe It: Black Verses in English from Africa, the West Indies and the U.S.* Ed. Paul Bremen. Baltimore: Penguin, 1973. 155.

"For My People." In *The Negro Caravan*. Ed. Sterling Brown, Arthur P. Davis, and Ulysses Lee. New York: Arno Press and The New York Times, 1941. 409–10.

"For My People." *Scholastic: High School Teacher Edition* 42.2 (1943): 21.

"For My People." In *American Negro Poetry*. Ed. Arna Bontemps. New York: Hill and Wang, 1963. 128–30.

"For My People." In *Black and Unknown Bards: A Collection of Negro Poetry*. Kent OH: Hand & Flower Press, 1963. 39–41.

"For My People." In *Kaleidoscope: Poems by American Negro Poets*. Ed. Robert Hayden. New York: Harcourt, Brace & World, 1967. 138–40.

"For My People." In *An Introduction to Black Literature in America*. Ed. Lindsay Patterson. New York: Publishers Company, 1968. 219.

"For My People." In *Black Voices: An Anthology of Afro-American Literature*. Ed. Abraham Chapman. New York: New American Library, 1968. 459–60.

"For My People." In *I Am the Darker Brother: An Anthology of Modern Poems by Negro Americans*. Ed. Arnold Adoff. New York: Macmillan, 1968. 107–9.

"For My People." In *Dark Symphony*. Ed. James A. Emanuel and Theodore L. Gross. New York: The Free Press, 1968. 495–96.

"For My People." In *Black American Literature*. Ed. Darwin T. Turner. Columbus OH: Charles E. Merrill, 1969. 97–99.

"For My People." *1969 Poetry Calendar*. Chicago: DuSable Museum of African American History, 1969.

"For My People." In *Afro-American Literature: Poetry*. Ed. William Adams, Peter Conn, and Barry Stepian. Boston: Houghton Mifflin, 1970. 2–3.

"For My People." In *The Black Experience: An Anthology of American Literature for the 1970s*. Ed. Francis E. Kearn. New York: Viking, 1970. 498–99.

"For My People." In *Afro-American Voices 1770s–1970s*. Ed. Ralph Kendricks and Claudette Levitt. New York: Oxford Book Co., 1970. 344–45.

"For My People." In *The Premier Book of Major Poets: An Anthology*. Ed. Anita Dore. Greenwich CT: Fawcett Publications, 1970. 204–5.

"For My People." In *Afro-American Literature: An Introduction*. Ed. Robert Hayden, David J. Burrows, and Frederic R. Lapides. New York: Harcourt Brace Jovanovich, 1971. 137–39.

"For My People." In *Black Insights: Significant Literature by Black Americans—1760 to the Present*. Ed. Nick Aaron Ford. Waltham MA: Xerox College Publishing, 1971. 95–96.

"For My People." In *Black Literature in America*. Ed. Houston A. Baker Jr. New York: McGraw-Hill, 1971. 261–62.

"For My People." In *Major Black Writers*. Ed. Alma Murray and Robert Thomas. Englewood Cliffs NJ: Scholastic Book Service, 1971.

"For My People." In *Poetry and Principle*. Ed. Gene Montague. Philadelphia: J. B. Lippincott, 1972. 104–6.

"For My People." In *Black Writers of America: A Comprehensive Anthology*. Ed. Richard Barksdale and Kenneth Kinnamon. New York: Macmillan, 1972. 636–37.

"For My People." In *By a Woman Writt: Literature From Six Centuries by and about Women*. Ed. Joan Goulianos. New York: Bobbs-Merrill, 1973. 333–35.

"For My People." In *The Poetry of Black America: Anthology of the Twentieth Century*. Ed. Arnold Adoff. New York: Harper & Row, 1973. 144–45.

"For My People." In *You Better Believe It: Black Verses in English From Africa, the West Indies and the U.S.* Ed. Paul Bremen. Baltimore: Penguin, 1973. 153.

"For My People." In *Understanding the New Black Poetry: Black Speech and Black Music as Poetic References*, by Stephen Henderson. New York: William Morrow, 1973. 163.

"For My People." In *American Negro Poetry*. Ed. Arna Bontemps. New York: Hill and Wang, 1974. 128–30.

"For My People." In *The New Negro Renaissance: An Anthology*. Ed. Arthur Paul Davis and Michael W. Peplow. New York: Holt, Rinehart and Winston, 1975. 383–84.

"For My People." In *By Women: An Anthology of Literature*. Ed. Linda Heinlein Kirschner and Marcia McClintock Folsom. Boston: Houghton Mifflin, 1976. 413–15.

"For My People." In *Celebrations: A New Anthology of Black American Poetry*. Ed. Arnold Adoff. Chicago: Follett, 1977. 248–50.

"For My People." *Ebony Magazine* (1980): 151.

"For My People." *The Black Nation* 2.1 (fall–winter 1982).

"For My People." In *For My People: Black Theology and the Black Church*, by James Cone. Maryknoll NY: Orbis Books, 1984.

"For My People." In *African American Literature: An Anthology of Nonfiction, Fiction, Poetry, and Drama*. Ed. Demetrice A. Worley and Jesse Perry Jr. Lincolnwood IL: National Textbook Co., 1993. 259–60.

"For My People." In *The Heath Anthology of American Literature*. 3rd ed. Ed. Paul Lauter. Boston: Houghton Mifflin, 1998. 1971–72.

"For Paul Laurence Dunbar (Centennial Celebration—Dayton, Ohio—1972)." In *Singer in the Dawn: Reinterpretation of Paul Laurence Dunbar*. Ed. Jay Martin. New York: Dodd, Mead, 1975. 11.

"From a Poem for Farish Street." *Iowa Review* 16.1 (1986): 127–29.

"Girl Held Without Bail." In *By a Woman Writt: Literature From Six Centuries by and about Women*. Ed. Joan Goulianos. New York: Bobbs-Merrill, 1973. 340.

"Girl Held Without Bail." In *The Poetry of Black America: Anthology of the Twentieth Century*. Ed. Arnold Adoff. New York: Harper & Row, 1973. 148–49.

"Girl Held Without Bail." In *Celebrations: A New Anthology of Black American Poetry*. Ed. Arnold Adoff. Chicago: Follett, 1977. 194–95.

"Girl Held Without Bail." In *Women Working: An Anthology of Stories and Poems*. Ed. Nancy Hoffman and Florence Howe. Old Westbury NY: McGraw-Hill, 1979. 201.

"Harriet Tubman." *Phylon* 5.4 (1944): 326–30.

"Harriet Tubman." In *Poetry of the Negro, 1746–1949*. Ed. Langston Hughes and Arna Bontemps. Garden City NY: Doubleday, 1949. 181.

"Harriet Tubman." In *People in Poetry*. Ed. Marjorie B. Smiley, Florence B. Freedman, and Domenica Paterno. New York: Macmillan, 1966. 17–23.

"Harriet Tubman." In *Black Poetry for All Americans*. Ed. Leon Weisman and Elfreda S. Wright. New York: Globe Book Co., 1971. 19.

"Harriet Tubman." In *Giant Talk: An Anthology of Third World Writings*. Ed. Quincy Troupe and Rainer Schulte. New York: Vintage, 1975. 28.

"Heritage." In *I, Too, Sing America: Black Voices in American Literature*. Ed. Barbara Dodds Stanford. New York: Hayden Book Co., 1971. 45–49.

"Hounds." *The New Challenge* 2.2 (fall 1937): 50.

"How Many Silent Centuries Sleep in My Sultry Veins?" In *An Anthology of Mississippi Writers*. Ed. Noel E. Polk. Jackson MS: University Press of Mississippi, 1979.

"I Hear a Rumbling." In *Confirmation: An Anthology of African American Women*. Ed. Amiri Baraka. New York: William Morrow, 1983. 369–71.

"Inflation Blues." *The Black Scholar: Journal of Black Studies and Research* 2.5 (1980): 74.

"Iowa Farmer." In *Kaleidoscope: Poems by American Negro Poets*. Ed. Robert E. Hayden. New York: Harcourt, Brace, and World, 1967. 144.

"Iowa Farmer." In *United States in Literature*. Ed. James E. Miller. Glenville IL: Scott Foresman, 1979. 474.

"I Want to Write." In *Third Woman: Minority Women Writers of the U.S.* Ed. Dexter Fisher. Boston: Houghton Mifflin, 1980. 249.

"Jackson, Mississippi." In *An Anthology of Mississippi Writers*. Ed. Noel E. Polk. Jackson MS: University Press of Mississippi. 362–63.

"Jackson, Mississippi." In *A Broadside Treasury*. Ed. Gwendolyn Brooks. Detroit: Broadside Press, 1971. 151–52.

"Jackson, Mississippi." In *The Forerunners: Black Poets in America*. Ed. Woodie King Jr. Washington DC: Howard University Press, 1975. 110–11.

"Kissie Lee." In *By a Woman Writt: Literature From Six Centuries by and about Women*. Ed. Joan Goulianos. New York: Bobbs-Merrill, 1973. 336–37.

"Kissie Lee." In *No More Masks! An Anthology of Poems by Women*. Ed. Florence Howe and Ellen Bass. Garden City NY: Doubleday, Anchor Books, 1973. 113–14.

"Kissie Lee." In *Black Sister: Poetry by Black American Women, 1746–1980*. Ed. Erlene Stetson. Bloomington: Indiana University Press, 1981.

"Lineage." In *Famous American Negro Poets*. Ed. Charlemae Rollins. New York: Dodd, Mead, 1965. 85–86.

"Lineage." In *Kaleidoscope: Poems by American Negro Poets*. Ed. Robert Hayden. New York: Harcourt, Brace & World, 1967. 141.

"Lineage." In *Black out Loud: An Anthology of Modern Poems by Black Americans*. Ed. Arnold Adoff. New York: Macmillan, 1970. 59.

"Lineage." In *Who Am I This Time? Female Portraits in British and American Literature.* Ed. Carol Pearson and Katherine Pope. New York: McGraw-Hill, 1971. 294–95.

"Lineage." In *By a Woman Writt: Literature From Six Centuries by and about Women.* Ed. Joan Goulianos. New York: Bobbs-Merrill, 1973. 336.

"Lineage." In *The Poetry of Black America: Anthology of the Twentieth Century.* Ed. Arnold Adoff. New York: Harper & Row, 1973. 148.

"Lineage." In *No More Masks! An Anthology of Poems by Women.* Ed. Florence Howe and Ellen Bass. Garden City NY: Doubleday, Anchor Books, 1973. 110.

"Lineage." *The Reporter,* 8 Nov. 1973, 3.

"Lineage." In *The World Split Open: Four Centuries of Women Poets in England and America, 1552–1950.* Ed. Louise Bernikow. New York: Vintage, 1974. 326.

"Lineage." In *Celebrations: A New Anthology of Black American Poetry.* Ed. Arnold Adoff. Chicago: Follett, 1977. 26.

"Lineage." In *Shifting Anchors.* Ed. Leo Fay and Paul S. Anderson. Chicago: Rand McNally, 1978.

"Lineage." In *Women Working: An Anthology of Stories and Poems.* Ed. Nancy Hoffman and Florence Howe. Old Westbury NY: McGraw-Hill, 1979. 49.

"Lineage." In *The Penguin Book of Women Poets.* Ed. Carol Cosman, Joan Keefe, and Kathleen Weaver. New York: Viking Press, 1979. 345–46.

"Lineage." In *Sturdy Black Bridges: Visions of Black Women in Literature.* Ed. Roseann P. Bell, Betty J. Parker, and Beverly Guy-Shestall. Garden City NY: Doubleday, Anchor Books, 1979. 339.

"Lineage." In *Black Sister: Poetry by Black American Women, 1746–1980.* Ed. Erlene Stetson. Bloomington: Indiana University Press, 1981.

"Lineage." In *Album U.S.A.* Ed. Olive Stafford Niles, Edmond J. Farrell, and Robert M. Leblanc. Palo Alto CA: Scott, Foresman, 1984. 72.

"Lineage." In *The Heath Guide to Literature.* Ed. David Bergman and Daniel Epstein. Lexington MA: D. C. Heath and Company, 1992. 710.

"Lineage." In *Trumpeting a Fiery Sound,* by Jacqueline Miller Carmichael. Athens: University of Georgia Press, 1998. 7.

"A Litany from the Dark People." *Phylon* 13.3 (1952): 252–53.

"A Litany from the Dark People." *Jackson College Bulletin* 2.2 (1953): 43.

"A Litany from the Dark People." In *A Voice Crying in the Wilderness: The Memoirs of Jacob L. Reddix,* by Jacob Lorenzo Reddix. Jackson MS: University Press of Mississippi, 1974. 231–32.

"A Litany From the Dark People." In *Poems (for Jackson College Diamond Jubilee).* Jackson MS: Jackson College, copyright applied for. 11–14.

"Long John Nelson and Sweetie Pie." In *By a Woman Writt: Literature From Six Centuries by and about Women.* Ed. Joan Goulianos. New York: Bobbs-Merrill, 1973. 337–38.

"Memory." In *Afro-American Writing: An Anthology of Prose and Poetry.* Ed. Richard A. Long and Eugenia W. Collier. New York: NYU Press, 1972. 521.

"A Message All Black People Can Dig (and a Few Negroes Too)." *American Libraries* (1970): 854.

"Mess of Pottage." *The New Challenge* 2.2 (fall 1937): 50.

"Micah." In *Understanding the New Black Poetry: Black Speech and Black Music as Poetic References,* by Stephen Henderson. New York: William Morrow, 1973.166.

"Micah." In *Keeping the Faith: Writings by Contemporary Black American Women.* Ed. Pat Crutchfield Exum. Greenwich CT: Fawcett Publications, 1974. 120–21.

"Molly Means." In *Black Sister: Poetry by Black American Women, 1746–1980.* Ed. Erlene Stetson. Bloomington: Indiana University Press, 1981.

"Molly Means." In *Story Poems, New and Old.* Ed. William Cole. New York: World Publishing Company, 1957. 202–3.

"Molly Means." In *American Negro Poetry.* Rev. ed. Ed. Arna Bontemps. New York: Hill and Wang, 1963. 130–31.

"Molly Means." In *Kaleidoscope: Poems by American Negro Poets.* Ed. Robert Hayden. New York: Harcourt, Brace & World, 1967. 142–43.

"Molly Means." In *Dark Symphony.* Ed. James A. Emanuel and Theodore L. Gross. New York: Free Press, 1968. 497.

"Molly Means." In *No More Masks! An Anthology of Poems by Women.* Ed. Florence Howe and Ellen Bass. Garden City NY: Doubleday, Anchor Books, 1973. 111–12.

"Molly Means." In *American Negro Poetry.* Ed. Arna Bontemps. New York: Hill and Wang, 1974. 130–34.

"Molly Means." In *Sharing Literature with Children: A Thematic Anthology.* Ed. Francelia Butler. New York: David McKay, 1977. 244.

"Molly Means." In *Arrangement in Literature,* by Edmond J. Farrell. Glenview IL: Scott, Foresman, 1979. 6–7.

"My Mississippi Spring." In *Afro-American Writing Today: An Anniversary Issue of the Southern Review.* Ed. James Olney. Baton Rouge: LSU Press, 1985. 240.

"My Mississippi Spring." *The Southern Review* 21 (1985): 827.

"My Truth and My Flame." In *Confirmation: An Anthology of African American Women.* Ed. Amiri Baraka. New York: William Morrow, 1982. 361.

"Now." In *Beyond the Angry Black.* Ed. John A. Williams. New York: Cooper Square Publishers, 1966. 156.

"Now." In *By a Woman Writt: Literature From Six Centuries by and about Women.* Ed. Joan Goulianos. New York: Bobbs-Merrill, 1973. 341.

"October Journey." In *Poetry of the Negro, 1746–1949.* Ed. Langston Hughes and Arna Bontemps. Garden City NY: Doubleday, 1949. 317.

"October Journey." In *Beyond the Blues: New Poems by American Negroes.* Ed. Rosey E. Pool. Kent OH: Hand and Flower Press, 1962. 180–82.

"October Journey." In *I Am the Darker Brother: An Anthology of Modern Poems by Negro Americans.* Ed. Arnold Adoff. New York: Macmillan, 1968. 28–30.

"October Journey." In *Poetry of the Negro, 1746–1970.* Ed. Langston Hughes and Arna Bontemps. Garden City NY: Doubleday, 1970. 176.

"October Journey." In *Black Insights: Significant Literature by Black Americans—1760*

to the Present. Ed. Nick Aaron Ford. Waltham MA: Xerox College Publishing, 1971.
96–98.

"October Journey." In *The Poetry of Black America: Anthology of the Twentieth Century.*
Ed. Arnold Adoff. New York: Harper & Row, 1973. 146–47.

"October Journey." In *American Negro Poetry.* Ed. Arna Bontemps. New York: Hill and
Wang, 1974. 132–34.

"October Journey." In *Poetry for the Earth: A Collection of Poems from around the World
That Celebrates Nature.* Ed. Sara Dunn. New York: Fawcett Columbia, 1991. 36.

"Ode on the Occasion of the Inauguration of Dr. John A. Peoples, Jr., as the Sixth
President of Jackson State College." In *Black Insights: Significant Literature by Black
Americans—1760 to the Present.* Ed. Nick Aaron Ford. Waltham MA: Xerox College
Publishing, 1971. 98–99.

"Palmettos." *Opportunity: Journal of Negro Life* 17.1 (1939): 14.

"People of Unrest and Hunger." *The New Challenge* 2.2 (fall 1937): 49–50.

"Poppa Chicken." In *Cavalcade: Negro American Writing from 1760 to the Present.* Ed.
Davis P. Arthur. Boston: Houghton Mifflin, 1971.

"Prophets for a New Day." In *A Broadside Treasury.* Ed. Gwendolyn Brooks. Detroit:
Broadside Press, 1971. 150–51.

"Prophets for a New Day." In *The Black Poets: A New Anthology.* Ed. Dudley Randall.
New York: Bantam Books, 1971. 160–62.

"Prophets for a New Day." In *Keeping the Faith: Writings by Contemporary Black American Women.* Ed. Pat Crutchfield Exum. Greenwich CT: Fawcett, 1974. 118–20.

"Solace." In *The Heath Anthology of American Literature.* 3rd ed. Ed. Paul Lauter. Vol. 2.
Boston: Houghton Mifflin, 1998. 1974.

"Sonnets to the Presidents of Jackson College." In *A Brief History of Jackson College,* by
B. Baldwin Dansby. Jackson MS: Jackson College, 1953. xvii–xix.

"Sonnets to the Presidents of Jackson College." *Poetry* (copyright applied for): 3–7.

"Sorrow Home." *Opportunity: Journal of Negro Life* 16.5 (1938): 139.

"Sorrow Home." In *Poetry for the Earth: A Collection of Poems from around the
World That Celebrates Nature.* Ed. Sara Dunn. New York: Fawcett Columbia,
1991. 75.

"Southern Song." In *Black and Unknown Bards: A Collection of Negro Poetry.* Kent OH:
Hand & Flower Press, 1963. 41.

"Southern Song." In *Afro-American Writing: An Anthology of Prose and Poetry.* Ed. Richard A. Long and Eugenia W. Collier. New York: NYU Press, 1972. 520.

"Southern Song." In *The Heath Anthology of American Literature.*, 3rd ed. Ed. Paul
Lauter. Boston: Houghton Mifflin, 1998. 1970–71.

"Southern Song." *The New Challenge* 2.2 (fall 1937): 49–50.

"The Spirituals." *Opportunity: Journal of Negro Life* 16.8 (1938): 237.

"Street Demonstration." In *The Black Poets: A New Anthology.* Ed. Dudley Randall. New
York: Bantam Books, 1971. 156.

"Street Demonstration." In *By a Woman Writt: Literature From Six Centuries by and
about Women.* Ed. Joan Goulianos. New York: Bobbs-Merrill, 1973. 340.

"Street Demonstration." In *Celebrations: A New Anthology of Black American Poetry*. Ed. Arnold Adoff. Chicago: Follett, 1977. 194.

"The Struggle Staggers Us." *Poetry: A Magazine of Verse* 52.4 (1938): 198.

"The Struggle Staggers Us." In *Trumpeting a Fiery Sound,* by Jacqueline Miller Carmichael. Athens: University of Georgia Press, 1998. 37.

"This Is My Century . . . Black Synthesis of Time." In *Confirmation: An Anthology of African American Women*. Ed. Amiri Baraka. New York: William Morrow, 1983. 361–63.

"Today." In *The Forerunners: Black Poets in America*. Ed. Woodie King Jr. Washington DC: Howard University Press, 1975. 112–13.

"Tribute to Robert Hayden, February 1980." *The Black Scholar* 4 (1980): 75.

"The Wall (For Edward Christmas)." In *Black Writers of America: A Comprehensive Anthology*. Ed. Richard Barksdale and Kenneth Kinnamon. New York: Macmillan, 1972. 721.

"We Have Been Believers." In *Poetry of the Negro, 1746–1949*. Ed. Langston Hughes and Arna Bontemps. Garden City NY: Doubleday, 1949. 180.

"We Have Been Believers." In *Beyond The Blues: New Poems by American Negroes*. Ed. Rosey E. Pool. Kent OH: The Hand and Flower Press, 1962. 179–80.

"We Have Been Believers." In *Soulscript: Afro-American Poetry*. Ed. June Jordan. Garden City NY: Zenith Books (Doubleday & Co.), 1970. 130–31.

"We Have Been Believers." In *Black Literature in America: A Casebook*. Ed. Raman K. Singh and Peter Fellowes. New York: Thomas Y. Crowell Company, 1970. 15.

"We Have Been Believers." In *Poetry of the Negro, 1746–1970*. Ed. Langston Hughes and Arna Bontemps. Garden City NY: Doubleday, 1970. 312.

"We Have Been Believers." In *Afro-American Literature: An Introduction*. Ed. Robert Hayden, David J. Burrows, and Frederic R. Lapides. New York: Harcourt Brace Jovanovich, 1971. 139–40.

"We Have Been Believers." In *Black Insights: Significant Literature by Black Americans— 1760 to the Present*. Ed. Nick Aaron Ford. Waltham MA: Xerox College Publishing, 1971. 96.

"We Have Been Believers." In *Cavalcade: Negro American Writing from 1760 to the Present*. Ed. Arthur Paul Davis. Boston: Houghton Mifflin, 1971. 530.

"We Have Been Believers." In *Black Perspectives*. Ed. Alma Murray. Englewood Cliffs NJ: Scholastic Book Service, 1971.

"We Have Been Believers." In *Afro-American Writing: An Anthology of Prose and Poetry*. Ed. Richard A. Long and Eugenia W. Collier. New York: NYU Press, 1972. 523–24.

"We Have Been Believers." In *The Poetry of Black America: Anthology of the Twentieth Century*. Ed. Arnold Adoff. New York: Harper & Row, 1973. 145–46.

"We Have Been Believers." *The Black Nation* 2.1 (1982): 36.

"Whores." In *By a Woman Writt: Literature From Six Centuries by and about Women*. Ed. Joan Goulianos. New York: Bobbs-Merrill, 1973. 339.

Algren, Nelson. "A Social Poet." *Poetry* 61 (1961): 634–36.

Barksdale, Richard. "Margaret Walker: Folk Orature and Historical Prophecy." In *Black American Poets Between Worlds, 1940–1960*. Ed. R. Baxter Miller. Tennessee Studies in Literature 30. Knoxville: University of Tennessee Press, 1986. 104–17.

Bell, Bernard W. *The Afro-American Novel and Its Traditions*. Amherst: University of Massachusetts Press, 1987.

Berg, Temma F. "Margaret Walker's *Jubilee*: Refocusing William Faulkner's *Absalom, Absalom!*" *Women's Studies International Forum* 10.5 (1987): 31.

Breman, Paul. "Poetry into the Sixties." In *The Black American Writer*. Ed. C. W. E. Bigsby. Deland FL: Everett/Edwards, 1969. 99–101.

Buckner, B. Dilla. "Folkloric Elements in Margaret Walker's Poetry." *CLA Journal* 33.4 (June 1990).

Carby, Hazel. "The Historical Novel of Slavery." In *Slavery and the Literary Imagination*. Ed. Deborah E. McDowell and Arnold Rampersad. Baltimore: Johns Hopkins University Press, 1989.

Carmichael, Jacqueline Miller. *Trumpeting a Fiery Sound: History and Folklore in Margaret Walker's "Jubilee."* Athens: University of Georgia Press, 1998.

Christian, Barbara. *Black Women Novelists*. Westport CT: Greenwood Press, 1980.

Emanuel, James A. Introduction to *Dark Symphony: Negro Literature in America*. Ed. James A. Emanuel and Theodore L. Gross. New York: Free Press, 1968. 350–73.

Evans, Mari, ed. *Black Women Writers (1950–1980): A Critical Evaluation*. Garden City NY: Doubleday, Anchor Books, 1984.

Fabre, Michel. "Margaret Walker's Richard Wright: A Wrong Righted or a Wright Wronged?" *Mississippi Quarterly: The Journal of Southern Culture* 42.4 (1989): 429–50.

Georgoudaki, Ekaterini. "The South in Margaret Walker's Poetry: 'Harbor and Sorrow Home.'" *Cross Roads* 2.2 (summer 1994): 66–79.

Giddings, Paula. "'A Shoulder Hunched Against a Sharp Concern': Some Themes in the Poetry of Margaret Walker." *Black World* (1971): 20–25.

Goodman, Charlotte. "From *Uncle Tom's Cabin* to Vyry's Kitchen: The Black Female Folk Tradition in Margaret Walker's *Jubilee*." In *Tradition and the Talents of Women*. Ed. Florence Howe. Champaign: University of Illinois Press, 1991.

Graham, Maryemma. Introduction to *"How I Wrote Jubilee" and Other Essays on Life and Literature*. Ed. Maryemma Graham. New York: Feminist Press, 1990. xiii–xxi.

———. Introduction to *On Being Female, Black, and Free: Essays by Margaret Walker, 1932–1992*. Ed. Maryemma Graham. Knoxville: University of Tennessee Press, 1997. xi–xix.

Gwin, Minrose. *Black and White Women of the Old South: The Peculiar Sisterhood in American Literature*. Knoxville: University of Tennessee Press, 1985.

———. "*Jubilee*: Black Women's Celebration of Human Community." In *Conjuring:*

Black Women, Fiction, and Literary Tradition. Ed. Marjorie Pryse and Hortense J. Spillers. Bloomington: Indiana University Press, 1985.

Harris, Trudier. *Exorcising Blackness: Historical and Literary Lynching and Burning Rituals.* Bloomington: Indiana University Press, 1984.

———. *From Mammies to Militants: Domestics in Black American Literature.* Philadelphia: Temple University Press, 1982.

Henderson, Stephen. "Survival Motion: A Study of the Black Woman Writer and the Black Revolution in America." In *The Militant Black Writer.* Ed. Mercer Cook and Stephen Henderson. Madison WI: University of Wisconsin Press, 1969. 101–21.

Hull, Gloria T. "Black Woman Poets from Wheatley to Walker." In *Negro American Literature Forum* 19.3 (1975).

Jackson, Blyden. "From One New Negro to Another." In *Black Poetry in America: Two Essays in Historical Interpretation.* Ed. Blyden Jackson and Louis Rubin Jr. Baton Rouge: LSU Press, 1974. 67–69.

Kent, George. *Blackness and the Adventure of Western Culture.* Chicago: Third World Press, 1972.

Klotman, Phyllis R. "'Oh Freedom'—Women and History in Margaret Walker's *Jubilee.*" *Black American Literature Forum* 11.4 (winter 1977): 139–45.

McDowell, Margaret. "The Black Woman as Artist and Critic: Four Versions." *Kentucky Review* 7 (1987): 19–41.

Miller, R. Baxter. "The 'Etched Flame' of Margaret Walker: Literary and Biblical Re-Creation in Southern History." *Tennessee Studies in Literature* 26 (1981): 157–72.

———. "The 'Intricate Design' of Margaret Walker: Literary and Biblical Re-Creation in Southern History." In *Black American Poets Between Worlds 1940–1960.* Ed. R. Baxter Miller. Knoxville: University of Tennessee Press, 1986. 118–35.

Payne, Ladell. *Black Novelists and the Southern Literary Tradition.* Athens: University of Georgia Press, 1981.

Pettis, Joyce. "Margaret Walker: Black Woman Writer of the South." In *Southern Women Writers: The New Generation.* Ed. Tonnette Bond Inge. Tuscaloosa: University of Alabama Press, 1990.

Powell, Bertie J. "The Black Experience in Margaret Walker's *Jubilee* and Lorainne Hansberry's *The Drinking Gourd.*" *College Language Association Journal* 21 (1977): 304–11.

Randall, Dudley. "The Black Aesthetic in the Thirties, Forties, and Fifties." In *The Black Aesthetic.* Ed. Addison Gayle. New York: Doubleday, 1971.

Redmond, Eugene B. *Drumvoices: The Mission of Afro-American Poetry—A Critical Evaluation.* New York: Doubleday, 1976.

Reid, Margaret. "The Defiant Ones: Black Female Voices in Poetic Protest." In *Amid Visions and Revisions: Poetry and Criticism in Literature and the Arts.* Ed. Barney J. Hollis. Baltimore: Morgan State University Press, 1985. 79–94.

Rubin, Louis D., et al., eds. *The History of Southern Literature.* Baton Rouge: LSU Press, 1985.

Russell, Sandi. *Render Me a Song: African American Women Writers from Slavery to the Present.* New York: St. Martin's, 1990.

Spears, James E. "Black Folk Elements in Margaret Walker's *Jubilee.*" *Mississippi Folklore Register* 14.1 (spring 1980): 13–19.

Thomas, H. Nigel. *From Folklore to Fiction: A Study of Folk Heroes and Rituals in the Black American Novel.* Westport CT: Greenwood Press, 1988.

Traylor, Eleanor. "'Bolder Measures Crashing Through': Margaret Walker's Poem of the Century." *Callaloo: An Afro-American and African Journal of Arts and Letters* 10.4 (1987): 570–95.

———. "Music as Theme: The Blues Mode in the Writing of Margaret Walker." In *Black Women Writers (1950–1980): A Critical Evaluation.* Ed. Mari Evans. Garden City NY: Doubleday, Anchor Books, 1984.

Wade-Gayles, Gloria. Introduction to *How I Wrote* Jubilee, by Margaret Walker. Chicago: Third World Press, 1972. 5–8.

Walker, Melissa. *Down from the Mountaintop: Black Women's Novels in the Wake of the Civil Rights Movement, 1966–1989.* New Haven: Yale University Press, 1991.

Williams, Delores S. "Black Women's Literature and the Task of Feminist Theology." In *Immaculate & Powerful: The Female in Sacred Image and Social Reality.* Ed. Clarissa Atkinson, Constance Buchanan, and Margaret Miles. Boston: Beacon, 1985. 88–110.

SELECTED ESSAYS BY MARGARET WALKER

"Agenda For Action: Black Arts and Letters." In *On Being Female, Black, and Free: Essays by Margaret Walker, 1932–1992.* Ed. Maryemma Graham. Knoxville: University of Tennessee Press, 1997. 86–97.

A Bicentennial Pamphlet: Black Culture. Washington DC, 1976.

"Black Studies: Some Personal Observations." *Afro-American Studies* 1 (fall 1970): 41–43.

"Black Women in Academia." In *"How I Wrote Jubilee" and Other Essays on Life and Literature.* Ed. Maryemma Graham. New York: Feminist Press, 1990. 26–32.

"Black Writers' Views on Literary Lions and Values." *Negro Digest* 17 (1968): 23.

"A Brief Introduction to Southern Literature." In *"How I Wrote Jubilee" and Other Essays on Life and Literature.* Ed. Maryemma Graham. New York: Feminist Press, 1990. 134–42.

"The Challenge of the 1970s to the Black Scholar." In *On Being Female, Black, and Free: Essays by Margaret Walker, 1932–1992.* Ed. Maryemma Graham. Knoxville: University of Tennessee Press, 1997. 183–88.

"Chief Worshippers at All World Altars." *Encore* 1.12 (1975).

"Critical Approaches to the Study of African American Literature (1968)." In *On Being Female, Black, and Free: Essays by Margaret Walker, 1932–1992.* Ed. Maryemma Graham. Knoxville: University of Tennessee Press, 1997. 121–31.

"Discovering Our Connections: Race, Gender, and the Law." *The American University Journal of Gender and the Law* 1.1 (1993).

"Dr. Nick Aaron Ford: A Man in the Classic Tradition." In *Swords upon This Hill*. Ed. Barney J. Hollis. Baltimore: Morgan State University Press, 1984. 116–20.

"Education in the Global Village." In *On Being Female, Black, and Free: Essays by Margaret Walker, 1932–1992*. Ed. Maryemma Graham. Knoxville: University of Tennessee Press, 1997. 189–91.

"The Education of a Seminal Mind, W. E. B. Du Bois." In *"How I Wrote Jubilee" and Other Essays on Life and Literature*. Ed. Maryemma Graham. New York: Feminist Press, 1990. 84–90.

"Faulkner and Race." In *The Maker and the Myth*. Ed. Evans Harrington and Ann J. Abadie. Oxford: University Press of Mississippi, 1978. 105–21.

Foreword to *I Wonder as I Wander*, by Langston Hughes. New York: Thunder's Mouth Press, 1986. xi–xii.

"Growing out of Shadow." *Common Ground* 4.1 (1943): 42–46.

"How I Told My Child about Race." *Negro Digest* 2 (1951): 42–46.

"The Humanistic Tradition of Afro-American Literature." *American Libraries* 1 (Oct. 1970): 849–54.

"Humanities with a Black Focus: A Black Paradigm." In *Curriculum Changes in Black Colleges III*. Washington DC: Department of Education, 1972.

"Jesse Jackson, the Man and His Message." In *On Being Female, Black, and Free: Essays by Margaret Walker, 1932–1992*. Ed. Maryemma Graham. Knoxville: University of Tennessee Press, 1997. 151–61.

"*Jubilee*: A Civil War Novel (an Excerpt)." *Northwestern Tri-Quarterly* (1964): 26–31.

"*Jubilee*: My Story." *Mississippi Magic* (1975): 3–6.

"A Literary Legacy from Dunbar to Baraka." In *"How I Wrote Jubilee" and Other Essays on Life and Literature*. Ed. Maryemma Graham. New York: Feminist Press, 1990. 69–83.

"Mississippi and the Nation." In *On Being Female, Black, and Free: Essays by Margaret Walker, 1932–1992*. Ed. Maryemma Graham. Knoxville: University of Tennessee Press, 1997. 145–50.

"Moral Education: Who Is Responsible?" *On Being Female, Black, and Free: Essays by Margaret Walker, 1932–1992*. Ed. Maryemma Graham. Knoxville: University of Tennessee Press, 1997. 198–207.

"My Creative Adventure." In *On Being Female, Black, and Free: Essays by Margaret Walker, 1932–1992*. Ed. Maryemma Graham. Knoxville: University of Tennessee Press, 1997.

"Natchez and Richard Wright in Southern American Literature." *Southern Quarterly* 29.4 (1991): 171–75.

"The Nausea of Sartre." *The Yale Review* 42 (1953): 251–61.

"New Poets." In *Black Expression*. Ed. Addison Gayle Jr. New York: Weybright and Talley, 1969. 89–100.

"New Poets of the Forties and the Optimism of the Age." *Phylon* 11.4 (1950): 345–54.

"The New Teachers." *Education Age* (1967): 4–6.

"Of Tennessee and the River." In *On Being Female, Black, and Free: Essays by Margaret Walker, 1932–1992*. Ed. Maryemma Graham. Knoxville: University of Tennessee Press, 1997. 108–16.

"On Being Female, Black, and Free." In *The Writer on Her Work*. Ed. Janet Sternburg. New York: Norton, 1980.

"On Money, Race, and Politics." In *On Being Female, Black, and Free: Essays by Margaret Walker, 1932–1992*. Ed. Maryemma Graham. Knoxville: University of Tennessee Press, 1997. 135–39.

"On the Civil Rights Movement in Mississippi." In *On Being Female, Black, and Free: Essays by Margaret Walker, 1932–1992*. Ed. Maryemma Graham. Knoxville: University of Tennessee Press, 1997. 140–44.

"Phillis Wheatley and Black Women Writers, 1773–1973." In *On Being Female, Black, and Free: Essays by Margaret Walker, 1932–1992*. Ed. Maryemma Graham. Knoxville: University of Tennessee Press, 1997. 35–40.

"Rediscovering Black Women Writers in the Mecca of the New Negro." In *"How I Wrote Jubilee" and Other Essays on Life and Literature*. Ed. Maryemma Graham. New York: Feminist Press, 1990. 91–101.

"Reflections on May, 1970." In *On Being Female, Black, and Free: Essays by Margaret Walker, 1932–1992*. Ed. Maryemma Graham. Knoxville: University of Tennessee Press, 1997. 177–82.

"Religion, Poetry, and History: Foundations for a New Educational System." *Vital Speeches of the Day* 34.24 (1968); Rpt. in *The Black Seventies*. Ed. Floyd B. Barbour. Vol. 284–95. Boston: Porter Sargent, 1970.

"Revolution and the University." In *On Being Female, Black, and Free: Essays by Margaret Walker, 1932–1992*. Ed. Maryemma Graham. Knoxville: University of Tennessee Press, 1997.

"Richard Wright." *New Letters* 38.2 (1971): 182–202.

"Some Aspects of the Black Aesthetic." *Freedomways* 16.2 (1976): 95–102.

"Southern Black Culture." In *On Being Female, Black, and Free: Essays by Margaret Walker, 1932–1992*. Ed. Maryemma Graham. Knoxville: University of Tennessee Press, 1997. 79–85.

"Symbol, Myth, and Legend: Folk Elements in African American Literature." In *On Being Female, Black, and Free: Essays by Margaret Walker, 1932–1992*. Ed. Maryemma Graham. Knoxville: University of Tennessee Press, 1997. 57–63.

"Their Place on the Stage." In *Their Place on the Stage: Black Women Playwrights in America*. Ed. Elizabeth Brown-Guillory. Westport CT: Greenwood Publishing, 1988.

"Tribute to Black Teachers." *The Lexington Banner*, 1975 [exact date unknown].

"What Is to Become of Us?" *Our Youth* (1932).

"Whose 'Boy' Is This?" *African American Women Speak Out*. Ed. Geneva Smitherman. Detroit: Wayne State University Press, 1995.

"Willing to Pay the Price." In *Many Shades of Black*. Ed. Stanton L. Wormley and Lewis Fenderson. New York: William Morrow, 1969.

"The Writer and Her Craft." In *Teaching Creative Writing: Proceedings of the Conference on Teaching Creative Writing, Library of Congress*, 1974.

SELECTED REVIEWS OF *JUBILEE*

Alante-Lima, Willy. *"Jubilee." Présence africaine* 72 (Fourth trimester 1969): 226–28.

"L'Autant en emporte le vent des noirs." *La Nouvelle Critique* 21 (February 1969): 58.

Arnothy, Christine. "Un Roman-Fleuve: *Jubilee* de Margaret Walker." *L'Oise-Matin and Le Parisien libéré* (August 20, 1968).

B., J. *"Jubilee* par Margaret Walker." *Syndicats* (October 19, 1968).

Barde, Jacqueline. "La Descente de Moïse." *Les Nouvelles littéraires* 2134 (August 15, 1968): 7.

———. "Margaret Walker: *Jubilee.*" *Le Papetier de France* (September 1968).

Barrow, William. *"Jubilee:* A Novel by Margaret Walker." *Negro Digest* (February 1967): 93–95.

Berger, Yves. "Splendeurs et misères du sud: *Jubilee* de Margaret Walker." *Le Mondes des Livres* 7732 (August 10, 1968): iii.

Bloch-Michel, Jean. "Autour du problème noir. *Jubilee* de Margaret Walker." *La Gazette de Lausanne* (1968): 1–2.

Bonnet, Melchior. "La Vie littéraire: *Jubilee*, roman de Margaret Walker." *La Nouvelle République de Centre-Ouest* (January 10, 1969).

Bouville, Eude. *"L'Autant en emporte le vent* des noirs américains: *Jubilee* de Margaret Walker." *L'Echo de la mode* (October 27, 1968).

Brierre, Annie. "Classiques et nouveaux venus." *France–U.S.A.* (October 1968): 2.

Bruls, J. "De l'esclavage au Black Power." *Eglise vivante* (1969): 66–68.

Buckmaster, Henrietta. "The Other Side of the Plantation." *Christian Science Monitor*, 29 Sept. 1966, 11.

Buhet, Gil. *"Jubilee* de Margaret Walker." *Résonances* 630 (November 1968).

Bussang, Françoise. *"Jubilee* de Margaret Walker." *Mobilier et décoration* (December 1968).

C., J.-P. *"Jubilee* de Margaret Walker." *Le Cri du monde* (November 1968): 55.

Cabau, Jacques. "Autant en emportent les blancs." *L'Express* 892 (August 12, 1966): 58.

Carvlin, Evanne. "A Review of *Jubilee.*" *Community* (February 1967): 13.

Chambers, Elsie Mae. "Great Novel by Jackson Woman Tells Other Side." *Jackson Clarion-Ledger*, September 19, 1966, 8.

Chapman, Abraham. *Saturday Review* 49 (September 24, 1966): 43.

Cousty, Paulette. *"Jubilee* de Margaret Walker: Un Pain noir américain." *Le Populaire du centre* (May 22, 1969): 6.

D'Aubarede, Gabriel. *"Jubilee* par Margaret Walker." *Livres et lectures* (November 1968).

———. "Un Grand Drame du racisme, *Jubilee.*" *Le Monde et la vie* (September 1968): 69.

"D'Autres Romans: *Jubilee* de Margaret Walker." *Pourquoi* (November 1968): 87–88.

Davenport, Guy. "Once More, a Little Louder." *National Review* 18.2(October 4, 1966): 1001–2.

Davis, Lester. "The Passing of an Era." *Freedomways* 3 (1967): 258–60.

Deransart, M. "Un Livre par mois: *Jubilee* de Margaret Walker." *L'Illustre protestant* (January 1969): 15.

Dollarhide, Louis. "Margaret Walker Opens New Windows in *Jubilee:* A Review." *Jackson Clarion-Ledger*, September 18, 1966, 4.

Dupré, Guy. "Livres: *Jubilee,* par Margaret Walker." *Centre-Presse* (September 25, 1968): 17.

Dykema, Wilma. *New York Times Book Review* (September 25, 1966): 52.

F., A. *"Jubilee." Nord-Matin* (October 2, 1968).

G., S. *"Jubilee* par Margaret Walker." *Saint-Etienne l'espoir* (August 20, 1968): 6.

Giesberg, Franz-Olivier. *"Jubilee* de Margaret Walker." *Paris-Normandie* (August 16, 1968).

———. "Le Problème numéro 1 des U.S.A.: *La Prochaine Fois, le feu." Paris-Normandie* (September 28, 1968): 7.

Giles, Louise. "Review of *Jubilee,* by Margaret Walker." *Library Journal* (October 15, 1966): 4978.

Grandmaison, Jacqueline de. "Les Livres: *Jubilee* de Margaret Walker." *La Semaine de Provence* (January 17, 1969).

Gros, L. G. "Liberté, ce mot interdit . . ." *Le Provençal-Dimanche* (July 14, 1968): 11.

Guissard, Lucien. "Ecrivains noirs américains. Margaret Walker: *Jubilee;* James Baldwin: *Face à l'homme blanc." La Croix* (August 4–5, 1968): 7.

Guyauv, Jacques. "Margaret Walker, Une Grande Romancière noir." *Le Journal de Charleroi* (August 17, 1968).

Guyot, Charly. "Hurrah the Flag that Makes You Free." *Journal de Genève* (November 30, 1968): 22–23.

Harris, Robert. "Review of the Afro-American Classics: An Essential Library." *Black Enterprise* (June 1984): 34–37.

Jardin, Claudine. "Un *Autant en emporte le vent* noir: *Jubilee* de Margaret Walker." *Le Figaro* (September 4, 1968).

Jean-Nesmy, Dom Claude. *"Jubilee,* de Margaret Walker." *L'Echo illustre de Genève* (December 7, 1968): 39.

"Jubilee de Margaret Walker." *L'Epicerie française* (November 16, 1968).

"Jubilee de Margaret Walker." *Femme pratique* (October 1968): 21–22.

"Jubilee de Margaret Walker." *Heures claires* 164 (January 1969): 36.

"Jubilee de Margaret Walker." *L'Humanité Dimanche* (October 27, 1968): 38.

"Jubilee de Margaret Walker." *Informations dieppoises* (March 7, 1969).

"Jubilee de Margaret Walker." *Le Journal du dimanche* (August 4, 1968).

"Jubilee de Margaret Walker." *Revue des cercles d'études d'Angers* 4.7 (1968): 57.

"Jubilee. Le Roman des esclaves noirs d'Amérique." *Bingo* 189 (October 1968): 77.

"Jubilee par Margaret Walker." *Jours de France* (October 5, 1968).

La Divenah, Patrick. "De l'esclavage à la liberté; *Jubilee* de Margaret Walker." *Combat* (September 5, 1968): 11.

Lamaire, Marcel. *"Jubilee* de Margaret Walker." *Le Soir* (August 1968).

Las Vergnas, Raymond. "Ce que n'emporte pas le vent: Lettres américaines. Margaret Walker: *Jubilee;* Hal Bennett: *Les Vignes sauvages.*" *Les Nouvelles littéraires* 2136 (August 29, 1968): 5.

Lipscomb, Ernestine. "Margaret Walker Wins Honors for *Jubilee.*" *Mississippi Library News* (December 1966): 218–19.

"Littérature américaine: *Jubilee* de Margaret Walker; *Face à l'homme blanc* par James Baldwin." *Clartés encyclopédiques* 14 (1968).

"Le Livre du mois: *Jubilee* par Margaret Walker." *La Vie catholique* (September 4, 1968).

"Margaret Walker: *Jubilee.*" *Les Echos* (August 23, 1968).

"Margaret Walker, *Jubilee.*" *Le Prêtre de Saint-François de Sales* (January 1969): 26.

Maroney, Sheila. "New View of the Plantation: Review of *Jubilee,* by Margaret Walker." *Crisis* (November 1966): 493.

Masselot, Felix. "Voici des livres: *Jubilee* de Margaret Walker." *L'Hôpital* (June 1969).

Mayer, Daniel. "Tribune libre: *Jubilee.*" *Combat* (November 19, 1970).

Mespouille, Jose. "L'Univers inconnu, tendre, cruel du sud esclavigiste. *Jubilee* par la romancière noir, Margaret Walker." *Vers l'avenir* (August 17, 1968).

Mullener, Elizabeth. "*Jubilee:* It Took Thirty Long Years, but Margaret Walker Kept Her Promise." *New Orleans Times-Picayune,* March 22, 1981: 8–9.

Neuveglise, Paule. "Deux grands romans étrangers." *France-Soir* (July 13, 1968).

"Nouveautés: *Jubilee* de Margaret Walker." *Revue de la Mercerie* (November 1968): 7.

Olivier, Daria. "Lettres étrangères: Feuilles d'automne." *Réforme* (September 21, 1968).

Oppenheim, J. E. "*Jubilee,* by Margaret Walker." *Best Sellers* 26 (October 1, 1966): 229.

Paret, Pierre. "Chronique littéraire: *Jubilee* de Margaret Walker." *La Dorgone libre* (September 1968).

Phillot, A. "Livres, *Jubilee* par Margaret Walker." *Eaux vives* (November 1968).

Porquerol, Elisabeth. "Margaret Walker: *Jubilee.*" *La Nouvelle Revue française* 191 (November 1968): 697.

Prevot-Laygonie, M.-F. "Le Livre du mois: *Jubilee* de Margaret Walker." *Educatrices paroissiales* (Mar.–Apr. 1969): 12.

"*La Prochaine Fois, le feu* par James Baldwin." *La Gazette littéraire* (August 17–18, 1968).

Renek, Morris. "*Jubilee,* by Margaret Walker." *Book Week* (October 2, 1966): 8.

"A Review of *Jubilee.*" *The Times Literary Supplement,* 29 June 1967.

Rivet, August. "*Jubilee,* les travaux et les joies des noirs américains au XIXème siècle." *Le Puy l'éveil de la Haute-Loire* (December 16, 1968): 4.

Rudel, Yves-Marie. "Lectures: *Jubilee* de Margaret Walker." *Ouest-France* (July 3, 1968): 6.

Sourillan, Jose. "Le Vieux Sud en négatif." *Minute* (September 12–18, 1968): 20.

Valogne, Catherine. "Quatre Romans d'auteurs 'Colored': La Parole est aux noirs." *La Tribune de Genève* (September 1, 1968).

"À la vitrine du libraire: *Jubilee* de Margaret Walker." *Le Petit Bastiais* (November 19, 1968).

SELECTED REVIEWS OF NONFICTION

Brodsky, Molly. "A Review of *How I Wrote* Jubilee." *Library Journal* 115 (1990): 110.

Brown, James. "*A Poetic Equation: Conversations Between Nikki Giovanni and Margaret Walker,* by Nikki Giovanni and Margaret Walker." *Library Journal* 99 (1974): 2464.

Burns, Ann. "*On Being Female, Black, and Free,* by Margaret Walker." *American Literature* 70 (1998): 223.

Campbell, Jane. "Bearing the Triple Burden." *Belles Lettres* 5 (1990): 32.

Davis, Tonya Bolden. "About People: Bookmarks." *Essence* 18 (1988): 26.

Fatch, Elizabeth G. "Keeping Faith." *Women's Review of Books* 8 (1990): 29.

Giddings, Paula. "Margaret Walker's *Richard Wright: Daemonic Genius.*" *Essence* 19 (1989): 30.

———. "A Review of *How I Wrote* Jubilee." *Essence* 21 (1990): 50.

Hubbard, Dolan. "A Review of *How I Wrote* Jubilee." *Callaloo* 13 (1990): 916.

———. "A Review of *Richard Wright: Daemonic Genius.*" *Callaloo* 13 (1990): 949.

Johnson, Carol Siri. "*How I Wrote* Jubilee, by Margaret Walker." *Journal of Popular Culture* 28 (1995): 268+.

Johnson, Charles R. "Richard Wright: Loved, Lost, Hated, Missed." *Los Angeles Times Book Review* (1989): 9.

Meltzer, Milton. "A Review of *Richard Wright: Daemonic Genius.*" *Library Journal* 112 (1987): 113.

"A Review of *How I Wrote* Jubilee." *American Literature* 62 (1990): 758.

Shuttaford, Genevieve. "*Daemonic Genius,* by Margaret Walker." *Publishers Weekly* 235 (1989): 50.

Ward, Jerry, Jr. "A Review of *How I Wrote* Jubilee." *African American Review* 27 (1993): 317+.

———. "A Review of *Richard Wright: Daemonic Genius.*" *African American Review* 27 (1993): 318+.

SELECTED REVIEWS OF POETRY

Anderson, Isaac. "Forthcoming Poetry." *New York Times Book Review,* 2 Aug. 1942, 10.

Bontemps, Arna. "A Review of *For My People.*" *Books* (1943): 3.

Cushman, Jerome. "*Prophets for a New Day,* by Margaret Walker." *Library Journal* 96 (1971): 641.

Dommergues, Pierre. "LeRoi Jones au théâtre." *Les Langues modernes* 60 (1966): 102–4.

Drew, Elizabeth. "A Review of *For My People.*" *Atlantic* 170 (1942): 166.

Dykeman, Wilma. "A Talent for Survival." *New York Times Book Review,* 25 Sept. 1966, 52.

Ezzard, Martha. "Two Views of a Segregated South." *Atlanta Journal/Atlanta Constitution,* 8 June 1996, sec. A, p. 10, col. 4.

Howe, Florence. "Poet of History, Poet of Vision." *The Women's Review of Books* 7.10–11 (July 1990): 41.

Hubbard, Dolan. "*This Is My Century,* by Margaret Walker." *Callaloo* 13 (1990): 912.

Hull, Gloria T. "African American Writers: Covering Ground." *Belles Lettres* 6 (1991): 2.

Littlejohn, David. "Negro Writers Today: The Poets." In *Black on White: A Critical Survey of Writing by American Negroes.* New York: Grossman, 1966. 80–83.

Muratori, Fred. "*This Is My Century,* by Margaret Walker." *Library Journal* 114 (1989): 92.

Overbea, Luix. "Margaret Walker's *This Is My Century.*" *Christian Science Monitor* 82 (1990): 13.

"A Review of *For My People.*" *Library Journal* 67 (1942): 910.

Stranchan, Pearl. "A Review of *For My People.*" *Christian Century* 59 (1942): 1495.

Thomas, Keith. "In the African Style." *Atlanta Journal/Atlanta Constitution,* 31 July 1990, sec. E, p. 1, col. 2.

Untermeyer, Louis. "New Books in Review: Cream of the Verse." *Yale Review* 32.2 (1943): 366–71.

———. "A Review of *For My People.*" *Yale Review* 32 (1942): 370.

Van de Water, Charlotte. "Poems to Remember." *Scholastic: High School Teacher Edition* 42.2 (1943): 21.

Ward, Jerry, Jr. "*October Journey,* by Margaret Walker." *African American Review* 27 (1993): 318.

———. "*Prophets for a New Day,* by Margaret Walker." *African American Review* 27 (1990): 317.

———. "A Review of *For My People.*" *African American Review* 27 (1993): 316.

———. "*This Is My Century,* by Margaret Walker." *African American Review* 27 (1993): 319.

Whipple, Leon. "A Review of *For My People.*" *Survey* 31 (1042): 597.

TRANSLATIONS OF MARGARET WALKER'S *JUBILEE*

Flieht wie ein Vogel auf eure Berge: Roman [Fleeing as a Bird to the Mountains]. 2nd ed. Zurich: Diana, 1968.

Huan Le. Trans. Hung-ch'an Huang. Shang-hi: I wen chu pan she, 1984.

Jubilee. Barcelona: Plaza & Janes, 1976.

Jubilee. Paris: Editions du Seuil, 1966.

Jubilee: Roman. 2nd ed. Paris: Editions du Seuil, 1968.

Contributors

TOMEIKO R. ASHFORD is a graduate of the University of North Carolina, Chapel Hill, where she was a teaching fellow and an Andrew W. Mellon Dissertation Fellow while completing a Ph.D. in English. Her dissertation, "'Daughters of Zion': Examining Spiritual Power in Black Womanist Narrative," reflects her interest in the intersection of literary and womanist theory and theology.

BERNICE L. BELL is a retired librarian from the Henry T. Sampson Library at Jackson State University, Jackson, Mississippi, where she served as a professional bibliographer, publishing a number of checklists on African American writers and holdings. Bell was a longtime friend of Margaret Walker and is currently completing a "Comprehensive Bibliography of Published and Unpublished Works by Margaret Walker."

B. DILLA BUCKNER is Professor of English at Jackson State University, Jackson, Mississippi. She has published widely on Margaret Walker. Her most recent work is "Spirituality, Sexuality, and Creativity: A Conversation with Margaret Walker," appearing in *My Soul Is a Witness,* edited by Gloria Wade Gayles.

JACQUELINE MILLER CARMICHAEL teaches English at Georgia State University in Atlanta, where she completed her Ph.D. Her most recent work is a book-length study, *Trumpeting a Fiery Sound: History and Folklore in Margaret Walker's "Jubilee".*

MICHELLE CLIFF is a Jamaican-born writer. After her widely acclaimed first volume, *Claiming an Identity They Taught Me to Despise,* she has gone on to publish *Abeng, The Land of Look Behind, No Telephone to Heaven, Bodies of Water,* and *Free Enterprise.* Her most recent work is the short story collection, *The Store of a Million Items.*

EUGENIA COLLIER is Professor Emerita at Morgan State University, Baltimore, where she served as chair of the Department of English for many years. Collier was an early contributor to studies of African American literature, with articles appearing in the *College Language Association Journal.* Her most recent publications include *Afro-American Writing: An Anthology of Prose and Poetry* (with Richard Long) and a prose collection, *Breeder and Other Stories.*

ESIM ERDIM, a native of Turkey, is currently Associate Professor of TESOL at the University of Mississippi after many years at Ege University in Izmir, Turkey. A former Fulbright scholar, she has had a long-standing interest in southern women's literature and has published in Turkish- and English-language journals.

EKATERINI GEORGOUDAKI is Professor Emerita in the Department of American Literature, the School of English, at Aristotle University of Thessaloniki, Greece. A past president of the Hellenic Association and board member of the European Association for American Studies, she has published widely in African American and American literature in the United States and in Europe. Her major research and writing focus is poetry.

CHARLOTTE GOODMAN is Professor of English at Skidmore College, Saratoga Springs, New York, where she teaches courses on American literature, women's literature, and drama. A past president of the Northeast Modern Language Association, she has written on Henry James, Faulkner, and American women writers and is author of *Jean Stafford: The Savage Heart.*

MARYEMMA GRAHAM is Professor of English and Director of the Project on the History of Black Writing at the University of Kansas, with five published books and numerous articles on nineteenth- and twentieth-century American and African American literature and the novel. Walker's *"How I Wrote Jubilee" and Other Essays on Life and Literature* and *On Being Female, Black, and Free* were both edited by Graham, whose current project is "A Life of Her Own: An Intellectual Biography of Margaret Walker."

MINROSE C. GWIN is Professor of English at the University of New Mexico, Albuquerque. Co-editor of *The Literature of the American South: A Norton Anthology,* Gwin is also the author of *Black and White Women of the Old South: The Peculiar Sisterhood in American Literature,* one of the first significant studies of Walker's work, and most recently *Feminine and Faulkner: Reading (Beyond) Sexual Difference.*

ROBERT A. HARRIS is a second-year graduate student in the Department of English at the University of Kansas, where he works as the computer specialist and bibliographer for the Project on the History of Black Writing. His major interest is in African American poetry, and he has presented papers at MELUS and CLA.

FLORENCE HOWE is founder and director of The Feminist Press in New York. In addition to being a publisher and advocate of women's rights issues, Howe has edited thirteen books of her own, including *Tradition and Talents of Women,* and *No More Masks: An Anthology of Twentieth-Century American Women Poets.*

PHYLLIS R. KLOTMAN is Professor of Afro-American Studies, Indiana University, Bloomington. A film historian and critic, she has authored and/or edited *Another Man Gone: The Black Runner in Contemporary Afro-American Literature, Frame by Frame: A Black Filmography,* and *Screenplays of the African American Experience.*

AMY LEVIN is Associate Professor of English and Director of Women's Studies at Northern Illinois University, where she specializes in nineteenth- and twentieth-century British and American women's writing. Her most recent book is *The Suppressed Sister: A Relationship in Novels by Nineteenth- and Twentieth-Century British Women.* She is currently completing a book-length study of Africanisms in novels by contemporary African American women.

R. BAXTER MILLER is Professor of English and Director of the Institute for African American Studies at the University of Georgia, Athens. He has published widely on African American poetry and theory. His book, *Black American Poets Between Two Wars,* includes two essays on Walker's poetry, one of the earliest books to treat Walker's work extensively.

JOYCE PETTIS is Professor of English at North Carolina State University, Raleigh, where she teaches undergraduate and graduate courses in African American literature. She is author of *Toward Wholeness in Paule Marshall's Fiction* and has also written articles on African American writing. Her current project is a reference book on African American poets.

HIROKO SATO is Professor of English at Tokyo Women's Christian University and Director of the Center for Women's Studies. A leading force in the American Studies movement in Japan, Sato is currently the president of the Japanese Association for American Studies. She has collaborated on eight book-length works on American and African American literature and is author of *Willa Cather* and *The American Domestic Novel.*

JAMES E. SPEARS retired from the University of Tennessee, Martin, in 1994 after many years as a professor of English. He is a pioneer in Black Studies scholarship, having first published his "Playing the Dozen" in 1969 and continuing to write on a spectrum of topics, including "Folk Oreo." Spears's work in folklore and dialect provided the basis for early studies of Walker, and his essays on *Jubilee* appeared in a number of journals.

CLAUDIA TATE is Professor of English at Princeton University and has most recently been a National Humanities Center Fellow. She has published widely on African American women writers and cultural theory. Her latest works include *Domestic Allegories of Political Desire: The Black Heroine's Text at the Turn of the Century* and *Psychoanalysis and Black Novels: Desire and the Protocols of Race.* Her current project is "Who's That Lady?", a visual representation of black femininity.

ELEANOR TRAYLOR is Professor and Chair of the Department of English at Howard University. Her writings and performances on African American literature and culture are well known. Her most recent book is *Broad Sympathy: An Oral Tradition Reader.*

MELISSA WALKER is author of *Down from the Mountaintop: Black Women's Novels in the Wake of the Civil Rights Movement, 1966–1989.*

JERRY W. WARD JR. is Lawrence Durgin Professor of Literature at Tougaloo College, Tougaloo, Mississippi, and a 1999–2000 Fellow at the National Humanities Center. He has published articles and poetry in many journals. His most recent books include *Black Southern Voices* and *Trouble the Water: 250 Years of African American Poetry.* He is currently completing *Delta Narratives: Memory, Testimony, and Social Change.*

DEBORAH ELIZABETH WHALEY is completing her Ph.D. in American Studies at the University of Kansas, where she specializes in ethnic studies and women's studies. She has presented papers and published on African American women and popular culture and teaches at the University of Kansas.

Index

Adams, Leonie, 21

Africa, 68, 124, 156; and Walker's poetry, 128–33

African American literature, xiii, 18, 30, 40–41, 69, 99, 238, 291; poetry, 114, 135

African American women, images of, 40–42; point of view of, 70

"Agenda for Action," xxiii

Alabama, xix, 11, 13, 44, 55, 56, 100–101, 113, 259

Alexander, Firnist James (husband), xx

Alexander, Firnist James, Jr. (son), xxi

Alexander, Joy Dale (granddaughter), xxiii

Alexander, Margaret Elvira (daughter), xxi

Alexander, Marion Elizabeth (daughter), xx

Alexander, Norma (daughter-in-law), xxiv

Alexander, Sigismund Constantine Walker (son), xxi

Alexander, Sigismund Walker, II (grandson), xxiv

Alpha Kappa Alpha Sorority, xx, xxii, xxvi , 315

American Prefaces, xx

"Amos," 93, 94

"Amos (Postscript, 1968)," 93, 94

Anderson, Margaret, 21

Anderson, Marian, xix, 11, 81

Angelou, Maya, 46, 57, 134, 197

Anvil, xx

architecture, folk, 256

Arnheim, Rudolph, 184

"At the Lincoln Monument in Washington, August 28, 1963," 52, 90–93

Attaway, William, 21–22

Aunt Sally (*Jubilee*), 198, 201, 202–4, 221, 236, 238, 246–47, 253, 261–63, 271–73, 282, 284, 296–97, 302, 310

autobiography, excerpt from, 28–31, 39

"Bad Man Stagolee," 51, 83

Bailey, Guy, *Language Variety in the South,* 249–50

Baker, Ella, 56

Baker, Houston A., Jr., 67, 244–45, 296; *The Journey Back,* 291

Baldwin, James, xxv, 37, 84, 134, 197, 242, 301; and the blues, 196; "Everybody's Protest Novel," 70; *Notes of a Native Son,* 84

"Ballad for Phillis Wheatley," 168

"Ballad of the Free," 52, 88, 108, 145–46

"Ballad of the Hoppy Toad," 52, 140–44, 148, 156–59, 162

Bambara, Toni Cade, 134, 197

Baraka, Amiri, 134, 197

Barksdale, Richard, 123, 180

Barthes, Roland, 180

Bell, Bernice L., xv

Bellah, Robert, 125

Benet, Stephen Vincent, 31–32, 45, 114, 117, 151

Bethune, Mary McLeod, 56

Bibb, Henry, 216

Bible as literature, 30

Bicentennial Symposium on American Slavery, xxiii

"Big John Henry," 51, 83

Bigger Thomas (character in *Native Son*), 70

"Birmingham," 130, 165–66

"Birmingham, 1963," 106, 165–66

Black Academy Conference to Assess the State of Black Arts and Letters in the United States, xxiii

Black Aesthetic, xxii, 180–81, 195

Black Arts Movement, xi, 81, 112

"Black Culture," xxiv

black historical fiction, 46–47

"Black Magic," 167

black myth, 99, 102, 106

black nationalism, 33, 37–38

"Black Paramour," 133

Blake, William, 96, 114

Blassingame, James, xxiii

Bloom, Harold, 180

blues. *See* music: blues

Bogan, Louise, 21, 37

Bontemps, Arna, xx, xxi, 21–22, 42, 45, 82, 197, 214, 242; *Black Thunder*, 211, 215

Bradley, David, *The Chaneysville Incident*, 47

Brewer, J. Mason, 247

Broadside Press, xxiii, 105, 107, 111

Brooks, Cleanth, 180, 248–49

Brooks, Gwendolyn, 31, 68, 75, 81, 119, 134; *Annie Allen*, 32; "The Children of the Poor," 83; *A Street in Bronzeville*, 31–32

Brother Ezekiel (*Jubilee*), 198–201, 202, 203–4, 216, 221, 227, 245–48, 255, 270, 272

Brown, Charles Brockden, 85

Brown, Elvira Ware (*Jubilee*). *See* Vyry

Brown, Innis (*Jubilee*), 58–59, 204, 217, 255–56, 263, 279

Brown, John, 89, 108, 146, 182, 189

Brown, Margaret Duggans Ware (great-grandmother), 12

Brown, Roscoe, xxii

Brown, Sterling, xxi, 18, 45, 51, 119, 241

Brown v. Board of Education, 56

Brown, William Wells, 197, 216, 309

Browning, Robert, 114

Burke, Kenneth, 114

Burroughs, Nannie, 12, 31

Burton, Annie L., 218

Byron, Lord George, 96

Carby, Hazel, 57

Carver, George Washington, 81

Cash, Wilbur J., 257

Cassill, Verlin, xxi

Catlett, Elizabeth, xx, xxiii

Cayton, Horace, 22, 35

Chesnutt, Charles, 242–43; *The Conjure Woman*, 245

Chicago Renaissance, 22

"Chief Worshippers at All World Altars," xxiii

"Childhood," 87, 91

Christian, Barbara, 68, 293, 308, 310; *Black Women Novelists*, 241

Christian Humanism, 18, 84, 220, 239, 284

Civil Rights Movement, 56, 58, 59, 61, 72, 88, 90, 91, 111, 117, 189

civil rights poems by Margaret Walker, 52, 69, 73, 74

Civil War, 46, 47, 48, 55, 58, 63, 64, 68, 70, 72, 115, 200, 225, 228, 239, 269, 276

Cixous, Hélène, 67

Cleaver, Eldridge, 94

College Language Association (CLA), xx, xxvi

Collier, Eugenia, 51, 167, 170

Collins, Patricia Hill, 68

Common Ground, xx

Communist Party, 20–21, 33–34, 37, 105. *See also* Marxism

Conference on Africa and African Affairs, xxiv

Congress of Racial Equality (CORE), 56

conjure and conjurers, 47, 52, 82, 84, 122, 140, 142–43, 148, 149, 172, 204, 228, 241

Cooke, Michael, 291–92, 299

Cooper, J. California, 283

Cooper, James Fenimore, 307

Coppin, Fannie Jackson, 12

Craft, Ellen and William, 216, 219, 309–10

Creative Writing, xx

The Crisis, xix, 17, 24, 34

"Critical Approaches to the Study of African American Literature," xxii

"The Crystal Palace," 129, 167, 182

Cullen, Countee, 81, 96, 111; "From the Dark Tower," 86

culture, folk, 241

Curry, Alleane, xv, xxii

Danner, Margaret, 81–82; "The Slave and the Iron Lace," 95

"Dark Blood," 51, 102, 104, 118, 120, 168, 197

Davis, Allison, 36

Davis, Angela, 68, 71

Davis, Frank Marshall, xx, 21–22

Davis, Ossie, xxii

"Daydream" ("I Want to Write"), xix, 17–20, 23, 108, 110, 116, 121

Dee, Ruby, xxii

Dégh, Linda, 254

Degler, Carl, xxiii

Delaney, Martin R., 197

Dell, Floyd, 21

"Delta," 50–51, 85, 92, 101–2, 124, 126, 167–70; and Isis, 118

Democratic National Convention, xxv

dialect. *See* language, folk

Díaz-Diocaretz, Myriam, xiii, xv

"Dies Irae," 142

Dillard, J. L., 249

Dillon, George, xix, 21

"Discovering Our Connection," xxvi

"Disillusion for Flower Children of Long Ago," 166–67

Dodson, Gwen, 119

Dolan, Jill, 162

Dorson, Richard, 140, 243, 255

Douglass, Frederick, 133, 196, 197, 216, 218, 252; *Narrative of the Life of Frederick Douglass,* 207

Dozier, Elvira Ware (grandmother), xix, xx, 12, 14, 209, 233

Dozier, Marion (mother), xix, xxiv, 11, 114

Drake, St. Clair, xx, 22

Dreiser, Theodore, 21

Du Bois, W. E. B. (William Edward Burghardt), xix, 11–12, 16, 42, 56, 81, 118, 124–25, 134, 189, 197, 248, 256, 292; *Dark Princess,* 41; *The Souls of Black Folk,* 247

DuCille, Ann, 316

Dunbar, Paul Laurence, xxiii, 42, 117, 145, 189, 241, 243

Dunham, Katherine, 21

Dutton, John Morris (*Jubilee*), 56–59, 71, 198–99, 201, 212, 269–70, 274, 277

Dutton, Lillian (*Jubilee*), 59, 72, 201, 210, 253, 275–76, 279, 295, 298, 311

Dutton, Salina (*Jubilee*), 57, 59, 70, 201, 213, 237, 270–71, 275–76, 278, 295

Ebony Magazine, 33

Edgerton, John, 262

education of Margaret Walker. *See* Gilbert Academy; New Orleans University; Northwestern University; University of Iowa

"Elegy," 52, 66, 93, 95

Eliot, T. S., 111; "Sweeney Among the Nightingales," 115; "Tradition and the Individual Talent," 114

Ellison, Ralph, xxvi, 134, 197, 217, 242, 290–91, 293, 301; and the blues, 196; *Invisible Man,* 84

Emerson, Ralph Waldo, 18

Encore, xxiii

Engel, Paul, xx, 32
"Epitaph for My Father," 71, 121, 126, 188
Evers, Medgar, xxi, 52, 70, 106, 132, 145, 189

Fabre, Michel, 34–36
fakelore, 140
"Fanfare, Coda, and Finale," xii, 190
Fanon, Frantz, 108
Farish Street. See [For] Farish Street
   [Green]
Farmer, James, 132
Farrell, James T., 21
Faulkner, William, 36, 39, 74, 270;
   Absalom, Absalom!, 71; Dilsey, 57; The
   Sound and the Fury, 41
Fauset, Jessie, 12
Federal Communications Commission,
   xxiii
Federal Writers Project, WPA, xix, xxv, 21,
   28, 45, 101, 210, 263
feminism, Margaret Walker and, xii, 26,
   67, 68, 70, 72
Feminist Press, xxv, 187
Fiedler, Leslie, Love and Death in the
   American Novel, 41
"Five Black Men," 118
folk: experience, 47, 216; history, 216, 220;
   imagination, xii; novel, 210, 225 (see
   also Jubilee: as folk novel); religion,
   99; tales, 82, 149; tradition, 51, 53, 163,
   139, 144, 148, 225, 234, 241–65. See also
   folklore; heroes, folk; idiom, folk;
   language, folk; medicine, folk; music:
   folk
folk ballads by Margaret Walker, 155–59,
   163–74; "Bad Man Stagolee," 51, 83;
   "Ballad of the Free," 52; "Ballad of the
   Hoppy Toad," 52, 140–44, 148, 156–
   59, 162; "Big John Henry," 51, 83;
   "Molly Means," 52; "Yalluh
   Hammuh," 83, 87, 145. See also For

My People; Prophets for a New Day
folklore, 102, 103, 139–40, 143, 242–45,
   301
Fontenot, Chester, 69
"For Andy Goodman, Michael
   Schwerner, and James Chaney," 52,
   91–92, 171, 189
[For] Farish Street [Green] (1986), xxv,
   111, 134, 167, 204–5. See also "Black
   Magic"; "The Crystal Palace"; "The
   House of Prayer"; "The Labyrinth of
   Life"; "Small Black World"
"For Gwen, 1969," 75, 119, 121
"For Malcolm X," 89, 189
"For Mary McLeod Bethune," 121
"For My People," xi, xx, 17, 25, 45, 50–51,
   67, 82–83, 88, 98–108, 118, 126, 148,
   159, 161, 162, 170, 179–85, 180–82, 184,
   188, 190, 210
For My People, xx, xxvi, 17, 24–25, 32,
   45, 82–83, 87–88, 100, 103–5, 111, 126,
   145, 180–84, 187–88, 317. See also
   "Bad-Man Stagolee"; "Big John
   Henry"; "Childhood"; "Dark Blood";
   "Delta"; "For My People"; "Iowa
   Farmer"; "Kissee Lee"; "Lineage";
   "Long John Nelson and Sweetie Pie";
   "Memory"; "Molly Means"; "Our
   Need"; "People of Unrest"; "Poppa
   Chicken"; "Since 1619"; "Sorrow
   Home"; "Southern Song"; "The
   Struggle Staggers Us"; "Today"; "We
   Have Been Believers"; "Yalluh
   Hammuh." See also folk ballads
"For Paul Laurence Dunbar," 121
Ford Fellowship, xix, 30, 35, 48
Foster, Gloria, xxii
Franklin, John Hope, 253–54, 257–58
Freedomways, xxiv
Freeman, Roland, xxvi, 182–83
Freibert, Lucy, 164
Fulbright-Hayes Fellowship, xxii

Gaines, Ernest, 42, 209; *The Autobiography of Miss Jane Pittman*, 46, 47, 239

games, folk, 254

Garland, Hamlin, 21

Garvey Movement, 56

Gates, Henry Louis, 244

Gayden, Fern, xx

gender, 41–42, 66–77, 153, 56

Genovese, Eugene D., 212, 252–53, 259, 262–63

Georgia, 55, 57, 60, 247

Gibbs, Philip, xxii

Gibson, Donald B., *Modern Black Poets*, xi

Giddings, Paula, 141–42

Gilbert Academy, xix, 15

Gilligan, Carol, 72

Giovanni, Nikki, xi, 32, 39, 46, 72, 108, 211, 293

"Girl Held Without Bail," 73

Gone with the Wind, 57, 205, 210, 225, 311

Goodman, Charlotte, 26, 243, 259

"Goose Island," 34

Graham, Maryemma, 26, 261

Granny Ticey, 204, 235, 245, 296

Grau, Shirley Ann, 46

Great Depression, 19–20, 45, 81

Green, James Earl, xxii

Green, Paul, 243

Greenlee, Sam, *Spook Who Sat by the Door*, 41

Grimes, Ed (*Jubilee*), 221, 245, 250–51, 257, 275, 284, 295–96

Grimke, Angelina Weld, 12

"Growing out of Shadow," xx

Gunn, Moses, xxii

Gwin, Minrose, 26, 238, 301

Haley, Alex, xi, 33, 36, 39, 209, 225; *Roots*, xi, 42, 225, 239; and suit by Margaret Walker, xi, xxiv

Hammon, Jupiter, 92

Harding, Vincent, 35

Harlem Renaissance, 11, 22, 42, 81

Harper, Frances E. W., 12, 116, 308; *Iola Leroy*, 42

"Harriet Tubman," 118, 121

Harris, Robert Anthony (Tony), xv

Harris, Trudier, xi, 243–44

Haven Institute for Negroes, xix

Hayden, Robert, xxi, 119, 123, 189

Hayes, Roland, 11, 81

Henderson, Stephen, 113, 118, 180–81

Henson, Josiah, 216

heroes, folk, 51, 103, 108, 145–46

Herskovits, Melville, 114

Hetta (*Jubilee*), 55, 57–58, 71, 198–99, 211–12, 220, 244, 271, 295, 311

Himes, Chester, 42

historical fiction, 46–47, 232, 292

Holland, Norman N., 180

Holman, C. Hugh, 290

hooks, bell, 68, 260

Hoovey, Alma, xxi

"Hosea," 93, 94

"Hounds" (poem), 22

"The House of Prayer," 167

"How I Told My Child About Race," xxi

How I Wrote Jubilee *and Other Essays on Life and Literature*, xii–xiii, xxiii, xxv, 48, 139, 210, 217, 241

"How Many Silent Centuries Sleep in My Sultry Veins," 51

Howard University Press, xxiii, xxiv, 28

Hubbard, Dolan, 248

Hughes, Langston, xix, xxi, xxii, xxiii, 11, 15, 18, 26, 42, 81, 96, 111, 116, 119, 123, 134, 197, 241, 243; and the blues, 196; "The Negro Speaks of Rivers," 89

humanism of Margaret Walker, 26, 53, 66–76, 82, 270, 301–2; defined, 69

"The Humanistic Tradition of Afro-American Literature," xxii, 26, 68

"Humanities with a Black Focus," xxiii
Hungerford, E. B., 16
Hurston, Zora Neale, xiii, 11, 42, 45, 51,
    81, 232, 241, 243; and the blues, 134,
    196, 197, 232, 241, 300, 306, 317; *Moses,
    Man of the Mountain*, 300; *Their Eyes
    Were Watching God*, 42, 306

"I Want to Write" ("Daydream"), xix,
    17–20, 23, 108, 110, 116, 121
idiom, folk, 148, 226–27, 249–50
"Inflation Blues," 190
Institute of the Black World, xxiii
"Iowa Farmer," 120
"Isaiah," 93
Iser, Wolfgang, 180

Jackson, Blyden, 36, 49
Jackson, Reverend Jesse, xxv
Jackson, Jimmie Lee, 65
"Jackson, Mississippi," 53, 74–75, 106,
    165–66
"Jackson State, May 15, 1970," 133, 166
Jackson State College (now Jackson State
    University), xxi, xxiii, xxiv, 29, 48, 82,
    210; Black Studies Program at, 30
Jacobs, Harriet, 216, 218–19, 284, 288
"Jeremiah," 93, 166
"Jesse Jackson," xxv
Jim (*Jubilee*, son of Vyry), 59, 249, 260–
    61, 274, 282, 288, 299, 309
Jim Crow, 24, 63–64, 83, 159, 188
"Jean Lafitte, the Baritarian," 116, 131
"Joel," 93, 94
Johnson, Barbara, 76
Johnson, Fenton, 82
Johnson, Georgia Douglas, 12, 111
Johnson, James Weldon, xix, 11, 41, 51,
    81, 217, 242; *Autobiography of an
    Ex–Coloured Man*, 114
Johnson Publishing Company, xxiii
Jones, James Earl, xxii

Jordan, June, 68
Joyner, Charles W., 263
Jubilee, xi, xvi, xix, xxi, 12, 16, 25, 31,
    46–49, 55–65, 67–74, 139, 197–200,
    210, 217, 232–39, 269, 297–302;
    abolitionists in, 213; and Civil Rights
    Movement, 46, 56, 68–69; as Civil
    War novel, 30, 46; composition of, 31,
    48–49, 55–56; contested spaces in,
    270–72; as folk novel, 139, 225–30,
    232, 241–65, 301; as historical fiction,
    47; and miscegenation, 41; and music,
    112–23, 226, 245–47; and naturalism,
    xii, 21; and protest tradition, 46;
    quilt/quilting in, 72, 237–38, 239,
    259–61; and realism, 48, 53, 70, 134;
    and religion, 64, 227, 300; and
    romanticism, 48, 96, 116; sequel to,
    39; as slave narrative, 70; structure
    of, 219–22; and voice and violence,
    relationship between, 286–87

Kane, Harnett T., 253
Kay, Ulysses, xxiv
Kennedy, John Pendleton, *Swallow
    Barn*, 41
King, Martin Luther, Jr., 33, 52, 56, 62–
    63, 70, 90, 91, 92, 94, 96, 106, 118, 132,
    145, 189
"Kissee Lee," 83
Klotman, Phyllis, 70, 246
Krieger, Dr. Otto Edward, 114
Ku Klux Klan, 61, 64, 88, 220, 221, 237,
    280
Kuhn, Manford, 95

"The Labyrinth of Life," 190
Landow, George, 181
Langston Hughes Festival, xxv
language, folk, 144, 226, 228, 249
Larsen, Nella, 12, 306
Levine, Lawrence W., 142, 248

Lewis, John, 132
Library of Congress Conference on
    Teaching Creative Writing, xxiii
Lincoln University (Pennsylvania), xxiv
Lindsay, Vachel, 21
"Lineage," 101, 133, 188
Liuzzo, Viola, 65
Livingstone College (North Carolina), xx,
    xxi, 29, 48
"Long John Nelson and Sweetie Pie," 148,
    153–56, 162
Lorde, Audre, 68, 72, 76
L'Ouverture, Toussaint, 89, 108, 145
"Love Song for Alex," 133
Lowell, Amy, 111
Lucy (*Jubilee*), 198, 203, 204, 214, 287, 296
lynching, 36, 64, 167, 182
Lyndhurst Foundation Fellowship, xxv
Lyotard, Jean-François, 67

Malcolm X (el-Hajj Malik el-Shabazz),
    91, 106, 133, 189
Mammy Sukey (*Jubilee*), 198, 200, 203,
    296, 311
Margaret Walker Alexander National
    Research Center, xxii, xxv, xxvii
*Margaret Walker Reads Margaret Walker
    and Langston Hughes* (recording),
    xxiii
Margaret Walker's "For My People"
    (Freeman), 182–83
Marshall, Paule, 134, 242
Marshall, Russell, xx
Marxism, 22, 26, 101, 105
Masters, Edgar Lee, 21
Mays, Benjamin E., 93, 132
McClendon, Willam H., 118
McDaniel, George W., 256, 258
McDavid, Raven I., 248
McDowell, John H., 254
McKay, Claude, 111, 116, 123, 134; "If We
    Must Die," 115

medicine, folk, 200, 228, 235, 241, 251–52
"The Medusa Head" (Louise Bogan), 37
Melville, Herman, 217
"Memory," 166
memory, in Walker's poetry, 140–42, 166,
    196, 199
"Mess of Pottage," 22
Methodist Episcopal Church (now
    United Methodist Church), 12
"Micah," 52, 93
Miller, R. Baxter, 68, 145, 171, 180
Minna (*Jubilee,* daughter of Vyry), 39, 55,
    232, 261, 282, 309
Minus, Marian, xx
miscegenation, 41–42
"Mississippi and the Nation," xxiv
Mississippi Arts Festival, xxii
Mississippi Committee for Humanities
    Conference, xxiv
Mississippi National Rainbow Coalition,
    xxiv
"Mississippi's Native Son," xxv
Modern Language Association, xxvi
"Molly Means," 52, 143–45, 148–51, 157–
    58, 162
"Money, Honey, Money," 190
Monroe, Harriet, xix, 16, 117
Montgomery, Michael B., 249
"Moral Education," xxiv
Morrison, Toni, xii, xxv, 134, 239, 241, 283;
    Beloved, 47, 283, 288; *The Bluest Eye,*
    239; *Song of Solomon,* 57, 240
"Mother Broyer" (unpublished
    manuscript), 39
Motley, Willard, 21, 82
mulatto, 304–14. *See also* Vyry: as
    mulatto
Murray, Albert, 197
music: blues, 39, 67, 110–12, 122–23, 133,
    155, 195–208; folk, 99, 105, 220, 226,
    235; spirituals, 44, 47, 127, 139, 154, 159,
    302

NAACP (National Association for the Advancement of Colored People), xxii, 56
"Natchez and Richard Wright," xxvi
Natchez Library Festival, xxvi
National Artists and Concert Corporation, xx
National Conference of Black Artists, xxv
National Endowment for the Humanities Senior Fellowship, xxiii, xxvi
National Urban League, 56
National Youth Administration (NYA), xx, 28
nationalism, 139–40
Naylor, Gloria, *The Women of Brewster Place*, 240
Negro Caravan, xx
Negro Digest, xxi
New Challenge, xx, 22, 24
New Haven Institute for Negroes, xix
New Orleans, 11, 13, 45, 113, 145, 182
New Orleans University (now Dillard University), xix, 12, 14–15, 114, 129
Nixon, Robert, 34
Northwestern University, xix, 14, 19, 28, 32–33, 45, 100, 116, 210
"Now," 73–74, 88

Obatala, 199
"October Journey," 53, 187–89
October Journey, xxiii, 46, 53, 107–8, 111, 119–21. *See also* "Ballad for Phillis Wheatley"; "Epitaph for My Father"; "For Gwen, 1969"; "For Mary McLeod Bethune"; "For Paul Laurence Dunbar"; "Harriet Tubman"; "I Want to Write" ("Daydream"); "October Journey"; "Ode on the Occasion of the Inauguration of the Sixth President of Jackson State College"
Ogun, 199–200, 204

"On Being Female, Black, and Free," xiii, xxiv, xxvii, 39, 69, 316
"On Police Brutality," 190
"On Youth and Age," 133
OperaSouth, xxiv
Opportunity, xx
oral tradition, 144, 159, 197, 232, 246–47
orality, and history, 209
Orisha, 199–200, 205
"Our Need," 114–15
Our Youth (magazine), xix
"Oxford Is a Legend," 74

Pan-Africanism, 38
Parks, Rosa, 70
Parrish, Lydia, 247
Payne, Ladell, 242
"People of Unrest [and Hunger]," 19–20, 22, 104
performance features in Walker's poetry, 163–64, 171–77
Petrarch, 114
Pettis, Joyce, 26, 248, 264
Phillis Wheatley Poetry Festival, xxiii, 38
plantation tradition, 39, 55
Plessy v. Ferguson, 63
Poe, Edgar Allan, 85
"Poem," 117
"A Poem for Farish Street Green," 111, 117, 119, 189
A Poetic Equation, xxiii, 32, 46, 72, 108, 211, 292
Poetry: A Magazine of Verse, xix, xx, 16, 21, 31, 117, 124, 159
The Poetry of Margaret Walker Read by Margaret Walker, xxiii
Poetry Society of America, 16
"Poppa Chicken," 148, 151–53, 162
Porter, Katherine Anne, 45
Pound, Ezra, 111
Powell, Adam Clayton, Jr., 94
"Power to the People," 190
Présence africaine, 38

President's Commission on Campus
  Unrest, xxii
"Prophets for a New Day," 92
Prophets for a New Day, xxi, xxii, 17,
  46, 49, 53, 87–95, 105–7, 111, 125–26.
  See also "Amos"; "Amos (Postscript,
  1968)"; "At the Lincoln Monument in
  Washington, August 28, 1963"; "Ballad
  of the Free"; "Ballad of the Hoppy-
  Toad"; "Birmingham"; "Elegy"; "For
  Andy Goodman, Michael Schwerner,
  and James Chaney"; "For Gwen,
  1969"; "For Malcolm X"; "Girl Held
  Without Bail"; "Hosea"; "How Many
  Silent Centuries Sleep in My Sultry
  Veins"; "Isaiah"; "Jackson,
  Mississippi"; "Jeremiah"; "Joel";
  "Micah"; "Now"; "Oxford Is a
  Legend"; "Prophets for a New Day";
  "Sit-Ins"; "Street Demonstration"
Prosser, Gabriel, 47, 52, 89, 108, 211

Quarles, Benjamin, xxiii

race, in Walker's work, 41, 66, 68–69, 72,
  73, 74, 154, 163, 175, 177
Radcliffe, Ann, 85
Randall, Dudley, 81–82, 105; "The Ballad
  of Birmingham," 83
Randolph, A. Philip, 56
Reagon, Bernice, 226, 247
reconstruction, 47, 48, 55, 70–71, 115, 200,
  242, 269
Reddick, Lawrence, 39
Reeb, James, 65
Reed, Ishmael, 134, 197; *Flight to Canada,*
  47
religion, folk, 99
"Religion, Poetry, History," xxii
"Richard Wright," xxii
Richard Wright, xi, xxiv, xxv, 33–36, 46.
  See also Wright, Richard: Walker's
  biography of

Richard Wright Symposium, 36
Richards, I. A., 180
rite de dessounin, 121, 130, 135
rite de possession, 135
Roach, Susan, 260
Robinson, Rowland, 243
Roots. See Haley, Alex
Rosenwald Fellowship, xx, 48
Rowell, Charles, xxiii, 35, 145, 241
Rukeyser, Muriel, xix, 21
Rustin, Bayard, 56

Sanchez, Sonia, 46, 134
Sandburg, Carl, 21, 120
"Setting the Record Straight," xxvii
Severens, Kenneth, 257
Shakespeare, William, 16, 82, 123
Shango, 199–200, 204
Shelley, Percy B., 96
"Since 1619," 49, 106
Sinclair, Upton, 21
"Sit-Ins," 52, 88
slave narrative, 55, 212, 216–18, 242, 245–
  46, 255, 269–70, 283–89
slave rebellions, 88–89
slavery and slave culture, 14, 40, 47–48,
  55, 70–71, 105, 115–23
"Small Black World," 167
Smith, Barbara, 241
SNCC (Student Non-Violent
  Coordinating Committee), 62
Sojourner Truth Festival, xxiv
"Some Aspects of the Black Aesthetic,"
  xxiv
"Sorrow Home," 50–51, 101, 104, 105, 118,
  120, 167–68, 182
South, the, in Walker's work, 22–24, 44–
  53, 56–64, 70–71, 82–83, 96, 101–8,
  116, 123, 164–74
South Side Writers Group, xix–xx, 21–22
"Southern Black Culture," xxiv
"Southern Song," 20, 22–23, 50, 101, 103,
  118, 167, 182

Spears, James, 139, 144, 245, 249–50, 261
Spelman College, xxvi
Spencer, Anne, 12
Spencer, Elizabeth, 46
spirituals. *See* music: spirituals
stereotype, 42, 47–48, 82
Stevens, Wallace, 111
Stowe, Harriet Beecher, 70, 236, 239–40;
    Uncle Tom's Cabin, 231–33, 236, 238–
    39, 308
"Street Demonstration," 52, 73
"The Struggle Staggers Us," 49, 142, 183, 190
Stuckey, Sterling, 253
Styron, William, *Confessions of Nat
    Turner,* 145
Sundquist, Eric J., 245, 246
Switzer, Jack, xxvi

Tate, Allan, 270
Tate, Claudia, 167; *Black Women Writers
    at Work,* xxiv
Tennyson, Alfred Lord, 96
Terry, Lucy, "Bars Fight," 123
"They Have Put Us on Hold," 190
Third World Press, xxii, xxiii
"This Is My Century," 133
This Is My Century, xxv, 46, 111, 115, 117,
    123–24, 126, 167, 187; as journey of
    memory, 138. *See also* "Birmingham,
    1963"; "Black Paramour"; "The
    Crystal Palace"; "Dies Irae";
    "Disillusion for Flower Children of
    Long Ago"; "Fanfare, Coda, and
    Finale"; "Five Black Men"; "Inflation
    Blues"; "Jackson State, May 15, 1970";
    "Love Song for Alex"; "Money,
    Honey, Money"; "On Police
    Brutality"; "On Youth and Age";
    "Poem"; "A Poem for Farish Street
    Green"; "Power to the People"; "They
    Have Put Us on Hold"; "This Is My
    Century"; "Tribute to Robert
    Hayden"; "Whores"

Thomas, H. Nigel, 242, 264
"Today," 52, 86–87, 120
Tolson, Melvin, xxi, 119
Toomer, Jean, 196, 197, 242–43
Traylor, Eleanor, 17, 101, 284
"Tribute to Robert Hayden," 119
Truth, Sojourner, 211, 215
Tubman, Harriet, 47, 189, 211, 214–15, 246
Turner, Darwin, 217
Turner, Henry McNeil, 221
Turner, Nat, 52, 89, 108, 145–46, 189, 221,
    246
Twain, Mark, 217
Tyson, Cicely, xxii

Udell, Geraldine, 21
University of Iowa, xx, 25, 31, 48, 101
University of Massachusetts (Amherst),
    xxiii
University of North Carolina Southern
    Historical Collection, xxi
University of Trondheim (Norway), xxii

Vassa, Gustavas, 216
Vesey, Denmark, 52, 89, 108, 145
Virginia Quarterly Review, xxi
Vlach, John Michael, 255, 257, 259, 261
Vyry (*Jubilee*), 39, 47–48, 55–56, 58–65,
    69–72, 197–208, 211–14, 217, 230–
    37, 245–46, 264–81, 304–5, 310–11;
    compared to other literary characters,
    57; and cooking/food, 59–60, 201,
    202, 236, 261–64, 273; and herbal
    cures, 115–16; and the lash, 119; and
    Lillian Dutton, 275, 287; as mulatto,
    62, 234, 304–13. *See also* Jim (*Jubilee,*
    son of Vyry); Minna (*Jubilee,*
    daughter of Vyry)

Walker, Alice, xii, 46, 68, 134, 241, 283;
    The Color Purple, 57, 239, 240;
    "Everyday Use," 238; *Temple of My
    Familiar,* 283

Walker, David, *Appeal,* 221

Walker, Margaret, 23; academic influence, 15; and Afrocentrism, 66, 67; Alpha Kappa Alpha Sorority, 315; anthologized, xi; awards, xix–xxvii, 29, 35, 202, 210, 217; on black women writers, 48–49; Chicago experiences, 15–22, 37, 45, 100–101, 182; comparison of works, 49–53, 106–7, 126–27; critical reception, xi, 24; cultural recovery, 14; and dialect, 144; dirges, 105; early life, xix, 11–15, 128; family influence, 12–15, 128–29; and feminism, xii, 26, 67, 68, 70, 72; film documentary, xi; folk ballads (*see* folk ballads by Margaret Walker); as folklorist, 139; and the Great Depression, 20; and historical fiction, 46–47, 232, 292; humanism of (*see* humanism of Margaret Walker); illness, xii, xiii; in Iowa, 101; journals, 128; literary influences, 12, 16, 21, 204, 241; and modernism, xii; and nationalism, xii, 33; as New Negro, 12; *oeuvre,* 66–67; as radical activist thinker, xii, 67, 72, 83; regional influence, 44; religious influence, 14, 18, 52, 64, 81–96, 103–6, 113–14, 128–29, 204, 243; response to Faulkner, 74; on Richard Wright, 33–38; and sexism, 29–30; as sonnets, 103; teaching career, 29–31; as "Whitmanesque," 18, 49, 91, 96, 120. *See also entries for specific works*

Walker, Mercedes (sister), 14, 27 (nn. 2, 5)

Walker, Reverend Sigismund Constantine (father), xix, xxi, 12–14, 45, 113, 119

Ward, Jerry, Jr., 149, 164

Ward, Ted, xx, 21–22

Ware, Randall (*Jubilee*), 58–63, 72, 204, 212–14, 217, 221, 226, 260–61, 270, 273–74, 288, 296, 312–13

Washington, Booker T., 134

"We Have Been Believers," 50, 84, 106, 182

Webb, Constance, 35

Welty, Eudora, 45, 270

West, Dorothy, 22

West Virginia State College, xx, 29

"What Is to Become of Us," xix

Wheatley, Phillis, xxiii, xxiii, 12, 38, 116, 123, 188

White, Hayden, 292

Whitehead, Tony L., 264

Whitlow, Roger, 242–43

"Whores," 181

"Whose Boy Is This?," xxvi

Wilkins, Roy, 132

Williams, Jarrett Jamal (grandson), xxiv

Williams, John A.: *Captain Blackman,* 47; *The Man Who Cried I Am,* 33

Williams, Patricia, 68

Williams, Sherley Anne, *Dessa Rose,* 46, 47, 72, 283

women writers, 68

Woodward, C. Vann, 290

Wordsworth, William, 114

WPA. *See* Federal Writers Project

Wright, Richard, xi–xii, xix, xxiii, xxv–xxvi, 21–22, 32–39, 42, 45, 68, 82, 101, 112, 113, 134, 197, 217, 242, 301; "Between the World and Me," 36; "Big Boy Leaves Home," 37; *Black Boy,* 36; and the blues, 196; *Eight Men,* 37; *Native Son,* 34, 70; *12,000,000 Black Voices,* 37; *Uncle Tom's Children,* 34; Walker's biography of, xi, xxiv, xxv, 33–36, 46, 82

"The Writer and Her Craft," xxiii

Wylie, Elinor, 21

Yaddo, xx

Yale Series of Younger Poets Award, xx, 24, 29, 31, 45, 126, 187

"Yalluh Hammuh," 83, 87, 145

Yerby, Frank, 21, 211

Yoder, Don, 251–53, 258